MILTON STUDIES

XXIII

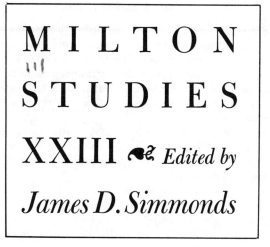

MILTON STUDIES

XXIII ~ *Edited by*

James D. Simmonds

UNIVERSITY OF PITTSBURGH PRESS

MILTON STUDIES

is published annually by the University of Pittsburgh Press as a forum for Milton scholarship and criticism. Articles submitted for publication may be biographical; they may interpret some aspect of Milton's writings; or they may define literary, intellectual, or historical contexts — by studying the work of his contemporaries, the traditions which affected his thought and art, contemporary political and religious movements, his influence on other writers, or the history of critical response to his work.

Manuscripts should be upwards of 3,000 words in length and should conform to the *MLA Style Sheet*. Manuscripts and editorial correspondence should be addressed to James D. Simmonds, Department of English, University of Pittsburgh, Pittsburgh, Pa. 15260.

Milton Studies does not review books.

Within the United States, *Milton Studies* may be ordered from the University of Pittsburgh Press, Pittsburgh, Pa. 15260.

Overseas orders should be addressed to Feffer and Simons, Inc., 100 Park Avenue, New York, N.Y. 10017, U.S.A.

Library of Congress Catalog Card Number 69-12335

ISBN 0-8229-3558-9

US ISSN 0076-8820

Published by the University of Pittsburgh Press, Pittsburgh, Pa. 15260

Copyright © 1988, University of Pittsburgh Press

Feffer & Simons, Inc., London

Manufactured in the United States of America

Dedicated to the memory of
Mother M. Christopher Pecheux
(1916–1982)

CONTENTS

MOTHER M. CHRISTO-
PHER PECHEUX — The Nativity Tradition in *Elegia Sexta* 3

JOAN S. BENNETT — Virgin Nature in *Comus* 21

EUGENE R. CUNNAR — Milton, *The Shepherd* of Hermas, and
the Writing of a Puritan Masque 33

LOUISE SIMONS — "And Heaven Gates Ore My Head":
Death as Threshold in Milton's Masque 53

BRUCE BOEHRER — Elementary Structures of Kingship:
Milton, Regicide, and the Family 97

LEE A. JACOBUS — Milton Metaphrast: Logic and Rhetoric
in Psalm i 119

MARY ANN
RADZINOWICZ — Psalms and the Representation of Death
in *Paradise Lost* 133

JOHN R. MULDER — The Lyric Dimension of *Paradise Lost* 145

CARROL B. COX — Citizen Angels: Civil Society and the
Abstract Individual in *Paradise Lost* 165

KING-KOK CHEUNG — Beauty and the Beast: A Sinuous Reflection of Milton's Eve 197

MICHAEL LIEB — Milton's "Dramatick Constitution": The
Celestial Dialogue in *Paradise Lost,*
Book III 215

LEONARD MUSTAZZA — The Verbal Plot of *Samson Agonistes* 241

HUGH MAC CALLUM — *Samson Agonistes:* The Deliverer as
Judge 259

MILTON STUDIES

XXIII

THE NATIVITY TRADITION
IN *ELEGIA SEXTA*

Mother M. Christopher Pecheux

T HE CONCLUDING lines of Milton's *Elegia Sexta* have given rise
to several problems. The first, chronologically, was articulated in
Salmasius's *Responsio*, published in England posthumously in 1660: referring to line 85, Salmasius says contemptuously, "He calls the sky 'stelliparum,' as if it would produce stars."[1] As far as I know, later scholars
have not been unduly exercised over this lapse; I shall return to the objection, however, at the end of this essay. A second problem, whether
these last lines are an excrescence which destroys the unity of the elegy,
has been answered by Anthony Low in a recent article.[2] Finally, there
is a question about the relationship of the passage to *Ode on the Morning
of Christ's Nativity*. *Elegia Sexta* was written in December 1629 as an
epistle to Charles Diodati; before he concludes the letter, Milton gives
an account of a poem he has just written. Is the ode, in fact, the poem
described in the elegy? And if it is, why do the details in the description
not correspond exactly with those in the English poem? Although there
has been some controversy on the subject in the past, it is generally agreed
that the ode is indeed the poem described in the elegy, composed, like
it, in the Christmas season of 1629.[3] I am concerned, therefore, only
with the final part of the third problem, the discrepancies between the
two poems.

The description of the English poem occupies only eight lines in the
elegy, with two lines of introduction and two of conclusion:

> At tu si quid agam, scitabere (si modò saltem
> > Esse putas tanti noscere siquid agam)
> Paciferum canimus caelesti semine regem,
> > Faustaque sacratis saecula pacta libris,
> Vagitumque Dei, et stabulantem paupere tecto
> > Qui suprema suo cum patre regna colit,
> Stelliparumque polum, modulantesque aethere turmas,
> > Et subitò elisos ad sua fana Deos.
> Dona quidem dedimus Christi natalibus illa,
> > Illa sub auroram lux mihi prima tulit.

3

Te quoque pressa manent patriis meditata cicutis,
Tu mihi, cui recitem, judicis instar eris.   (79–90)

[But if you will know what I am doing (if only you think it of any importance to know whether I am doing anything) — I am singing the heaven-descended King, the bringer of peace, and the blessed times promised in the sacred books — the infant cries of our God and his stabling under a mean roof who, with his Father, governs the realms above. I am singing the starry sky and the hosts that sang high in air, and the gods that were suddenly destroyed in their own shrines. These are my gifts for the birthday of Christ — gifts which the first light of its dawn brought to me. For you these simple strains that have been meditated on my native pipes are waiting; and you, when I recite them to you, shall be my judge.][4]

Despite many obvious similarities between these lines and the Nativity ode, there are some differences, which have been duly noted by critics and editors. Parker, for example, in referring to the elegy, says: "Milton here emphasizes — *as his ode does not* — the infant wails and humble roof of the Christ-child."[5] Louis Martz attempts to explain the variations by the theory that the infant cries and the stabling under a mean roof in the elegy stem from the naive tradition of the Christmas carol as part of the decorum of simplicity.[6] Because I do not think simplicity is precisely what Milton was aiming at in either the elegy or the ode, and because, in any case, the theory does not explain why some details are in one poem and not the other, I do not find this explanation entirely satisfactory, even though I am grateful to Martz for providing by his hypothesis the impetus to my own investigations.

Before attempting an answer I should like to emphasize the problem. Milton himself cannot have failed to notice the variations; both poems were composed in 1629 but not published until 1645, and there was certainly time to polish and reconcile. Bentley's favorite hypothesis concerning the handicap of the poet's blindness did not apply in 1645. Moreover, when the poems were reissued, again in the same volume, in 1673, the only change in these concluding lines of the elegy was a minor one, perhaps accidental, in punctuation (CM I, 584). Salmasius himself alludes to the fact that the alleged errors could not be excused on the grounds of youth, since Milton had reached mature years before the poems were published.[7] Leo Miller suggests the possibility that Salmasius's criticisms, which were published only in 1660, may have been read to Milton (who of course was blind by that time) before the second edition of the poems; some of the changes in the 1673 edition correspond to some of Salmasius's examples.[8] At any rate, it is certain that Milton allowed the lines in question to remain unaltered, and the premise from which all Miltonists start is that Milton knew what he was doing.

In demonstrating the unity of *Elegia Sexta*, Anthony Low has shown that the classical festive spirit and the religious are not incompatible, that the overtly classical surface of the elegy has typological implications which lead naturally to the direct mention of Christian revelation in the last lines, and that the kind of poetry celebrated in the elegy is not only epic but any kind of divine poetry, including St. Paul's psalms, hymns, and spiritual songs.[9] That the lines constitute in some sense a declaration of the young poet's dedication to Christian poetry seems to be an inevitable corollary.[10]

Milton makes a graceful transition from the role of classical bard to that of Christian singer. In lines 77–78 he declares: "Diis etenim sacer est vates, divûmque sacerdos, / Spirat et occultum pectus, et ora Jovem" ["Truly the bard is sacred to the gods and is their priest; his hidden heart and his lips alike breathe out Jove"]. There follows immediately: "But if you will know what I am doing . . . I am singing the heaven-descended King." Besides making explicit the Christian implications of the preceding part of the poem, the final passage refers to the particular poem that this poet has just written; and that poem, after its introductory stanzas, is a *hymn*, as Milton is careful to entitle the main part of the ode, a hymn which he is offering as a gift to the Infant. At this moment, therefore, he is taking his place in the genus "Christian poet" and in the species "hymn writer." Moreover, because he has demonstrated in the elegy his mastery of classical Latin poetics, he is not in any sense disavowing this heritage but rather declaring that a Christian poet can use all that he has learned from classical masters in the service of the Christian God. In this twofold role he resembles the group of poets—late Latin, early Christian—who performed a similar function at the dawn of the Middle Ages: Hilary, Juvencus, Paulinus of Nola, Ambrose, Sedulius, Prudentius, Fortunatus. By their overt statements and their practice these poets were the logical model for the young Milton.

There is good reason to believe that even in 1629 Milton would have been familiar with these poets. The translation of Latin hymns was a regular part of the curriculum in schools of the period.[11] John Colet, the founder of St. Paul's School, had included in his list of recommended authors Prudentius, Sedulius, and Juvencus, as well as Lactantus, Proba, "and suche other as shalbe thoughte convenyent and moste to purpose unto the true laten spech."[12] Although Clark finds no evidence that they were still being studied when Milton attended St. Paul's a century later, the probability that they were is attested by various sources. Baldwin shows that Colet's ideas on the curriculum had remained popular; his words were borrowed many times by other foundations, the statutes at

St. Saviour's in Southwark, for example, being closely modeled on Colet's and including the same list of Christian poets.[13] Vives assigned readings from their works both for Princess Mary and for Charles Mountjoy (see the citations below). The works of the poets continued to be published; Prudentius had been included in five collections by 1625, and there had already been twelve editions of his works.[14] A collection of Latin poetry published in London in 1603, with later editions in 1611 and 1627, included poems by Juvencus, Paulinus, Prudentius, and Fortunatus; most of the examples I shall cite below can be found there.[15]

More significant than the availability of these writers are the reasons for their inclusion in the curriculum. Subject matter alone would not have been sufficient to justify a Renaissance educator in presenting impeccable matter in lame verse. It is precisely the combination of lofty matter with excellent classical verse that recommends them. Vives's instructions to Princess Mary illustrate this point:

There are also Christian poets whom it will be pleasant and fruitful to read, as Prudentius, Sidonius, Paulinus, Arator, Prosper, Juvencus, who in many places might compare with any of the ancients — I speak of the elegancies of verse. For in subject matter they are as much superior, as good things surpass the evil and the divine the human (Baldwin, p. 187).

Similarly, in his instructions to Charles Mountjoy, Vives mentions Prudentius, Prosper, Paulinus, Servilius, Juvencus, and Arator, pointing out that not only do they have the highest kind of matter but that they have many passages which by eloquence and charm of verse equal or even surpass the ancients (Baldwin, pp. 187, 191). Even Erasmus, who was less enthusiastic in his estimate of these poets, includes Prudentius in his list of recommended authors as "the most truly eloquent Christian poet" (Baldwin, p. 85).

Baldwin (p. 680) cites a "prefatory puff" to Haddon's *Lucubrationes*, published in 1567, which seems to put the later Christian poets on a level with earlier classical authors:

> Eloquium quis non Ciceronis laudet, et artem,
>   Quis non Nasonis nobile carmen amet?
> Cui non Sedulius, Prudentius atque Iuvencus
>   In pretio? Quis non scripta vetusta probet?

[Who would not praise the eloquence of Cicero and his art? Who would not love the noble song of Ovid? Who would not prize Sedulius, Prudentius, and Juvencus? Who would not approve these old writings?]

Baldwin comments that Haddon "was trying to be a Christian poet, along with Sedulius, Prudentius, and Juvencus." I believe that it was in this tradition, rather than that of the naive Christmas carol, that Milton placed his poetic efforts.

Renaissance humanists like Colet, Vives, and Haddon evidently recognized the importance of the role played in the history of Western culture by these early Christian poets, men who had been well educated, and educated in the classical tradition; who knew that the best way to appeal to their educated readers was to clothe their new ideas in accepted style. Paulinus, for example, has been recognized as "demonstrably the literary disciple of Virgil, Horace, and Ovid"; he was writing "primarily for the edification and instruction of men who scrutinise Christian claims through classical spectacles."[16] If Milton wanted a model for his own efforts to use Christian material without sacrificing his classical heritage, he could find it in some of their explicit statements. Juvencus, after speaking of the immortality which poets bestow on those whose deeds they celebrate, claims no less immortality for the poets themselves, especially the Christian poets:

> Nec minor ipsorum discurrit gloria vatum,
> quae manet aeternae similis, dum saecla volabunt
> et vertigo poli terras atque aequora circum
> aethera sidereum jusso moderamine volvet.
> Quod si tam longam meruerunt carmina famam,
> quae veterum gestis hominum mendacia nectunt,
> nobis certa fides aeternae in saecula laudis
> immortale decus tribuet, meritumque rependet.
> Nam mihi carmen erit Christi vitalia gesta,
> divinum populis falsi sine crimine donum.   (11–20)

[For the poets too no less a fame is heralded far and wide, which shall endure well-nigh eternal, as long as the ages will run, as long as the spinning pole sweeps round through starry space the lands and seas in their unchanging orbits. And if poems, that weave lying fables into the deeds of the ancients, have merited so great praise, then our unshaken faith will win for us immortal glory and earn the reward of eternal praise through all the ages. For my song shall be the life and deeds of Christ, God's gift to mankind, without any falsehood.][17]

"I, in my proportion, with this over and above of being a Christian" were the words in which some years later Milton was to express his poetic aspirations.[18] The sentiment is elaborated in *Carmen X* (the first letter to Ausonius), by Paulinus of Nola. Formerly, he says, he had begged for poetic power from Apollo and the Muses:

Nunc alia mentem vis agit, major Deus;
    aliosque mores postulat,
sibi reposcens ab homine munus suum,
    vivamus ut vitae Patri.   (29–32)

[But now a new power, a mightier God animates my soul; a different life he demands of man, requiring that we should live for him alone, the author of life.][19]

Like Milton's water-drinking poet, Paulinus responds to the demand that he renounce vanities, a life of ease, or sinful gain, experiencing in their place a chaste joy at belonging wholly to God. But Paulinus insists that in rejecting the muses he has not rejected his old master; if there is in his talent now anything fit for the service of God, the first thanks are due to Ausonius, as well as the glory, "for by your training was born in me what Christ loves" ("cujus praeceptis partum est quod Christus amaret," 146).

Paulinus's attitude to Ausonius is simply a particularization of what is recognized by literary historians as the general posture of all these early Christian poets: to write on Christian subjects without sacrificing the techniques they had learned in the pagan schools from the pagan poets. This is surely at least part of what Milton means by his transition to the last part of *Elegia Sexta*, where the adversative force of "but" in line 79 is qualified by the typological thrust of the lines that precede it: "For truly, the bard is sacred to the gods and is their priest. His hidden heart and his lips alike breathe out Jove." The terminology suggests that the Christian poet is going beyond those water-drinking poets who could see the true vision only darkly but that he recognizes his affinity with them. I have been speaking, he says equivalently, of pagan poetry, and of pagan poetry that is implicitly Christian; but what I have been doing, in the poem I have just been writing, is to take a further step, to write on a specifically Christian subject. That in so doing I have not renounced my old classic masters is attested by the fact that I describe my Christian subject here in the same elegant elegiacs I have used in the earlier parts of the poem. Neither the English ode, meditated on my native pipes, nor my description of it, is to be dissociated from the classic masters who were my first inspiration.

In noting some of the resemblances between the Latin hymn writers and *Elegia Sexta* I am aware, of course, that any poet writing on the Nativity has only a limited number of details on which to draw, with Luke, chapter ii, and Matthew, chapter ii as his only primary sources. Obviously, then, there will be parallels between the early Christian writers and Milton. However, since I am placing these resemblances in the context of a larger problem — why the elegy includes some details which the ode does not — I believe that they acquire some added significance.

Most of the Latin Christmas hymns that have come down to us emphasize the contrast between the eternal generation of the Son of God and his temporal birth at Christmas, the light of the miraculous star, the role of the Child as a bringer of peace between God and man, and the presentation of gifts. All of these motifs appear in both the elegy and the ode, as does the flight of the pagan gods (which is not a part of the hymn tradition but which Milton could have known from a number of sources, including Prudentius's *Apotheosis*).[20] Some of the hymns emphasize also, however, the two chief details which Milton includes in the elegy but not in the ode: the Infant's cry (which is not mentioned in the Gospel accounts either), and the poverty of the stable (implied but not explicit in the Gospel or the ode).

The fourth-century Hilary of Poitiers was the first to introduce Latin hymns into the Church, as attested by Jerome and Isidore. The three hymns, certainly by Hilary, were discovered only in the nineteenth century; but another poem formerly attributed to him, "Hymnum dicat turba fratrum," was extant in the Middle Ages and the Renaissance. Addressing Christ as the creator of all things, born of the Father, the hymn moves to a mention of the Virgin birth and then to the coming of the Magi, who follow the star and offer their gifts: "rem novam nec ante visam, virginem puerperam. / tunc magi stellam secuti primi adorant parvulum, / offerentes tus et aurum, digna regi munera" ("something new and never seen before, a virgin giving birth; then the Magi, following the star, are the first to adore the Child, offering incense and gold, gifts worthy of a king"; 13–15). The end of the poem is especially significant in that it refers to the coming dawn, which, as Walpole points out, had special meaning for the early Christians: "ante lucem nuntiemus Christum regem saeculo. / galli cantus, galli plausus proximum sentit diem" ("before the light dawns, let us announce Christ, the king of the ages. The song of the cock, the crowing of the cock, announce the coming of day"; 69–70).[21] The dawn has a prominent place at the end of *Elegia Sexta:* "Illa sub auroram lux mihi prima tulit. ("These [gifts] the first light of dawn brought me"). The morning light which on one level brought inspiration to the poet symbolizes on another level the shattering of the darkness of paganism.

The real founder of the Christian hymn tradition was Hilary's slightly younger contemporary, Ambrose. One of the best known hymns attributed to him is "Christe Redemptor omnium" (sometimes given as "Jesu Redemptor omnium"). Like Milton, the author contrasts the divine origin of the Infant with his lowly birth in time, putting special emphasis on the occasion for the hymn: it is *this* annual occurrence of the commemoration of the Nativity which inspires *this* new hymn:

> Hic praesens testatur dies
> Currens per anni circulum,
> Quod solus a sede patris
> Mundi salus adveneris.
>
> Hunc caelum, terra, hunc mare,
> Hunc omne, quod in eis est,
> Auctorem adventus tui
> Laudat exsultans cantico.   (13–20)

[This present day, as it comes around each year, bears witness that you alone have come from the seat near your Father to be the world's salvation. The heavens, the earth, the sea, and everything in them joyfully praise in song this day of your coming.][22]

The immediacy of the occasion comes to a climax in the final stanza, where the hymn itself becomes a birthday gift:

> Nos quoque, qui sancto tuo
> Redempti sanguine sumus,
> Ob diem natalis tui
> Hymnum novum concinimus.   (21–24)

[And we too who have been redeemed by your holy blood, sing together a new hymn for your birthday.]

So too Milton presents his poetic gift at the end of the elegy: "These are my gifts for the birthday of Christ."

In the fifth-century alphabetical hymn by Sedulius, "A solis ortus cardine," the familiar contrast between the dignity of the creator of the world and the lowliness of the human body which he puts on is followed by several stanzas which describe the details of the nativity scene:

> Faeno iacere pertulit,
> praesepe non abhorruit,
> parvoque lacte pastus est,
> per quem nec ales esurit.
>
> Gaudet chorus caelestium
> et angeli canunt Deum,
> palamque fit pastoribus
> pastor, creator omnium.   (21–28)

[He was content to lie on hay; he did not shrink from the manger; and he through whose care not even a bird suffers hunger was fed with a little milk. The choir of heavenly spirits rejoices, and the angels sing to God; the Shepherd, the creator of all things, is made known to the shepherds.][23]

The specific evidences of the poverty of the surroundings are in line with Milton's more succinct phrase, "stabling under a mean roof."

In the stanza which deals with the coming of the Magi, the real significance of the miraculous star and of the gifts, two elements stressed by Milton, suggests a movement beyond realism:

> Ibant magi qua venerant
> stellam sequentes praeviam;
> lumen requirunt lumine,
> Deum fatentur munere.   (33–36)

[The Magi set out, following the star which they had seen leading the way; by its light they seek the Light, and by their gifts they acknowledge him to be God.]

Here the symbolism of light adds a poetic aura to the realistic description.

Fortunatus, like Sedulius, combines some specific details of the Nativity scene with a reflection on the contrast between these and the Infant's real dignity:

> praesepe poni pertulit,
> qui lucis auctor exstitit:
> cum Patre caelos condidit,
> sub matre pannos induit.   (17–20)

[He suffered himself to be placed in a manger, he who is the author of light; he who with his Father created the heavens puts on the clothes made by his mother.][24]

This stanza, as might be expected, comes from a Nativity hymn. More unexpectedly, there is a similar passage in Fortunatus's hymn to the Cross, "Pange, lingua, gloriosi proelium certaminis":

> quando venit ergo sacri plenitudo temporis,
> missus est ab arce patris natus, orbis conditor,
> atque ventre virginali carne factus prodiit.
>
> vagit infans inter arta conditus praesepia,
> membra pannis involuta virgo mater adligat,
> et pedes manusque, crura stricta pingit fascia.   (10–15)

[When therefore the fullness of the sacred time had come, the Son, the creator of the world, was sent from the citadel of the Father, and clothed in flesh he proceeded from the virginal womb. Hidden in a narrow manger, the Infant cries; the Virgin Mother binds his members, wrapped in rags, and marks with a tight band his hands and feet.][25]

The main theme of this hymn is the divine dispensation whereby the instrument of man's fall, the tree, is replaced by the wood of the redeeming cross, so the two stanzas devoted to the Nativity are something of a digression. Probably Fortunatus wanted to single out from the beginning of the Savior's life some features which might be thought to foreshadow the Passion. Whatever his motive, it is interesting that he combines in a single line the infant cry and the lowly manger ("Vagit infans inter arta conditus praesepia") much as Milton combined them: ("Vagitumque Dei, et stabulantem paupere tecto").

Most successful of all these early poets in uniting classical and Christian traditions was Prudentius, who wrote about the year 400. "The culture represented by Prudentius's hymns," says E. K. Rand, "and which he passed on to the coming generations, cannot dispense with the ancient authors who had contributed to its making." "He was filling the framework of Pindaric and Horatian hymns with Christian feeling and belief."[26] Even aside from the fact that most modern editors of Milton cite some parallels between Prudentius and the Nativity ode,[27] his possible influence on *Elegia Sexta* deserves exploration.

Outstanding among Prudentius's contributions to the hymn genre was the *Cathemerinon*, a collection of twelve hymns. In *Cathemerinon IX*, entitled "A Hymn for Every Hour" and dealing with the entire life of Christ, the first twenty-seven lines celebrate the Nativity, and they include some of the more abstract and theological concepts (as distinguished from realistic details) used by Milton in the elegy.

The poet presents himself at the beginning of the poem as a successor to David, the priest-king:

> Christus est, quem rex sacerdos adfuturum protinus
> infulatus concinebat voce, chorda et tympano,
> spiritum caelo influentem per medullas hauriens.   (4–6)

[Christ it is whose speedy coming the priest-king in his priestly vestment sang with sound of voice and string and tambour, drinking deep the inspiration that flowed on him from heaven.][28]

Milton uses a similar image in his transition to the conclusion of his poem: "For truly, the bard is sacred to the gods and is their priest. His hidden heart and his lips alike breathe out Jove" ("Diis etenim sacer est vates, divûmque sacerdos, / Spirat et occultum pectus, et ora Jovem").

Prudentius devotes several stanzas to describing the role of the Son as the manifestation of the Father's love, the beginning and end of all creation, before he speaks of the "blessed birth" and exhorts the angels in heaven and all on earth to sing the praises of God. He then returns to one of Milton's themes:

> ecce, quem vates vetustis concinebant saeculis,
> quem prophetarum fideles paginae spoponderant,
> emicat promissus olim: cuncta conlaudent eum.   (25–27)

[Lo, he whom seers in ancient times foretold, and the faithful pages of the prophets pledged, comes forth, promised of old: let all things join in praise of him.]

In distinguishing between the "seers" and the "prophets," Prudentius seems to be referring to both pagan and Hebrew figures; a Christian of the era would probably think of the Sibylline Books and Virgil's Messianic Eclogue as true prophecies by pagan seers. Milton's allusion to "the blessed times promised in the sacred books" seems to include, through its generalized phrasing, the sacred books of both pagan and Christian cultures.

Cathemerinon XI is a hymn for Christmas day which comes close in many ways to the emphasis and spirit of Milton's elegy. It begins where Milton's poem ends, with the returning light:

> Quid est quod artum circulum
> sol iam recurrens deserit?
> Christusne terris nascitur,
> qui lucis auget tramitem?   (1–4)

[What means it that the sun is now returning, leaving his narrow circle behind him? Is not Christ, who enlarges the path of light, born this day on earth?]

The hymn continues with an explanation of the way in which the word and wisdom of the Father in the fullness of time put on a mortal body, thereby inaugurating a new golden age:

> o quanta rerum gaudia
> alvus pudica continet,
> ex qua novellum saeculum
> procedit et lux aurea!   (57–60)

[What joys for the world that chaste womb holds, whence comes forth the new age with its golden light!]

In the sixteenth stanza this new age is said to be inaugurated by the crying of the Infant:

vagitus ille exordium
vernantis orbis prodidit,
nam tunc renatus sordidum
mundus veternum depulit.   (61–64)

[That child's crying showed forth the beginning of the world's spring, for then the
world reborn put away its foul torpor.]

The golden age and the holy manger are the focus of the next several
stanzas, and the hymn concludes with a vision of the last judgment.

The resemblance of this part of the hymn to *Elegia Sexta* invites special comment. In the first place, Prudentius uses the word "vagitus," which
constitutes in the elegy the most evident departure from the ode. In the
second place, this "vagitus" is closely related by Prudentius to the beginning of a new era; and Milton too combines these two ideas in lines 83
and 84: "Faustaque sacratis saecula pacta libris, / Vagitumque Dei" ("the
blessed times promised in the sacred books and the infant cry of God").

These two hymns of Prudentius offer analogues to some features of
Milton's lines not usually present in the traditional hymns: the seasonal
motif of light, the figure of the poet-priest, the golden age. In common
with many other hymns they include the singing angels and the paradox
of the mighty creator lying in a manger. Taken as a whole, these early
Christian Latin hymns include in one form or another every detail used
by Milton at the conclusion of *Elegia Sexta* except the destruction of the
pagan gods; and Fortunatus and Prudentius emphasize the cry of the
Infant which figures in the elegy but not in the ode. I am less interested
in arguing for a direct influence from these hymns, although I think Prudentius does offer such an example, than in placing the concluding lines
of the elegy against a tradition which, both in general context and specific details, provides an appropriate framework for the lines. Both this
passage and the English ode are recapitulations of the themes of their
predecessors, offshoots from a common parent stem. Both reveal discreetly
their ancestry and inherit the same traits, while each also retains its own
individuality. From this viewpoint, the question of whether they correspond exactly with each other becomes less important. Milton had indeed written a Nativity poem in English, but the passage in the elegy
must be approached on its own merits. Because of its language and form
it is a closer analogue to its predecessors; moreover, it does not stand alone
but is closely related to the earlier parts of the poem. It goes beyond
them, however, to declare allegiance to an important tradition which
could praise Christ without denying the claims of Apollo.

Whether the declaration of allegiance is strengthened by verbal reminiscence is difficult to ascertain. Certainly Milton's training would have sharpened his awareness of distinctive word uses. The common practice in the schools of translating verses from Latin to English and English to Latin in itself demanded careful attention, and extensive use was made of lists of synonyms and epithets. The pupils were encouraged to keep their personal lists of words and phrases used by different authors; and if the more ambitious boys did this, as Bradner suggests, Milton would most probably have been among their number.[29]

Renaissance authors were expected to use allusions to the classics but not make them too obvious.[30] The *Variorum* cites several classical parallels to phrases in the last part of the *Elegia;* the use of these is consistent with the retention of classical meter in the poem. There are similar parallels with the Christian hymn writers, but they cannot be pressed too far, since the vocabulary available for the similar subject matter inevitably would be limited. I believe, however, that there may be some special significance in Milton's use of the word "vagitus," the most important motif that appears in the elegy but not in the ode. As has been seen above, the Infant's cry is especially significant in Prudentius's hymn, where it is closely related to the renewal of the world. Two sixteenth-century commentaries on this passage of Prudentius elaborate this significance. Erasmus remarks: "In Christo . . . vagitus indicabat mundum renasci: quandoquidem qui baptizantur in Christum, per illum renascuntur." ["In Christ, the cry indicated that the world was being reborn: seeing that those who are baptized in Christ are reborn through him."][31] Fabricius makes a similar comment:

Vagitus in aliis hominibus miseriae exordium est, in puero Christo initium solatii, et orbis quasi juvenescentis praesagium; quia ejus ortu in novam dignitatem restitutus est, non aliter ac post hyemis sterilitatem ver novum efflorescit.

[A cry in other men is a prelude to misery, but in the infant Christ it is the beginning of consolation and as it were a presage of the renewal of the earth; because at his birth man is restored to new dignity, just as the new spring bursts into bloom after the sterility of winter.][32]

Since Milton incorporated echoes of Virgil and Horace into his verse, he may have deliberately and consciously treated the later Latin writers in the same way. Many of the words he uses in lines 81–88, even those which were part of the vocabulary of the classic writers as well, had been consecrated by usage in the Christian hymns. One of the characteristics of early Christian Latin poetry was its tendency to revive obsolete words, use old words with new meanings, and even, when necessary, to coin new words when the older vocabulary was inadequate for conveying subtle theological points.[33] The result was the creation of a somewhat distinctive Christian tone.

At any rate, considerations of vocabulary bring us finally to Salmasius and his problem with the word "stelliparum." It is not clear whether he is objecting to the idea that the sky could bring forth anything—that is certainly part of his meaning—or whether he is upset even more by an apparent neologism. Objection to the concept itself seems unusually captious, even for Salmasius; surely, such personification has always been a recognized poetic device, and Milton's English phrase near the end of the ode, "Heav'n's youngest-teemed Star," is recognized by most readers as a happy phrase. Since Salmasius's citation of "stelliparum" occurs in the context of a list of alleged errors in grammar and scansion, perhaps his criticism is directed at the more technical aspect of the word.

The combination of "stella" and "pario" does seem to be Milton's innovation. "Stellifer," "stelliger," and "stellimicans" are known, however, especially in poetry, and "stelliger" was increasingly used in Late Latin.[34] "Gero" can mean "to bring forth," and Milton could have used that word instead of "pario," as he did in the third epigram on the Gunpowder Plot, line 7: "Et, si stelligeras unquam penetraveris arces" ("And if ever you attain the starry citadels"). Possibly the choice of "pario" was a reflection of the practice of the hymn writers, who used the word frequently, in either its noun or its verb form, when they emphasized, as they so often did, the virgin birth. The choice of the word had theological as well as lexical implications, since it was often said that the Virgin had been exempted from the pains that usually accompany childbirth.[35] Milton's combination of "pario" and "stella" was a license similar to that assumed by Prudentius and the others, who often had to modify classical vocabulary in order to express new ideas.

Another possible defense against Salmasius's criticism may lie in the sound of the word. These last lines contain a good deal of alliteration. Although the earlier parts of the elegy have also made use of this device, I have not detected such an extended use: the alliterative pattern is confined to one or two lines, whereas here the "p" and the "s" are repeated over six lines, 81–86. The pattern is marked, even if only initial alliteration is considered, and it becomes still more marked if each syllable is noticed. The italicized letters demonstrate the design:

> Paciferum canimus caelesti semine regem,
>   Faustaque sacratis saecula pacta libris,
> Vagitumque Dei, et stabulantem paupere tecto
>   Qui suprema suo cum patre regna colit,
> Stelliparumque polum, modulantesque aethere turmas,
>   Et subitò elisos ad sua fana Deos.

This yields an interesting series: psss, ssssps, spp, spsp, sppss, sssss. The "p" in "stelliparum" is one element in the series. One might notice also the rhyme in "paciferum," "vagitum," and "stelliparum."

Such overtly musical devices as alliteration and rhyme became more and more common as Christian hymnody developed. Most of the writers wanted their hymns to be sung. St. Ambrose adapted to this end without sacrificing quantitative meters; eventually, for his followers in the Middle Ages, accentual and rhymed poetry became the rule. Most Renaissance scholars deplored this development as far as Latin poetry was concerned (vernacular hymns were a different matter), and Milton would no doubt have hesitated to stray too far from classical models; but perhaps the additional musical element provided by the marked alliteration was an acknowledgment of his inheritance from the hymn tradition in which he now had a secure place.

That hymn tradition is carried on in English by the ode which Milton wrote on Christmas morning, 1629. When, a few days later, he ended his letter to Diodati, it seems that the tradition loomed larger for him than the hymn itself; otherwise, he would have made sure that there was no discrepancy between the concluding lines of *Elegia Sexta* and the English poem. The relationship between the two is indeed close, but it is not exactly equivalent; rather, the former carries the concentrated weight of the same tradition that is diffused in the longer poem. Paradoxically, the relationship can sustain surface dissimilarities because of the firmness of the foundation on which it rests.

The early hymn writers consciously united classical tradition (which in their period included the use of the Latin language) with Christian content. Milton, in a later age, was free to use either Latin and English, and in this instance he showed his virtuosity by writing in both. The decorum of the Nativity ode did not permit the kind of statement possible in the elegy, where by various means he designates himself as the imitator and successor of the earlier writers, the inheritor of a dual tradition. The two poems taken together constitute the beginning of his lifelong dedication to demonstrating the continued viability of that tradition.

College of New Rochelle

NOTES

The most complete collection of Latin hymns is *Analecta Hymnica Medii Aevi*, 58 vols., ed. G. M. Dreves, C. Blume, and H. M. Bannister (Leipzig, 1886–1923). More manageable are two one-volume collections which are confined to the early period: *Early Chris-*

tian Latin Poets from the Fourth to the Sixth Century, ed. Otto J. Kuenmuench (Chicago, 1919), and *Early Latin Hymns*, ed. A. S. Walpole (Cambridge, 1922; rpt. Hildesheim, 1966); I have used these for most of my citations. For citations from Prudentius I have used the Loeb Classical Library edition, 2 vols., trans. H. J. Thomson (Cambridge, Mass., 1949). Also useful are Matthew Britt, *The Hymns of the Breviary and Missal* (New York, 1948), and Joseph Connelly, *Hymns of the Roman Liturgy* (Westminster, Md., 1957); however, since these use the texts as revised for the Roman Breviary of 1632, they are more helpful for translations and notes than for texts. Kuenmuench provides English translations for some of the hymns. When no reference for the English is given to one of these sources, the translation is mine.

1. *The Life Records of John Milton*, ed. J. M. French (New Brunswick, N.J., 1956), vol. iv; pp. 345–47 (text and translation).

2. Anthony Low, "The Unity of Milton's *Elegia Sexta*," *ELR*, XI (1981), 213–23.

3. See the evidence summarized in *The Latin and Greek Poems*, vol. I of *A Variorum Commentary on the Poems of John Milton*, ed. Douglas Bush (New York, 1970), pp. 125–26; hereafter cited as Bush, *Variorum*.

4. Text from *The Works of John Milton*, 18 vols., ed. Frank Allen Patterson et al. (New York, 1931–40), vol. I, pp. 212–14 (hereafter cited in the text as CM); translation from *John Milton: Complete Poems and Major Prose*, ed. Merritt Y. Hughes (New York, 1957), pp. 52–53.

5. William Riley Parker, *Milton*, 2 vols. (Oxford, 1968), vol. I, p. 69.

6. Louis L. Martz, *Poet of Exile* (New Haven, 1980), pp. 53–55. For an earlier presentation of this idea see Martz's essay "The Rising Poet" in *The Lyric and Dramatic Milton*, ed. Joseph H. Summers (New York, 1965), pp. 23–28.

7. French, *Life Records*, p. 347.

8. Leo Miller, "Milton, Salmasius, and *vapulandum*: Who Should Be Flogged?" *MQ* IX (1975), 73.

9. Ephesians v, 18–19; see note 2.

10. This is another matter that has been disputed, but the affirmative position has strong scholarly support; see Bush, *Variorum*, vol. I, pp. 113–15.

11. T. W. Baldwin, *William Shakspere's Small Latine and Lesse Greeke*, 2 vols. (Urbana, 1944), vol. I, p. 152.

12. Donald Clark, *John Milton at St. Paul's School* (New York, 1948), p. 101.

13. Baldwin, *William Shakspere's Small Latine and Lesse Greeke*, pp. 128, 424. See also A. F. Leach, "Milton as Schoolboy and Schoolmaster," *Proceedings of the British Academy* III (1907–08), 309.

14. *A Milton Encyclopedia*, 9 vols., ed. William B. Hunter, Jr. (Lewisburg, Va., 1975), vol. VII, p. 51.

15. This two-volume collection is entitled *Corpus Omnium Veterum Poetarum Latinorum*. I have used standard modern editions for my references to early hymns, but the texts of the following can also be found in volume II of this collection (1603 ed.): Juvencus, p. 673; Paulinus, pp. 803–05; both hymns by Fortunatus, pp. 809–10; both by Prudentius, pp. 803–05.

16. *The Poems of St. Paulinus of Nola*, ed. P. G. Walsh (New York, 1975), p. 4. For other comments on the role and the attitude of the early Christian poets, see F.J.E. Raby, *A History of Christian Latin Poetry* (Oxford, 1927), chapters 1–4.

17. Kuenmuench, *Early Christian Latin Poets*, pp. 18–19.

18. *The Reason of Church-government*, in CM III, p. 236.

19. Kuenmuench, *Early Christian Latin Poets*, pp. 210–17.

20. Lines 436–46; Loeb Classical Library, pp. 152–55.

21. The text is in Walpole, *Early Latin Hymns*, pp. 5–15; translation mine. Walpole comments in his introduction on the symbolic significance of the dawn for the early Christians (p. 3). The texts from Jerome and Isidore can be found in J.-P. Migne, *Patrologia Latina*, 23.738–39 and 83.743.

22. *Analecta hymnica medii aevi*, ed. Guido Maria Dreves, Clemens Blume, and Henry Marriott Bannister. 55 vols. (Leipzig, 1886–1922), vol. LI, 49; translation mine. According to John Julian, *A Dictionary of Hymnology*, rev. ed. (London, 1915), p. 936, this hymn was in use in 1575 at the Thame Grammar School among the prayers before leaving school.

23. Walpole, *Early Latin Hymns*, pp. 151–58; translation Britt, *Hymns of the Breviary*, pp. 85, 96.

24. Walpole, *Early Latin Hymns*, pp. 195–98; translation mine.

25. Ibid., pp. 167–73; translation mine. The progressive diminution in these stanzas from the Father's citadel to the virginal womb to the narrow manger to the swaddling bands is similar to the descent from the Trinal Throne to the darksome house of clay in the Nativity ode; the security of the Throne is contrasted in the latter poem with the destruction of the pagan shrines. I am indebted to James Freeman for these observations.

26. E. K. Rand, "Prudentius and Christian Humanism," *Transactions of the American Philological Association* LI (1920), 80; *Founders of the Middle Ages* (Cambridge, Mass., 1928), p. 212.

27. See the summary in *A Variorum Commentary on the Poems of John Milton*, vol. II, part 1, *The Minor English Poems*, ed. A.S.P. Woodhouse and Douglas Bush (New York, 1972), 35–36, and in the notes passim.

28. Loeb edition, vol. I, *Cath. IX* is on pp. 76–85; *Cath XI* is on pp. 94–103.

29. Leicester Bradner, *Musae Anglicanae* (New York, 1940), pp. 3–4. See also Clark, *John Milton at St. Paul's School*, pp. 175–77.

30. Rand, "Prudentius and Christian Humanism," p. 119.

31. *Prudentii opera omnia cum notis et interpretationibus in usum Delphini* 2 vols., (London, 1824), vol. II, pp. 1001–02; translation mine.

32. Prudentii, *Opera Omnia*, vol. II, p. 1135; translation mine.

33. Richard C. Trench, *Sacred Latin Poetry*, 3rd ed. (London, 1874), p. 6.

34. Alexander Souter, *A Glossary of Later Latin* (Oxford, 1949); A. Ernout and A. Meillet, *Dictionnaire étymologique de la langue latine* (Paris, 1939).

35. Thus St. Ambrose (on Psalm xlvii, 11) says: "Ideo eum Maria non parturivit, sed peperit" (Migne, *Patrologia Latina*, vol. XIV, p. 1206); "Therefore Mary did not go through labor, but she brought forth."

VIRGIN NATURE IN *COMUS*

Joan S. Bennett

R EADERS OF *Comus* continue to struggle with the young Milton's radical proclamation of the "sage and serious doctrine of Virginity." By some, the poem's high mystery of virginity is read as synonymous with "chastity" and as serving to symbolize virtue itself, the expression in action of the soul's chaste love (charity) of God.[1] In these readings, the masque is viewed primarily as a Christian moral statement extolling temperance. On the other hand, virginity is seen by some as a dogmatic elevation of the Lady's (and Milton's) literal virginity, most recently as "a reaction-formation to oedipal temptation" and as "hoarded [poetic] power."[2] In this view, the "doctrine" is seen to be one which the mature Milton repudiated.

Readers who are not willing to view the masque primarily through its author's early psychological complexes — who sense that *Comus* is essentially of a piece with Milton's later work — are left with some problems in the currently formulated Christian reading of the poem. William Madsen's 1958 summary of the problem still stands: "It has been alleged that the Lady's doctrine of virginity takes back what her doctrine of temperance grants. . . . The Lady's doctrine of temperance, it is said, suggests a reconciliation of the conflicting claims of the natural and spiritual, her doctrine of virginity a repudiation of nature."[3] A.S.P. Woodhouse and many subsequent readers see a continuum in the masque from the realm of nature to that of grace; more recently, Georgia Christopher has argued for an absolute (Protestant) disjunction between grace and nature. In Christopher's view, Milton's faith in *Comus* is made "more murky than mysterious," however, by the trappings of the humanistic masque genre: the nymphs, demons, and allegorical forms.[4]

While not at all devaluing either the fascination of reading the masque in terms of biography and contemporary psychology or the necessity of understanding theological modes of thought, I would like to readdress the Christian humanist literary context in which the poem also has roots; for these roots, throughout Milton's life and poetry in ever more radical forms, sustained all of his personal, religious, political, and poetic commitments — from virginity and Presbyterianism through marriage, revolution, and poetry. They are what give life to that virtue

21

which "alone is free" and to that freedom toward which Milton directed his creative powers. To reach back into the tradition, we can draw upon the work of the artist-scholars of the "twelfth-century Renaissance," whom C. S. Lewis characterizes as unifiers: "The great work which they attempted was to reunite the courtly and religious ideals. In an age of wilful asceticism and wilful *Frauendienst* they asserted the wholeness of the nature of man; it is this far more than their prosecution of classical studies, which entitles them to the name of Humanists."[5] The reuniting agent for the members of the school of Chartres was — as it was for the author of *Comus* — a concept of Nature. This is the same Nature that Milton defined in theological terms in the *De Doctrina:* "Nature cannot mean anything except the wonderful power and efficacy of the divine voice which went forth in the beginning, and which all things have obeyed ever since as a perpetual command."[6] Believing that faith may be expressed and explored even more fully through poetry than through theology, Christian humanists from Bernard Sylvestris and Alain de Lille through Edmund Spenser ("better teacher than Scotus or Aquinas"), and Milton himself have sought the challenge of giving poetic being to this *Natura.*

Spenser broke off his own attempt to elaborate a description of Natura in the mutability cantos of the *Faerie Queene* to defer, as had Chaucer before him, to the monumental achievement of Alain in his *Complaint of Nature (Plaint of Kindes)*, where the beauty and grandeur of the "great goddesse" is "set forth so as it ought":

> So hard it is for any living wight,
>   All her [Nature's] array and vestiments to tell,
>   That old Dan Geffrey (in whose gentle spright
>   The pure well head of Poesie did dwell)
>   In his Foules Parley durst not with it mel,
>   But it transferd to Alane, who he thought
>   Had in his Plaint of Kindes describ'd it well:
>   Which who will read set forth so as it ought.
> Go seek he out that Alane where he may be sought.[7]

The *Plaint of Kindes* could presumably "be sought" by Milton in the early seventeenth century since printing, in the sixteenth century, had given the work a new circulation.[8] Whether or not he was thinking of Alain in particular, however, Milton wrote *Comus* within a literary tradition whose concept of chastity was rich and whose figures of virginity offered a wealth to artists that has been unavailable since Milton's time. Alain's *Complaint of Nature* offers us a glimpse back into this fruitful artistic mode.[9]

Portraying Nature-as-God's-Voice called for allegory, but for allegory of a certain type. The generic difference between a tropological allegory, whose moral abstractions prescribe for us courses of action, and the allegory that Milton saw to be possible in the masque genre has been well characterized by Rosemond Tuve, who says of *Comus*, "We have imaged before us in the entire piece the greater beauty, superior reasonableness, and naturalness of all that we can lodge within the insufficient word *virtue* (the figure *castitas* is better)."[10] Her observation about *Comus*'s genre is paralleled by Lewis's comment about the genre developed by the school of Chartres, which, he says, "set the example of allegory on a large scale" that "enlarged upon the narrowly ethical scheme of Prudentius and [showed] itself capable of dealing with any subject the author cared to attempt" (p. 111).

The masque genre for Milton invited the paradoxical possibility of Platonic forms being made visible — of metaphysical qualities becoming the audience's felt experience. We hear Milton's Lady exclaim that she is able to "see visibly" the true "forms" of faith, hope, and chastity; but it is the Lady herself who is the object of the audience's vision. Because she is such an image, she can function at one level for us as a "form" made "visible"; in particular, her personal virginity, the object of Comus's attempted seduction, can call to mind and figure forth for us the ultimate virginity of the divine Nature which informs all being.

Like Milton's Lady, Alain's allegorical figure Natura, whose "Complaint" is against all human Comuses, has two often reiterated identifying traits besides her amazing beauty; these are her temperance and her virginity. A brief philosophical reminder might be useful here to recall how in the realm of ethics it can have been held that "virginity — even perpetual virginity — can be considered a mean."[11] Then we can go on to see how virginity could have seemed an appropriate trait for the allegorical Natura, endlessly fertile mother of all being, whose creative principle is temperance.[12]

The noun "temper" has in the past been used to mean "being," "creature," or "nature" — to refer, that is, to the essential nature of a thing. Thus, in *Paradise Lost*, Book IV, when Milton refers to Uthuriel as a "celestial temper" he means he is a celestial being, that is, an angel (cf. *PL* II, 211). This usage is related to Aristotle's notion of the mean as the "formal cause" of a human being, as that complex balance of all its elements which defines the whole individual being. Since the circumstances of each individual differ, the mean which would preserve the balanced identity of the agent in ethical decisions is to be identified "not in the object but relatively to us."[13]

Madsen points out that the whole context in which each Christian must "temper" his or her acts includes the realm of grace as well as the realm of Nature and that grace might, for a particular individual, call for celibacy. However, for the twelfth-century humanists in whose mode I believe Milton was working in *Comus*, the realms of grace and nature were not really distinct. In spite of the Fall, Natura in the masque remains "the wonderful power and efficacy of the divine voice" or, as Alain calls her, the perpetual "deputy of God the creator," "God's vice-regent" (Sheridan, pp. 117, 146).

A recent writer on Alain's theology finds his theological works orthodox but his poetry theologically puzzling. The surprise occurs first in Alain's *Anticlaudianus*, an extensive allegory in which Natura, grieved by human sinfulness, recreates a perfect man who does not fall to temptation and who shows it possible for a human being to live a perfect life. This schema, according to G. R. Evans, "amounts to an alternative to the Incarnation."[14] The schema really is not "alternative," however, but complementary.

The primary value of allegory, for Alain, is in its ability to lift us imaginatively out of the mode of thought in which nature and grace are differentiated, to invite us to imagine perfection. C. S. Lewis points out that in the *Anticlaudianus* "it is not a question of grace redeeming Nature: it is a question of sin departing from Nature."[15] Nature herself is eternally, purely good. Thus, in Alain's *Complaint of Nature*, when the poet, who has been severely depressed by the sinful world he sees around him, encounters Natura herself — descended from the heavens as a virgin of astounding beauty, who shines with dazzling light and on whose vestments (which Chaucer and Spenser would despair of describing) are depicted in patient, flamboyant detail all of her creations from constellations to fishes — he addresses her as holy: "O child of God, mother of creation, bond of the universe . . . peace, love, virtue, guide, power, order, law, end, way, leader, source, life, light, splendor, beauty, form, rule of the world: you, who by your reins guide the universe [and] . . . wed heaven to earth in a union of peace . . . you, at whose nod the world grows young again" (Sheridan, pp. 128–29). Alain's Natura journeys "out of the coasts of the heavenly region into the hovel of the world passible"[16] and we may identify her home with that of Milton's Attendant Spirit, that realm above this world where "the spruce and jocund Spring" and "eternal Summer" dwell. At the virgin's approach, Alain tells us, "You would think that all the elements were having a celebration by having . . . their native powers renewed" (Sheridan, p. 109). In Milton's Nativity ode it was Christ for whom the wind and waves stopped and the winter earth sought a covering; in *Comus* we are offered another mode of imagining the same reality.[17]

The divine power symbolized in the virginity of Natura is reflected in figures and metaphors used by Milton after he had largely given up the allegorical mode, as when, in *Paradise Lost*, Book V, Nature, in the Creation "wantoned . . . and plaid at will / Her Virgin Fancies" (294–96)[18] and when the Satan of *Paradise Lost* is struck with awe at the "virgin majesty" of Eve (IX, 270, 452). The Lady of *Comus* is identified by the Elder Brother as virgin in this large sense; she is, like Eve, strongly natural; that is, purely fulfilling the human "temper" Nature gave her. Natura herself shone for Alain "with no borrowed sheen" (Sheridan, p. 73). "Virtue," in the words of the Elder Brother, "could see to do what virtue would / By her own radiant light" (373–74). The light is the mean, Nature's ordering principle; it results in all things' growth from within to perfection.[19] For humans in an ideal (virginal) realm, the nature of the metaphysical order, the mean, will always determine the expression of that order in ethical action, in temperance. God created "passions within us, pleasures around us" because "these rightly *tempered* are the very ingredients of virtue" (*Aereopagitica*, YP II, 527; emphasis added). And Virtue means, as the angel tells Adam, holding one's "place / By wisdom" (*PL* IX, 636–37).

Holding one's place, maintaining one's identity, is the task of Wisdom. Throughout, Milton's Lady is identified with Wisdom. Hence the comparison to the virgin Minerva, who is a standard type of Wisdom, and the Elder Brother's identification of the Lady with "Wisdom's self" (*Comus* 375); hence the whole great Circe myth (treated so competently by Tuve) in which the Lady (as the Ulysses figure) stands for wisdom, right reason in the face of Circe-Comus (libertine nature), which tries to degrade her humanity into a half-animal monster for his herd. Hence also is the ordering of the Elder Brother's speech on chastity; he ascends (in lines 429–63) from the folklore magical concept of virginity's powers, through allegorized Greek mythology, to direct reference to the soul's chastity in this world, and, finally, to the virginity of the immortal soul, "The divine property of her first being" (469).

In his second speech (*Comus* 584–608), the Elder Brother can with confidence assert that "Virtue may be assailed but never hurt" (589) and that "evil on itself shall back recoil, and mix no more with goodness" because what he is talking about — and what the Virgin is — is a definition, the definition of the virtuous, or natural, human being. "If this fail," he says, "The pillar'd firmament is rott'nness" (597–98); if this virgin Lady, our image of the humanity Natura created, were to fail, there would be no such thing as a human being by God's definition. Alain's *Complaint of Nature* ends with Natura's "excommunication," pronounced by Genius, of all intemperate humans: "By the authority of the superessential Usia [Being] and his eternal Idea, with assent of the heavenly army, with the combined aid and help of Nature and the other recognised virtues, let every . . . [sinner] be separated from the kiss of heavenly love as his ingratitude deserves . . . let him be set apart from the harmonious council of the things of Nature" (Sheridan, p. 220). In the *Complaint*, the "pillar'd firmament" is firm; "rott'nnes" is expelled.

The immediate occasion of the *Complaint* is the poet's dismay at the widespread practice of sodomy, "a Venus turned monster" (Sheridan, p. 67). What the speaker perceives as sexual perversion stands in his mind aptly for all vice and crime, for that state in which "the essential decrees of Nature are denied a hearing." "Alas!" he cries, "Where has Nature with her fair form betaken herself?" (p. 67).

When Natura herself appears, she exclaims: "I regret that . . . I have honoured man's nature with so many graces and privileges (Sheridan, p. 134). Every other creature, she says, "obeying the edict I have promulgated, completely discharges the duties imposed by my law as the raison d'etre of its native condition demands," but man alone, "stripping himself of the robe of chastity . . . dares to stir up . . . strife against the dignity of his queen, and . . . fan the flame of civil war's rage against his mother" (p. 131). The first examples it occurs to her to list are sexual and depict the generation of nonhuman creatures like those in Comus's herd: "Pasiphae, also driven by the madness of inordinate lust, in the form of a cow corruptly celebrated her bestial nuptials with a brute animal, and, concluding with a viler error, ended by miscreating the enormity of the bullock [Minotaur, half bull and half man]" (Moffatt, p. 37).

Not all humans will be excommunicated by Genius's pronouncement, however. Natura's sister Wisdom, "although she grows weak from being held too cheaply in the many who live like animals in brutish sensuality, does not, however, cheat out of her gift of fame . . . those who have restored the little spark of reason to its original fire." Wisdom, Natura tells Alain, is "the one remedy for your exile, the only solace in human misfortune, the one and only morning star to end man's night. . . . No darkness in the heavens confuses her keen vision, no thickness of earth blocks her operation, no water's depth dims her vision" (Sheridan, p. 179).

In answer to Alain's question: "what irrational reason . . . has so forced man's little spark of reason to slumber, that he, drunk with the Lethean cup of sensuality, not only has become an apostate from thy laws, but also unrighteously rebels against them" (Moffatt, p. 42), Natura replies that this fall has come about because Wisdom — the steadfast perception of the mean — has been held too cheap. The "Lethean cup" is, of course, Comus's "crystal glass." Unlike the other wayfarers who have drunk from the glass, however, no darkness in the heavens confuses her vision of the holy forms that guide her, no thickness of earth blocks the efficacy of the root that protects her brothers, no water's depth dims the vision of the river goddess who rescues her. In all of the forms through which it appears in the masque for the Lady and her brothers, Wisdom is the one remedy for their exile.

The cup/glass is the second of Comus's three-step temptation of the Lady in the scene in his palace, and the order of the temptations follows the process by which, Natura tells Alain, "the ruinous evil of [1] idleness has produced inordinate love; how the excess and deluge of [2] drink has brought to pass love's raging [3] lust" (Moffatt, p. 57). Comus tries to put the Lady through three such steps; he wants her first to be idle, to "sit" (*Comus* stage directions and line 659) when she should be most on guard, then to drink and refresh herself, and finally to lust: "There was another meaning in these gifts" (754). As Tuve points out, however, although Comus follows the pattern for a literal seduction, he is really attempting a "rape of the mind."[20] It is thus, according to Natura, that "the whole world is shipwrecked on the most universal flood of intemperance" (Moffatt, p. 59).

"Intemperance" means in the *Complaint* what it means in *Comus*, the rape of the mind, the loss of wisdom or right reason. Natura describes the daughters of Idolatria, who accomplish the rape, and says that at the beginning of all is Bacchilatria. Bacchus himself in Alain's version is not unnatural, but he is dishonored by the intemperance of the victims of Bacchilatria, "who steals the spark of reason from her lover, and exposes him to the darkness of brutish sensuality, after the manner of a harlot so intoxicates him that he is forced to desire wine beyond measure . . . and [have] a canine greediness for eating" (Moffatt, pp. 59–60). "For swinish gluttony," the Lady declares to Comus, "Ne'er looks to Heav'n amidst his gorgeous feast, / But with besotted base ingratitude / Crams and blasphemes his feeder" (*Comus* 776–79). When sensual evil holds sway, Natura laments, then humanity "disregards the restraints of temperance, breaks to pieces the seals of my chastity, pays no heed to the graciousness of my bounty. For though my liberality distributes to men so many dishes of food, and rains upon them such flowing cups, yet they, ungrateful for my favors, [misuse] lawful things in ways beyond all measure of law" (Moffatt, pp. 62–63). The misuse of Natura's gifts extends beyond the food and drink of Bacchilatria to the vices induced by the other four daughters of Idolatria: Avarice, Pride, Envy, and Flattery.

Comus has tempted many readers with his appeal to the fruitful-

ness of Nature's gifts: "Wherefore did Nature pour her bounties forth /
With such a full and unwithdrawing hand, / Covering the earth" (*Comus*
710–12). In the *Complaint*, there is just one of the Virtues who sheds tears
at the damnation of a sinner; that is Generosity, mourning for one condemned of Prodigality. Natura, seeing her sister's bowed head, reminds
Generosity that "the one who misuses the gifts of nature by an excessive
flood of prodigality" can be deceptively attractive; "while a harlot-like
relationship with Prodigality lyingly advertises itself as a tribute of respect to Generosity, the torrent of riches flows away leaving an arid waste
of poverty, the bright star of wisdom goes off its course to set in folly,
the steadfastness of magnanimity weakens into the bravado of rashness"
(Sheridan, p. 214).

Generosity replies that "a golden chain of love" links her with her
sister Natura, "first principle of all things born . . . special preserver of
all things," and that therefore he who affronts Nature with prodigality
also revolts against Generosity: "Although he may be deceived by a belief in shades and phantoms . . . and think that he is bearing arms under
the flag of my interests, and men, deceived by a staged display of prodigality, may scent traces of Generosity in him, yet he is suspended from
the benefit of friendly relationship with us by banishment to a far-off
place" (Sheridan, p. 214).

Chastity in Alain's poem is "a virgin, the dawn of whose beauty
charmed all things." On her garments are depicted types, male and female, literally virgin and not, of those whom she governs: Hyppolytus,
Daphne, Lucretia, Penelope, and endless numbers more; the design is
"careful not to cheat any daughter of chastity of her need of praise"
(Moffatt, p. 79). Temperance, on the other hand, appears as " a matron
with moderate and measured gait." We can tell from the description of
the matron Temperance why this personification does not offer the possibilities for allegory that the figure of the virgin Chastity does. First,
on her garment there are no traditional individual heroes to stand as her
exemplaries; so the allegory, since it can not be embodied in whole persons with their possibilities for complexity of symbolic meaning, is merely
tropological, narrowly ethical, prescriptive. Second, since tropology demonstrates a rather limited idea of temperance, only the context of Natura's
expository definition of the fuller temperance makes it possible for this
traditionally limited idea to stand for something larger. The passage reads:
"On her garments a picture showed with faithful characters what circumscription ought to be in the words of man, what circumspectness
in his deeds, what moderation in dress, what serenity in bearing, what
bridling of the mouth in eating, what reproof of the throat in drink"

(Moffatt, p. 180). The lovely matron Temperance can stand for what a human being does to triumph "o'er sensual Folly and Intemperance" (*Comus* 975); but the radiant beauty of the virgin can show what that victor is, or—said another way—can show the identity which it is the function of temperance to maintain.

For Alain to apprehend and convey to his readers the sublime notion and high mystery of the Virgin Natura, the agent of God's divine reality, and his eternal Idea, a considerable accommodation has had to occur. He reports a dream-vision, but even within the vision, he tells us, at the Virgin's approach, he had fainted "prostrated by stupor of mind and all buried in the delirium of ecstacy, and the powers of my senses imprisoned; and, neither in life nor in death, I struggled between the two" (Moffatt, p. 23). Once Natura had revived him, she had addressed him by depicting "for [his] mental perception the image of a real voice, and by this brought into actual being words which had been, so to speak, archetypes ideally preconceived" (p. 24).

To hear Natura is hard for Alain; for Comus it is impossible. He has "nor Ear nor Soul to apprehend" (*Comus* 784) the truths of Natura that would empower him to speak a truth about the more limited subject of human virginity. The Lady "had not thought to have unlock'd [her] lips / In this unhallow'd air" (757–58) for the same reason that Natura is indirect with Alain; I have determined "to cover the face of my might," she explains, "in very many ways, preserving its mystery from commonness. . . . Aristotelian authority declares that he lessens the majesty of mysteries who divulges secrets to the unworthy" (Moffatt, p. 29).

"For many I have decided to cloak my face in figures," Natura says, "lest, if I should grant them an intimate knowledge of myself, [I] . . . should when known . . . be regarded as of less value" (Sheridan, p. 123). Eight hundred years later, she is indeed regarded as of less value. That the figure of virginity could for five hundred years have symbolized the divine purity of the principle of all creation, however, is not a sign of any impoverishment in that period's view of the power of human sexuality. On the contrary, our inability to value virginity as a fertile emblem reflects one of the routes by which we have cut ourselves off from an encounter with Natura.

Milton's Attendant Spirit invites us to follow him along that old route, upward, "Higher than the Sphery chime." Natura's way leads to the same place, as Milton was later to explain in his *Apology*, where the virgins of the parable wed the heavenly bridegroom, where the chaste receive their "high reward of ever accompanying the Lamb with those celestial songs to others incomprehensible" (YP I, 892–93). In *Comus*,

Milton's choice of genre offered him the same figures Alain had worked with, Venus and Cupid.

Natura warns Alain against misconstruing Venus's nature because of the stories told about her: "Many men, as we know from the testimony of the poets, have misused, by a literal interpretation, the terms applied to Venus." However, "this account of theirs which falsely states that there is a plurality of gods or that these gods have wantoned in the playgrounds of Venus, comes to the evening and sunset that await extreme falsehood" (Sheridan, p. 141). Venus and her son Cupid are in truth "connected with me by a certain bond of true consanguinity" (p. 154), and "I bring no charge of dishonourable conduct against the basic nature of Desire" (p. 135). Natura had, in fact, made Venus her own vice-regent since "without the help . . . of an assisting worker" she "could not perfect so many classes of things" in the ongoing creation and maintenance of the universe. While Natura herself sojourned "in the grateful palace of the eternal region," she tells Alain:

In the outskirt world I stationed Venus, who is skilled in the knowledge of making, as under-deputy of my work, in order that she, under my judgment and guidance, and with the assisting activity of her husband Hymen and her son Cupid, by laboring at the various formation of the living things of earth . . . might weave together the line of the human race in unwearied continuation, to the end that it should not suffer violent sundering at the hands of the Fates. (Moffatt, p. 45)

Even though he learns that the gods are innocent of abusing Venus's gifts, however, Alain knows too well that humans are not. Alain offers a myth to account for these unnatural events: they are perpetrated by the victims of Venus's bastard son, Jocus, born of an affair with Antigenius, for whom Venus — tired of the endless, meticulous work of creation — forsook her husband Hymenaeus, father of Cupid, her true son. (Jocus demonstrates what the true behavior of "Nature's bastards" would be like; cf. *Comus*, line 727.)

There may remain a suggestion of the need to restore humanity's relation to Venus, this vice-regent goddess of Nature, in Milton's reference to a place "up in the broad fields of the sky" where we are to imagine a representative of humankind "waxing well" of a wounded nature. Once human sensuality is restored to its original wholeness, once earthly love resumes her original role, then the route of the human psyche (soul) to divine love is again straightforward and fruitful.[21]

I do not mean to suggest that Milton was using Alain as a literary model for the epilogue or for the poem as a whole; Milton was engaged in his own vastly superior Spenserian sort of mythmaking within the masque genre. But Milton's heroine has a relationship to that dazzling virgin who visited Alain, the goddess whose ethical spokesman is Aristotle, the heavenly vice-regent who is entrusted with the power to "create a soul / Under the ribs of Death" (*Comus* 561–62). We may feel more fully the strength of Milton's strange Lady if we have met Natura.

University of Delaware

NOTES

1. See, for instance, Maryann McGuire, *Milton's Puritan Masque* (Athens, Ga., 1983).

2. William Kerrigan, *The Sacred Complex: On the Psychogenesis of "Paradise Lost"* (Cambridge, 1983), p. 55.

3. William G. Madsen, *Three Studies in the Renaissance: Sidney, Jonson, Milton* (New Haven, 1958), p. 205.

4. A.S.P. Woodhouse, *The Poet and His Faith* (Chicago, 1965); Georgia B. Christopher, *Milton and the Science of the Saints* (Princeton, 1982), p. 57.

5. C. S. Lewis, *The Allegory of Love* (Oxford, 1958), pp. 110–11.

6. *Complete Prose Works of John Milton*, 8 vols., ed. Don M. Wolfe et al. (New Haven, 1953–82), vol. VI, p. 131. This edition of the prose works is hereafter cited as YP.

7. *The Faerie Queene*, VII, vii, 9, in *The Poetical Works of Edmund Spenser*, ed. J. C. Smith and E. de Selincourt (London, 1963).

8. Ernst Robert Curtius, *European Literature in the Latin Middle Ages*, trans. W. R. Trask (New York, 1963), p. 126.

9. Quotations of Alain's *Complaint of Nature* are from either *The Plaint of Nature*, trans. James J. Sheridan (Toronto, 1980) or *The Complaint of Nature*, trans. Douglas M. Moffat (New York, 1908). Quotations from these editions are hereafter cited in the text.

10. Rosemond Tuve, "Image, Form, and Theme in *A Mask*," in *A Maske at Ludlow: Essays on Milton's* Comus, ed. John S. Diekhoff (Cleveland, 1968), p. 150.

11. Madsen, *Three Studies in the Renaissance*, p. 213.

12. Christian humanism presumably inherited from prehistoric matriarchal religions (if we look back far enough) a generalized figure of a goddess as virgin. Carol Ochs, in *Behind the Sex of God: Toward a New Consciousness — Transcending Matriarchy and Patriarchy* (Boston, 1977), pp. 68–69, summarizes: "The nature of this virginity is not consistent with the usual understanding of the term, but is compatible with being ravished by the gods, shedding hymenal blood, and bearing children. For example, Persephone, daughter of Demeter, is ravished by Pluto, sheds hymenal blood from which a pomegranate tree grows, and bears a son; yet she is still called *Kore*, the maiden or virgin. It encompasses an essential purity which cannot be touched by the exigencies of external fate."

13. *Ethica Nicomachea*, trans. W. D. Ross, in *The Works of Aristotle*, 11 vols., ed. W. D. Ross et al. (Oxford, 1925), vol. IX, Book II, line 6, p. 1106b. R. A. Gauthier and J. Y. Jolif, in *L'Ethique à Nicomaque* (Paris, 1958), p. 44, comment: "le juste milieu n'est pas distinct de la cause formelle."

14. G. R. Evans, *Alan of Lille: The Frontiers of Theology in the Later Twelfth Century* (Cambridge, 1983), p. 148.

15. C. S. Lewis, *The Allegory of Love*, p. 104.

16. Ibid., p. 106; Lewis's translation.

17. "The saintly veil of maiden white," *Ode on the Morning of Christ's Nativity*, II, 42. The twelfth-century humanists experimented with an allegorical form called a ternary, "a combination used to reflect and help understand the Trinity." Nature, Genius, and Truth form a ternary (Sheridan, p. 218, n27).

18. All quotations of Milton's poetry are from *Complete Poems and Major Prose*, ed. Merritt Y. Hughes (New York, 1957). Joseph E. Duncan observes in *Milton's Earthly Paradise* (Minneapolis, 1972), p. 238, that "Milton's Nature is so strongly personified that she is almost another character."

19. C. S. Lewis, *The Allegory of Love*, p. 330.

20. Tuve, "Images, Form, and Theme," p. 148.

21. A.S.P. Woodhouse, in *A Variorum Commentary on the Poems of John Milton*, gen. ed. Merritt Y. Hughes (New York, 1972), vol. II, iii, p. 985, points out: "Boccaccio says: 'Psyche is the soul . . . and there is joined with her that which preserves the rational element, that is pure Love' . . . from this love is born Pleasure which is eternal joy and gladness."

MILTON, *THE SHEPHERD* OF HERMAS, AND THE WRITING OF A PURITAN MASQUE

Eugene R. Cunnar

WHEN MILTON argued in *The Reason of Church Government* that the ideal spiritual community should, like Republican Rome and the early Christian communities established by Paul and Clement, reform man's recreations because wisdom may be found in "solemn Paneguries, in Theaters, porches, or what other place," he may well have been remembering his own earlier effort to reform one of England's more aristocratic pastimes, the masque.[1] At the time Milton agreed to write *Comus* he had not yet aligned himself with the radical reformers, but he was in the process of developing his concepts of poetic reform and spiritual regeneracy.[2] The close imagistic and thematic relationship between Milton's *Comus* and his early antiprelatical tracts reveals a strong continuity in his emerging attempts at both ecclesiastical and poetic reforms.[3] The theme of regeneracy is present throughout Milton's early work, but is especially poignant in *Elegia Quinta*, where Milton transforms the common *topos* of the advent of spring into a statement about the need for each generation to renew poetry, and in *Elegia Sexta*, where he informs Charles Diodati of his dedication to forms of poetry higher than classical or mythological poetry and of his developing sense of the self-discipline and virtue necessary to his new pursuit.[4]

Milton's early commitment to ecclesiastical and poetic reform partially explains why a young Puritan would agree to write a masque, a literary genre generally despised by Puritans. As Margot Heinemann has recently shown, all Puritans did not automatically disparage and oppose drama and masques. In fact, many Puritans actively supported drama and when they did oppose it, the opposition was often based on political rather than religious grounds. At times, they supported drama that opposed and criticized the court, while political or moral opposition to the drama often focused on the masque as one of the more obvious political dramatic forms associated with the courtly politics of the Stuarts.[5] Puritans objected to most forms of ceremony including the Anglican liturgy, and they particularly disliked the masque since it was perceived as a form

of court ceremony that echoed liturgical ritual particularly objection-
able to them. However, as it was not uncommon for Puritans to employ
dramatic forms for their own propaganda, it seems likely that Milton
took the opportunity of writing *Comus* to express his own growing dis-
illusionment with a corrupt court and its political and ecclesiastical policies as a symbol for a deeper spiritual malaise he wished to correct. One
of poetry's functions for Milton was to carry out the evangelical work
of transforming man into a vision of regeneracy. For Milton, God will,
through his poet/prophets, strive to "Forme and regenerate in us the lovely
shapes of vertues and graces the sooner to edifie and accomplish that im-
mortall stature of Christs body" (YP I, p. 755). Thus, agreeing to write
Comus, Milton perceived an opportunity to express his commitment to
reform those genres invested with ideologies and world-views repugnant
to his new calling of poet/prophet.

Masques were associated with the court and aristocracy and were
designed to flatter noble personages and their values. Flourishing during
the Stuart and Caroline periods when new ideologies were threatening
the monarchical assumption of divine right, masques became a means
of supporting the political, and by extension, the ecclesiastical *status quo*.
The establishment of a new courtly aesthetic to reflect Stuart absolutism
in politics and theology manifested itself in painting, music, and literature and spawned reactions from Puritans. Quite early, masques, those
"publique Spectacles" as Ben Jonson called them, and the licentious behavior of the court became the target of Puritan invective, and, in some
cases, a focal point for opposition to court policies.[6] Apparently, the
moral reputation of the Caroline court reached such a low level that
Thomas Carew and Inigo Jones produced a masque, *Coelum Britanni-
cum*, celebrating the chastity and virtue of Charles I as a countermea-
sure to the adverse public opinion about court morality. Ben Jonson, who
quarrelled with Inigo Jones over the latter's emphasis on spectacle to the
denigration of serious poetry in the masque, attempted to reform the
court by writing masques that simultaneously criticized and upheld court
policies while also self-consciously validating the masque as a serious and
proper form of literature.[7]

Milton adopts a more radical approach to the masque as a literary
genre. Part of Milton's strategy emerges from his later attitudes toward
the masque. In *Eikonoklastes* (1649) he condemns the portrait of Charles
I that prefaced *Eikon Basilike* by complaining about "the conceited por-
traiture before his book, drawn out to full measure of a masking scene,
and set there to catch fools and silly gazers." He goes on to argue "But
quaint emblemes and devices begged from the old pagentry of some

Twelfthnight's entertainment at Whitehall, will do but ill to make a saint or martyr" (YP III, pp. 342, 343). Later, in *Paradise Lost*, as Enid Welsford and John Demaray have shown, Milton emphatically criticizes the courtly context of the masque by associating Satan and the fallen angels with the most corrupt and courtly aspects of the genre.[8] Milton's strong distaste for the masque's courtly context becomes apparent in *Comus*, where though he had to satisfy his aristocratic audience's generic expectations, he imitates the form in order to radically transform its ideology and courtly context.

Like Jonson, Milton employs the antimasque/masque structure. Like the Jonsonian masque, Milton's masque is highly symbolic and incorporates the audience into its symbolic and imaginary world. Court masques attempt to compliment the noble personages by creating an equation between the harmony prevailing at the masque's end with the actual hierarchy at court. Moreover, as Stephen Orgel and Roy Strong demonstrate, the masque attempts to transform masquer and spectator alike into living embodiments of the ideas and values expressed through the masque's verbal and visual symbolism.[9] So too does Milton in *Comus*. Quite clearly, Milton understands the conventions of the masque and its essential ingredients of poetry and spectacle. John Demaray argues that *Comus* "succeeds in all those ways in which a masque can succeed, by reflecting in words the essential masquing arts and by uniting those arts in decorous accord with the invention and the occasion."[10]

But *Comus* is more than just a successful masque that transcends the limitations of the genre to become a lasting work of art. One of the characteristics of Milton's poetic genius is the ability to use a poetic form in order to undermine and subvert the values associated with that form. More and more we have become aware that Milton employed the Bible, and especially the prophetic books, such as the Book of Revelation, to create a tradition of prophecy and a "visionary poetics."[11] For Milton, the vision of prophecy meant a reformation of human forms, a reshaping of them into biblical and prophetic patterns. Milton's purpose, as Joseph Wittreich claims, is not "to acknowledge superficial likeness . . . [but] to dissolve the literary relationship his poem implies."[12] Perhaps more than in any previous work, in *Comus* Milton's desire for theological reform and his understanding of dissolving literary form coalesce, producing the radical transformation of genre that typifies his mature aesthetic. It is my contention that Milton discovered in *The Shepherd* of Hermas, a work little known today, but well known in the Renaissance, an apostolic model that would allow him to create *Comus* in the superficial likeness of a masque while simultaneously dissolving its literary and courtly associations. *The Shepherd* of Hermas furnished Milton with concepts from the apostolic era that were compatible with his variety of Puritanism and that would influence and guide his transformation of the masque genre from "publique Spectacle" to the spectacle of prophesy.

I

The Shepherd of Hermas was written, according to tradition, in the second century by the Hermas at Rome mentioned by Paul (Rom. xvi, 14). Probably on the basis of the attribution (which is problematical according to modern scholarship), the work was briefly held as canonical.[13] Although later excluded from the Bible and relegated to the ranks of the deutero-canonical, it remained known in Latin versions from the Middle Ages through the Renaissance.[14] *The Shepherd* is a perplexing work thought to embody genuine prophesyings of the apostolic age. It is divided into three parts: first come five visions, in the last of which appears the shepherd from which the work derives its name, followed by twelve mandates or commandments, and finally by ten similitudes or parables. As a whole, the work reflects the tribulations of the early church in reforming itself through purification and penance in order to survive persecutions.

The Shepherd is both a dream vision, in which the author moves in and out of visions, and a pastoral apocalypse set in a visionary landscape. In it, Hermas is both recipient and promulgator of the revelations. In the first vision Hermas sees the Lady Rhoda, whose slave he had once been in Rome, bathing in the Tiber, and he begins to lust after her with ardent passion. Later, journeying to the city of Cumae, he falls asleep and has a dream in which Rhoda appears as an old lady and accuses him of lust and sin. Rhoda, as an old lady, derived from the Wandering Woman of the Apocalypse, represents the church and accuses both Hermas and his family, who are apparently involved in some scandal, of sinning against her. The doubts created about his own chastity and the purity of his family become the motivating force for a series of dream visions that Hermas experiences. During the first four visions Hermas perceives the church as an elderly woman who grows progressively younger as he follows her directions, leading him to purification and penance. The lady's transformation suggests the eternal youth of the church and symbolizes the resurrection of the faithful. The woman reveals to Hermas the process of the church being built through the metaphor of the construction of a stone tower. The white stones employed in the tower's construction are "apostles, bishops, teachers, and deacons, who have lived in godly purity, and have acted as bishops and teachers and deacons chastely and reverently to the elect of God" (p. 14). The stones that are discarded represent those who "through doubt have abandoned the true road," and those who "thinking, then, that they could find a better . . . wander and become wretched, and enter upon pathless places" (p. 15). Others cast away as unfit for the building of the church are those "who have heard the word, and wish to be baptized in the name of the Lord; but when the chastity demanded by the truth comes into their recollection, they draw back and again walk after their own wicked desires" (p. 15). Hermas receives this vision in order to encourage him to become one of the chaste. The fourth vision presents an apocalyptic scene based on Revelation and includes an encounter with a terrible beast, who poses no threat to true prophets or the faithful. In the fifth vision, Hermas sees the angel of repentance who comes to him in the guise of a shepherd. The shepherd proves to be Michael and dictates to him the twelve mandates.

Both the mandates and the similitudes that follow emphasize the need for repentance and purification if Hermas and his family are to be among the elect. The lady earlier makes clear to Hermas the stages of salvation: "for from Faith arises Self-restraint; from Self-restraint, Simplicity; from Simplicity, Guilelessness; from Guilelessness, Chastity; from Chastity, Intelligence; and from Intelligence, Love. The deeds, then, of these are pure, chaste, and divine. Whoever devotes himself to these, and is able to hold fast by their works, shall have his dwelling in the tower with the saints of God" (pp. 16, 18–19). In addition, the guardian angel or shepherd will show Hermas not only the punishment for lust and adultery, but also he will show him a false shepherd and his flock, who suggest Comus and his crew (pp. 27–28).

The experiences of Hermas's family may be viewed as an allegory of the Christian's as well as the apostolic church's need for renewed repentance.[15] In this context Hermas's encounter with revelators, and his receiving and rendering of revelations, become prophetic and apocalyptic. In the eleventh mandate, Hermas concerns himself with distinguishing between true and false, Christian and pagan prophets. The false prophets mislead the people and congregation, especially those who are in doubt; that is, those who are unwilling to cooperate with the Grace of Atonement because their barren spirit renders empty prophecies (p. 28). Ultimately, the false prophet can cheat those who listen to him of their souls. In contrast, the true prophet is known by his moral, virtuous, and chaste life — values that Hermas is in the process of acquiring through the visions. The angel Michael fills the chaste with the spirit of prophecy. Accordingly, Hermas stresses the need for individual, familial, and congregational virtue or chastity in order to receive true prophecy. The work ends with Hermas achieving a state of virtue and repentance, celebrated by his being allowed in the company of dancing virgins who represent the purified church.

II

The various deutero-canonical works, popularly known as the Apostolic Fathers and including *The Shepherd* of Hermas, were of some importance in the debate between Anglicans and Puritans over the question of episcopacy. Those favoring the authority of bishops, such as Bishops Hall and Ussher, cited the deutero-canonical epistles of Clement, Ignatius, and Polycarp to show that bishops were employed and sanctioned in the apostolic church. In refuting his adversaries, Milton severely questioned the use of extrascriptural and noncanonical evidence regardless of how early or ancient, urging instead the sufficiency of scripture.[16] However, in refuting his adversaries' use of church fathers and deutero-canonical sources, Milton cites ancient and apostolic sources such as Eusebius and *The Shepherd* of Hermas when they support his positions.

Milton's knowledge of the Apostolic Fathers seems fairly extensive, as witnessed by his citation of many of them in the antiprelatical treatises. During the early seventeenth century and during the period Milton wrote *Comus* and the antiprelatical treatises, he had available any number of editions of the Apostolic Fathers that included *The Shepherd* of Hermas. In 1513, Jacques Le Fevre published the Latin version in *Liber trium virorum et trium spiritualium virginium: Hermae liber unus . . .* (Paris), followed by an edition by Nicholas Grebelius, *Hermas, Pastoris nuntii poenitentiae, visiones . . .* (Argentorati, 1522). These early editions of *The Shepherd* were followed by a number of fully annotated editions of the Apostolic Fathers, including *The Shepherd*, that summarized the problems with its authorship, dating, and scriptural status.[17] In 1633, just prior to the production of *Comus*, Patrick Young, keeper of the King's Library, brought out a Latin edition of Clement's epistles based on a new manuscript, followed by an English translation by William Burton, both of which called further attention to the status of the Apostolic Fathers. Later in the century, William Wake, Archbishop of Canterbury, brought out the first English translation of the Apostolic Fathers, *The Genuine Epistles of the Apostolic Fathers* (London, 1693). Wake's introduction provides an excellent summary of both ancient and modern opinion and interpretation of *The Shepherd*, most of which Milton could have learned from the earlier editions.

Milton's familiarity with *The Shepherd* is seen in his citing Hermas's arguments in *Of Reformation* (1641) and *The Reason of Church Government* (1642) as an apostolic example of how the early church was governed.[18] Unlike Ignatius, Clement, or Polycarp, all cited by Hall and Ussher, Hermas, among the Apostolic Fathers, argues that the church should be governed, not by bishops, but by individual self-control or spiritual discipline. During the course of the visions, Hermas experiences scenes in which the church is purged of overly wealthy and worldly bishops, being governed instead by chaste presbyters in a loose and democratic fashion. Quite obviously, Hermas's position on church government appealed to Milton's Puritan opposition to the bishops of the state religion and was a useful apostolic source in refuting the reliance of Hall, Ussher, and others on apostolic sources.

However, *The Shepherd* was important to Milton for more than polemical purposes. In *The Shepherd* of Hermas, Milton encountered an enigmatic work made up of apocalyptic visions coinciding, in part, with his own developing beliefs, especially his concern for prophetic, visionary, and apocalyptic structures and meanings. In spite of his polemical criticism of the Apostolic and Church Fathers, Milton was serious about the nature and expression of the primitive church, especially its corruption and the possibilities of its regeneration in the present.[19] As a visionary and apocalyptic work mixing genres, *The Shepherd* appealed to Milton's growing understanding and appropriation of John's *Book of Revelations* with which it shared similarities. The shepherd of the title is named after the angel of revelation and repentance appearing as a shepherd and bears marked similarities to Christ as the Good Shepherd in John's gospels and to the angel of apocalypse in Revelation.[20] Moreover, the Lady Rhoda in one of her manifestations parallels the Wandering Woman of Revelation, chapters xii and xiii, who, as Alice-Lyle Scoufos shows, was interpreted as the church by Protestant commentators and is transformed by Milton in *Comus* into a figure of both the corruptible visible church or the Church of England and the figure of tried and living faith.[21]

These and other similarities between *The Shepherd* and Revelation perhaps caused Milton to look more closely at the former, where he would have discovered a work that, although stressing repentance, placed faith in a primary position, revealing in Hermas's progressive experiences of purification the need for a continuously tried and living faith if the true church were built. In addition, *The Shepherd* exposed the emptiness of mere works and excessive ritual while criticizing lax family and individual spiritual discipline and unsanctified wealth (pp. 4–6). Hermas's concerns for the corruption of the early church and the apocalyptic warnings from the Lady Rhoda about the approaching great tribulations were compatible with Milton's growing concept of himself as an apocalyptic prophet who would spiritually regenerate individuals, the nation, and the English Church.

The Shepherd of Hermas provided Milton with themes and prototypes for several of his major thematic and aesthetic concerns in Comus. On one level The Shepherd traces the spiritual regeneration of a fallen man and his scandal-ridden family, which anticipates Milton's motive in producing Comus as a purification ritual for the scandal-tainted Egerton family.[22] On a second, and perhaps more significant level for Milton, The Shepherd provides one of the first apostolic attempts to establish the type of spiritual discipline or chastity needed for both the individual's and the early church's regeneration. Hermas's visionary and apocalyptic treatment of chastity and virginity as forms of spiritual discipline brought about by moral choice provided Milton with further support for his adaptation of Luther's concept of virginitas fidei in characterizing and distinguishing the Lady as Protestant.[23] Lastly, Milton found in The Shepherd a model of literary regeneration compatible with his own early efforts at reforming genres in the service of prophecy. Origen, Eusebius, Jerome, and later, Bellarmine in the sixteenth century, among others, attributed authorship of The Shepherd to the Hermas mentioned in Rom. xvi, 14, which led many to view the work as an early example of the type of apostolic prophesying urged by Paul as a means of countering heathen and Sibylline oracles. Milton may have regarded The Shepherd as an apostolic equivalent to the masque much as he perceived various segments of the Bible to be specific literary genres.[24] Its dream framework is filled with dramatic scenes, dialogue, and what amounts to spectacular and prophetic visions. At the end of The Shepherd, Lady Rhoda as the church deems Hermas to have achieved a sufficient level of faith and chastity to allow him into the company of twelve dancing virgins. Representing the Pauline fruits of the spirit found in Galatians and the Isaaic messianic gifts, these virgins dance what was a form of pagan revel, but now is transformed by Hermas into an allegory of chaste Christian life celebrating grace and faith. During the dance Hermas becomes younger and, at the end, the angel arrives to take the maidens and the shepherd away, promising that they will return to Hermas's house in the future.

Early in his career, Milton explored the possibilities of writing a prophetic drama, and, in The Reason of Church Government, wrote that:

the Scripture also affords us a divine pastoral Drama in the Song of *Salomon* consisting of two persons and a double *Chorus*, as *Origen* rightly judges. And the Apoclypse of Saint *John* is the majestic image of high and stately Tragedy, shutting up and intermingling her solemn Scenes and Acts with a sevenfold *Chorus* of halleluja's and harping symphonies: and this my opinion the grave autority of *Pareus* commenting that booke is sufficient to confirm. (YP I, p. 815)

Even earlier the young poet attempted to work out in "The Passion" a comparison between Christ, the "Perfect hero," and a masquer.[25] Clearly, Milton's early interest in creating a prophetic drama influenced his decision to write *Comus* and to find a means of transforming the court masque into a prophetic genre. By combining the transformational goal of the Jonsonian masque with theological precedent thought to be from the apostolic church, Milton hoped to transform and reform the masque into a prophetic mode. The association of the masque with Old Testament prophecy was cogently stated by John Smith, who, in comparing the mystical experience of the biblical prophets Hosea, Jeremiah, and Ezekiel to the court masque, argued for the role of the imagination on the "Stage of Prophesie":

That the prophetical scene or Stage upon which all apparitions were made to the Prophet, was his *Imagination;* and that there all those things which God would have revealed unto him were acted over *Symbolically,* as in a *Masque,* in which divers persons are brought in, amongst which the Prophet himself bears a part: And therefore he, according to the exigency of the Dramatical *apparatus,* must, as the other Actors, perform his part, sometimes by speaking and reciting things done, propounding questions, sometimes by acting that part which in the *Drama* he was appointed to act by some others. . . . And therefore it is no wonder to hear of those things done which indeed have no *Historical* or *Real* verity; the scope of all being to represent something strongly to the Prophet's Understanding, and sufficiently to inform it in the Substance of those things which he was to instruct that People in whom he was sent. . . . And therefore in these recitals of *Prophetical Visions* we find many times things less coherent then can agree to a true History.[26]

Anticipating Smith, Milton transcends the public and private occasions for *Comus* and produces on the "Stage of Prophesie" his own unique form of the prophetic masque.

　　The major concerns of *The Shepherd* of Hermas — apocalypse, dream visions, the purification of the individual and the church, the distinction between true and false prophets, the need for chastity in each of these endeavors — were also Milton's concerns during the period in which he produced *Comus.* When Milton was commissioned to create *Comus* to celebrate the earl of Bridgewater's appointment, he must have realized the occasion presented him with an opportunity to transfer his concerns with religious and political corruption and the Puritan insistence on the regeneracy of man and the church to serious poetic expression. A Masque Presented at Ludlow Castle is more than a family cleansing ritual; it is also an invitation to the earl of Bridgewater, members of whose family at the time may have been sympathetic to some Puritan causes,[27] to join in the continuing process of reforming the church. Thus, Milton, like the angel Michael in The Shepherd, is not presenting the Egerton family a courtly masque, but a visionary statement of the need for further regeneracy, which itself reveals in its transformation of genre how regeneracy may be achieved.[28]

III

The conflict between Comus, son of Circe and representative of pagan and courtly culture, and the Lady, representative of the church in need of liberation and the steadfastness of faith, may also reflect Hermas's concern for man's ability to distinguish between true and false prophets, classical divination and Christian prophecy.[29] In the Animadversions, Milton echoes Hermas when he says "nor can there be a more proper object of indignation and scorne together then a false Prophet taken in the greatest dearest and most dangerous cheat, the cheat of soules" (YP I, p. 664). It is precisely Comus's goal to cheat the Lady of her soul by being a false prophet. And, as symbolic of the church's plight, Comus will attempt to lead the Lady into the spectacle of the antimasque's paganism as manifested by the classical and courtly context of the masque itself. Milton established an imagistic and thematic comparison between his condemnation of the church's corruption and Comus's lineage and behavior, and the masque genre. Comus presents himself as a false guide or prophet to the Lady: he has the power to "cheat the eye with blear illusion." Indeed, the traditional courtly masque attempts the same thing through its employment of spectacle, artifice, and visual illusion, all of which glorify king, court, and a social elite.[30] Moreover, as Andrew Milner suggests, Comus and his courtly aesthetics represent both contemporary Cavalier morality and Archbishop Laud, the representative of "rites" and "canon law," concepts repugnant to Milton.[31] Neither the court and its rites — the masque — nor the Laudian church and its rites are, for Milton, the proper agents to carry out the church's reform since they are like false prophets misleading the English nation.

The distinction between true and false prophets that Milton establishes echoes Hermas's warning that false prophets not only fool the unvirtuous, but they also may be known by their unholy, unchaste lives (pp. 27–28). Fallen man, the corrupted church, the courtly masque, the scandal-ridden Egerton family — all are in need of purification. In their fallen condition they may succumb to Comus's temptation to join the "sensual sty" of the false prophet. Milton's message is similar to that of Hermas to the leaders of the early church: "You will tell, therefore, those who preside over the church, to direct their ways in righteousness, that they may receive in full the promises with great glory (p. 11). For Milton, the antimasque features of the masque, the riotous spectacle of Comus's crew, become indicative of the corruption in the church. Accordingly, the earl of Bridgewater, as newly appointed political leader, is being asked to set an example of the chastity necessary for the church's reform.

The Lady's rigid adherence to the concepts of chastity and virginity protect her physically from Comus, but it does not free her. Although heaven protects her through the Attendant Spirit, the Lady must confront Comus or be accused of exhibiting nothing more than a cloistered virtue. Her chastity allows her prophetically to see her own situation:

> These thoughts may startle well, but not astound
> The virtuous mind, that ever walks attended
> By a strong siding champion of Conscience. . . .
> O welcome pure-ey'd Faith, white-handed Hope,
> Thou hov'ring Angel girt with golden wings,
> And thou unblemish't form of Chastity,
> I see ye visibly, and now believe
> That he, the Supreme Good, t'whom all things ill
> Are but as slavish officers of vengeance,
> Would send a glist'ring Guardian, if need were,
> To keep my life and honour unassail'd.   (209–19)

These lines point out more than the actual dramatic realities of the masque; they also state strongly that the chaste are open to visionary reception on the stage of prophecy. In similar fashion, Hermas's virtue allows him to both receive and communicate the visions necessary to his and the early church's reformation.

The Elder Brother's long discourse on his sister's chastity as a means of protection makes clear that heaven is guarding the Lady: "Virtue could see to do what virtue would / By her own radiant light, though Sun and Moon / Were in the flat Sea sunk" (372–74). And later:

> So dear to Heav'n is Saintly chastity,
> That when a soul is found sincerly so,

A thousand liveried Angels lackey her,
Driving far off each thing of sin and guilt,
And in clear dream and solemn vision
Tell her of things that no gross ear can hear,
Till oft converse with heav'nly habitants
Begin to cast a beam on th'outward shape,
The unpolluted temple of the mind,
And turns it by degrees to the soul's essence,
Till all be made immortal: but when lust
By unchaste looks, loose gestures, and foul talk,
But most by lewd and lavish act of sin,
Lets in defilement to the inward parts,
The soul grows clotted by contagion,
Imbodies, and imbrutes, til she quite lose
The divine property of her first being.   (452–68)

The Elder Brother's speech tells the audience and the actors that the Lady's chastity both protects her and enables her to receive visions as part of that protection. Moreover, like Hermas, she receives and renders prophetic visions as a major means of combatting evil and insuring regeneracy. The same opportunity "in clear dream, and solemn vision" is being offered Milton's audience, who may also choose the chastity of faith and hear the prophetic message of reformation.

Milton adapted both the secular and sacred celebrations for Michaelmas Day to his masque, as James G. Taaffe and William B. Hunter have demonstrated.[32] On Michaelmas, a quarter day on which officials traditionally assumed office for the coming year, secular offices were treated as the symbolic, earthly manifestations of their heavenly counterparts. Taaffe shows how the civil rituals of misrule are applied to Comus, while Hunter points out how Milton adapted Anglican liturgy for St. Michael's Day, especially its reading of passages from Revelation treating the Wandering Woman and Michael's defeat of the satanic dragon. By adapting both civil and religious rites to his own masque, Milton could also conflate passages from Hermas to his text, thereby adding another prophetic dimension. In Hermas, the guardian angel Michael appears as a shepherd who can lead the repenters and the virtuous to salvation, warning the congregation to "Heal yourselves, therefore, while the tower [church] is still building" (p. 54). Milton's early prose, in similar fashion, urges ethical harmony and self-discipline as a prerequisite for spiritual regeneracy in both the individual and the church. In Comus, the Lady's character and actions, but especially her chastity, are symbolic of the inner integrity that Milton, like Hermas, considers necessary for true prophecy and regeneracy. When Hermas encounters the apocalyptic beast as a form of anti-Christ symbolizing the tribulation to come if the purification process is not completed, he, like Milton's Lady, does not overcome the beast through physical strength, but through internal spiritual purity, discipline, faith, the help of Lady Ecclesia, dressed in white and representing a higher form of purity or chastity, and the guardian angel (pp. 18–19).

Although the Lady's chastity will protect her, it will not free her from Comus's grip of enchantment. To be completely freed from the clutches of the false prophet or evil minister something more is needed, as the Attendant Spirit indicates to the Elder Brother:

> Alas good vent'rous youth,
> I love thy courage yet, and bold Emprise,
> But here thy sword can do thee little stead;
> Far other arms and other weapons must
> Be those that quell the might of hellish charms,
> He with his bare wand can unthread thy joints,
> And crumble all thy sinews.   (608–13)

In this spiritual struggle, the Attendant Spirit reveals to the brothers that the Lady may be saved through the use of *haemony* and the offices of Sabrina.[33] The intervention of Sabrina, whom Milton found in Geoffrey of Monmouth and Spenser and rehabilitated for her role in *Comus*, has most often been interpreted as a form of divine grace.[34] In creating the Lady's predicament, Milton emphasizes the roles of both chastity and deity, which Angus Fletcher maintains are paradoxical absolutes in the creation of a transcendental form, "the conversion of one medium into another."[35] While Sabrina represents divine grace, she also represents a higher form of chastity symbolic of the liberating power potential in the Lady's chastity. In this sense, she is like Hermas's Lady Rhoda, who, after he vanquishes the beast through his newly gained spiritual purification and faith, appears to him as a virgin totally dressed in white, "adorned as if she were proceeding from the bridal chamber" (p. 18) and symbolizing his now regenerated soul. In *Comus*, unlike the Lady in her present condition, Sabrina has the power to change and still preserve her chastity: she "underwent a quick immortal change," but "still she retains / Her maid'n gentleness" (841–43). Although Comus can immobilize the Lady's body in the enchanted chair, he can not capture her mind or spirit; nor can the Lady free herself. In *The Shepherd*, Hermas's "Lady Ecclesia" is confined in a great white chair while she tells Hermas that he is in a state of sin and scandal, and the false prophet sits in a chair while he deceives the people (pp. 10, 58). By having the Lady imprisoned in the enchanted chair, Milton suggests the imprisonment of the true church of saints in the proverbial chair of St. Peter and by the English throne. However, Sabrina's chastity and song free the Lady, and by implication will free the church. Milton implies that liberation does not just come from chastity, but chastity expressed through song or prophecy. His own attempt to transform the courtly masque as spectacle into a visionary and prophetic mode parallels Sabrina's freeing of the Lady. As the Lady becomes free, Milton's masque strives to become chastity visible as prophecy.

The freeing of the Lady by Sabrina and the end of the masque — with its happy reunion of children with their parents and the subsequent joyous dancing — have received extensive commentary. However, there is a small and significant detail of the masque's symbolic landscape at the end that has gone unnoticed. This is the description of Sabrina's local dwelling place "By the rushy-fringed bank, / Where grows the Willow and the Osier dank" (889–90) that occurs in her song. Most often the description is taken to be that of the local River Severn. Even Terry Kohn, who sees many of the significant and mythological qualities of the masque's landscape, interprets the line realistically.[36] I want to suggest that the reference to the willows also echoes the eighth similitude in Hermas concerning the willows of chastity (pp. 39–43) and plays an important role in explaining Milton's use of chastity as a liberating force.

Milton's inclusion in Sabrina's song of this small but significant detail of scenery reinforces the doctrine of chastity in strong terms by repudiating the classical concept of willows. Just as Milton recreates the context of Comus and his lineage, he also recreates the context of the willows in book X of the *Odyssey*. In that book, Circe urges Odysseus to journey to Hades, even providing him with directions that include the instruction to pass by "where there are both tall poplars and willows that lose their fruit."[37] For classical antiquity, according to Hugo Rahner, the willow became a symbol of a tree of both death and life.[38] The early Greeks observed that the willow drops its blossom before fruit begins to grow and that it propagates not through seed but through suckers. Thus, the willow seems to have life and death at work in it simultaneously. Because of these properties the willow became associated with chastity and the mysteries celebrating child-bearing. The willow was both chaste and fruitful. The dual symbolism of the willow was quickly absorbed into Christian symbolism, especially in the writings of the early church fathers.

The early exegetes interpreted the dual symbol of the "water-loving" and "fruit-destroying" willow along two lines. On the one hand, commentators such as Origen, Cassidorus, and Methodius interpret the willows in Leviticus, chapter xxiii, and Isaiah xliv, 3 as symbols of the chaste and faithful soul and as prophecy of the new life or Messianic kingdom to come.[39] On the other hand, exegetes such as Gregory the Great and Augustine interpreted the willows in Psalm cxxxvii as "fruit-destroying," that is as symbolic of spiritual sterility.[40] It is precisely this dual and contradictory meaning of chastity that characterizes Milton's paradoxical treatment of the Lady. Her chastity preserves her, but does not free her. The early church's working out of the paradoxical symbolism of the willows of chastity provides Milton with a solution to his own dilemma.

The first major reference to the willows as Christian symbol appears in *The Shepherd* of Hermas where, following the reference to willows in Isaiah xliv, 3 Hermas interprets the tree as symbolic of the liberation of the church's martyrs, who reap the fruit of their chastity in heaven, thereby encouraging the renewal of the earthly church. Moreover, the Lady explains to Hermas that the willow which eternally renews itself symbolizes Christ's Incarnation, an event which gives power to the martyrs (pp. 40–41). Following Hermas, Eusebius, commenting on Isaiah, chapter xliv, and the faithful who shoot up like "willows by the watercourses" in the Messianic kingdom, says, "For the willow with its everlasting greening and the youthful vigour of its growth, is a symbol of the abundance of that spring in the Church of the Logos."[41] Exegetes such as Origen, Cassidorus, and Methodius extended the meaning of the willow as symbolic of chastity into a symbol of grace transcending all nature, especially in the mystical dying or renunciation of earthly values. Gregory of Nyssa, in his discussion of virginity, adds an element to the tradition which is important for Milton's characterization of the Lady. Gregory says that virginity, which is characterized by *apatheia*, represents the earthly spiritual life destined to participate in angelic purity after death.[42] For these church fathers chastity on earth foreshadows the fruitful life of heaven. Thus, the willow tree that stood at the gates of the Homeric underworld becomes symbolic of the true Christian life.

The exegetical tradition of the willows of chastity provided Milton with a symbolic framework that reinforced his own unique theme about the chastity needed to reform and free the church, making it fruitful once more. The Lady's impassibility should not be seen as a character flaw or limitation, but instead as a trait required for any serious movement toward individual or ecclesiastical regeneracy. In liberating the Lady from Comus's spell, Sabrina symbolically functions as the guardian of virgins and as the grace that will allow the chastity of faith to liberate the individual and the church from worldly corruption or the *carpe diem* approach to nature that Comus advocates. Comus's argument that the Lady should experience the fecundity of nature (706–42) echoes Hermas's description of those bound by sin and the love of this world (pp. 20–25). Comus invites the Lady to participate in courtly spectacle by appealing to her vanity: "Beauty is nature's brag, and must be shown / In courts, at feasts, and high solemnities / Where most may wonder at the workmanship" (745–47). In rejecting Comus's appeal, the Lady rejects both his values and courtly spectacle.

After Comus is routed, the children are returned to their father's house, the symbolic heaven that is the true fruit of the willow of chastity. Like Methodius, who interprets Psalm cxxxvii as "the joyous hymn of praise sung by souls that have returned home to everlasting security and now, together with Christ, wander through the heavens, for they manage to escape being engulfed in the material and fleshy waters,"[43] Milton returns the children in triumph "O'er sensual Folly and intemperance" (975). By having the children return to a household that may have been sympathetic to some Puritan causes, Milton further strengthens his theme of reformation.

Obviously, Milton's praise of the Lady, the young Alice Egerton, does not achieve the absolute apotheosis accorded the king in a courtly masque; but it was not meant to. The Egerton family is not being complimented for its scandalous past. Instead, Milton is inviting them to become examples of the chastity, virtue, and self-discipline that will restore the church, just as his chaste masque has restored spectacle to its role in achieving prophecy. In addition, just as the family has been purged of bondage to sensual corruption through this chaste masque, so too may the church if such tried individuals will but join the effort before the church's mission on earth is completed. On the one hand, Milton has effectively celebrated the earl of Bridgewater's political appointment and purged the family of unseemly sexual scandal. On the other, he has clearly provided an example of how that reformation may be accomplished by reforming the courtly context of the masque. In preserving the Lady's chastity, Milton is preserving the faith necessary for the invisible church, the community of saints, to achieve its goal.

Instead of transforming history into just myth — or even poetry — as a means of complimenting noble personages, Milton transforms history into visionary prophecy and offers the Egerton family the opportunity to participate in the reform of the church. At the end of the masque, when masquers and spectators merge and when masquers reveal themselves as the living embodiment of the virtues acted out, Milton is including the Egerton family in more than political compliment. Like Hermas, who both rendered and received visions, Milton compliments the Egertons by suggesting that they are the inspiration for his rendering of a visionary masque prophesying the reformation of the church. They, also like Hermas, have motivated and received their own special prophetic vision, *A Masque Presented at Ludlow Castle*, from the hand of England's budding poet/prophet. The theme of chastity and *The Shepherd* of Hermas provided Milton with the means of resolving the dialectical tensions inherent in his attempt to write a courtly masque. By writing a masque that replaces neo-Platonic allegory and spectacle with chaste vision, Milton effectively destroys the courtly context of the masque: he achieves the aesthetic equivalent of *virginitas fidei* by writing a Puritan masque.[44]

New Mexico State University

NOTES

Funds for this study were provided in part by a grant from the New Mexico State University Arts and Sciences Research Center, for which I am thankful.

1. *Complete Prose Works of John Milton*, ed. Don M. Wolfe et al. (New Haven, 1953–82), vol. I, pp. 820, 831–32. Hereafter cited as YP in the text.

2. Christopher Hill, *Milton and the English Revolution* (New York, 1977), pp. 33–49, provides an account of Milton's early and growing radicalism. Milton's development as a poet, priest, and prophet has recently been reexamined by John Spencer Hill, *John Milton: Poet, Priest and Prophet* (Totowa, N.J., 1979).

3. Arthur E. Barker, *Milton and the Puritan Dilemma* (Toronto, 1956), pp. 19–59, and John M. Via, "Milton's Antiprelatical Tracts: The Poet Speaks in Prose," in *Milton Studies*, vol. V, ed. James D. Simmonds (Pittsburgh, 1973), pp. 87–127. Both provide illuminating accounts of the relationship between Milton's early poetry and his antiprelatical activities.

4. John Milton, *Complete Poems and Major Prose*, ed. Merritt Y. Hughes (New York, 1957), pp. 37–41, 50–53. D. C. Allen, "Milton as Latin Poet," in *Neo-Latin Poetry of the Sixteenth and Seventeenth Centuries* (Los Angeles, 1965), pp. 30–52.

5. Margot Heinemann, *Puritanism and Theatre: Thomas Middleton and Opposition Drama Under the Early Stuarts* (Cambridge, 1980), pp. 18–47, 200–36. For the masque as a form critical of court corruption, see my "The Wedding Masque's Moral Vision in *The Maid's Tragedy*," Selected Papers from the West Virginia Shakespeare and Renaissance Association, VII (1982, 37–45. For examples of the association of court policy and drama see Heinnemann, Lawrence Stone, *The Crisis of the Aristocracy* (Oxford, 1965), p. 688, and Hill, *Milton and the English Revolution*, p. 45.

6. See Leah Sinanaglou Marcus, "The Occasion of Ben Jonson's *Pleasure Recon-*

ciled to Virtue," SEL XIX (1979), 271–93; Stephen Orgel, *The Illusion of Power: Political Theater in the English Renaissance* (Berkeley and Los Angeles: University of California Press, 1975); Gary Schmidgall, *Shakespeare and the Courtly Aesthetic* (Berkeley and Los Angeles: University of California Press, 1981), pp. 27–98; *Ben Jonson,* 11 vols., ed. C. H. Herford, Percy and Evelyn Simpson (Oxford, 1925–52), vol. VII, p. 755; vol. X, pp. 522, 533; Christopher Hill, *Society and Puritanism in Pre-Revolutionary England* (New York, 1964), esp. pp. 168–94; Heinemann, *Puritanism and Theatre,* pp. 26–36; and Leah Sinanaglou Marcus, "Present Occasions and the Shaping of Ben Jonson's Masques," *ELH* XLV (1978), 201–25.

7. Roy Strong, *Splendor at Court: Renaissance Spectacle and the Theatre of Power* (London, 1973), pp. 33–43; Stephen Orgel and Roy Strong, *Inigo Jones: The Theater of the Stuart Court* (Berkeley and Los Angeles: University of California Press, 1973), vol. I, pp. 66–70; D. J. Gordon, "Poet and Architect: The Intellectual Setting of the Quarrel between Ben Jonson and Inigo Jones," in *The Renaissance Imagination,* ed. Stephen Orgel (Berkeley and Los Angeles: Univeristy of California Press, 1975), pp. 77–101; Stephen Orgel, *The Jonsonian Masque* (New York, 1965), pp. 186–202.

8. John G. Demaray, *Milton's Theatrical Epic* (Cambridge, 1980), pp. 57–72; Enid Welsford, *The Court Masque* (1917; rpt. New York, 1912), p. 312.

9. Orgel and Strong, *Inigo Jones,* vol. I, pp. 1–14; Orgel, *Jonsonian Masque,* pp. 6–7.

10. John G. Demaray, *Milton and the Masque Tradition* (Cambridge, 1968), p. 142. See also Angus Fletcher, *The Transcendental Masque* (Ithaca, 1971), esp. pp. 147–94, and Jeanne S. Martin, "Transformations in Genre in Milton's *Comus,*" *Genre* X (1977), 195–213.

11. See especially Joseph Anthony Wittreich, Jr., *Visionary Poetics: Milton's Tradition and His Legacy,* (San Marino, 1979).

12. "Milton's 'Virtuoso' Forms: A Review Article," *Genre* V (1972), p. 308.

13. *The Ante-Nicene Fathers,* ed. Alexander Roberts and James Donaldson (1896; rpt. Grand Rapids, 1962), p. 6. Unless otherwise noted all references are to this edition, cited hereafter by page numbers in the text.

14. For the status of *The Shepherd* and for available editions in the Renaissance see Johannes Quaesten, *Patrology* (Utrecht-Antwerp, 1966), vol. I, pp. 92–93; *The Apostolic Fathers,* ed. Kirsopp Lake (Cambridge, 1912), vol. II, pp. 2–5; and John Chapman, "Hermas," in *The Catholic Encyclopedia* (New York, 1910), vol. VII, pp. 268–71.

15. J. Reiling, *Hermas and Christian Prophecy* (Leiden, 1973), pp. 24–25.

16. See the "Introduction" in YP I, pp. 1–120 by Don M. Wolfe and the various prefaces and notes to the antiprelatical treatises by Wolfe, William Alfred, J. Max Patrick, Rudolf Kirk, William P. Baker, and Ralph A. Haug. For Milton's views, see YP I, pp. 569, 624–29, 632, 651.

17. Major editions were: Johann Basilius Heroldt, *Orthodoxographa Theologie Sacrosanctae ac Syncerioris Fidei Doctores* . . . (Basil, 1555); Johann Jacob Grynaeus, *Monumenta S. Patrum Orthodoxographa* . . . (Basil, 1569); Margarinus de La Bigne, *Bibliothecae Vetrum Patrum ac Auctorum Ecclesiasticorum tomi octo* (Paris, 1609); La Bigne, *Magna Bibliotheca Vetrum Patrum* . . . , 15 vols. (Colon, 1618–22); and Jean Baptiste Cotelier, *S. Patrum, qui temporibus apostolicis floreunt, Barnabae, Clementis, Hermae, Ignatii, Polycarpii opera* . . . (Amsterdam, 1624).

18. YP I, pp. 616, 780–81. *The Shepherd* may have aided Milton in making what Thomas Kranidas calls a "Politics of Vision" in the antiprelatical treatises: "Milton's *Of Reformation:* The Politics of Vision," *ELH* XLIX (1982), 497–513.

19. On this point see Thomas Kranidas, "Words, Words, Words, and the Word: Milton's *Of Prelatical Episcopacy*," in *Milton Studies*, vol. XVI, ed. James D. Simmonds (Pittsburgh, 1982), p. 159.

20. *The Shepherd*, p. 29. Some commentators have argued that the angel is a figure for Christ. If so, this identification would probably make the work more attractive to Milton. See Halvor Maxnes, "God and His Angel in the *Shepherd* of Hermas," *Studia Theologia* XXVIII (1974), 49–56; and *The Shepherd*, pp. 18–19.

21. "The Mysteries in Milton's *Masque*," in *Milton Studies*, vol. VI, ed. James D. Simmonds (Pittsburgh, 1974), pp. 113–42. My interpretation is compatible with Scoufos's account.

22. Barbara Breasted, "*Comus* and the Castelhaven Scandal," in *Milton Studies*, vol. III, ed. James D. Simmonds (Pittsburgh, 1971), pp. 201–24. The theme of familial regeneration is found in *The Shepherd*, pp. 10–12.

23. Georgia B. Christopher, *Milton and the Science of the Saints* (Princeton, 1982), pp. 31–58.

24. Barbara Kiefer Lewalski, *Protestant Poetics and the Seventeenth Century Lyric* (Princeton, 1979), pp. 7–13, 31–71.

25. *Complete Poems*, pp. 61–63. Demaray, *Milton and the Masque Tradition*, pp. 41–42.

26. John Smith, *Select Discourses*, 2nd ed. (London, 1673), pp. 215–17.

27. William Riley Parker, *Milton: A Biography* (Oxford, 1968), vol. II, pp. 792.

28. Cf. John D. Cox, "Poetry and History in Milton's Country Masque," *ELH* XLIV (1977), 622–40.

29. Comus's lineage and association with courtly culture is traced by John M. Steadman, "Iconography and Renaissance Drama: Ethical and Mythological Themes," Research Opportunities in Renaissance Drama, vols. XIII, XIV (1970–71), 73–122.

30. Orgel, *Illusion of Power*, pp. 37–58.

31. *John Milton and the English Revolution* (Totowa, N.J., 1981), pp. 134–35.

32. James G. Taaffe, "Michaelmas, the 'Lawless Hour,' and the Occasion of Milton's *Comus*," *ELN* X (1972), 11–15; William B. Hunter, "The Liturgical Context of *Comus*, *ELN* X (1972), 11–15.

33. The numerous interpretations of *haemony* are summarized in A.S.P. Woodhouse and Douglas Bush, eds., *A Variorum Commentary on the Poems of John Milton*, gen. ed. Merritt Y. Hughes (New York, 1972), vol. II, pp. 932–38. In addition see Charlotte Otten, "Homer's Moly and Milton's Rue," *HLQ* XXXIII (1970), 361–72, and "Milton's Haemony," *ELR* V (1975), 81–95; and John C. Ulreich, Jr., "'A Bright Golden Flow'r': Haemony as a Symbol of Transformation," *SEL* XVII (1977), 119–28.

34. See Woodhouse and Bush, *Variorum Commentary*, vol. II, pp. 818–19, 827–29.

35. *Transcendental Masque*, pp. 175, 150–75, 209–18.

36. "Landscape in the Transcendent Masque," in *Milton Studies*, vol. VI, ed. James D. Simmonds (Pittsburgh, 1974), pp. 160–61.

37. *The Odyssey*, trans. Albert Cook (New York, 1974), p. 142.

38. *Greek Myths and Christian Mysteries* (New York, 1963), pp. 286–327. I am indebted to Rahner's excellent study for many of the subsequent references.

39. Origen, *Homily on Exodus*, vol. IX, p. 4 (GCS, vol. VI, p. 244), and *Comment in Leviticus*, 6 (*Patrologiae Latina*, vol. LXX, col. 975C); Methodius, *Symposium*, IV, IX, as quoted in Rahner, *Greek Myths*, pp. 315–20.

40. Gregory the Great, *Moralia in Job*, XXXIII, 5 (PL, vol. LXXVI, col. 676B/D);

and Augustine, *Enrratio in Psalmum*, 136, 6 (PL, vol. XXXVII, 1764 CD), as quoted in Rahner, *Greek Myths*, pp. 311–13. However, the willows in Psalm cxxxvii were also interpreted in terms of the Babylonian exile and the prophecy concerning its destruction.

41. Eusebius, *Commentarius in Isaiam*, vol. XLIV, p. 4 (*Patrologiae Graeca*, vol. XXIV, col. 401D), as quoted in Rahner, p. 305.

42. See Jean Danielou, *The Angels and their Mission* (Westminster, 1957), pp. 90–91.

43. Methodius, *Symposium*, IV, 2, as quoted in Rahner, *Greek Myths*, p. 317.

44. This essay was substantially completed when Maryann Cole McGuire's *Milton's Puritan Masque* (Athens, 1983) appeared. My use of *The Shepherd* as a source for themes and structures compatible with Milton's desire to reform the church and literary expression supports her general approach to the masque and her conclusions about its Puritan content and form.

"AND HEAVEN GATES ORE MY HEAD": DEATH AS THRESHOLD IN MILTON'S MASQUE

Louise Simons

MILTON'S COURTLY entertainment, *A Mask Presented at Ludlow Castle*, was written for performance at Ludlow Castle in 1634. In theatrical terms, Milton's masque is a household entertainment: members of the earl of Bridgewater's household commissioned the writing, acted in the spectacle, attended the performance. The household itself further takes part in the masque's action because it is to Ludlow Castle that the three lost children are making their way. Comus's household also plays a part. He images a fantastic household for the Lady, "a low / But loyal cottage" (320); he guides her to his actual home, "a stately Palace, set out with all manner of deliciousness . . . his rabble, and . . . an inchanted Chair" (s.d.).[1]

In terms of the masque's attitude toward death, however, a dialectic is established between thematic enclosure, which is tropically figured as the earthly household, and thematic release, which comes through death and is symbolized as the heavenly threshold. The author affirms celestial reward for virtue: ultimately, death crowns the chaste Lady with eternal life. For virtuous individuals, then, death provides an entryway to renewed existence. Betokening mythic and celestial possibilities, the Attendant Spirit's dwelling place is mentioned, as is Sabrina's; and an additional reference is made to Jove's court. Death serves as a threshold, or passageway, by offering a means of release from terrestrial containment. Thus, at the close of the masque, when return of the children (especially of the Lady) to the Bridgewater family's household has been effected — when the mundane journey has been successfully transacted — we must consider the larger significance of the theme of return, including return to the parental home.

I

A Mask opens with the Attendant Spirit's entrance into "a wild wood" (s.d.). His introductory speech initiates the series of oppositions on which the drama is built. "Before the starry threshold of *Jove's* court," he says,

"My mansion is" (1–2). Milton sets in to establish antithetical images; one is containing (a wild wood), and one is expansive (a starry threshold). The conceptual image of the mansion at the bright threshold serves to oppose the visual image of the dark wood, which the Attendant Spirit extends synecdochally to become "this dim spot, / Which men call Earth" (4–5). The tangled, threatening forest, then, is an emblem for the constricted opportunities, the narrow margins, of the material world. Dim and disordering both visually and metaphorically, mundane existence contrasts to celestial existence, with its stellar vastness, its enlarging occasions framed by the extensive and expansive portals opening onto Jove's court. Allusively, the mansion and its location, "In regions mild of calm and serene air . . . where those immortal shapes / Of bright aereal spirits live insphear'd" (4, 2–3), suggest both classical and biblical antecedents. The Attendant Spirit (who is called a "Guardian Spirit, or Daemon" in the Trinity manuscript, a "guardian spiritt or demon" in the Bridgewater) "descends" (s.d.) to the action of the *Mask* from "Before the starry threshold of *Joves* court" (1). This emphatic designation of *threshold*, a stressed word in the opening line, is particularly appropriate for our consideration. The masque illustrates an early expression of a Miltonic theme — the liminality of death for the virtuous, as the entryway to mild and aerial renewed life.

The primary confrontation of the masque takes place between Comus and the Lady — a woodland enchanter and a young noblewoman lost in his part of the forest.[2] In the context of Milton's life-work, Comus and the Lady initiate the series of confrontations that have their most compelling moment in Milton's rewriting of the biblical Fall from Eden. Hence the critic is tempted to understand the *Mask* through a revisionary ratio that casts Comus and the Lady as canonical precursors, valued for shedding light on Milton's later antithetical structures. Through the pair's opposition, the poem presents us with an exploration of one of Milton's abiding preoccupations, that of resistance to evil. Because the Lady's resistance to Comus is depicted early in Milton's writing, her role acquires a special significance. She becomes the prototypical figure who is "Sufficient to have stood, though free to fall" (*PL* III, 99). She does not fall, but freely and virtuously withstands temptation, learning thereby her own sufficiency; her virtue leads to her eventual incorporation with other like spirits through ascent into the heavenly realm of mythologized sainthood. Thematically, then, her testing is linked both to that of other specified characters, especially in *Paradise Lost, Paradise Regained,* and *Samson Agonistes,* and also to that of entire nations, such as the Britons as a people in *The History of Britain.* Similarly, Comus is an early Miltonic figure of temptation and oppression, especially foreshadowing Satan's demonry in *Paradise Lost* and *Paradise Regained*.

II

In the masque, Milton's pastoral images take on the characteristics of reversed, or negative, transparencies, causing the earthly realm to be sensed as the constricting household of withheld or dead-ended possibilities and of closure. Interestingly, modern science verifies our earth's cycle as indeed a closed system. In Milton's *Mask*, mortal life becomes identified with the circular: social interaction is perceived as a restless "rouling" in the "pleasure" of carnality, illustrated by the activity of those who make up the debased herd of the antimasque (77). Antithetically, the Lady envisions for herself a different kind of movement, a different social order: hers is an upright and sedate "walking attended" (211) by guardian virtues. The trope serves as a kind of earthly prolepsis of the heavenly "solemn troops, and sweet societies" of *Lycidas* (177). Figuratively, thus, the Lady sallies out on the direct path to a self-realization that is derived from "blest providence" (329). Mundane life withholds nurture and fulfillment; in contrast, for the worthy individual, death provides ultimate meaning and promise of renewal, or rebirth into higher existence. Life entails a ceaseless traversal of a time-bound maze, or "leavy Labyrinth" (278), a "gloomy covert" (945) whose shady lanes circumvent arrival at the desired clearing of self-recognition; death affords a rising above the seasonal recurrences of history into the self-expressing sacred harmonies of eternality. Crucially, it is the earthly boundary, earth's household, that the Lady transcends.

Although the *Mask* has often been categorized as a pastoral poem (beginning in the eighteenth century with Joseph Warton, who called the poem a "Pastoral Drama"),[3] still, its *stylus humilis* is misleading. The evergreen of immortality shades with great rapidity from classical to biblical myth. One such quick transition is to be seen in the Spirit's description to the two brothers of the three musical episodes that take place earlier in the evening: first, the Spirit's own music-making as Thyrsis; next, the wild dance of Comus's throng; and last, the Lady's song to Echo. To begin, the Spirit narrates an account of himself as Thyrsis, a pastoral swain, playing the lowly shepherd's pipe:

> I sate me down to watch upon a bank
> With ivy canopied, and interwove
> With flaunting honiesuckle, and began
> Wrapt in a pleasing fit of melancholy
> To meditate my rural minstrelsie. (543–47)

Next, he recapitulates what the audience has just heard and seen, the "barbarous dissonance" (550) of the rout's antimasquing interlude, followed presently by the exalted "soft and solemn breathing sound" (555) of the Lady, which he says

> Rose like a steam of rich distill'd perfumes
> And stole upon the air, that even silence
> Was took e're she was ware, and wish't she might
> Deny her nature, and be never more
> Still to be so displac't.   (556–60)

The disguised spirit's description of the Lady comprises the conventional courtly compliment; it is appropriate to the masque itself and to Lawes speaking of Lady Alice Egerton in a public spectacle viewed by her parents and social circle. Next, however, the Spirit adds the Miltonic trademark, the subsuming of the classical by the biblical: "I was all ear, / And took in strains that might create a soul / Under the ribs of Death" (560–62). In recounting the quality of their relative music making, the Attendant Spirit, as Thyrsis, attaches himself to the classical world and the Lady, imagistically, to the biblical. Both the Spirit-as-shepherd and the Lady would be understood by a contemporary audience as exemplary masque figures of virtue, but a break occurs between their two forms of music, which separates the forms not so much as one musical harmony from another, but as one kind of musical harmony from another. In that Comus prevents the piped song from reaching an end, he functions, as usual, to represent rupture: the shepherd says that "ere" his music reached "a close / The wonted roar was up amidst the woods" (548–49). Here, the rout's unruly noise prevents the piping swain from completing his song; a bit later the rout's wild dance abruptly breaks off at the Lady's footsteps. The disruptive antimasque danced by Comus's thronging followers establishes an artistic difference, or change of pace, between the two harmonious modes that surround it; in addition, it serves a separate but related function, a special authorial purpose of discreet disjuncture: it displaces the classical by the biblical.

Notably, Thyrsis's remarks about the antimasquing "roar" (549), or disharmony, coming as they do between the description of the two kinds of masque harmony, are diversionary. Notice of the dissonant intrusion of the antic rout's customary hubbub serves as a break, or cover, behind which Milton can rank linguistic modes without attracting notice. The shading of classical, or pagan, into biblical is so consistently a Miltonic device that its appearance in the masque seems unremarkable enough.

Earlier, in *Ode on the Morning of Christ's Nativity*, the newborn infant overtly defeats the classical figures. The "flowr-inwov'n tresses" of the nymphs are "torn" (186), in token of the jagged, disruptive ending of pagan hold on the world, including the literary world; for the power of the *word* is at stake: "The Stars . . . Stand fixt . . . And wil not take their flight . . . Untill their Lord himself *bespake*, and *bid* them go" (69, 70, 72, 76, my emphasis). The pagan gods, typified by Osiris, are consigned to be "shrouded" in "profoundest Hell" (218), a restless, blank death, associated with deepest darkness, from which there is no possibility of return or rebirth: "In vain with *Timbrel'd Anthems dark* / The *sable-stoled Sorcerers* bear his worshipt Ark" (219–20; my emphasis). The association of darkness with sorcery, frenzied music, orgy, and perverse ritual is continued in the *Mask*'s deep woods with "black shade imbowr'd," where Comus performs "noctural . . . rights" to "Dark-vaild Cotytto" (62, 125, 128, 129).

III

The character of the Attendant Spirit presents us with a prefiguring of a repeated type in Milton's canon. In *Paradise Lost*, he reappears as the sociable angel Raphael, archetypal messenger. The two celestial messengers are well-connected and gorgeously attired. The Attendant Spirit appears first to the audience in his "sky robes spun out of *Iris* woof" (83). The "heavens" he would desend from is the technical term for the area above stage (presuming the masque was performed indoors in the great hall at Ludlow Castle).[4] Raphael leaves heaven "from among / Thousand Celestial Ardors, where he stood / Vaild with his gorgeous wings," and descends in an unobstructed, cloudless "vast Ethereal Skie" to earth (*PL* V, 248–50, 267). When Raphael alights, he resumes "his proper shape" (*PL* V, 276).

In effect, both the Attendant Spirit and Raphael are salvation figures who first fail to avert human confrontation with deceptive evil and then, additionally, cannot save the endangered woman — the Lady or Eve. Yet from the outset, they are altogether figures of sympathy to the audience. As an amiable shape-shifter, each serves in an adversarial role to a wily shape-shifter, one who is "mutable" in the most deplorable sense. Second, both messengers figure in a protective role toward the innocent and unprotected human characters, who are in need of sociable guidance. Finally, they are given the genial role of narrator of off-stage events, which makes them handily available for shaping human response — of both characters and audience. Basically, their role is a decentered one, as mediator of events in which other characters play the central part.

As it happens, the Spirit is occasionally mistaken and ineffective. In his continued narration to the brothers of the evil befallen their sister, by associative imagery he misapprehends the Lady, who is indeed stalked by Comus, but who is not a "poor hapless nightingale" about to be "snared" (566, 567). The Lady is neither Philomela nor Daphne, as Comus imagines, adding his own descriptive epithet, "Root-bound" (662). She transcends others' interpretations of her, including the fearful projections of her danger by her youngest brother.

Perhaps the Elder Brother is most attuned to her true worth because, as William Kerrigan points out, he functions on one level as a stand-in for Milton himself.[5] Although the Lady proves that she is unbounded by classical precursors, including Diana and Minerva who are mentioned by the Elder Brother, these two goddesses are most closely allied to her as emblems of her ennobling qualities. The Elder Brother speaks of them, respectively, as "for ever chaste" and "unconquer'd virgin" (442, 448). In miniature, the Elder Brother's reassurance to the Younger Brother imitates the poem's greater movement in describing the sacred attributes of the Lady, which grow, in turn, from chastity to virginity. The Elder Brother initially likens her to "a quiver'd nymph" (442), who is protected by "the sacred rayes of chastity" (425). The description of the Lady as encircled by "sacred rayes," a nimbus conferred upon her by her state of chastity, admits the Lady to the company of those human beings whom Michael Lieb defines as "earmarked," or "set apart from the profane." Lieb says these sanctified individuals are ones who personify, even in their earthly life, a "positive notion of holiness."[6]

As the Elder Brother develops his description, by increments the Lady's power is enhanced, from the more moderate "quiver'd nymph" to the resplendent "Fair silver-shafted Queen" (442), a difference in wording that implies her radiance, or her impending radiance. Moreover, her "saintly chastity" endows her with visionary powers — "cleer dream, and solemn vision" of discourse from "heav'nly habitants" — and an imminently glowing "beam on th' outward shape" (453, 457, 459, 460). What she is in preparation for is the turning of the "unpolluted temple of [her] mind . . . by degrees to the souls essence, / Till all be made immortal" (461–63). The Elder Brother thus confirms a theme begun in the Attendant Spirit's opening speech, that "human countnance" is "Th' express resemblance of the gods" (68, 69). By repetition of such forecasts as these, the teleology of the masque is made manifest through the other characters' assessments of the Lady. The various descriptive analogies that are furnished by the brothers, the Attendant Spirit, and Comus, all function in preparation for her eventual release through death to higher life.

Hence, the diverse strands of the *Mask* gather together harmoniously in her eventual triumph, in which she is led, literally, to the threshold of her earthly father's home, and, figuratively, to the threshold of her heavenly father's home.

Although she may be thought a helpless songbird, unfledged and untried, the Lady proves herself worthy as she resolutely faces her impending "triall" (329), her virtue being proven neither "fugitive" nor "cloister'd," those opprobrious qualifiers Milton said he could not praise (*Areopagitica*, YP II, p. 515). It is to herself that the Lady gives birth "Within the navil of this hideous wood" (520): through hardy resistance to evil in time of trial, her full-fledged selfhood emerges into preparation for final rebirth. Even though the words, or lyrics, of her song to Echo depend upon pagan myths as their codes, the harmony of the Lady's song is heavenly—"divine . . . holy" (245, 246). In song, the Lady calls upon Echo as "Sweet Queen of Parly" (241), and during the masque's events she becomes both the shadow and type of Echo. First, as we shall see, in the stichomythia of her dialogue with Comus, she speaks the echoing line. Next, in Comus's palace, it is the Lady herself who becomes the "Queen of Parly," the coequal to Echo.

The Lady's discourse has significance on a spiritual level. Strategically, Milton removes the rhetorical power of chastity from the category of magic: her speech-making ability is not merely a kind of magical charm to ward off a charming magician. Indeed, her more simple rhetoric lacks the adornment, and hence, to the "fallen" audience and readership, the verbal power, or magic, of those protean figures, the Attendant Spirit and Comus, both of whom assume a disguise during the masque. As Angus Fletcher reminds us, "The chaste person has no mask."[7] David M. Miller points out, "When the demonic assumes a mask, the purpose is to deceive; when the divine assumes a mask, the purpose is to instruct. As is always the case in Milton's poetry, demonic accommodations must be discredited before divine accommodations can be understood."[8] Hence, the "navil" of the poem signals a coming into selfhood, with self-knowledge and self-recognition as central, and, as we shall see in the actions of Sabrina and the Attendant Spirit, with acknowledgment by the community as a concomitant. There is an implicit ranking of linguistic modes, and as an adjunct we find an adumbration of a Miltonic theme: assurance of ultimate resurrection for the Lady is in some sense equally a guarantee of Milton's own ultimate reward. The underlying suggestion of a self-referential authorial voice within *A Mask* will become even more insistently explicit when Milton writes *Lycidas*, with its layered singing voices.

IV

In *A Mask,* Milton interlards his text with tropes signifying a pervasive earthly swinishness. The Lady fears to meet up with "swill'd insolence" (178), a derogate that promotes the masque's connection of drink with base behavior. Unknowingly, the Lady echoes the Spirit's early reminder to the audience that Bacchus and Circe are connected through perversion of the powers of wine. In fact, their use of wine is as a death-dealing, or death-related, poison, the very antitype to wine's religious connection with eternal life. It is Bacchus who "first . . . Crush't the sweet *poyson* of *mis-used* wine" (my italics), and Circe's "charmed cup" which caused the "upright" to become "groveling swine" (46, 47, 51, 53, 54). In words that allusively discredit all kinds of excessive ingestion, the Lady castigates "swinish gluttony" with a pun on gorging—"gorgeous feast":

> for swinish gluttony
> Ne're looks to Heav'n amidst his gorgeous feast,
> But with besotted base ingratitude
> Cramms, and blasphemes his feeder.   (776–79)

Threaded through her language are dialectics: her own elevated connection to "Heav'n" is opposed to the "baseness" and implicit "blasphemy" of the "besotted." Linguistically, the letters *b, g, s,* and *t,* which predominate in the piled-up negatives, are not present in "Heav'n" and in "feeder," setting apart the two words attached to holiness as distinct from the words cataloguing carnal appetites. In *An Apology Against a Pamphlet,* Milton speaks of "chastity and love . . . whose charming cup is only vertue" (YP I, p. 891).

As the Spirit notes, the "brutish" change that Comus can cause in humans through the folly of their "intemperate thirst" (70, 67) is only to those unfortunates who stray into his woods. For whereas the Egerton children find themselves temporarily stranded in the "perplext paths" of the mazy woods—which for the virtuous is related to being "Confin'd and pester'd" in a "pinfold"—Comus is present in his natural habitat where he confidently boasts of knowing "each lane, and every alley green / Dingle, or bushy dell . . . And every bosky bourn" (37, 7, 311–13). Screened by night shadows, which he terms "dun shades" (127), Comus perverts the ethical powers of others, impelled by a fantasy of exerting his own magical power. It is the shape-shifting abilities of the Attendant Spirit and Comus that provide most of the *Mask's* spectacle.

By nature, a masque, although literary in execution, is spectacular (a viewed spectacle) in presentation. As Ben Jonson said in exasperation,

"Painting & Carpentry are ye Soule of Masque!"[9] Generically, or by definition, then, the masque is an imaginal, or specular, form of expression.
"Ben Jonson was correct, of course," writes John G. Demaray, "in claiming that the *enduring* soul of the masque is poetry, but Aurelian Towns-
hend disclosed something of the *theatrical* soul of the masque when he
referred to 'these showes' as 'pictures with Light and Motion.'" Moreover, Demaray links the spectacular effects of the performance with the
spectacular gaze of the audience. "In *Comus* [as in other masques] the
ruling power of the seated nobility is related to that of the gods," says
Demaray, "and order is restored in a place clearly ruled by the nobles. . . .
Even the scenery on the masquing stage is, in effect, 'proportioned' by
the nobles; the scenic perspectives are absolutely true only when viewed
from the chair of state."[10] In Milton's masque, the chair of state, the
central point from which the performance was to be watched, was occu-
pied by the earl of Bridgewater, father to the three children and para-
mount viewer. By their specular power, then, the viewers were incorporated, both physically and psychologically, into the scenic spectacle
itself. Milton portrays Comus as an essentially spectacular character,
which makes him an exemplary masque figure.

Comus grasps in either hand the "charmed cup" (51) of Circe, his
mother, and the "charming rod" (s.d.) of Bacchus, his father. Through
these visual symbols, the badges of his parents' means of enchantment,
Comus's interior, mental level is easily ascertained. True to the masque
tradition in which identifying character traits are made visual, Comus
exteriorizes his attributes of power by carrying emblems easily recognized
by an audience. His fragmented ego is thus spatially verifiable. Brandish-
ing phenomenal manifestations of his power, he presents an external-
ized, or spectacular, display of the objectifying and fragmenting of his
own body-image. In the case of Comus, the identifying objects, the cup
and the rod, are not merely emblematic of generalized sexuality, but pertain specifically to the gender-identity of his own parents: he predicates
his own identity on the signs of enchantment of both his parents. Hence,
Milton's description of Comus as "a son / Much like his father, but his
mother more" (56–57), which overtly refers to Circe's enchantment
powers, now deepens in residual meaning. Comus displays and retains
the fragmented nature of his own self-image by clutching iconic images
of the genitalia of both sexes. Seen from this perspective, Milton's wording conveys gender confusion and a lack of dominance of male attributes.

Although the character resemblance is slight, Milton probably based
his conception of Comus in part on the title figure in a work by Hendrik
van der Putten, or Puteanus, that was printed in 1608 and reprinted at

Cambridge in 1634, the year in which Milton wrote *A Mask*. Linkage with the Comus of Cartari's *Imagines* and Philostratus's *Icones* is also probable. "It was from Puteanus," says Merritt Y. Hughes, "that Milton learned to give life to the shadowy classical genius of revelry whom Philostratus described as an allegorical figure, gracefully drunk, standing with an inverted torch in his hand."[11] Through the symbolism attached to the "inverted torch" that he carries, we find the clue to Comus's need to use guile and force in order to win the Lady. Comus is invested with no clearly dominant masculine sexuality, having instead a fragmented, or uncombined, psychic *melange* of sexual attributes. In fact, Comus's behavior reveals the outermost manifestations of gender typing—powerless guile of the female, brute force of the male. Therefore, it follows that his desire for the Lady is a perverse one, compounded rather of alienating wishes than of incorporating ones. What Comus offers to the Lady, then, is the opposite to Eros, or true affirmation of life; with his false enticement— his "poisoned cup of pleasure"—what he proffers to the Lady is Thanatos, or benumbing death."[12]

In Milton's depiction, Comus maintains a forest existence as an alien from orderly society. In the Trinity manuscript, Milton marks Comus's first speech with "intrant κωμάζοντες," or *revelers* (p. 58). Cedric C. Brown develops Comus's identification with the rites of *komos*, or *nocturnal debauchery and revelry*. Through Milton's notation of a possible topic for tragedy, "Comazontes or the Benjaminits Jud. 19.20 &c. or the Rioters," Comus and his "rabble" (s.d.) are tied by Brown to Milton's description of debauchees in Book I of *Paradise Lost*.[13] In the epic, Milton refers to a rape episode in Judges xix, 22, in which the iniquitous Benjamites are named בְּנֵי־בְלִיַּעַל, or *sons of belial*, a derogate that carries the meaning of *worthlessness*. Although in the Old Testament *belial* is an abstract concept, in New Testament writing *Belial* becomes personified. Accordingly, in *Paradise Lost*, Belial is a fallen angel, associated with "the noyse / Of riot . . . And injury and outrage"; Milton continues, "And when Night / Darkens the Streets, then wander forth the Sons / of Belial, flown with insolence and wine" (*PL* I, 498–500, 500–02). The zeugmatic "*flown* with insolence and wine" indicates Milton's conjunction of *overflowing* drink with *swollen* antisocial behavior. Thematically, the opposed concepts of alienation and community underlie the masque's dialogue and action as powerful forces for, respectively, evil and good. In *A Mask*, Comus, who incarnates alienation, or estrangement from the organized social order, is driven off the stage alone at the end, whereas the Lady, enspirited by the social virtues, is rescued and released by communal effort.

The linkage of Comus with riot and *belial* has significance among other suggestive connections in the Milton canon. The episode in Judges opens, "In those days when there was no king," a reiterated phrase that indicates the necessity for self-imposed morality among the people. The account tells of a man whose status as a Levite connotes his connection with religion and ethics. In the biblical story, his concubine is unfaithful — "played the harlot against him" — and returns to her father's house. After four months pass by, the Levite goes after her, "to speak kindly unto her and bring her back." The woman's father welcomes him and detains him for feasting. On their return trip, the couple stay overnight in Gibeah, where they have trouble finding a host among the local Benjamites, "for there was no man that took them into his house to lodge." Finally, an old man, a field hand who came originally from the hill-country of Ephraim, takes them into his home as guests. Later that night, a crowd of riotous Benjamites, "men that are sons of belial," demand that the guest, the Levite, be sent out into the streets to be sodomized. The host offers his own daughter, who is a virgin, and also the concubine, but the mob of revelers will not be appeased. Eventually, in his own place, the guest opens the door and puts out the concubine, who is "abused all the night until the morning." The next day, the Levite finds her fallen down for dead in the doorway, "with her hands upon the threshold." He takes her up on his ass, goes home, hacks her into twelve pieces, and sends the pieces, like Truth, throughout Israel. A battle is prepared, and on the third day, the Benjamites, or fallen angels, are beaten (Judges xix, 1–35).[14]

Milton makes multiple uses of this narrative in his works. In *The Doctrine and Discipline of Divorce*, his comments show that he had read the Judges account in at least one rabbinical Bible, probably in the edition printed by Buxtorf about 1620. For this passage, Milton refers to three opinions, those of Rabbis Kimchi, Rashi, and ben-Gershon. From the rabbis, we find that the notion that the concubine was sexually unfaithful to her husband is a later and less logical telling of the story. According to the Masorah, or rabbinical commentary, the woman is wayward but not promiscuous. She leaves her husband after nothing more serious than a tiff, or marital spat. Part of the supporting evidence for this reading is syntactical and part is legal; a Levite could not lawfully have reclaimed the woman had she strayed sexually and hence been unclean. Our English translation that the man goes to her father's home to speak to her kindly is literally "goes to speak to her heart," which also indicates that a squabble occurred. Her father's taking her in and the cordial relationship between the two men, father and husband, again supports the rabbinical reading. In the divorce tracts, evidently Milton equates the headstrong woman with Mary Powell and the long-suffering and conciliatory husband with himself. This personalizing of the story lends an intimate and psychological significance to the *Paradise Lost* wording that the husband "Expos'd a Matron" to the Benjamite rabble in order to "avoid *worse rape.*" Emotionally, Comus is more clearly antithesized to the Lady, a Milton-figure threatened by rape. This point serves to refute the critical notion that Comus is "less demon than fertility god" and that the Lady's "triumph is equivocal" because "Comus' rich inducements simply do not appeal to her as they ought."[15] Through his alienated, profane nature, Comus shares kinship with "*Ely's* Sons, who fill'd / With lust and violence the house of God" (*PL* I, 495–96).

In fact, the dialectic between alienation and communality is subtly present in the language of *A Mask* even at seemingly unrelated moments. Milton prepares for the combined rescue of the Lady by linguistic seeding of the dialogue. When the Elder Brother says that "evil on it self shall back recoyl . . . Self-fed, and self-consum'd" (593, 597), the thanatotic isolation of the paradoxical "*self*-fed . . . *self*-consum'd" shows evil's innate estrangement from domestic or social connections. Robert M. Adams comments that "the forces which the Lady opposes to [Comus] are by no means simple. Some of her strength is her own, some is her brothers', some is the Attendant Spirit's." Also, he notes that the combinations formed by the Lady's "own strength" and that of the other figures of rescue are "complex" and ambiguous, including "the power" of the water nymph Sabrina.[16] In his opening speech, the Attendant Spirit signals a motif that becomes thematic: the oppositional function of horizontal and vertical movement. Rescue for the Lady, for instance, will be extra-earthly, appearing vertically both as descent from "regions . . . Above the smoak and stirr of this dim spot, / Which men call Earth" and as ascent from "*Neptune*" who has "Imperial rule of all the sea-girt Iles" (4, 5–6, 18, 21). In terms of the nonhuman figures of magical power, the Attendant Spirit descends and Sabrina rises, but Comus — who is tied to "sin-worn" (17) earth — enters laterally.

Comus's "rout" (s.d.) of followers are typical masque figures of vice. As such, they not only reinforce Comus's own fragmentary identity, but they extend the concept of specularly identifiable markings even further. Cavorting monstrously, they display psychic fragmentation in their physical being: they are described as "headed like sundry sorts of wild beasts, but otherwise like men and women" (s.d.). Their bestial heads on human bodies present a visual confirmation of the disjunctive reification that Comus imposes on his own "herd" (152). Comus's followers give oracular confirmation of their own physical mutability, thus, theoretically, opposing themselves to stability of societal order. Moreover, the dance in which they "beat the ground / In a light fantastick round" (143–44), was originally described by Milton in the Trinity manuscript as "a wild rude & wanton antick" (p. 64). In reinforcement of the thought that Comus externalizes his internal attributes, Barbara Howard Traister points out that Comus's magic actually "brings about few changes; it merely makes visible the inner state of his victims."[17] Comus functions as an instigator of social disorder. He achieves a further disordering of his rout's "wanton" revels with his command to "Break off, break off" their dancing abruptly, as he "feels . . . the different pace" of the Lady's "chast footing" (145–46).

V

Parted from her two younger brothers in the forest and out of their sight in the gathering dusk, the Lady calls upon a kind of self-image, "Sweet Echo, sweetest nymph that liv'st unseen," for guidance in reuniting her with the pair of boys "That likest thy *Narcissus* are" (230, 237). When Comus hears the Lady's song to Echo, he imagines aloud, "Ile speak to her / And she shall be my Queen" (264–65). In effect, he operates from passionate desire based on uncontrolled fantasies of domination; the imperative grammatical structure of the intention, "she *shall* be," bears evidence of his tendentious thought patterns. Wish leaps to fulfillment: the Lady becomes his object of desire, and hence, according to his fantasy, available for his appropriation by force. Comus's obsession with seduction of the Lady is a function of his indulging in an impossible desire. As such, his longing for her is compounded more of imagined perversion of her purity than of appreciation of it. Although Comus is superhuman in some respects, especially through his parentage and his powers of magical enchantment, he is less than human in others. Indeed, his herd seconds his own animalistic level. Milton implies Comus's serpentlike nature:

> I under fair pretence of freindly ends
> And well-plac't words of glozing courtesie
> Baited with reasons not unplausible
> Wind me into the easie-hearted man,
> And hugg him into snares.   (160–64)

If gender-confusion indeed occurs in Milton's writing,[18] in this passage the serpent is an ambiguated symbol of insinuating guile (male: the snake as phallus; female: the woman as temptress). What is most clear, however, is the presence of menace.

Even though, as we shall see, the Lady claims powers for her chastity that remain unsubstantiated rhetorically, purity governs her actions. Her plane of spirituality is above Comus's debased level of comprehension. He compares her song to remembered experience of what he has "oft heard":

> My mother *Circe* with the Sirens three,
> Amidst the flowry-kirtl'd *Naiades*,
> Culling thir Potent hearbs, and balefull drugs,
> Who as they sung, would take the prison'd soul,
> And lap it in *Elysium; Scylla* wept,
> And chid her barking waves into attention,
> And fell *Charybdis* murmur'd soft applause:
> Yet they in pleasing slumber lull'd the sense,
> And in sweet madnes rob'd it of it self.   (252–61)

Through his limited understanding, Comus constructs a model of what he takes to be the feminine type. Interestingly, based on his familiarity with, and approval of, treachery, he builds a false concept, or structure, with just the insufficiency of understanding that the Lady later recognizes about his other constructs. He bases his reasoning on feminine figures from his own experience—mythological personages of wile and destruction—in fact, those whose allure brings a kind of death to their victims, a death of *ratio*, or sensibility. He then connects, or *equates*, the Lady's song to Echo with the speech-model of his own understanding. He believes, or "reasons," that her singing contains actual enchantment, or magic. Comus's first impressions depend on memory. He harks back to what he can comprehend, the kind of songs that are used as lures or preludes to magical enslavement, which leads him to equate the Lady's song with those of Circe and the Sirens. Also, Comus desires to captivate the Lady, and as Jacques Lacan establishes, desire is the psychological equivalent of the metonymic pole of language.[19] In the tropic axis of metonymy, relationships are expressed through contiguity, or proximity. Comus's thoughts have been on his own practice of magic for purposes of entrapment: "Thus I hurl / My dazling spells" (153–54). By contiguity, then, his ideas are projected diachronically from concentration on his own magical enchantments to the notion that others also have enchantment abilities.

For this reason, he self-consciously attributes magical power to the Lady. His "sober certainty" (263) indicates he believes the Lady enchants him not through "cordial Julep" (672) such as he proffers but through magical aid from Echo, a *water* nymph. By a parallel contrast, the Lady's effect on him of "waking bliss" (263) indicates her superiority to his mother's "pleasing slumber"; again, his mother's effect of "madnes" is inferior to the Lady's of sobriety. In sum, his understanding of a non-magical effect is insufficient to comprehend the Lady's spiritual powers. Later in his palace, her kinship with the water nymph Echo is recalled, as her kinship with Sabrina is anticipated, by the "cold shuddring dew" that besprinkles Comus as he "feels . . . fear" at the "superior power" of her discourse (802, 800, 801). Water, of course, is the *Mask*'s primary symbol of spirituality and regeneration. It is essentially antithetical to the "magick *dust*" (165, my emphasis) with which Comus manages his "blear illusion" (155).

The word *dust* may signify life-givingness elsewhere in Milton's writing, especially in the grateful thoughts of Adam: "needs must the Power / That made us . . . Be infinitly good . . . That rais'd us from the dust and plac't us here / In all this happiness" (*PL* IV, 412–13, 414, 416; see also V, 514–18 and Raphael's words to Adam, VII, 524–27). In Milton's masque, however, *dust* indicates the thanatotic aridity of Comus's powers. A *Mask* presents the restless sterility of Comus's forest existence as an evil option. His sensual round, a sprawling, endless *danse macabre* of heedless gratification, has only one type of renewal, the enticing of new victims into the spiral. This mode of existence is mindless, sophisticated, effete, freakish. In Milton's depiction, such sprawling, hectic existence poisons its participants with incomprehension of their true status, forgetfulness of the higher life, and foul disfigurement of that which in humans reflects their creator and paradisal origin. Put differently, through the artifice of his "brew'd inchantments," "visor'd falshood," "lickerish baits," Comus closes off the avenues to rational and truly generative life (696, 698, 700). In due time, the Lady rejects opiate, treason, and lust when she opts for "well-govern'd and wise appetite" (705). Her just and reasonable temperance is life-affirmative.

Comus's first address to the Lady is marked by a certain rhetorical flourish:

> Hail forren wonder
> Whom certain these rough shades did never breed
> Unless the Goddes that in rurall shrine
> Dwell'st heer. (265–68)

Comus exalts the Lady to the status of a "wonder," a "Goddes" to be "hailed," "enshrined," elevated, worshipped. The Lady replies to Comus's greeting with a mildness that contains a small reproof:

> Nay gentle shepherd, ill is lost that praise
> That is addrest to unattending ears,

> Not any boast of skill, but extreme shift
> How to regain my sever'd company
> Compell'd me to awake the courteous Echo
> To give me answer from her mossie couch.   (271–76)

Despite her words of rebuke, the Lady seems not altogether displeased with Comus's lofty, or "gentle," salutation. Through a system of false echoes, which Milton uses to cheat the ear of the unwary auditor, it seems that the greeting by Comus in "answer" to her song becomes "the courteous Echo" the Lady "awakes." Indeed, the ensuing dialogue suggests the Lady's and Comus's temporary linkage, or pairing, on the linguistic level. In the imaginary conjunction that appears to take place between Comus and the Lady, their essential differences are obscured in the dappled shadows of the disordering forest. Through innocence, the Lady accepts the appearance of a kind of courtier-shepherd in the gloomy woods despite the fact that they stand on the very spot from which she has just heard "the sound / Of riot and ill-manag'd merriment" (171–72).[20]

Thus, in their meeting, manipulated as it is by Comus, Milton establishes the basis for a disjunctive relationship between his two characters. Through a confronting of masque virtue by masque vice, Milton provides his poem with a dramatic tension that is atypical of the genre. Psychologically, the relationship of Comus and the Lady comes about because their approach to each other is based on an innocent sureness of her own safety on the part of the Lady and a perverse fantasy of his prevailing might on the part of Comus. For a brief time during their meeting, then, the outcome of Comus's cheating illusion is in doubt. During this period, the characters seem to be doubled, their parallel, or echolike, status reinforced by the lines of stichomythic dialogue they immediately share:

> *Comus:* What chance good Lady, hath bereft you thus?
> *Lady:* Dim darknes, and this leavy Labyrinth.
> *Comus:* Could that divide you from neer-ushering guides?
> *Lady:* They left me weary on a grassie terf.
> *Comus:* By falshood, or discourtesie or why?
> *Lady:* To seek i'th valley som cool freindly spring.
> *Comus:* And left your fair side all unguarded, Lady?
> *Lady:* They were but twain, and purpos'd quick return.
> *Comus:* Perhaps fore-stalling night prevented them.
> *Lady:* How easie my misfortune is to hit!
> *Comus:* Imports thir loss, beside the present need?
> *Lady:* No less then if I should my brothers loose.
> *Comus:* Were they of manly prime, or youthfull bloom?
> *Lady:* As smooth as *Hebe's* thir unrazor'd lips.   (277–90)

Comus dominates in initiating and shaping the rhetorical movement of their dialogue, with the Lady allowing herself to give the echoing answer. Because he manipulates the dialogue, the sound of courtship is to be heard in their exchange. Indeed, when Comus next varies the rhetoric in his full answer (291–304), the stichomythia ends lingeringly on the Lady's word *lips*, which closes a line flowing with sensuous imagery and sibilance. We see the two figures involved in a possible seduction, a relationship whose rhetorical expression, at least, appears to be of a complicitous nature.

In the Lady's seeming collaboration may be read her security under her father's watchful eye, even in the mazy lanes and concealing dimness of the forest. On the importance of the attentive figure of the father in seventeenth-century thought, Boyd M. Berry remarks, "Quite obviously, the Father was the center of Puritan theology, which we often term 'paternal' and 'patriarchal.'"[21] As we have seen, Comus's fantasy of power arises from the fragmenting of a physical attribute of the parent. Indeed, a fragmented image of the parent — for Comus, the symbolized genitals of both parents; for the Lady, the specular ability of her father — is made thematic by Milton in his *Mask*, whose very title suggests the hidden and the specular. Even though she is enclosed by disorderly overgrowth, she "walks attended / By a strong siding champion conscience" (211–12), the patriarchal superego, the all-seeing eye of her father. It is in the paternal gaze that the Lady believes herself to be unobscured. For this reason, the Lady is immune to Comus's act of "hurling . . . magick dust . . . to cheat the eye with blear illusion." Traister emphasizes the dramatic convention that magic "can affect one's body, but never one's unwilling mind." She quotes from an anonymous late sixteenth-century drama, *The Wars of Cyrus*, whose language could have served Milton as a pattern: "Araspas: 'Must Magicke yeeld to vertue?' . . . Magician: 'Magicke cannot commaund the soule.'"[22] Temporarily, the Lady may willingly delude herself that, no matter how unlikely, the "glozing" Comus is really a "good shepherd" (307). Yet it is a virtuous motive that governs her thought: ultimately, she desires to end with safe conduct from the woods.

VI

In the first decade of the nineteenth century, William Blake painted two series of illustrations of *A Mask*.[23] Although Blake's interpretation alters only somewhat between the first and second set of illustrations, the differences tend to support and emphasize my commentary. Significantly, there is one unchanging aspect Blake stresses: the feminine and nonthreatening appearance that Comus presents to the Lady and her brothers when he is in disguise. In scene 1 (fig. 1) of the first series, Comus, undisguised and accompanied by his rout, is unseen by the Lady as he moves fluidly toward the center of the picture. His left hand is empty; the "charming rod" in his right hand is cut off by the top of the painting, leaving limitless space above him. He thus presents the appearance of possessing extensive power. Irene Taylor comments, "Comus' starward gesture [is] welcoming night and its dark confusion."[24] In scene 1 of the second series (fig. 2), Comus is more static in posture and appears more constrained. He is decentered at top right in a more awkward stance. He holds both glass and charming rod, raised aloft in his left and right hands respectively. The signs of his magical powers form a flattened circle above his head, now giving the impression of limitation on his potency.

Scene 2 of Blake's series (figs. 3 and 4) shows Comus disguised before the Lady as a "harmles villager" (166). His curly hair is here hanging limp on his shoulders, its slack appearance in contrast with its usual springy vitality. Later, in valiant, if boastful, projection, the Elder Brother says of Comus, "Ile . . . drag him by the curls and cleave his scalp / Down to the hipps" (606, 608–09). Thus, although the pictoral depiction of Comus's appearance to the children—one which shows the magician with lank hair drooping downward—may seem to be factually inaccurate, Blake's sensitivity to the enticing attractiveness of youthful curls is accurate indeed. Blake transposes the wand and cup to a walking staff and hat, which Comus now carries in either hand, both items held downward; the inside of the hat faces outward toward the Lady. Although in scene 2 the figures of Comus, the Lady, and the Attendant Spirit are similarly located in both series, the second series (fig. 4) supports my interpretation more precisely, for, as Stephen C. Behrendt notes, Blake "more carefully delineates in the second set what is already implicit in the first":[25] Comus's rod/cane (sign of masculine power) is in his left hand, held just behind him, out of the Lady's sight. The cup/hat (feminine sign) in his right hand is propelled just slightly before his body, its placement presenting the Lady with an unassertive vaginal symbol held just parallel to her genital area. Pictorially, the projected, vulvar hat centers on to itself Comus's benign and submissive appearance. As the Lady is enframed in her own space by a gothic arch of trees, not only is her matching feminine appearance emphasized and enhanced but also her true virginity, which for Blake, of course, is a spiritual condition rather than a physical state.[26] In accord with the *Mask* in which they appear, Comus masks his real nature. In his subtle rendering of Comus's deceptively humble approach to the Lady, Blake illustrates in part what Madelon Gohlke defines as "structures of dominance and submission":[27] in Comus's disguise, we must read submission as merely a strategic *mask* of humility, a pretense of weakness.

VII

Significantly, even as she is on the point of setting off with him, the Lady recognizes the risk involved in departing with Comus. She voices a negative presentiment about her situation despite her innocent acceptance of his seeming gallantry. She frames her appeal for heavenly aid in terms of specular body-imagery — the detached, all-seeing eye of the father: "Eye me blest providence, and square my triall / To my proportion'd strength. Shepherd lead on" (329–30). Through the bewildering power that Comus exerts, the Lady's song to Echo appears to be answered by the Lady's echo, or *imago*, in Comus. When the Lady first enters, she recapitulates the sounds she has just heard from Comus's rabble, revising wanton dance into music she can comprehend. She says, "This way the noise was, if mine ear be true, / My best guide now" (170–71). Her opening line of discourse bespeaks her reliance on fragmentation of her body to receive and make sense of events in the phenomenal world, even as she recognizes her father (omniscient as both her paternal and spiritual father incorporated in one) — her guardian, guide, champion, conscience — metonymically, as a watchful eye. Not only does she turn her ear, which is unaccustomed to interpreting disharmonious music, into her "best guide," but also she disjoins herself from her feet that have carried her to the spot: "yet O where els / Shall I inform my unacquainted feet" (179–80). In addition to perceiving her bodily parts as detachments, she personifies internal abstractions and then markedly fragments and externalizes them as physical phenomena:

> These thoughts may startle well, but not astound
> The vertuous mind, that ever walks attended
> By a strong siding champion conscience —
> O welcom pure-ey'd Faith, white-handed Hope,
> Thou flittering Angel girt with golden wings,
> And thou unblemish't form of Chastity,
> I see ye visibly.   (210–16)

A masque is a form of writing whose logic is essentially visual. What the Lady "sees . . . visibly" (her phrase is put in doubled terms of specularity) climaxes with fragmented body-images of the "pure-ey'd," the "white-handed," and the "unblemish't form."

The Lady changes the third term of the biblical triad from *Charity* to *Chastity*. This movement, a wrenching of a formula, forcibly focuses

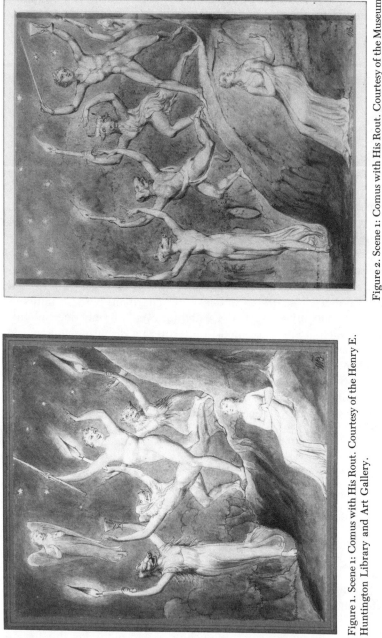

Figure 1. Scene 1: Comus with His Rout. Courtesy of the Henry E. Huntington Library and Art Gallery.

Figure 2. Scene 1: Comus with His Rout. Courtesy of the Museum of Fine Arts, Boston; gift of Mrs. John L. Gardner and George N. Black.

Figure 3: Scene 2: Comus Addressing the Lady. Courtesy of the Henry E. Huntington Library and Art Gallery.

Figure 4: Scene 2: Comus Addressing the Lady. Courtesy of the Museum of Fine Arts, Boston; gift of Mrs. John L. Gardner and George N. Black.

audience attention on *Chastity*. That Milton paused over his wording is evident from the Trinity manuscript. He crossed out "unspotted" and replaced it by "unblemish't"; also, after "I see ye visibly" there follow two and a half lines crossed out and dropped from printed editions (p. 74). The introductory line, "These thoughts may startle well, but not astound," guides the audience to react properly to Milton's coming reformulation into what A.S.P. Woodhouse defines as "the doctrine of chastity . . . the central theme in the argument of the poem."[28] The Lady's soliloquy has been much studied because, as Fletcher states, "Chastity is the final cause of the Lady's destiny, and the masque may be regarded as the demonstration of what follows, magically as well as logically, from this cause."[29] In considering the larger context of the role of women as the sixteenth century ended, Lisa Jardine says, "The female personification on which the cult of Elizabeth finally centered was chastity." She continues, "Virginity is the acme of female virtue. It is to femaleness what valour is to maleness."[30] Milton's high regard for chastity, however, transcends the conventional assumptions of a masque's audience that chastity is the ultimate female virtue. In his writing, the unchaste are thematically identified as the prideful; moreover, in taking up his own defense, he claims for himself the status of the chaste man (YP I, pp. 888–89).

Comus's assault on the Lady's "vertue . . . chastity . . . Virginity" is the subject of the Lady's "triall," the temptation scene in his palace, where she is "set in an inchanted Chair" amidst "all manner of deliciousness: soft Musick, Tables spred with all dainties" (s.d.). *A Mask* in many ways foreshadows *Paradise Regained*, which also moves "through highth or depth of natures bounds" (*PL* I, 13); what we see adumbrated thematically in *A Mask* is finally "full summ'd" in *Paradise Regained* (I, 14). The scene of the Lady's temptation by Comus is especially precursive of Milton's depiction of the temptations set out by Satan in the wilderness in Book II, lines 340–65. The Lady proves herself resolute and virtuous when urged to carnal indulgence. "Heer dwell no frowns, nor anger," coaxes Comus. "See here be all the pleasures / That fancy can beget on youthfull thoughts," he tempts the Lady, holding out the enchanted cup of youth and pleasure. "This will cure all streight, one sip . . . Will bathe the drooping spirits in delight / Beyond the bliss of dreams," he says, fearful himself for his own immortality, but dissembling before the Lady. "Be wise and tast," he ends his appeal, saving the most potent temptation — the desire for wisdom — for the last stratagem (667, 668–69, 813).

The Lady refuses both Comus's offer of fantasy and his offer of wisdom, preferring, as "holy dictate," to have "a moderate and beseeming share" of earthly wealth (767, 769). Against Comus's enchanting cup of giddy pleasure, the Lady opposes the "chastity and love . . . whose charming cup is only vertue" that Milton describes in *An Apology* eight years later. Milton continues to say that this pure draft is borne by hand only "to those who are worthy," whereas the "rest are cheated with a thick intoxicating potion which a certaine Sorceresse the abuser of loves name carries about" (YP I, pp. 891–92). The Lady refutes Comus's lustful notions, which she terms "false structures," by showing that what he presents as *nature's bounty* is actually *"natures bounds."* Comus, the "Sorceresse's" son, continues to carry about the abusive "thick potion," with *thick* indicating both the impurity of the drink and its agency as a thickener, or stupefier, of reason and perception. The thick potion causes foolishness. For Milton, to be "fondly," or dotingly and foolishly, "overcome with Femal charm" is the worst fate in man's life (*PL* IX, 999). This is how Adam falls in *Paradise Lost:* "Against his better knowledge, not deceav'd, / But fondly overcome with Femal charm." Milton assigns the Fall to Book IX, line 999, which, as Shawcross points out, is the "inverse number of the sign of the beast of Revelation (666), assigned in book II to Death."[31] Thus, for the Lady to succumb to Comus would mean the inversion of the formula. She summons up a kind of clearheaded resistance to Comus's blandishments, and withstands deceit and death masquerading in the form of male charm: magical charm of the magician-charmer.

The Lady's moderate wishes reveal the bounteous replenishment possibilities of natural purity, with its far-reaching consequences of salvation and everlasting life for both the individual and the community. In her wholesome respect for "a well-govern'd and wise appetite" (705) — for what Milton writes of elsewhere as a "neat repast . . . light and choice" (*Sonnet XX*, 9) — the Lady shows herself to be endowed with the private virtues that enable her to resist, or to transcend, public evils. Her inward *nomos*, morality, renders her impervious to Comus's life of *anomie*, lawlessness. She demonstrates that Comus's "engulfing appetites are the demonic parody of transcendental virtue."[32] Dialectically, Comus's unrestrained carnality reveals the stunted and impotent perversions that result from indulging in the all-engrossing appetites of death itself.

At this point in the masque, Comus and the Lady operate on two distinct levels of visual acuity. Comus believes himself to be infolded within a shielding screen of darkness that masks his hectic activity. The Lady, however, sits calmly within, and also *exposed by*, an aura, the beam of light the Elder Brother describes. She is protected by a kind of "snaky-headed *Gorgon* sheild," her own "rigid looks of chast austerity" (447, 450). Once again, the slight alterations made by Blake in his masque illustrations reinforce my comments about the trial episode. In Blake's portrayal of scene 5, The Magic Banquet (figs. 5 and 6), the Lady is sitting on a thronelike, heavy chair, set just apart from the banqueting table, with the rout ranged about in a row behind her and the spread table. Comus stands with her in the foreground, his wand held above her head to cause her "nervs" to be "all chain'd up in alablaster" (660). In the depth perspective of the first portrayal (see fig. 5), there are four levels, with Comus in the nearest; thus, his figure physically dominates the scene. He stands firmly, legs apart, at ease in the solidity of the stable triangle created by his own body. His muscular legs are flexed, his expression forceful, his bulky shoulder emphasized by the gladiatorial cloak of faint reddish tinge. The wand, his male sign, is now boldly extended toward the Lady. His glass containing the magic potion, his female sign, which is held away from the Lady, is extended in the direction of the audience, enticing the viewer's eye into the scene.

In the revised second series (fig. 6), the Lady and Comus are foregrounded together, with their figures now of equal proportion. His body shows more torsion than in the first illustration, the cape now fallen behind lightly, like drooping blue wings. A reddish wash is underfoot on the floor beneath him, suggesting spilled wine, or blood. The Lady is surrounded, or encircled, by an indistinct, cloudy brightness. A shadowy, lizardlike serpent hisses at Comus from along his wand; the serpent is contained within her encircling nimbus, which the snake echoes by its curvilinear outline. The Lady's surrounding area, including two servitors, is distinctively different in the second depiction. In the first, her seat is pictured as carved in bas-relief, with root-bound, columnar women, caryatids, shown entwined in serpentine loops. Also, the Lady's hands are crossed over her breast, seemingly in subjection and modesty, covering herself from evil. The two rout figures behind her, both of which are either tailed or winged with dragon scales, have their hands clasped as if in supplication, pictorially shadowing the Lady's hands. In the second depiction, however, the demonic serpent and dragon images on the chair and behind the rout members are deleted and even are reversed through the hissing snake, whose forked tongue points back along the rod toward Comus.[33] Also, and most important, in the second illustration, the Lady's hands are at rest. She is in a position of patient, confident waiting, set comfortably within her enframing brightness.

In Blake's most significant change in scene 5 (see fig. 6), that of the Lady's posture, she is shown as one who "May sit i'th center, and enjoy

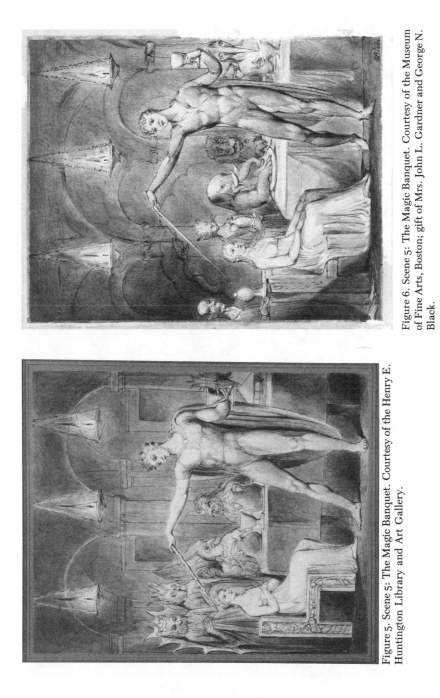

Figure 5. Scene 5: The Magic Banquet. Courtesy of the Henry E. Huntington Library and Art Gallery.

Figure 6. Scene 5: The Magic Banquet. Courtesy of the Museum of Fine Arts, Boston; gift of Mrs. John L. Gardner and George N. Black.

bright day." The Elder Brother has described this spiritual state of blessedness:

> He that has light within his own cleer brest
> May sit i'th center, and enjoy bright day,
> But he that hides a dark soul, and foul thoughts
> Benighted walks under the midday sun;
> Himself is his own dungeon. (381–85)

Indeed, Comus — whose thoughts turn automatically to what is unseen and who earlier mentioned "hidd'n residence" (248) — imagines himself to be hidden in the darkness of the foul thoughts of his own dungeon, a form of mental enclosure that contaminates the entire woodland in which he roams. The concept of self-containing darkness is proleptic of Satan's famous evaluation, "my self am Hell" (*PL* IV, 75), which conveys not merely the outer hell, but more importantly, the hell within:

> And like a devillish Engine back recoils
> Upon himself; horror and doubt distract
> His troubl'd thoughts, and from the bottom stirr
> The Hell within him, for within him Hell
> One step no more then from himself can fly
> By change of place. (*PL* IV, 17–22)

Hectic, satanic activity characterizes Comus's machinations: distracting doubts and feverish activity, generated by an infected cup of pleasure.

Opposed to Comus, all of whose processes, both physical and mental, are befouled by images of enclosing darkness, we have the essential liminality of the *Mask* itself and of Milton's thought in general. The enlightened Lady moves by degrees back to the supernal source from whence she was "created . . . Such to perfection":

> Indu'd with various forms, various degrees
> Of substance, and in things that live, of life;
> But more refin'd, more spiritous, and pure . . .
> Till body up to spirit work. (*PL* V, 471–75, 478)

Hence, the Lady on the chair may be in the patient posture of one who is to be found "waiting in readiness," which is how Lieb describes the ancient Israelites: "Waiting in readiness, the Israelites revealed their faith in God's providence. After all their fighting and all their acts of heroism, their ultimate inaction was their most triumphant act."[34] Thus, the trial on the enchanted chair is held, in one sense, only within the false structure of Comus's fantasy. Moreover, when the time of trial arrives, even though the Lady's "Soul" may be "more bent / To serve," or to affirm life actively, than to "wait," she must await providence patiently (*Sonnet XIX*). And finally, in the most profound sense, the trial is a temptation of the Lady's *ratio*, not *sensatio*. When "ultimate inaction" is paradoxically (illogically) one's "most triumphant act," the mental route to understanding runs not through logic, but through faith. What enables the Lady to withstand Comus, with his structurally false logic, is the harmonious grace, or spirit, that she embodies. As Paul Stevens says, hers is the "perception of the mind in a state of rational harmony — a state of harmony that ultimately depends on reason informed by revelation."[35]

The Lady's encircling radiance, which centers her on the masquing stage, has a corresponding reciprocal in her father and mother as the central viewers. They are represented by the omniscient eye, of which she is always conscious. Orgel notes,

That Milton was constantly aware of his work as a real masque — as a symbolic representation of the milieu in and for which it was created, as a production wherein, when the lords and ladies became masquers, the real world became indistinguishable from the world of the masque — is obvious from the frequency and complexity with which references to the audience, the Earl of Bridgewater and his family and court, are woven into the fabric of the piece.[36]

The linguistic patterns of the Lady's speeches show a heightened awareness of the audience as fragmented into its specular ability, and especially an awareness of the fragmented, centered eye of the attentive parents. As Kerrigan puts it, "The gaze and the light inside the virtuous mind of the Lady have been dismantled and reexternalized in her 'Noble Lord, and Lady bright.' Surely the most common metaphors for the vigilance of the superego are the sun and the eye, often merged in iconographical traditions."[37] In corresponding fragmentation, the Lady's speech is itself disjoined from its physical origin. Using language that insists on images of dissociation, she says,

> Fool do not boast,
> Thou canst not touch the freedom of my mind
> With all thy charms, although this corporal rind
> Thou hast immanacl'd, while Heav'n sees good.   (662–65)

This is a valiant defense of herself on the Lady's part. Her chastity becomes a kind of "spiritual Armour" (*PL* XII, 491), enabling her to withstand Comus's blandishments and his rhetoric. Her assuredness in speech is based on the certainty that this armor "of chast austerity" is a shield to deflect and ward off his force, a shield so bright that his thrusts must glance off harmlessly. In effect, what she recognizes in herself is a status of double privilege. She valorizes her chastity as providing her both with a protective armor sanctioned by "Heav'n" and also with special rhetorical powers. Comus is the masque equivalent of those whom Milton later was to call "th' unfaithful herd, / The enemies of truth" (*PL* XII, 481–82). Recognizing his debased state, she disputes his ability to understand her elevated, "sublime" language:

> Thou hast nor Ear, nor Soul to apprehend
> The sublime notion, and high mystery
> That must be utter'd to unfold the sage
> And serious doctrine of Virginity.   (784–87)

Meeting no immediate demand for explanation, the Lady involves herself in her prior affirmation more explicitly, relating the deeply felt knowledge that arises from her state of transcendent piety. Although she is trapped and immobilized in Comus's "stately Palace" (s.d.), she calls the dwelling an unsubstantial "magick structure," which "brute Earth" would topple at her behest. Put differently, she places faith in the holiness of the word, thus recognizing her own untested powers of narrative as able to conquer and topple his proven powers of magic. She says that even though he would not be "fit" (792) to hear her words:

> Yet should I try, the uncontrouled worth
> Of this pure cause would kindle my rapt spirits
> To such a flame of sacred vehemence,
> That dumb things would be mov'd to sympathize,
> And the brute Earth would lend her nerves, and shake,
> Till all thy magick structures rear'd so high,
> Were shatter'd into heaps o're thy false head.   (793–99)

She declares her narrative to have the "vertue" and "the Sun-clad power of Chastity" (761, 782). If the "vertuous . . . power" of her chastity were to be put into words, the speech would take on an "uncontrouled" quality of a *sacred* force that can alter *natural* events. This "power" would contrast with Comus's enchantments, which are under his control, but which are *artificial*, or "false." The Lady's concept claims explosive force for her speech-making ability. She asserts possession of rhetorical power that is the equivalent of an avalanche or a volcanic eruption and that could bury Comus under his own disintegrated illusions, the "structures" of his "false head." Thus, the Lady's concept of herself is indeed of fragmented body-image, of linguistic abilities as activated by the "uncontrouled worth" of her "pure cause." By means of the speech energy thus released, she acknowledges her relationship with the outer world to be one of ability to cause changes — either through the primary power of chastity or through the power of speech thereby engendered. In fact, what she claims to have is "resounding grace" in her earthly, or natural, abilities, just the quality she expects Echo to have eventually when the nymph is "translated to the skies" (242). The Lady's speech *re-sounds*, or replaces, all Comus's *din*, his disruptive and bewildering *sounds* and gives to them her own *harmonious grace*.[38]

VIII

In her meeting with Comus in the shadowy forest, the Lady encounters the underside of desire itself. It is Cotytto, "Dark-vaild . . . goddess of nocturnal sport," whom Comus "hails" as her priestly devotee; and even the debauched, brutish Comus names his rout's licentious rites, or "dues," as "sin," to be performed "till utmost end," while "conceal'd" from the "nice morn" (129, 128, 137, 126, 136, 142, 139). In the Lady's perilous travel, she is to be seen as a kind of microcosmic Ulysses, discovered wandering "In the blind mazes of this tangl'd Wood" (181), attempting to return home. Further enforcing the masque's Ulysses image is the response the Lady attracts, which comes from the "swill'd insolence" of the son of Circe. J. B. Broadbent remarks that in "the Renaissance the main literary escape-area was the classical world."[39] Milton, however, first joins classical elements with Christian and then empties the classical, as pagan and precursive, into the Christian, as true and final. In *A Mask*, the major means of joining is through the introduction of Sabrina and other nymphs into the poem. A system of false echoes controls the rhetorical and dramatic patterns before Sabrina appears as true echo. Indeed, as Sabrina's "viold liquors" reverse Comus's "lickerish baits," so her lustration of the Lady, a form of baptism, washes away the baneful influence to these woods of Comus — possessor of the "banefull cup" (525) — as one of the Baptes, or orgiastic priests of Cotytto.[40]

The Lady answers Comus's "insolent," presumptive fantasies with what appears to be a kind of bravado, in that she affirms, seemingly by arrogating to herself, suprahuman or heavenly powers of speech. As it happens, the relationship of powers of speech to powers of action is an underlying motif of Milton's *Mask*, in which language and action exist in a decidedly negative ratio. The Lady's two brothers are ineffective in finding or rescuing her. That they therefore engage in lengthy dialogue accords with a rule of thumb: in this poem language becomes the substitute for potency. It seems that the equation Milton employs actually measures the extent of the brothers' helplessness by the protraction of their speech-making. Similarly, the Attendant Spirit, who narrates the opening and closing, and is thus verbally "active," is unable to effect a rescue or even to "guard" the Lady from falling into danger in the first place. Yet he has declared that precisely this protective function is both his "task" (18) and his intention:

> A noble peer of mickle trust and power
> Has in his charge, with temper'd aw to guide
> An old and haughty nation proud in Arms;
> Where his fair offspring nurs't in princely lore,
> Are comming to attend thir fathers state
> And new-entrusted Scepter, but thir way
> Lies through the perplext paths of this drear wood,
> The nodding horror of whose shady brows
> Threats the forlorn and wandring passinger.
> And heer thir tender age might suffer perill,
> But that by quick command from Soveran *Jove*
> I was dispatcht for thir defense, and guard.   (31–42)

The greater the verbal influence, the lesser the actual influence. Comus, who loses most, has rhetorically the most imagistic mode of speaking, and is perhaps even the most persuasive, in terms of usual mundane ranking of speech abilities. Not only does he persuade the Lady against all reason that he is a gentle swain, but the graceful movement and witty sophistication of his first alliterative, metaphoric speech may serve to confuse the audience's own sense of reason about this "classical . . . allegorical figure":

> The star that bids the shepherd fold,
> Now the top of Heav'n doth hold,
> And the gilded car of day
> His glowing axle doth allay
> In the steep *Atlantick* stream,
> And the slope sun his upward beam
> Shoots against the dusky pole,
> Pacing toward the other goal
> Of his chamber in the East.
> Mean while welcom Joy and feast,
> Midnight shout, and revelry,
> Tipsie dance, and jollity.
> Braid your locks with rosie twine
> Dropping odours, dropping wine.   (93–106)

Comus's syntax, however, is misleading: he says he expects to be "well stock't" with a "fair . . . herd" (152) and in order to gain this end uses "fair pretence . . . And well-plac't words" (160, 161). Thus, through repeated use of oxymoronic constructions as a cover for paradoxical false-hoods, his language seeks to disguise the brutish changes he effects on others.

In addition, we find that Comus's enbroidered, "glozing" language masks, or substitutes for, absent significance. And in a related conception in *A Mask*, the more "insolent," or boastful, the disguising language, the more it covers or replaces its own lacking signifier. When Comus resolves, "Ile speak to her / And she shall be my Queen," his speech precedes the action that initiates his eventual downfall. Bent on deception, Comus flies about the stage in a burst of hasty activity—hustling the rout out of sight, shifting his shape, sprinkling dust—that eventually comes to nothing. He leaves his concealment—his "shrouds within these brakes and trees" (147), which serve as externalizations of the internal self-misrecognition behind which he hides—and opens dialogue with the innocent Lady. Instead of causing their eventual joint woodland monarchy, however, he brings about his own abdication, an actual flight, as all his antimasquing disruptions culminate in this final rupture. On the other hand, in true theodicean pattern, when the Lady, in her awakened moment of self-recognition, declares that she could save herself with sublime speech powers, she remains motionless and speechless. In the calm stillness that signals a state of *implicitness*, she awaits her intervening rescue. That is to say: in a state of providential grace, or true liminality, she awaits Providence.

IX

Held within the conjunction of speech and powerlessness we have been following is the reverse equation: that silence and power reside together. Thus, the function of the parents is important to the total activity of *A Mask*, in that the parents contribute to the action by their absent, silent awareness. For the Lady, this parental care is figured by their alert and guarding eye. For Comus, the more than proper influence of his mother is a primary antecedent of his embruted existence; he has become "the prison'd soul" lapped "in slumber," his senses "lull'd" into "madnes" by "potent hearbs, and balefull drugs" (256, 260, 261, 255). Hence, his possible liberation from narcosis is indicated by a remarkable moment of rupture—the shattering of Circe's cup: "The brothers rush in *with Swords drawn*, wrest his Glass out of his hand, and break it against the ground" (s.d.; my emphasis).

Blake accentuates Comus's fixation on the brothers' swords in scene 3 of his first series of illustrations (fig. 7). The brothers are gathering berries (186), or as Blake says, "plucking grapes." Comus is again garbed

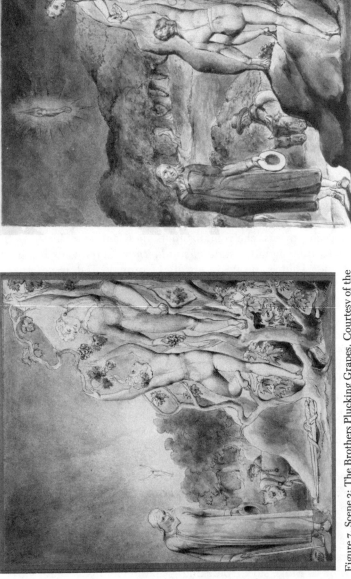

Figure 7. Scene 3: The Brothers Plucking Grapes. Courtesy of the Henry E. Huntington Library and Art Gallery.

Figure 8. Scene 3: The Brothers Plucking Grapes. Courtesy of the Museum of Fine Arts, Boston; gift of Mrs. John L. Cardner and George N. Black.

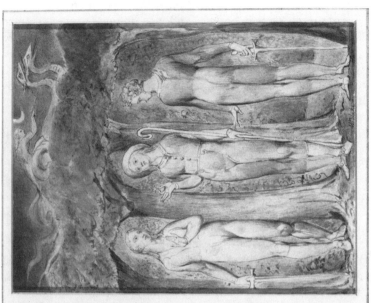

Figure 10. Scene 4: The Brothers with the Attendant Spirit. Courtesy of the Museum of Fine Arts, Boston; gift of Mrs. John L. Gardner and George N. Black.

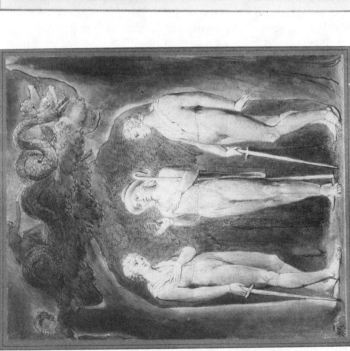

Figure 9. Scene 4: The Brothers with the Attendant Spirit. Courtesy of the Henry E. Huntington Library and Art Gallery.

as a villager, his walking stick is obscured at his side, and his hat is now held forward submissively in his *left* hand, as a pretense of even lessened potence. He looks modestly downward, his gaze intent on the paired swords, which are centered and point across the width of the scene, connecting him to the self-contained tableau of the graceful brothers. Blake's revisions in the same scene of the second series (fig. 8) emphasize my analysis of *A Mask*. The brothers' two swords are not visible, yet Comus is menaced just as surely but more subtly by a surrogative pair of oxen (290; Blake makes "the labour'd ox" plural), whose upright horns point to the open, vulvar hat. Once again, the illustration from the second series alters Comus's presenting of the deceptive female sign, the cuplike hat. Comus, who here wears a cloak that resembles a kind of skirted dress, turns his hat more dramatically toward the unmindful, foregrounded brothers. Centered in a dominant position in the sky above is the Attendant Spirit, now triumphantly phallic in appearance.

Significantly, in scene 4 (figs. 9 and 10), when the brothers and Attendant Spirit meet in the wood, the sword handles are subtly changed in appearance. Arched by overhanging trees, the brothers hold their swords mildly, with the cruciform shape of the swords made prominent. The Spirit is centered; he holds in one hand the golden-flowered Moly and in the other the shepherd's crook. In the second series (fig. 10), the three are each enframed in his own arch of trees. The brim of the Spirit's hat halos his head. What the tableau suggests, of course, is a religious tryptich. In the sky above, however, Diana drives her chariot of monsters. In the first series (fig. 9), the figure is indistinct and could be Cotytto, who in Comus's narrative rides in an ebony chair with Hecate and appears to Comus "when the dragon womb / Of Stygian darknes spitts her thickest gloom" (131–32). This infernal trio, comprised of Cotytto and two dragons, would allow Comus some power of menace over the holy trio of men below. When Blake reillustrates the scene for the second set (fig. 10), the steeds pulling the chariot are less dragons than serpents, and he indicates clearly that the figure driving the chariot is Diana; he shows just before her forehead the cupped horns of the sickle moon, whose pale radiance illuminates the scene.

When the melee caused by the brothers' entrance into the palace is over and Comus and his followers are put to flight, no longer is Comus the "sly . . . wisard" with the "banefull cup" (571, 525). He escapes from the palace, half debunked. His leaving comprises his final moment of rupture. Since he retains his father's wand, his disappearance has the same quality of jagged, or torn, edges as did his masque appearances. He gets away before the Lady can be freed, and what seems a calamitous event, a blemish on the smoothness of the masque action, has two interesting ramifications. First, Comus's accession into incorporating heterosexuality is indicated, or at least is made possible, through his keeping the rod of the father. No longer is he to be Philostratus's figure who "stands at the entrance . . . with his torch ready to fall from his hand."[41] Comus now is able to achieve a kind of entry — into the world of adulthood. "For," as Jameson says, "the phallus . . . comes to be considered . . . the fundamental signifier of mature psychic life."[42] In an unanticipated outcome of the struggle, Comus is liberated into the possibility of heterosexual existence by the brothers' valiant action; as such, the event instances another problematic moment of doubt as to whether the Attendant Spirit is a reliable interpreter. He rebuked the brothers in bustling complaint:

> What, have you let the false enchanter scape?
> O ye mistook, ye should have snatcht his wand
> And bound him fast; without his rod revers't
> And backward mutters of dissevering power,
> We cannot free the Lady that sits heer
> In stony fetters fixt and motionless. (814–19)

Although the concept is dramatized in formula appropriate to masque conventions, the escape of Comus anticipates a Miltonic theme of the human household, with the alienated outsider barking at the entryway: that the ordered, civilized realm of everyday life is, historically, interfered with through opposition or trial by the disordered force of the satanic tempter. In masque terms, the threat of the molesting presence at the gate causes the people living within the walls to greet and welcome an actual political ruler/protector, the earl of Bridgewater (the appointed father) and also a symbolic domestic icon/protector, the Lady (his virtuous daughter). In *The Doctrine and Discipline of Divorce*, Milton mentions "the brood of Belial" as "the dross of men" who exist with "unbridled and vagabond lust without pale or partition" (YP II, p. 58). Comus retains his wand, or scepter, in emblem of his sway over, and also membership in, the ranks of the disordered *rabble*, or fallen *rebels*, or *rebellious* sons, who do not recognize the proper boundaries demarcating the sphere of the father. In *Paradise Lost*, when the Father instructs the Son, "Be thou in *Adam*'s room" (III, 285), the denotative meaning of the words is that the Son is to serve in Adam's stead, but one underlying connotation is that worthy humans inhabit a *household*, a mortal room, that is always imperiled by the profane intruder.

In *A Mask*, the two sons of the Bridgewater household adumbrate

a victory won by the Son in *Paradise Lost,* who in the battle in heaven
against the rebellious angels

> check'd
> This Thunder in mid Volie, for he meant
> Not to destroy, but to root them out of Heav'n:
> The overthrown he rais'd, and as a Heard
> Of Goats or timerous flock together throng'd
> Drove them before him Thunder-struck, pursu'd
> With terrors and with furies to the bounds
> And Chrystal wall of Heav'n.   (VII, 853–60)

In an expulsion appropriate to their inherently swinish nature, Comus
and his "flock" are "rooted out of Heav'n," driven "timorously thronging" outside the "Chrystal wall."[43] The excluded demonic and threatening presence, a repetition figure in Milton's work, is to be understood
as a historic, or temporal, being, one who will remain in existence through
the offices of sin and death until the Apocalypse brings the end of time.
Relating Milton's eschatological perception of evil to the convention-filled
world of *A Mask,* we see the crux in the plot thematically: the boys do
not "sease" Comus's "wand" (653) because he is to be "rooted *out*" (both
searched out and driven out) but not destroyed. He retains the badge
of his magistral/magical sway over the wild wood outside the polis. The
inherent thought is that Comus can not be entirely disarmed, and thereby
rendered harmless, by the brothers; through his own evil desires — an internal evil, which ever "on it self shall back recoyl" (593) — the tempter
remains a presence. Though an external force, he is repelled by the internal eye of vigilant faith.

X

The rescue of the Lady is complicated. Centrally, she must be saved
from Comus; and in a wider perspective, the encircling false resonances
that have included the audience in the action of the masque must be cor-
rected. Therefore, to rescue the Lady, a general cleansing is required:
a system of true echoing must take over that will revise everyone's mis-
perceptions and reincorporate the audience into the masque's and society's ordered and true patterning. As a first matter, the bewildering spirit
of the demonic has infected the forest and thus has touched all characters who stray into the paths. In response, the guardian genius of the
place, the water nymph Sabrina, is invoked by the worthy characters,
which revises the invocation of Cotytto by the demonic figures. There
are "two well defined rites," says Thomas B. Stroup of the invocations
of the two goddesses. "In fact, the two oppose each other, the one used

to complicate the plot, the other to resolve it; the one evil, the other good."[44] Also, as Fletcher points out, the Lady's song to Echo is reinterpreted, or echoed, by the Spirit's song to Sabrina, even though, as Fletcher says, the second song is "without precise musical duplication."[45] In addition, this "warbled song" (854) to Sabrina, completed and answered, brings to conclusion two of Comus's interruptions: the Spirit's piped song that is broken off by the din of the rout and the Lady's song that is misanswered by Comus. As I have noted, Sabrina's vial of pure drops of water reverses Comus's glass of brewed potion. Life wins over death; water replaces swill; the fountain washes out the cup.

Most significantly, the major moment of reversal comes with an aspersing that is not a magical but a purifying ritual. This second aspersion involves not dust but water. As Comus sprinkles his hellish dust to "cheat" and "blear" the eye, Sabrina sprinkles hallowing water to cleanse the entire community. "Brightest Lady," Sabrina commands, "look on me," recalling the Lady's own welcome to "pure-ey'd Faith." Sabrina recites:

> Thus I sprinkle on thy brest
> Drops that from my fountain pure,
> I have kept of pretious cure,
> Thrice upon thy fingers tip,
> Thrice upon thy rubied lip. (910–15)

Shawcross gives a lucid explanation of the significance of Sabrina's revivifying, or re*hallowing*, of the Lady's "brest . . . fingers tip . . . lip."[46] Put in slightly different terms from Shawcross's, the breast houses the emotions, or "spirit"; for the Lady, the "brest" represents the "unblemish't form of Chastity." The finger tip, or "white-handed Hope," has been sullied *metaphorically* by Comus's "ill greeting touch" (406), which was presented in the masque visually as an offer of an enchanted drink. In discussing the charge to Adam and Eve "not to touch the interdicted Tree" in Eden (*PL* VII, 46), Lieb notes, "Touching and tasting, in a sense, become interchangeable, two acts derived from the same root, one *tangere* that implies them both."[47] Moreover, the Lady's lips must be included in the hallowing ritual because they were "unlockt" in an "unhallow'd" place, Comus's palace.

Sabrina continues:

> Next this marble venom'd seat
> Smear'd with gumms of glutenous heat
> I touch with chast palms moist and cold,
> Now the spell hath lost his hold. (916–19)

What Sabrina most must erase are "the gumms of glutenous heat," the symbol of Comus's seductive wiles. The description of the seat as "*marble venom'd*" recollects Comus's threat to turn the Lady to "alablaster," a statue, an imitation Daphne, immobilized, nerveless. These changes are a mutability to a lesser state, the kind of transformation Comus comprehends. The Lady, however, rises to a higher state. In transcending the palace of sensuality and its inhabitants, she is in preparation for "a quick immortal change," like Sabrina. The Lady, though, is not to be "Made goddess of the river," but is to be acclaimed a symbol of chastity for Ludlow town and castle (841–42). In continued thought, "marble *venom'd*" recollects Comus's dreaded power over the Lady and her community: his is the satanic, or serpentlike, phallic and disordering power of the seducer, who gains shelter in the chiaroscuric shadows outside the gates of orderly, imperial courts. The "cure" Sabrina effects has personal and also societal consequences for the Lady. In placing her "chast palms moist and cold" on the enthralling chair of satanic desire, Sabrina indicates she reverses and washes away the warmth of Comus's demonic ardor. Confronted with evil seduction, the Lady becomes immobilized, or stilled in waiting, but as Shawcross indicates, metaphorically this immobility translates as "remaining unmoved and thus unenthralled and unhurt."[48]

The perceived "perill" (40) to the Lady lies in the fact that the "sin-worn" earth itself is venal, that its "nodding . . . shady brows" (38) confine humanity (as in a "pinfold") to "low-thoughted care" (6). In her "unspotted" innocence, the Lady says, "Shepherd, I take thy word," (322). The speech of acceptance, the bodily excursion into the "pinfold" of mortal existence, and the brush with the molesting stranger, all necessitate Sabrina's reversal of the community's — including the audience's — imaginary fear of the Lady's having come to harm. Sabrina's "pure drops" wash away Comus's "magick dust." The Lady's concept in her opening soliloquy of "the gray-hooded Eev'n / Like a sad votarist in palmers weeds" (188–89) finds a linkage — a true reciprocal, or fuller type — in Sabrina's "chast palms." Sabrina becomes the palmer who has attained the final state of chastity to which the Lady dedicates herself. The Lady's state of readiness focuses upon the inward self in preparation for ultimate life.

Just as Comus is routed without uttering a word, so in the silence of the three children the close of *A Mask* itself is correspondingly sedate. In the Lady's final silence we may read a realistic, or socially imposed, replacement of the loquacious flow of her imaginary, or masquing, speech of dispute with Comus. Thus, for the virtuous Lady herself, Sabrina's sprinkling is not a washing away of sin so much as a consecration. In reward for her private virtues, the Lady is publicly acclaimed. In courtly fashion, the daughter is affirmed a virgin; the family embodies propriety and virtue. The dance at the end of the masque proclaims a kind of conjunction: the earl and his family join the land through their own deservingness and also through heavenly intercession. In her stillness and silence, the Lady indicates her acceptance of her lot. Immobilization in the chair in the palace of evil is a kind of epic journey to the underworld, a voyage into the cave of self-contemplation, a type of death from which the Lady is revived by her community and her saving–figure, Sabrina.

The Lady undergoes the kind of ritualistic testing often associated with the *artes moriendi,* in which good and evil wage a cosmic struggle for possession of the dying individual. Self-composed and aware, however, the Lady is not a mere prize or "alablaster . . . statue." Though rescued by intercession of her appointed guardian Spirit, she shows her deservingness. Further, Milton suggests that a future psychic transformation will come about for the Lady "After this mortal change" (10), when at last she will be transformed and exalted symbolically to an otherworldly level to gain for herself a heavenly reward, "the crown that vertue gives" (9). Ultimately, her steadfast resistance on Comus's enchanted seat destines her to join "the enthron'd gods on sainted seats" (11). Her journey, finally, is not to "Ludlow Town and the Presidents Castle" but to "the palace of Eternity" (14). These verbal echoes serve to complete the true echoing begun by the appearance of the virtuous Lady's echo in Sabrina. In final outcome, the Lady joins Echo, Sabrina, and Psyche in the mythic symbolic register. Indeed, in a speech predictive of the ending, Comus's first words to the Lady hail her as a goddess. Released both from her alienating image in the false appearance of Comus in the woods and also from her objectified status of sanctified symbol in her parents' home, she is initiated into the heavenly realm in the capacity of free subject. For her successful endurance of the trial in the wilderness — her virtuous denunciation of Comus's palace of pleasure as a sty and his julep as swill — the Lady is sanctified by lustration into mythic, celestial rebirth by Sabrina.

A *Mask* twice involves the Lady in precursive ascent: once when she forecasts that Echo will "be translated to the skies" for her help and once when she "puts by" the cup of Circe at Comus's palace and "goes about to rise" (242, s.d.). Instead of succumbing to temptation, which in specular metaphor is called falling "downward . . . into a groveling swine," she exhibits virtuous temperance, which is similarly called retaining an "upright shape," (53, 52); this latter vertical image remains an important concept in Milton's writing. In line with Milton's usual fusion of classical and Christian imagery, the Lady's "mould" is understood intuitively by Comus to be not earth's sin-mould but "divine . . . holy" (244, 245, 246). Sabrina's action confirms that the Lady is indeed the "*Brightest* Lady," worthy to be elevated "Above the smoak and stirr of . . . *dim* . . . Earth." Sabrina certifies the Lady: affirms her worthiness to be included among those who undergo the "mortal change" by degrees, to sit eventually "amongst the enthron'd gods on sainted seats." Sabrina's lustration, then, is an initiation of the ephebe into the ranks of the sanctified. Shawcross says of withstood temptation that for Milton "trial and resistance are emphasized if the person involved is a type of Christ":

The Christ legend, undisguised myth in the human world, insures man's recognition of the need for loss or separation (a version of the *felix culpa* which, however, avoids loss or fall while emphasizing the recognition of need), the nature of man's quest and the form that initiation takes (in the Temple, where the learned doctors may be confounded, as well as in the Wilderness), and the means to effect return.[49]

"Undisguised myth" is not properly a part of *A Mask,* yet Milton hints that a masque may move "From shadowie Types to Truth" (*PL* XII, 303).

XI

Return to parents is problematic in Milton's work and must be interpreted carefully. Milton seems to distinguish between return to the father and to the mother. Samson is returned to his father's house at the end of *Samson Agonistes,* but the return is made in terms of endless stasis (1733–44). In *Paradise Regained,* however, Christ "Home to his Mothers house private return'd" (IV, 639), thereby completing a successful reunion. The Lady's way out of the forest turns the shady paths into a compressed version of "this dim spot . . . Earth"; indeed, return to her father's earthly residence is a horizontal journey in a poem whose sanctified journeys are vertical. Apparently, return to the maternal dwelling place is more successful than to the paternal. It is typical of Milton, of course, that the ultimate significance of the Lady's journey—with its magistral blessings and order conferred by a symbolic maternal figure instead of an earthly paternal one—subverts the aristocratic genre of court masque. By convention, the masque's compliment is paid to a ruling figure. In terms of Milton's *Mask,* the lord who is to receive the compliment is one who holds the "pinfold" earth as his realm; indeed, restoration of order has little to do with *temporal* monarchy. As the Attendant Spirit informs their parents in his song, the children have won "a crown of *deathless* praise" for "triumph . . . O're sensual folly, and intemperance" (973–75, my emphasis). Milton thus refashions the value system of the political order of the masque itself, *masking* his revisions under conventional forms.

The Lady's journey through the woodlands, then, with its appeal to the conventionally spectacular images of the masque, prefigures a future symbolic journey in which she is to be united, or reunited, on a celestial plane with all her "family." The enabling figures are her substitute mothers — the trio of nymphs, Echo, Sabrina, Psyche. *Nymph*, in reference to the Lady, takes on its etymological root meaning of *bride*, for in the closing lines the Lady becomes identified with "*Psyche* sweet intranc't / After her wandring labours long" (1005–06). Since in *A Mask* Psyche, the soul, is next called an "eternal bride" from whose "fair unspotted side / Two blissful twins are to be born" (1008, 1009–10), we may read in this description a preview of the Lady's parallel status as a figure of chastity: an "eternal bride," eventually to give birth by "unblemish't," or "unspotted," means.

Although one kind of reunion is to be with the mothers — Echo, Sabrina, Psyche — the ultimate reunion is a Christian return to the heavenly Father and also to the Son, who is conjoined with her two brothers. Her offspring, if twins, would be surrogative replacements for the brothers, who also are exalted by the Attendant Spirit as meriting an afterlife of "deathless praise." In *An Apology*, immediately after the description of the "charming cup . . . virtue" that is handed to those who are "worthy," meaning the ones who have "chastity and love," Milton says that "the first and chiefest office of love begins and ends in the soule, producing those happy twins of her divine generation, knowledge and virtue" (YP I, p. 892). Christopher Hill states that in part the conclusion "celebrates . . . the heavenly love of Christ for his eternal bride, who is both the church and the individual soul, Psyche."[50] In an eternal reunion, the Lady "finds" the two boys from whom she has become separated, a repetition in the text that brings a kind of figural closure. The Lady gathers into herself all the diverse patterns of *A Mask*, by bringing her earthly journey to an end, even while "heaven gates ore [her] head."[51]

Upsala College

NOTES

An early version of this essay was read at the Milton Festival, State College University at Buffalo, 1984. I am grateful for helpful suggestions from Cedric Brown, Margaret Ferguson, Christopher Kendrick, William Kerrigan, William Shullenberger, John Shawcross, and Joseph Wittreich.

1. My citations of Milton's poetry are from *The Complete Poetry of John Milton*, rev. ed., ed. John T. Shawcross (Garden City, 1971). Citations of the Trinity College, Cambridge, manuscript are from *John Milton: A Maske: The Earlier Versions*, ed. S. E. Sprott (Toronto, 1973). Milton's prose is cited from *Complete Prose Works of John Milton*, 8 vols., ed. Don M. Wolfe et al. (New Haven, 1953–82), hereafter cited as YP in the text. Citations of Shakespeare's work are from *The Riverside Shakespeare*, ed. G. Blakemore Evans (Boston, 1974). Bible citations are from *The Holy Scriptures* (1917; rpt. Philadelphia, 1955). Stage directions are indicated throughout the text by the abbreviation s.d.

2. Most commentators concur; see E.M.W. Tillyard, "The Action of *Comus*," in *A Maske at Ludlow: Essays on Milton's Comus*, ed. John S. Diekhoff (Cleveland, 1968), p. 43. Some consider the primary conflict to be between Comus and the Attendant Spirit; see Angus Fletcher, *The Transcendental Masque: An Essay on Milton's Comus* (Ithaca, 1971), pp. xiii, 167, and Barbara Howard Traister, *Heavenly Necromancers: The Magician in English Renaissance Drama* (Columbia, 1984), p. 171. To Cedric C. Brown, *John Milton's Aristocratic Entertainments* (Cambridge, 1985), pp. 58, 72–73, *A Mask* interrogates aristocratic festivity itself.

3. Joseph Warton is cited by J. B. Leishman, *Milton's Minor Poems* (London, 1969), p. 199.

4. For discussion of whether the masque was performed indoors or out, see Brown, *John Milton's Aristocratic Entertainments*, pp. 36–37; William B. Hunter, Jr., *Milton's Comus: Family Piece* (New York, 1983), p. 48; and Mindele Anne Treip, "*Comus* as 'Progress,'" *Milton Quarterly* XX (1986), p. 5.

5. William Kerrigan, *The Sacred Complex: On the Psychogenesis of "Paradise Lost"* (Cambridge, 1983), pp. 40–42.

6. Michael Lieb, *Poetics of the Holy: A Reading of "Paradise Lost"* (Chapel Hill, 1981), p. 21.

7. Fletcher, *The Transcendental Masque*, p. 210.

8. David M. Miller, *John Milton: Poetry* (Boston, 1978), p. 45.

9. Ben Jonson, *The Poems, the Prose Works*, ed. C. H. Herford, Percy and Evelyn Simpson (Oxford, 1947), vol. VIII, p. 404.

10. John G. Demaray, *Milton and the Masque Tradition: The Early Poems, Arcades, and Comus* (Cambridge, 1968), pp. 26–27; see also pp. 125–43.

11. John Milton, *Complete Poems and Major Prose*, ed. Merritt Y. Hughes (1957; rpt. Indianapolis, 1980), p. 87. But see Brown, *John Milton's Aristocratic Entertainments*, p. 65, for another viewpoint.

12. William Hazlitt, (in *The Examiner* 11 June 1815) is quoted in *Milton: Comus and Samson Agonistes*, ed. Julian Lovelock (London, 1975), p. 29.

13. Brown, *John Milton's Aristocratic Entertainments*, pp. 58, 66–68.

14. Compare the Judges narrative with the Holiness Code (Lev. xix, 33), of great significance in Jewish thought: "And if a stranger sojourn with thee in your land, ye shall not do him wrong. The stranger that sojourneth with you shall be unto you as the home-born among you, and thou shalt love him as thyself; for ye were strangers in the land of Egypt: I am the LORD your God" (Lev. xix, 33–34).

15. W.B.C. Watkins, *An Anatomy of Milton's Verse* (Hamden, Conn., 1965), pp. 98, 96.

16. Robert M. Adams, *Ikon: John Milton and the Modern Critics* (Ithaca, 1955), pp. 8, 17; see pp. 8–27. In discussing freedom and paralysis, Roger B. Wilkenfeld provides a detailed analysis of balance and symmetry, including horizontal and vertical action, in "The Seat at the Center: An Interpretation of *Comus*," *ELH* XXXVI (1969), pp. 123–50.

17. Traister, *Heavenly Necromancers*, p. 176.

18. See Kerrigan, *The Sacred Complex*, pp. 49–50.

19. Jacques Lacan, "The agency of the letter in the unconscious or reason," in *Ecrits: A Selection*, trans. Alan Sheridan (New York, 1977), p. 156.

20. "The insinuating and courtly overtones in his speech ('And left your fair side all unguarded, Lady?') have made no impression upon her innocent mind, and she has accepted him on his own showing as a simple shepherd." A. E. Dyson, "Virtue Unwavering: Milton's *Comus*," in *Comus and Samson Agonistes: A Selection of Critical Essays*, ed. Julian Lovelock (London, 1975), p. 122.

21. Boyd M. Berry, *Process of Speech: Puritan Religious Writings and "Paradise Lost"* (Baltimore, 1976), p. 34.

22. Traister, *Heavenly Necromancers*, pp. 176, 57.

23. The full sets of both series are reprinted in Fletcher, *The Transcendental Masque*, following p. 256; Fletcher describes their history, present location, and pictorial story on pp. 253–56; and in Pamela Dunbar, *William Blake's Illustrations to the Poetry of Milton* (Oxford, 1980), following p. 208; Dunbar interprets the illustrations on pp. 9–34.

24. Irene Tayler, "Say First! What Mov'd Blake? Blake's *Comus* Designs and Milton," in *Blake's Sublime Allegory: Essays on The Four Zoas, Milton, and Jerusalem*, ed. Stuart Curran and Joseph Anthony Wittreich, Jr. (Madison, 1973), p. 248.

25. Stephen C. Behrendt, "The Mental Contest: Blake's *Comus* Designs," in *Blake Studies*, vol. VIII (1978), p. 68.

26. In interpreting Blake's designs, Behrendt's and Tayler's analyses differ from each other, and from mine even more particularly. For instance, Behrendt finds in Blake's designs a revision of Milton's poem where I see a more sympathetic critique.

27. Madelon Gohlke, "'I wooed thee with my sword': Shakespeare's Tragic Paradigms," in *The Woman's Part: Feminist Criticism of Shakespeare*, ed. Carolyn Ruth Swift Lenz et al. (Urbana, 1980), p. 166.

28. A.S.P. Woodhouse, "The Argument of Milton's *Comus*," in *A Maske at Ludlow: Essays on Milton's Comus*, ed. John S. Diekhoff (Cleveland, 1968), p. 23; see also pp. 17–42.

29. Fletcher, *The Transcendental Masque*, p. 169; see also pp. 209–13.

30. Lisa Jardine, *Still Harping on Daughters: Women and Drama in the Age of Shakespeare* (Totowa, 1983), pp. 175, 176.

31. Shawcross, *Complete Poetry*, p. 445, n. 73.

32. Fletcher, *The Transcendental Masque*, p. 245.

33. Dunbar, *Blake's Illustrations*, p. 13, notes the "markings on the enchanted chair, which in the Huntington version take the form of serpent-entwined figures (a common emblem in Blake's works for the self-imprisoned personality) and in the Boston plate an ear of corn—a Christian and pre-Christian symbol of resurrection."

34. Lieb, *Poetics of the Holy*, p. 298. Critics have discussed the Miltonic concept of patient readiness in other contexts: see Jackie Di Salvo, "'The Lord's Battels': *Samson Agonistes* and the Puritan Revolution," in *Milton Studies*, vol. IV, ed. James D. Simmonds (Pittsburgh, 1972), pp. 39–62; Stanley Fish, "Inaction and Silence: The Reader in *Paradise Regained*," in *Calm of Mind*, ed. Joseph Anthony Wittreich, Jr. (Cleveland, 1971); Edward Tayler, *Milton's Poetry: Its Development in Time* (Pittsburgh, 1980), pp. 170–72.

35. Paul Stevens, *Imagination and the Presence of Shakespeare in "Paradise Lost"* (Madison, 1985), p. 31.

36. Stephen Orgel, *The Jonsonian Masque* (Cambridge, 1965), p. 102.

37. Kerrigan, *The Sacred Complex*, p. 25; see also pp. 25–26.

38. See Fletcher, *The Transcendental Masque*, p. 169. John Carey, in *John Milton: Complete Shorter Poems* (1968; rpt. London, 1981), p. 188, n. 242, points out that the last line of the Lady's song to Echo, "And give resounding grace to all Heav'ns harmonies," "is the only alexandrine in *Comus*, mimicking the lengthening of heaven's song by echo."

39. J. B. Broadbent, "Pastoral in *Comus*," in *Comus and Samson Agonistes: A Selection of Critical Essays*, ed. Julian Lovelock (London, 1975), p. 72.

40. The priests of Cotytto, Thracian goddess of lewdness, were called Baptes. Their name derives from the Greek verb *bapto*, to wash, because of their so-called purification ceremonies.

41. A.S.P. Woodhouse and Douglas Bush, eds., *A Variorum Commentary on the Poems of John Milton*, gen. ed. Merritt Y. Hughes (New York, 1972), vol. II, iii, p. 769.

42. Fredrick Jameson, "Imaginary and Symbolic in Lacan: Marxism, Psychoanalytic Criticism, and the Problem of the Subject," in *Literature and Psychoanalysis*, ed. Shoshana Felman (Baltimore, 1982), p. 355.

43. This reference may extend Milton's use of swinish imagery. According to Mother M. Christopher Pecheux, in "The Conclusion of Book VI of *Paradise Lost*," the likening of driven angels to timorous creatures refers to "the swine that perished with the devils expelled by Jesus" (*SEL* III, pp. 109–17), quoted in Shawcross, *Complete Poetry*, p. 386, n. 60.

44. Thomas B. Stroup, *Religious Rite and Ceremony in Milton's Poetry* (Lexington, 1968), p. 8.

45. Fletcher, *The Transcendental Masque*, p. 200; see pp. 198–209.

46. John T. Shawcross, "Two Comments," *Milton Quarterly* VII (1973), p. 98.

47. Lieb, *Poetics of the Holy*, p. 98.

48. Philippe Aries, *Western Attitudes toward Death: From the Middle Ages to the Present*, trans. Patricia M. Ranum (Baltimore, 1974), pp. 37, 38; see pp. 33–39.

49. John T. Shawcross, *With Mortal Voice: The Creation of "Paradise Lost"* (Lexington, 1982), p. 118.

50. Christopher Hill, *Milton and the English Revolution* (New York, 1978), p. 48.

51. The quotation is from a crossed out line in the Trinity manuscript. The Lady welcomes "Faith," "Hope," and the "forme of chastity," which she sees "visibly." Next follows a crossed out section: "& while I see yee / this dusky hollow is a paradice / & heaven gates ore my head," in John Milton, *A Maske: The Earlier Versions*, p. 74. Although *gates* would usually be understood as a noun, in this case it seems to me to function with the force and feeling of a verb: the threshold of heaven spreads open over the Lady's head.

ELEMENTARY STRUCTURES OF KINGSHIP: MILTON, REGICIDE, AND THE FAMILY

Bruce Boehrer

WHEN CHARLES I knelt at the headsman's block on January 30, 1649, his death marked the climax of an extended sequence of negotiations, accusations, orations, oaths, expostulations, and entreaties, in which the king had fought vainly to improve his position between the various rebel factions seeking to influence the character of English government. This entire process had been carried out more or less in public, commented upon copiously by an army which was fast becoming (in Merritt Hughes's phrase) "a political debating society";[1] and the events leading up to the execution were conducted under the watchful eye of the entire European intellectual community. Moreover, the execution itself was conceived and performed as a public and corporate activity, even a grimly carnivalesque one, whose principal actors well knew their roles and their audience. The event itself was carefully observed and recorded.[2]

As king, Charles was especially aware of the theatrical nature of his trial and execution. Having made detailed arrangements beforehand so as to present himself with the greatest possible dignity, he proceeded under guard to the execution-place at Whitehall. Once upon the scaffold, he delivered his farewell speech which restated his position regarding the crimes of which he stood convicted; significantly enough, while the speech was delivered per expectation and in the open air, the parliamentary guard had placed sufficient barrier between the king and his subjects for him to be unable to make himself heard at large; while the execution was technically a public event, it was also, in a sense, a stiflingly private one.[3] After the obligatory farewell speech, the king knelt at the executioner's block; he spent a moment in devotions and then gave the sign that the headsman should do his office.

If Charles's final words failed to reach his subjects' ears, his blood nonetheless spoke to them with most miraculous organ. After the execution was done, the spectacle did not cease; instead, the crowd pressed close to the scaffold in order to dip handkerchiefs and other items in the blood of the new martyr-king. The parliamentary guard, for its part, took advantage of the moment as one might expect; the soldiers charged money for admission to the scaffold area and then sold chunks of blood-soaked board to the highest bidders.[4] Nor did the soldiers' pecuniary exercises end at the execution-place. After Charles's body was embalmed at Whitehall, it was placed on display at St. James's, where the army once again charged admission to the public, with such gratifying results that one soldier is reported to have remarked, "I would we could have two or three such Majesties to behead, if we could but make such use of them."[5]

The soldier's request would eventually be answered, though not quite as he would have wished. There would be more majesties, if not more beheadings, and the Roundhead cause would suffer lethal embarrassment from its inability to control its own political symbology. The execution was in this sense the final action of the English Civil War, and it proved a victory for Charles that would, in its way, compensate for Naseby and Marston Moor and much else besides. For even after Charles himself was finally laid to rest, the spectacle of his execution continued, and the critical issues it raised would ultimately be thrown into action once again, to restore the monarchy that the Rump had sought to extirpate.

In this respect, Charles's trial and execution were arranged along traditional lines; a quick glance at Foxe's *Actes and Monuments* will demonstrate the overwhelmingly rhetorical character of such events in the Renaissance. The killing itself was regularly preceded by elaborate dialectic, both written and spoken, and in many cases — as Foxe again illustrates — the debate continued well after the killing stopped. It is almost, indeed, as if the rhetoric — itself initially invoked as justification for the taking of life — were in fact the object of the entire display, as if the execution itself were a mere appurtenance designed to extend the boundaries of the universe of discourse. And to a degree this is indeed the case; as Charles's execution and the failure of the Protectorate suggest, one has but a blind hold on power if one cannot control the terms in which it signifies.

By 1649, political power in England had clearly become the property of Cromwell and the Independents; however, they chose to inscribe their authority in manners not always congenial to their purposes. The sham adjudication of Charles's trial proved a case in point. Before a satisfactory conclusion could be determined, and in fact before the trial could even begin, Charles's fate had to be settled by the clumsy manipulations of a power scarcely concerned with justifying itself: by George Joyce's abduction of the king from Holdenby and by the crucial gesture of Pride's Purge. And these manipulations showed like outsized bones beneath the skin of judicial procedure; the body politic of inter-regnum England, from Parliament's Rump to King Charles's head, was ill-proportioned and out of joint.

Naturally enough, the royalist prescription for setting matters to rights depended upon a traditional notion of the relationship between king and subjects, with the king serving as the father of a glorified family, with paternal rights and responsibilities extending over all his people. This was of course the Jacobean vision of kingship; James himself, in his parliamentary address of 1609, was only too pleased to elaborate:

As for the Father of a familie, they had of olde under the Law of Nature *Patriam potestatem,* which was *Potestatem vitae et necis,* over their children or fami-lie. . . . Now a Father may dispose of his Inheritance to his children, at his pleasure: yea, even disinherite the eldest upon iust occasions, and preferre the youngest, according to his liking; make them beggers, or rich at his pleasure: re-straine, or banish out of his presence, as hee finds them give cause of offence, or restore them in favour againe with the penitent sinner: So may the King deale with his Subjects.[6]

In altogether too many ways we may see here how little distance royal thinking had traversed since the days of Henry VIII. Monarchy is still buttressed by reference to natural law; it is still intimately associated with the private family order; it is as uncompromising as ever in its preten-sions to absolute authority, both public and personal, over its subjects. Elizabeth and James *had* contributed to the myth of English monarchy, but principally by way of refinement, by gradually rearticulating the precise nature of the family authority accruing to the ruler; they had left the Henrician foundation of that authority untouched.

Charles paid for this myth of monarchy with his life, and therefore it is fitting, in a way, that his view should have triumphed at the Restora-tion. Even now it is difficult not to be overwhelmed by the force and appeal of the *Eikon Basilike,* the King's Book; yet the work with which Parliament aimed to refute the *Eikon,* Milton's *Eikonoklastes,* is most memorable only for its hard and unrelenting hatred. These two books formed the core of the rhetorical debate surrounding the execution, a debate in which Milton did yeoman's service, composing first *The Ten-ure of Kings and Magistrates,* then *Eikonoklastes,* and finally the first and second *Defence of the English People.* The two *Defences* would give Milton his first great victory in the world of scholarship and letters; yet his *Eikonoklastes* survives as perhaps his most dismal defeat. Milton could vanquish the king's men; but even he was powerless against the king himself.

Milton's relative success with the *Defences* and his embarrassing failure with *Eikonoklastes* are easily explained. With the King's Book, as with Salmasius and the *Regii Sanguinis Clamor*, he found himself in the role of respondent, working as official apologist for Parliament and the English people. Yet he seems not to have grasped that the *Eikon* was a very different kind of book from the others that he would soon be refuting. Indeed, possibly the most noteworthy relation between Milton's regicide tracts is the rhetorical one; Milton in the *Second Defence* sounds very much like Milton in *Eikonoklastes*. There is no significant attempt to adjust the tone of the polemic in accordance with circumstances. Like Milton's God, his prose seems here to know no respect of persons; yet *Eikonoklastes* and the *Second Defence* address entirely different people in utterly different situations, and the rhetoric that would be so effective against Alexander More succeeds far less well when applied to the dead king.

With the *Defences*, Milton was fighting a more or less conventional rhetorical battle; written in Latin and against scholarly opponents, the long stretches of *argumentum ad hominem* in the *Defences* were at once more private and more esoteric than anything in *Eikonoklastes*. Moreover, they were more properly provoked. Salmasius's *Defensio Regia pro Carolo I* and the *Regii Sanguinis Clamor* by Peter du Moulin (which Milton attributed incorrectly to Alexander More) are theologico-political polemics in the old tradition: labyrinthine in their arguments, bulging with references to scholastic authority, and — to put it mildly — uncompromising in their rhetoric. Not only do they provoke opposition; they virtually demand it. And they do so upon the very same ground held by English royal supremacists for a hundred and twenty years already.

In this respect, Charles's apologists insist upon the supremacy and independence of the temporal sovereign within the system of natural law. They emphasize the scriptural character of royal supremacy, deriving their arguments for divine right ultimately from the precedents of Old Testament monarchy. And, most importantly, they characterize the relation between subjects and sovereigns as a *family* relation, and they thus present crimes against sovereigns as *family* crimes — as a disruption of the system of sexual significations upon which both divine and positive law are predicated. For Salmasius, the correspondence between king and father is to be taken absolutely literally; divine right monarchy is purely patriarchal and biblical in nature, and the nature of Parliament's sin against Charles is self-evident:

Idem Petrus regem honorandum esse in eadem epistola [ad Romanos] pronuntiat . . . *Deum timete, regem honorate.* Ita parentes honorari mandat Apostolus

Paulus. Hoc & unum est ex Decalogi praeceptis quo patrem & matrem honorare jubemur. Regem quippe parentis locum apud subditos tenere, semper & ab omnibus creditum est. Quem qui occidit, plusquam homicidam, plusquam parricidum censendum esse, vel ipsi gentilium auctores testantur.[7]

[Likewise in the same epistle [to the Romans], Peter proclaims that the king must be honored . . . *Fear God, honor the king.* In this way the Apostle Paul commands that parents be honored. There is this, and one of the commandments of the Decalogue in which we are enjoined to honor our father and mother. Indeed everyone has always believed that the king takes the place of parent among his subjects. Whoever kills him must be condemned of more than homicide, more than parricide, as even the Gentile authors themselves bear witness.]

This is the emotional heart of Salmasius's argument; firmly in the divine right tradition, he relies upon the notion of family responsibility to convince his readers that the king's dilemma is also theirs; and he reviles the parliamentary evildoers in the most immediate and personal terms possible—as sinners against family order and as filial ingrates.

From this point it is easy for the royalists to expand almost infinitely upon the evils of regicide. Salmasius has claimed that it is a worse crime than murder or even parricide; Du Moulin agrees and elaborates, writing of the Parliament's actions that

Immanissimo omnium Paricidio accedunt horribile Sacrilegium, Legum omnium eversio, Jurium divinorum & humanorum violatio, Naturae extinctio, Justitiae traductio, trium Regnorum uno ictu contrucidatio, Ecclesiae demolitio, Religionis proculcatio, Evangelii per totum orbem defamatio, Reformatorum . . . infestis dominorum securibus objectio; & quod caput est rei, Deo Opt. Max. horrenda offertur injuria.[8]

[To this most heinous parricide of all are added horrendous sacrilege, the overturning of all laws, the violation of divine and human rights, the destruction of nature, the disgrace of justice, the cutting down of three kingdoms at one blow, the ruin of the church, the trampling of religion, the defamation of the gospel throughout the world, a reproach to the wicked authority of the lords of the Reformers, and, what is the heart of the matter, a horrific injury is inflicted upon God, greatest and best.]

Regicide becomes in fact the royalist equivalent of Milton's Fall, the crime that comprehends all other crimes and is the necessary condition for their existence.[9] For any violation of the king's authority is also a violation of paternal dignity and of heavenly commandment; the figures of God, king, and father constitute the axis of Renaissance political authority, an axis upon which the individual conscience is to spin obediently. To offend one of these figures of power is simultaneously to offend all three, and any gesture that might question their authority carries within itself the figurative overthrow of kingship, and paternal dignity, and heavenly order. One cannot rebel in even the smallest way without murdering the royal image in one's heart.

The result of such rhetoric is of course to solidify the figure of the king in personal terms while rendering the evils of tyranny at once remote and theoretical. In service of these ends, Salmasius adduces the following reading of history, in which kingship proceeds both naturally and literally from family patriarchy:

Inde enim origo Regum Regiique regiminis petenda est. Haec cum primo homine & cum sole novo coepit, quoniam primum parentem numerosus ex eo descendens natorum & qui ex his nati sunt populus pro Rege habuit & observavit ut primum sui generis auctorem. Ad hoc instar Reges postea alios, nihil pertinentes ad genus stirpemque & cognationem priorum, a gentibus electos vel sumptos liquet a quibus regerentur & quos pro patribus colerent, qui & *Patriae Patres* exinde nuncupati sunt. Ut patres veri, ita Reges qui pro patribus sunt, non ejusdem moris & naturae omnes esse possunt. (Sig. A1v)

[For from this point we must seek the origin of kings and monarchy. This began with the first man, at the dawn of time, since the populous race of his children descendent from him, and those born from them, held their first parent to be their king, and revered him as the founder of their race. After this fashion, it is clear that later, other kings who did not belong to the family, line, and kin of the earlier kings were chosen or adopted by the people to rule them, and to be loved by them in place of their fathers. Hence they were called *fathers of their country.* Like real fathers, kings who stand in the place of fathers cannot all be of the same character and nature.]

In this argument we may see the ultimate literalization of metaphor; the word (i.e., the analogy whereby kings are likened to fathers) is simply made flesh through the figurations of historical fiction; after this gesture, the analogy itself ceases to be a mere learning aid, a convenient method of *representing* the royal prerogatives. The representation becomes the thing itself.

And it is through this rhetorical maneuver that we may see the ultimate applicability of the term "parricide" to Charles's execution. For acceptance of the historical fictions of divine-right royalism ultimately demands a literalization of the sexual analogy; only by actually viewing the king as father may one fully accept the first premise of divine-right monarchy: that the king is the earthly author of social relations and identity, and hence that he is the immediate source of all social authority. Once this point has been recognized, the royalist insistence upon the parricidal nature of the king's execution becomes far more understandable;

that insistence is not simply a propagandistic scare tactic, a stick with which to beat the parliamentarian rebels; it is the heart and soul of royalists thought on the nature of regicide. For Salmasius and Du Moulin — and for Charles himself — a social order without royal authority was as absurd as speech without utterance, or children without parents.

Thus the peculiar ferocity with which Salmasius and Du Moulin stress the parricidal character of Charles's execution: parricide is the only term adequate to their comprehension of the act, and it takes pride of place in their writings, appearing as the first word of the *Defensio Regia*, and occuring again within the title of the *Regii Sanguinis Clamor*. And indeed, the word "parricide" recurs on virtually every page of both tractates; it is invoked to explain and elucidate practically every detail of Parliament's behavior. The image of the king as father looms over every syllable of the royalist arguments, and with good reason. For the execution itself may have been (in Salmasius's words) "plusquam parricidum," but only by virtue of the fact that it was parricide first and foremost.

Salmasius stresses the equivalence of paternal and royal power whenever possible, and in the most uncompromising of terms. The result is an open assertion of Jacobean divine right in which the two bodies or capacities of the king — his identity as private individual and his character as public representative and embodiment of the state — merge indistinguishably. This conflation of the private with the public is essential to the royalist cause, and Salmasius buttresses it with historical references whenever possible:

Nam ut Pater naturalis quamvis asperior sit & iniquior, atque etiam saevior, non potest sine scelere summo a natis tolli, ita eum qui vicem parentis publici gerit, licet molesta & iniusta dominatione subiectos premat, sine parricidii crimine fas non est occidi. Quippe ut pater non desinit esse pater, quamvis in liberos ius Patriae potestatis severius exerceat, sic Rex qui imperium in subditos durius exercet, non perdit appellationē *Patris patriae*, ut ait Iustinianus. (Sig. L3v)

[For as a natural father, although he may be too harsh, too wicked, and even too cruel, cannot be removed by his children without the greatest crime, so it is not right that he who plays the role of public parent, although he may oppress his subjects with burdensome and unjust rule, be killed without the crime of parricide. Indeed as a father does not stop being a father, although he exercises the right of a father's power over his children too severely, so the king who exercises his power over his subjects too harshly does not lose the title, Father of his Country, as Justinianus says.]

Similarly, the *Eikon Basilike* would argue for a "frame of [church] government which is paternal, not magisterial";[10] and indeed this peculiar insistence upon the *family identity* of public officials is one of the principal points uniting the policies of Laudian Anglicanism and Stuart divine-right royalism. Despite the elegant Latin and the labored erudition of their arguments, the royalists' thesis was at heart a simple one; no bishop, no king; no king, no God; no God, no father.

In this fashion the royal authority could be integrated with matters of which the king's subjects generally had more experience: matters pertaining to the governance of the family. And this representation of royal concerns as family concerns would reinforce, in its turn, the extended familial analogy by which Christian theology represented the relationship between God and creation. In both of these instances, political figurations would depend directly upon gender and upon the system of sexual difference upheld within the family unit; and the discourse of royal and divine authority would blend into the discourse of family order, just as Charles's own fleshly sacrifice would become one more rhetorical gesture in an ongoing doctrinal debate. Indeed, it is this rhetorical character of the physical act, not the cruelty of the execution itself, that seems to trouble Du Moulin most; writing of the regicides, he maintains,

Non sunt simpliciter parricidae, sed parricidium in doctrinam vertunt; eamque Reformatarum Ecclesiarum consensione, capiunt quidem non audent, apertore defendere. (Sig. H9v)

[They are not simply parricides, but they turn the crime of parricide into doctrine; and they take this doctrine to be in agreement with the Reformers of the churches, yet they do not dare to defend it openly.]

Perhaps it is sheer coincidence that Du Moulin's concern with the doctrinal quality of the execution, with its *logos*, should lead him to mention ecclesiastical matters; yet if so, it is a coincidence that is repeated almost infinitely within the pages of the royalist tractates. For the bedrock of authority in these works — whether that authority be temporal or divine — never varies. To the royalists, power is purely and simply sexual identity.

And this observation helps to explain the royalist attacks on Milton's alleged libertinism; for those attacks were prompted by more than a mere idle desire to discredit Milton as an individual. It could not have seemed accidental that the man who had already created a furor through his advocacy of divorce should now defend regicide, too. Indeed, Du Moulin sees a logical consistency in this behavior, a consistency that must have seemed apparent to many:

Modo enim [Miltonus] a matrimonium dissociatione ad Regnorum divortium transit. (Sig. B6r)

[For now he [Milton] turned from the dissolution of marriage to the divorce of kingdoms.]

The charge is not without grounds; Arthur Barker, commenting upon this passage from the *Clamor*, largely agrees that "the political pamphlets did in fact apply to a larger field the ideas developed in the divorce tracts."[11] In a sense, the vehement rhetoric that is such an ugly characteristic of the royalist regicide tracts is a natural outgrowth of the ideas being handled; if we conceive of power and authority in the royalist sense as somehow consonant with sexuality and family identity, then it is hard to avoid charging Milton with both doctrinal error and sexual depravity. Salmasius's and Du Moulin's rhetoric is in the worst tradition of Renaissance controversial prose, and the violence of Renaissance polemic has become a scholarly cliché. But that violence exists for good reason, as a necessary consequence of the field of representation the controversialists themselves have chosen. And in this sense Milton's own rhetoric is predetermined, too; for in his role as respondent to the royalist arguments he has no choice but to neutralize whatever patterns of representation the royalists find most useful. By and large, he succeeds in the cases of Salmasius and Du Moulin, whereas with the *Eikon Basilike* he fails.

In a way, Milton could not help but fail with the *Eikon*, for in responding to the King's Book he was seeking to use traditional rhetoric against an adversary for whom the rules of rhetoric simply did not apply. This is not to say that the king himself did not need to present his case persuasively and intelligently; but the field of royalist discourse automatically privileged his arguments, and the patterns of that discourse enabled Charles to be tender and magnanimous where his men could only be strident. Moreover, the *Eikon Basilike* made no attempt to fit itself into the accepted structures of political debate: it was not written in Latin or addressed to a specifically academic audience; it presented itself as first and foremost a private and personal work, as a series of meditations prepared by the king for his own benefit and preserved for the further benefit of his son; and it had the luck to be, in one manner of speaking, an author's commentary upon the text under debate: the text of Charles's execution. It spoke to the individual conscience in a particularly powerful and subtle way, for it spoke with the personal voice of the king himself. Milton simply never had a chance.

For all of these reasons, it might have been better to ignore the *Eikon* altogether, yet it is easy to see why Parliament found this course of action unacceptable; the King's Book was the ideal royalist polemic precisely because it was not polemical in nature; it demanded rebuttal most urgently exactly because it invited none. Thus Milton's position as respondent to the *Eikon* was weakened from the very outset. As Joseph Jane would later note in *Eikon Aklastos:*

The author [of *Eikonoklastes*] might have done well to shew, why his Majest: booke seemed a Challenge, it provokes no answeare, nor handles any thing by way of controversie but his very devotions, and instructions to his son. . . . Evidence of worth in the sufferer torments the persecutour, and they cannot rest, while the vertues live, though the bodies are laid in the dust by their wicked hands.[12]

The king's words are lifted above the plane of controversy; they do not invite discussion, nor do they even permit it. Instead, the language of the *Eikon Basilike* operates like that of God at the creation; hermetic and self-reflexive, it is language that denies the fundamental condition of rhetoric in denying the centrality of its audience.

In this respect the *Eikon* stands in stark contrast to Milton's regicide tracts, for Milton, as Merritt Hughes has noted, "wrote as a rhetorician. His object was to convince."[13] And in service of that object Milton was forced to address himself, at least perfunctorily, to his audience, to confer upon that audience — at least implicitly — the superiority of the judge. The fact that Milton is not very graceful in according his audience this political centrality does not detract from the fact that he must do so; Milton writes as a man addressing other men, Charles as a creator to his creatures. In this sense the text of the *Eikon* does not *ignore* its audience; the King's Book simply does not permit the audience to take part in its discourse. Indeed, instead of presuming that the reader will read the book, the *Eikon* seems to assume that the author will inscribe the reader. That is to say, the audience that appears in the *Eikon*, in all its many forms, appears as the king's *creation;* the analogy to God's language in the first two chapters of Genesis becomes most frighteningly manifest in this gesture. The narrative voice of the *Eikon* is solitary and superb, issuing from an eminence that both comprehends and transcends all other voices, and it operates in this way by virtue of its sexual identity; if the author of the King's Book has created his readers, it is because he is a father first and foremost, and his readers are his children.

What is especially curious about this rhetoric, though, is that it is most impressive when it is supported least by the trappings of political power. It is as if the authority of the king's voice increased in inverse proportion to the security of his person. When Charles invokes his paternal status to protest his personal treatment, the *Eikon* is at its most affecting. Thus the *Eikon* compares the exposure of the king's letters after Naseby to Ham's exposure of Noah's nakedness:

> I am sure they [Parliament] can never expect divine approbation of such inde- cent actions, if they do but remember how God blest the modest respect and filial tenderness which Noah's sons bare to their father; nor did his open infirmity jus- tify Cham's impudency, or exempt him from the curse of being servant of ser- vants. . . . Nor can their malicious intentions be ever excusable . . . who thought by this means to expose me . . . forgetting that duty of modest concealment which they owed to the father of their country. (P. 160)

Never content merely to *assert* Charles's paternalism, the *Eikon* reinforces the assertion once more through scriptural reference, pointing toward that treasure-trove of divine-right precedents, the Old Testament. Yet the particularly successful quality of this passage derives from its vision of the king's "infirmity" and its concomitant sense of the subject's duty to the king as essentially a species of filial obligation. It is not proper on the personal level to pry into another person's private correspondence; and the *Eikon* effectively denies the special circumstances surrounding Parliament's capture of Charles's letters by stressing the king's character as *private* person. It is no accident that the scriptural patriarch to whom this passage refers is not a king, but a father. Charles could not afford to distinguish between fatherhood and kingship in any substantive way.

And thus the arguments of the *Eikon* come ultimately to rest upon the *sexual* character of patriarchy, for it is the act of *begetting* that fi- nally unites fatherhood to kingship. This begetting can be literal, of course; a principal responsibility of both father and of king, after all, is simply to create heirs. But one can also beget in a figurative sense: laws, authority, tradition, order. And it is this figurative potency to which the *Eikon* appeals when explaining how government must operate. While thus acknowledging Parliament's legislative capacities, the king voices his central objection to rule by Parliament alone:

> But . . . I cannot allow their [Parliament's] wisdom . . . to exclude myself . . . without whose reason concurrent with theirs (as the sun's influence is necessary in all nature's productions), they cannot beget or bring forth any one complete and authoritative act of public wisdom. (P. 69)

In this case, as in so many others, the debate over royalism simply re- solves into a question of priority, of who was there first. Do kings create nations and laws, or do nations and laws create kings? And in settling questions of priority, the royalist father/king nexus is particularly con- venient. After all, priority is the great prop of paternal authority. The father governs his children because he *made* them; and if the analogy of father to king is accepted and appropriated by political theorists, then the entire question of priority is settled before it can ever be raised.

This measure licenses the most effective elements of royalist rhetoric, for it involves language that is at once authoritative and protective. Just as the father, in consequence of his historical priority, gains political preeminence, his subjects, by virtue of their posteriority, acquire their own political identity. And the two conditions of that identity are subservience and dependence. Traditionally, royalist polemic had emphasized the former of these conditions in arguing for divine right, and the regicide tractates of Salmasius and Du Moulin follow suit; but it is in the *Eikon* alone that we find consistent reference to the *dependence* of subjects upon their king. Indeed, if we consider matters closely enough, it is this emphasis upon dependence that animates each of the passages of the *Eikon* that we have already examined; only if we accept the literal nature of the king's paternal authority can we then accept, for instance, that Parliament cannot function as an independent and self-sufficient legislative unit. The king's argument assumes dependence to be the immediate consequence of posteriority: the king exists before his nation, creates his nation, and embodies his nation, while the nation itself derives all order and identity from him.

The final result of this concept of kingly authority is a book that abandons the customary browbeating of royalist polemic in favor of something very like a father's love for his children. The author of the *Eikon* held before his eyes a vision of nurturing paternity, and it is this vision that accounts for the book's stunning success as propaganda. While the blunt assertions of divine-right authority alienate, the tender mercies of the *Eikon* seduce; the insistence upon the king's role as *sustainer* of his nation-family would lead later writers to liken him to the pelican, nourishing his offspring with his own blood.[14] And this analogy between sacrificial blood and sustenance would reintroduce the paternal character of the Christian God to the pattern of royalist language. Certainly King Charles — as represented in the *Eikon* — sees himself occupying the concurrent roles of king, father, and prophet/martyr; and the gentleness with which he insists upon those roles lends his claims authority. In one of his many expressions of fondness for his people, Charles remarks in the *Eikon* that "My own subjects . . . are, next to my children, dear to me, and for the restoring of [their] tranquillity I could willingly be the Jonah" (p. 102). And finally, in this last passage, we can discover the ultimate effect of the *Eikon*'s rhetoric. The King's Book is not a polemic or an academic work in the traditional sense; it is a personal, private communication from the king to his son, and through his son to his family-at-large: the subjects of his kingdom. The special, intimate relationship presumed by royalist theory to obtain between the sovereign and each one of his people is at last the subject of the *Eikon*, and it is spoken in every line and syllable of the book. The *Eikon* is a family document, the last meditations of a father facing execution, directed and addressed to each surviving member of his family. Charles would in fact be the Jonah for his children; as Maureen Quilligan has observed, "What is left after reformation and regicide is—to put it at its most basic—the political unit of the individual nuclear family."[15] And that nuclear family would be the king's.

To turn from the *Eikon Basilike* to Milton's regicide tracts is anticlimactic. To be sure, the *Defences* are effective pieces of Renaissance polemic, but they necessarily appealed to a far narrower audience than did the King's Book; and *Eikonoklastes* is almost a blemish upon Milton's character. Indeed, these three works do little to distinguish themselves from the mass of political vituperation provided by the English Renaissance; yet, as disheartening as it may be to contemplate the bitterness of Milton's political prose, it is important that we recognize it for what it is: an integral part of a dreary tradition of backbiting and mud-slinging. It is to Milton's enduring credit that he was ultimately able to abandon the patterns of Renaissance political controversy; yet, with all compassion, it is still necessary to recognize in the Milton of *Eikonoklastes* an author mired in the things of this world, a writer full of hatred and bitterness and the determination to put that hatred and bitterness into action. It is unjust to deny Milton the ultimate triumph his poetry and spirit achieve; but it is equally irresponsible to ignore the vehemence and vitriol that preceded it. The Milton of *Eikonoklastes* does not compare well to the author of the King's Book.

Perhaps the principal reason for this unfortunate fact is that Milton never betrays, in any of these three works, the least recognition of his changing rhetorical situation. Certainly the two *Defences* are addressed to different men—Salmasius and More—and *Eikonoklastes*, too, is directed at a specific figure—King Charles. Yet Milton speaks to these men as if they were one and the same person; his hostility, vehemence, and scurrility are the same everywhere. And further, Milton does not seem to recognize the special rights and requirements of his audience. One suspects that *Eikonoklastes* is in English not, like the *Eikon*, in order to touch the reader more closely, in order to establish a more intimate bond between author and audience, but rather simply because the *Eikon* had already been written and Milton had no choice but to answer it in his native tongue. And the grudging condescension with which Milton undertakes his rebuttal places him at further disadvantage; the English king writes in his own language to his own children, but Milton appears to scorn any such intimacies. His language is that of the alien, his demeanor that of the autocrat.[16]

On the question of kingly authority, Milton thus finds himself in no easy position. For in opposing the royalist theory of monarchy, he must at the same time oppose a venerable tradition of representation that ultimately involves not only the king, but also God, created nature, and the very structure of the family. His task is not lightened by the brilliant rhetoric of the *Eikon;* on the contrary, his response to the King's Book must necessarily challenge a whole series of established social structures, and it does so in self-conscious inflammatory language. Where the *Eikon,* for instance, gains strength from repeated reference to proper family order, Milton has no choice but to respond in terms of perversion, effeminacy, and sexual degeneracy; of the *Eikon*'s tender praise for Henrietta Maria, Milton sneers,

He [Charles] ascribes *Rudeness and barbarity worse then Indian* to the English Parlament, and *all vertue* to his Wife, in straines that come almost to Sonnetting: How fitt to govern men, undervaluing and aspersing the great Counsel of his Kingdom, in comparison of one Woman. Examples are not farr to seek, how great mischief and dishonour hath befall'n to Nations under the Government of effeminate and Uxorious Magistrates. Who being themselves govern'd and overswaid at home under a Feminine usurpation, cannot but be farr short of spirit and autority without dores, to govern a whole Nation.[17]

This passage is typical of Milton's rhetoric throughout *Eikonoklastes.* Where the *Eikon* professes devotion, Milton responds with contempt; where the *Eikon* praises wifely virtue, Milton makes lewd suggestions; where the *Eikon* extols family government and filial piety, Milton urges committee rule and tyrannicide. We may admire the gumption with which Milton played the rebel; but it is not hard to see from this why Christopher Hill should claim that "liberty for Milton was always largely negative. It involved criticism, destruction, iconoclasm."[18] Nor is it hard to see how fundamentally unattractive such an approach to liberty could be for the English reading public after Charles's execution.

But not only was Milton's conception of liberty negative and largely unattractive; it was also utterly relentless. Not content to accuse Charles himself of uxoriousness, for instance, Milton raises the issue again when confronting Salmasius:

You have at home a barking bitch who rules your wretched wolf-mastership, rails at your rank, and contradicts you shrilly; so naturally you want to force royal tyranny on others after being used to suffer so slavishly a woman's tyranny at home. (YP IV, p. 380)

It is at moments like this that Milton's rhetorical discrimination appears most suspect. For if discrimination is merely the ability to distinguish between things, then Milton has signally failed to discriminate between Charles the king and Salmasius the pedant, who receive virtually the same treatment at his hands. One wonders, indeed, whether Milton ever had a clear vision of his adversaries *as individuals* in his own mind. Certainly the sexual rhetoric of *Eikonoklastes* and the *Defences* is interchangeable; the references to uxoriousness could be multiplied almost *ad nauseam*.

We may dispense here with Milton's innumerable jibes at Salmasius, all of which seem calculated to portray the man as a henpecked ninny, incapable of governing his family at home and hence unqualified to discuss the proper governance of nations abroad. We may even disregard Milton's subsequent references in the *Eikonoklastes* to Charles's uxoriousness. But after we have discarded the fistful of relevant passages in *Eikonoklastes* and *The First Defence*, we are still left with Milton's obscene attack on Alexander More in *The Second Defence*, which once more seizes upon the themes of sexual ambiguity and family anarchy. Of More's alleged affair with Pontia, Salmasius's servant-girl, Milton writes:

From the union resulted at length a marvellous and unnatural prodigy; not only the female but also the male conceived — Pontia a little More, which for a long time afterward persecuted even that persecutor of Pliny, Salmasius; and More conceived this empty wind-egg, from which burst forth the swollen Cry of the King's Blood. (YP IV, pp. 569–70)

Unlike Charles and Salmasius, More has no wife to whom Milton can assign the privileges of family rule; yet Milton nonetheless includes More in the pattern of his sexual discourse, challenging More's status as *potential* husband by virtue of the necessary precondition for that status: masculine sexual identity. To Milton, More is "a hermaphrodite, as fit to give birth as to beget" (YP IV, p. 571), and therefore constitutionally unfit for the masculine business of government.

What is perhaps most curious about all of these passages from Milton's tracts is that, while they are revolutionary in tenor, they are derivative in formulation. They offer no new perspective upon the nature of government; instead, they merely reiterate the royalist premise that a ruler is the father of his people. Milton uses assertions of uxoriousness and sexual ambiguity to discredit his opponents' *political status;* but in order for such arguments to work, one must first assume that sexual identity and political authority somehow correspond, that they are in some way equivalent. One is thrown, in other words, back upon family structure as the model for national government, and it is this model that the royalists have been using all along. Moreover, it is a model that Milton goes to great lengths to deny at other points in his work; responding to Salmasius's use of the royal/paternal analogy, for instance, he makes his position clear:

You are wholly in the dark in failing to distinguish the rights of a father from those of a king; by calling kings fathers of their country, you think this metaphor has forced me to apply right off to kings whatever I might admit of fathers. Fathers and kings are very different things: Our fathers begot us, but our kings did not, and it is we, rather, who created the king. It is nature which gave the people fathers, and the people who gave themselves a king; the people therefore do not exist for the king, but the king for the people. (YP IV, pp. 326–27)

At moments such as this, Milton struggles mightily to rid himself of the encumbrances of royalist sexual metaphor; yet once he has expelled royalist theory from his political edifice, it merely slips in again at the back door. His political arguments are of the king's party without knowing it,[19] for they rely ultimately upon the very rhetorical figurations that constitute the notion of the king as *parens patriae.*

Is the royal scepter a metaphorical penis? At the very least it may be said that Milton conceived of government as a fundamentally sexual or sex-specific, fundamentally masculine activity, one properly performed by men and *only* by men; the ability to govern properly, indeed, is for Milton a manifestation of *virtus.* And it is this conception of matters that licenses Milton's most outstanding sallies against King Charles. Consider, for instance, the following oblique reference in *Eikonoklastes* to Henrietta Maria's influence over her husband:

It happn'd once . . . to be a great and solemn debate in the Court of *Darius*, what thing was to be counted strongest of all other. . . . One [councillor] held that Wine was the strongest; another that the King was strongest. But *Zorobabel* Prince of the Captive Jewes, and Heire to the Crown of Judah, being one of them, proov'd Women to be stronger then the King, for that he himself had seen a Concubin take his Crown from off his head to set it upon her own: And others besides him have lately seen the like Feat don, and not in jest. (YP III, pp. 582–83)

What seems to disturb Milton most in this passage is not that Charles is king, bu that as king he defers to a woman; and in a sense it is this objection which caps and undoes all his arguments against monarchy. To argue that absolute monarchy itself is not a desirable form of government is one thing; but to argue that it is not desirable *except insofar as it preserves the family relation* is something entirely different; and Milton seems to be doing both at one and the same time. Opposed to theories of divine-right monarchy, Milton cannot yet bring himself to sever the inveterate connection between government and family; yet this connection points directly toward monarchy, toward the centralization of power in the hands of a single — preferably male — individual.

The results of this conflict in Milton's rhetoric can at times be preposterous, or even amusing. When driven to respond to the royalist equation of king to father, Milton generally does so simply by denying that any such equivalency exists; and having made that denial, he then proceeds as quickly as possible to matters with which he is more comfortable. But on occasion, he comments on the subject more fully, and when he does so, he almost always seeks to appropriate the royalist discourse of government-as-family to his own ends. Thus, in response to the *Eikon's* claim that the king's concurrent reason is necessary for the begetting of authoritative laws, he comments,

So that the Parliament, it seems, is but a Female, and without [Charles's] procreative reason, the laws which they can produce are but wind-eggs. . . . He ought then to have so thought of a Parliament, if he count it not Male, as of his Mother, which, to civil being, created both him, and the royalty he wore. And if it hath been anciently interpreted the presaging sign of a future Tyrant, but to dream of copulation with his Mother, what can it be less then actual Tyranny to affirme waking, that the Parlament, which is his Mother, can neither conceive or bring forth *any autoritative Act* without his Masculine coition . . . What other notions but these, or such like, could swell up *Caligula* to think himself a God. (YP III, p. 467)

Milton here presses the maternal identity of Parliament as earnestly as Salmasius or Du Moulin ever insisted upon the paternal character of the monarchy; yet where the royalist analogy succeeds, Milton's merely appears ludicrous: the king, after all, could act reasonably like a father to his people, but who could believe for a moment that the gentlemen of the Rump might be anyone's mother?[20] The central issue here is that of the relation between the family structure and monarchy — between kinship and kingship — presupposed by Renaissance thought and social order. For the royalist figure of the father-king appeals to Milton the family autocrat at the very moment that it repels Milton the republican revolutionary. The result is this bemusing vision of incest-by-committee, with King Charles committing his rape upon the Rump.

In a way, Milton's problem here is purely representational. Royalist theoreticians had long made capital of the ease with which two distinct discursive fields — that of family structure and that of political order — could merge in the figure of the king. This was a mode of representation that in many ways left Milton speechless: how was he to oppose monarchy without appearing at the same time to oppose family? In general, his tactic was to ignore the problem, to accuse his polemical opponents of uxoriousness and hermaphroditism on the one hand, while on the other hand blandly denying that family had anything to do with politics. And this fissure in Milton's rhetoric leads me to one final observation: Milton's political prose is bad political prose. It is bad in the sense in which George Orwell has called most modern political writing bad: it opposes clarity of thought in order to mask a fundamental insincerity of purpose.[21] After all, Milton's immediate purpose in *Eikonoklastes* and the *Defences* is not to prove that Charles was an incestuous rapist or that Salmasius is a hen-pecked pedant; nor is it his primary goal to assert a particular relation between royal and parliamentary power. These are all means to an end, and that end, purely and simply, is to get away with killing another human being.

Again and again in Milton's regicide tracts, as I have already noted, the private vision vanishes; there is no clear picture of Charles or of Salmasius or of More in these works, any more than there is a clear picture of incestuous rape in Charles's figurative abuse of Parliament; the concrete, the private, the personal is again and again trammeled and dismembered in favor of the theoretical. In a sense, we have here the origin of what T. S. Eliot would call Milton's lack of visual imagination.[22] And that origin, at least within the context of the regicide tracts, is a fundamental tension between autocratic action and egalitarian ideals. Milton hides behind the vehemence of his own rhetoric, spitting out phrases that are the Renaissance equivalent of "capitalist lackey," "jack-booted tyranny," and "making the world safe for democracy"; and he does so precisely to avoid the private, personal object under consideration, the object with which this analysis began: the dead, headless body of King Charles I.

In the immediate scheme of things, Milton's defense of regicide was not particularly successful; it was in Cromwell's soldiers, not Milton's pen, that the Independents found their ultimate justification. King Charles's party won the war of words, almost as a natural consequence of Parliament's military victory. And Milton, although generally successful in his more conventional debates with Salmasius and Du Moulin, was utterly baffled by the stunning popularity of the *Eikon Basilike*. His bafflement would eventually contribute, through the *Eikon*'s rhetorical victory, to the Restoration, and the regicide tracts would serve as a proving-ground for the sexual language of Milton's later poetry, for what Kester Svendsen has called "the motifs of miscegenation, hermaphroditism, and disnatured conception" that abound in *Paradise Lost*.[23]

But of more immediate concern for this study is the political nature of these sexual references. For in Milton's political prose we may witness the ultimate exhaustion of a particular view of royal power, a view of royal power as originally sexual and familial in nature and of the king's authority as both patriarchal and paternal. It is this political perspective that is championed in the *Eikon* and its sister tracts, and it proves signally unadaptable to the purposes of Milton's own political discourse. After Milton, the nature of kingship would be so fundamentally altered that this unique strain of sexual reference would not reappear in English literature; never again would the king's two bodies, the private and the public, be so conflated as they were in the figure of Charles.

I have argued that the failure of *Eikonoklastes* was principally a failure of rhetoric, that Milton was unable to refute a concept of kingship that manifested itself, on the personal level, in the figurations of family order. In this sense, one may gain a certain ironic satisfaction from the spectacle of the arch-patriarch of English literature being beaten at his own game. In a way, indeed, one may say that Milton could not bring himself to view the king as father and therefore chose not to view him as anything at all, at least not as anything credible. But the royalist triumph of the father-king over Milton's rhetoric would be the last such triumph; the condition of victory was self-destruction, both of the divine-right view of kingship and of the king himself. And thus the ultimate royalist text would prove to be nothing less than the king's dead body, the self-consuming artifact implicit in all the literature of the regicide. And the royal martyrdom, Charles's great personal work of art, would redeem his dynasty, while leaving him and his world in ashes.

University of Pennsylvania

NOTES

I would like to thank Maureen Quilligan, Margreta de Grazia, Robert Y. Turner, and Ellen Pollack for reading and commenting upon various versions of this study; I also wish to thank Elizabeth Beckwith for her extensive help in preparing translations from the Latin.

1. *Complete Prose Works of John Milton* 8 vols. ed. Merritt Y. Hughes (New Haven, 1962), vol. III, p. 1.

2. See, for instance, the account given in *A Perfect Diurnall of Some Passages in Parliament . . . from Munday the 29 of January till Mund. the 5 of February 1648* (London, 1649). This description of Charles's last day includes such personal details as the refreshment he took before execution, as well as a verbatim transcript of proceedings on the scaffold. Other contemporary accounts of the execution include those of Richard Collings, *Kingdom's Weekly Intelligencer*, 30 January–6 February 1648 (1649), and Gilbert Mabbot, *A . . . Narrative of the Proceedings of the High Court of Justice . . . Concerning the Tryal of the King* (London, 29 January 1648 [1649]). The latter was the official parliamentary version of the event.

3. Thus the *Perfect Diurnall* (30 January 1649) records the odd *non sequitur* with which Charles's death-speech begins: "I shall be very little heard of any body here, I shall therefore speak a word unto you here."

4. C. V. Wedgwood, *A Coffin for King Charles* (New York, 1964), p. 242, provides an informative account of the extraordinary powers that were immediately attributed to these relics.

5. Cited in John Bowle. *Charles I: A Biography* (London, 1975), p. 336.

6. Parliamentary speech of 1609, in *The Political Writings of James I*, ed. Charles Howard McIlwain (1946; rpt. New York, 1965), p. 308.

7. Claude de Saumaise, *Claudii Salmasii Defensio Regia pro Carolo I* (Paris, 1651), sigs. E4v–F1r. Further citations will be to this edition.

8. [Pierre Du Moulin], *Regii Sanguinis Clamor ad Coelum Adversus Paricidas Anglicanos* (The Hague, 1652), sigs. B2v–B3r. Further citations will be to this edition.

9. Cf. *De Doctrina Christiana*, I, xi, in *The Complete Prose Works of John Milton*, 8 vols, ed. Don M. Wolfe et al. (New Haven, 1953–82), vol. VI, pp. 383–84.

10. [John Gauden], *Eikon Basilike*, ed. J. L. Scott (London, 1880), pp. 126–27. Further citations will be to this edition.

11. Arthur Barker, *Milton and the Puritan Dilemma: 1641–1660* (Toronto, 1942), p. 123.

12. [Joseph Jane], *Eikon Aklastos: The Image Unbroaken* (n.p., 1651), sig. B1v.

13. Hughes, *Complete Prose Works*, vol. III, p. 128.

14. See, for instance, *The Princely Pellican: Royal Resolves Presented in Sundry Choice Observations, Extracted from his Majesties Divine Meditations* (n.p., 1649), which presents Charles as a "pious indulgent and gracious . . . Prince; whose Bloud onely was held fit to appease the implacable fury of a remorcelesse Enemy" (sig. E4r).

15. Maureen Quilligan, *Milton's Spenser: The Politics of Reading* (Ithaca, 1983), p. 13.

16. In this respect it is useful to consider T. S. Eliot's remark that "It is not so unfair, as it might at first appear, to say that Milton writes English like a dead language" ("Milton I," in *On Poetry and Poets* [1943; rpt. New York, 1968], p. 159).

17. John Milton, *Eikonoklastes*, in *Complete Prose Works of John Milton*, 8 vols., ed. Don M. Wolfe et al. (New Haven, 1953–82), vol. III, pp. 420–21. All citations to Milton's prose will be to this edition, to be denoted by YP, with volume and page numbers.

18. Christopher Hill, *Milton and the English Revolution* (New York, 1977), p. 178.

19. In this respect it is valuable to consider Joan Bennett's argument in "God, Satan, and King Charles: Milton's Royal Portraits," *PMLA* XCII (1977), p. 441, that references to Charles in *Eikonoklastes* serves as a principal source for the later characterization of Satan in *Paradise Lost*. If, as Blake has asserted, Milton was of the devil's party without

knowing it, we may thus arguably trace the source of his diabolical allegiance to the nature of royalist family politics.

20. Also consider Joseph Jane's response to this passage in the *Eikonoklastes* (Jane, *Eikon Aklastos*, sig. Aa1v): "Parliaments can be noe Mothers to kings, that are created by kings. The king is by the law of England Father of the Countrey, & the life, and soule of the law, but [Milton] will find out a step Mother an Athalia to destroy the seede Royall, and sett her incestuous brood upon the throne."

21. George Orwell, "Politics and the English Language," in *The Orwell Reader*, ed. Richard H. Rovere (1933; rpt. New York, 1956), pp. 362–63.

22. Eliot, "Milton I," p. 158: "At no period is the visual imagination conspicuous in Milton's poetry. . . . His language is . . . *artificial* and *conventional.*"

23. Kester Svendsen, *Milton and Science* (Cambridge, 1956), p. 188.

MILTON METAPHRAST:
LOGIC AND RHETORIC IN PSALM I

Lee A. Jacobus

COMMENTARY ON Milton's translations of the Psalms has begun to move from concern with his knowledge of Hebrew, and with the motives for his efforts of 1648 and 1653, toward considering his artistic achievement and its relation to questions of prosody and his preparation for writing his major works.[1] Most of the close and comparative work has been done in regard to the paraphrases of 1648, particularly because of their political tone and the facts regarding a probable motive for their composition. The problems of motive for the metaphrases of 1653 are more difficult and seem to be connected to personal rather than public pressures.[2] Yet, these eight psalms represent a greater artistic effort on Milton's part, and seem to point to a deeper personal involvement. Each is in a different meter and none in the meter of the original. I consider these to be metaphrases because of Ascham's definition: "*Metaphrasis . . .* is all one with *Paraphrasis* saue it is out of verse, either into prose, or into some other kinds of meter."[3] The term helps distinguish between Milton's stated and apparent motives for translating the Psalms. The 1648 group is preceded by the note: "Nine of the Psalms done into metre, wherein all, but what is in a different character, are the very words of the text translated from the original." The use of common meter, reflecting the Westminster Assembly's needs, demonstrates that Milton sought to produce a singable translation, a "public" version of the Psalms which would suit the needs of Presbyterian worship. The discipline implied in the group of 1653, resulting in an unusually clear dating of each (except the first) metaphrase, suggests that Milton may have had a private motive for continuing through the entire Psalter, translating a psalm a day (although he "rested" on one day, August 11). The ending of the Rump and the calling of the fractious Nominated Parliament coincided with his efforts, and public business may have intervened on private discipline.

The group of 1648 is more clearly of public use. The Presbyterian view was that the Psalms were to be a cornerstone of public worship. The Ordinance for 4 January 1644 (1645) reads:

119

It is the duty of Christians to praise God publiquely by singing of Psalmes together in the Congregation, and also privately in the Family.

In singing of Psalms the voice is to be tunably and gravely ordered: But the chief care must be, to sing with understanding and with Grace in the heart, making melody unto the Lord.

That the whole Congregation may joyn herein, every one that can read is to have a Psalm-Book, and all others, not disabled by age or otherwise, are to be exhorted to learn to read. But for the present, where many in the Congregation cannot read, it is convenient that the Minister or some other fit person appointed by him and the other Ruling Officers, do read the Psalm line by line, before the singing thereof.[4]

In discussing Richard Neile, bishop of Winchester and archbishop of York (appointed by Charles at the age of seventy), Ronald Marchant notes that "Psalms were sung before, and often after, the sermon, in the same way in which a hymn is sung today" (Marchant, p. 65). Neile, an adversary of Puritanism, made changes in other aspects of the form of worship, but not, apparently, in the singing of psalms. Sternhold and Hopkins were not easily supplanted. The Puritans were interested in better translations, but they were generally happy with the old tunes.

Even if Neile were content with the singing of the Psalms, it is clear that there was discontent in some corners concerning the ordinance. Milton's sonnet on the "new forcers of conscience" does not seem pointed in the direction of the singing of psalms, although it is important to note that the question of conscience has been repeatedly connected with the Psalms, and that they represent an expression of conscience that was very close to Milton's personal interests. Henry Lawes's dedication of *Choice Psalms* begins with the observation that if he did not offer his songs to Charles, "I could not answer mine owne Conscience" (Boddy, p. 2). Although it was established in Geneva by exiles from the Marian persecutions and continued in English churches when the exiles returned in 1553, the singing of psalms became controversial after the ordinance of 1644 (1645). The controversy centered on the issues of metrics, with the versions of Sternhold and Hopkins coming under scrutiny for their additions to scripture. The fear was that in such translations much that was not scripture had entered in. This is why Milton was so cautious in his 1648 group to point out his attention to accuracy. The primary purpose of the Westminster Assembly's desire for a new Psalter was accuracy, although the question of delight was not entirely ignored. Beyond accuracy, there may have been other reasons for objection to the ordinance on the part of Independents who were unwilling to be told how to treat the Psalms.

Nathaniel Holmes approached the question of singing the Psalms from a typically logical point of view. In *Gospel Musick*, 1644, he says,

In handling the Questions, or Case of Conscience touching singing of the Psalmes found in the Scriptures, being translated into English metre, you have these 6. generals presented to you.
1. The warrantablenesse of it from the word of God.
2. The unquestionablenesse of it in all Ages.
3. The ancientnesse of it in all Ages.
4. The necessarinesse of it with other Ordinances.
5. The usefulnesse of it for God's glory and man's comfort.
6. The unjustnesse of mens exceptions against it, and their objections answered. (Sig. A1v)

In recommending the Psalms, he says, "every well minded family by singing can make themselves a little church. And every church make themselves a little heaven" (p. 12). However, Holmes's primary concerns are with accuracy and the question of English meter. On the one hand he admits that if unsoundness of doctrine crept into the Psalms because the poet had to serve meter, "the people would fall in love with it, and as *Zanchy* saith very well, there would be no removing it" (p. 17). But if every church had a different meter, then "it would not so tend to the union of churches, and anticipating of emulations" (p. 17).

On the larger issue of singing in the churches, there is the fear that it emulates too much the Roman Catholic practice, and Holmes attempts to explain the distinctions:

Davids Psalmes sung in our English Meeter differ much from Cathedral singing, which is so abominable, in which is sung almost every thing, unlawfull Letanies, and Creeds, and other prose not framed in Meeter fit for singing. Besides they do not let all the Congregation, neither sing, nor understand what is sung; *Battologizing* and quavering over the same words vainly. Yea nor do all they sing together, but first one sings an Anthem, then half the Chore, then the other, tossing the Word of God like a Tenice-ball. Then all yelling together with confused noise. This we utterly dislike as most unlawful. (P. 19)

By 1657 the question of singing the Psalms had not subsided entirely, but prompted Cuthbert Sidenham to cite the singing of psalms and the baptizing of infants as "the Two Grand Practical Controversies of These Times" (title page). As he saw it, Satan, in raising these controversies to create confusion, called psalm-singing into question, "to deprive the Saints of the benefit of that soul raising & heart-ravishing Ordinance, by which God is publickly and solemnly praised & the spirit filled with the glory of God" (p. 171).

Milton's family created their own little church of psalm singers, and it is difficult to imagine John Milton taking issue with the Ordinance. In 1648 his intention was to help supply accurate paraphrases that fit the common meter and which would then perhaps help extend the union of churches.[5] However, by 1653 it is not clear that his intentions were to supply a version which would in any way relate to the Ordinance. Rather, by choosing a highly idiosyncratic approach to meter, his metaphrase implies personal purposes which relate to individual conscience and perhaps even to artistic needs. Mary Ann Radzinowicz suggests that Milton "numbered himself not only with Homer, Tiresias, and Phineus but also with the Psalmist" (p. 207), and it may be that the intention of creating a personal Psalter seemed to him an ambition similar to that of creating a tragedy or an epic.

Marian Studley observes that the group of 1653 was "not necessarily for use in the church, because he does not use the service form, but as if to satisfy an ambition to write a metaphrase more worthy of his model and of his own powers" (pp. 366–67). She also observes that the custom of paraphrase and metaphrase was widespread in the first half of the seventeenth century in England, and may have served as wide a variety of purposes as there were poets.

Among those available to Milton were the version by Henry Ainsworth, with commentary and explanations (1617); the version by John Calvin, with commentary translated by Arthur Golding (1571), as well as Calvin's Latin version (1578), with the Hebrew text to the right of the Latin. In addition to the Sternhold and Hopkins Psalter, Milton also had recourse to the *Bay Psalm Book* (1640), George Wither's version of 1631, George Sandys's version of 1636, Richard Braithwaite's of 1638, as well as the widely circulated manuscript version by Sir Philip Sidney and his sister, the countess of Pembroke (responsible for the forty-fourth to final Psalms). There were also numerous examples of parts of the Psalter paraphrased — not all of them published.

Milton's purposes, if they were personal and artistic in the group of 1653, would have been to produce the finest poetry possible, beginning from the original language. Hunter's demonstration of the communal nature of the Psalms (1961) is most dependent on the group of 1648 for its examples. The Psalms of 1653 are less communal, and while Milton is not explicitly concerned with absolute accuracy in "the very words of the text translated from the original" as he was in 1648, these psalms represent an effort of a special kind: to raise the spirit of the metaphrast to that of the original psalmist by a performance of a like act: making a prayer in the best poetic form possible.

The use of a different metrical form for each psalm is not unique with Milton. Although he may have repeated himself if he had continued, the precedent set in the French Psalter of 1562, by Clement Marot and Theodore Beza, would have permitted him to emulate their own variety: one hundred and ten different meters for the one hundred and fifty psalms. These were designed for singing, with music written by Claude Gondiure. Sir Philip Sidney's psalms are equally various: "Each of the Psalms is cast in a different stanza" (Ringler, p. 501) with no repetitions. Only two of the forty-three appear in other poems by Sidney, and Ringler assumes that Sidney's model was Beza's: "the Psalms were either versified from English prose or translated from French metrical versions" (p. 500). Sidney, like Milton, had commented on the importance of the Psalms in his daily life, and their efforts have much in common.

An appreciation of Milton's effort depends in part on observing some of the versions available to him in his own work. We can see from an act of comparison the extent to which Milton was willing to move from traditional phrasing and from absolute literalness in his effort to make his metaphrases full and expressive. Below are a number of important translations of Psalm i. We can presume that Milton saw all or most of them, since none was obscure in 1653.

Henry Ainsworth's prose version of Psalm i begins with a brief but typical analysis in two parts, a common pattern of the logically trained commentator and one that, as we will see, affected numerous translators:

1. The happiness of the godly whose conversation is described, & their prosperity, like a fruitfull tree.
4. The contrary course of the wicked, for which they and their way doe perish.

   Blessed *is* the man, that does not walk, in the counsel of the wicked; nor stand in the way of synners: nor sit, in the seat of the scornful. But, *hath* his delight, in the law of Iehovah: and in his law doth he meditate, day and night. And he shalbe, as a tree, planted by brooks of water; which shal give his fruit, in his time; and his leaf shal not fade: and whatsoever he shal doe, shal prosper. Not so the wicked: but as the chaff, which the wind driveth away. Therefore, the wicked shal not stand-up, in the judgement: and synners, in the assembly of the just. For Iehovah knoweth, the way of the just: and the way of the wicked shal perish.

Ainsworth's commentaries on Psalm i are often rudimentary, restating Beza's observations, or rendering the language on the simplest level possible. Occasionally, he cites some of the more significant views of psalmody, such as the allegorical implications of the verse: "Christ is called the *Fountain of the Gardens*, that is, of the churches . . . the godly man is likened to a tree planted by waters, which thrusteth out his roots by the river, and feeleth not when the heat commeth, and careth not for the year of drought, nor ceaseth from making (or yielding) fruit" (Sig. A3v). Calvin's commentary includes mention of the artistic choices of the psalmist, concerning image and trope, including the allegory. Rathmell regards such concerns as important for the artistic choices of the translator, citing a number of the countess of Pembroke's metrical choices as being inspired by the commentary (pp. xvii–xx).

Golding's translation of Calvin follows:

1. Blessed is the man that walketh not in the Counsell of the vngodly, and standeth not in the way of the wicked, and sitteth not in the seat of the skorners:
2. But delighteth in the law of the Lord, and occupieth himselfe in his law day and night
3. And he shalbe like a tree planted by the riuers syde, which shall yelde his frute in dew season, and whose leafe shall neuer fall awaye: and what soeuer he doeth it shall prosper.
4. So are not the vngodly, but as the chaffe which the wynde scattereth.
5. Therefore shall not the vngodly stand in the iudgement, nor the wicked in the congregation of the rightuouse.
6. For the Lord knoweth the waye of the rightuouse, and the waye of the vngodly shall perishe.

Richard Bernard's translation is of particular interest because it professes to involve a logical analysis of the Psalms, something which had been done earlier by William Temple. The analyses are typically dichotomous and Ramistic, including in Bernard's case a Ramist chart. His version of the psalm is:

1. Blessed is the man that walketh not in the counsell of the vngodly: nor standeth in the way of the sinners, nor sitteth in the seate of the scornfull,
2. But his delight is in the law of the Lord. And in his law doth he meditate day and night.
3. For hee shall be like a tree, planted by the riuers of waters, that bringeth forth his fruit in due season, whose leafe shall not fade, and whatsoeuer he doth shall prosper.
4. The wicked are not so, but as chaffe which the winde driueth away.
5. Therefore the wicked shall not stand in iudgement, nor sinners in the assemblie of the righteous.
6. For the Lord knoweth the way of the righteous: And the way of the wicked shall perish.

Bernard's chart, as shown in figure 1, offers a schematic analysis.

William Temple, the Ramist controversialist, earlier analyzed some twenty psalms, although without benefit of charts. Temple was secre-

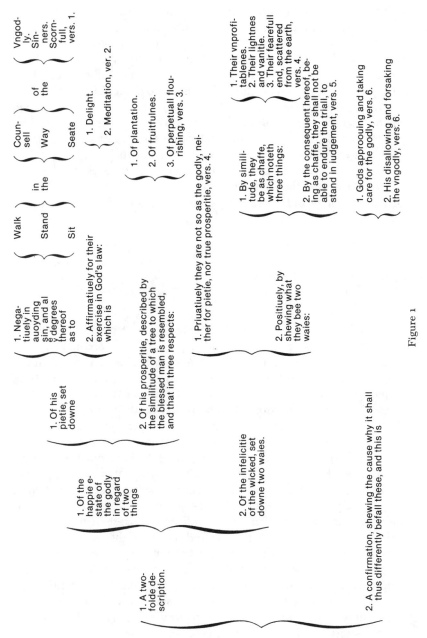

Figure 1

tary to Sir Philip Sidney and is reputed to have held him in his arms as he died. Later, in 1594, he joined the household of Robert Devereaux, then after considerable struggle capped his career by becoming provost of Trinity College, Dublin, in 1609. He assumed that "there is no subject of what nature soever, falling within the reach of naturall reason, which by Logike the express image thereof cannot be disputed" (fol. 3). His approach was to treat the Psalms as disputations, finding the issues disputed and the arguments by which they were resolved. His method depends upon the use of disjunct and conjunct syllogisms (compound syllogisms of the sort explicitly devalued by Aristotle and promoted by Ramus).

Temple asserts that "The question disputed by the Prophet in this Psalme is this: That the Godlie man onelie is blessed." He begins his discussion of the logic of the psalm by establishing the core of its argument in a conjunct syllogism:

> If the godly man only be blessed, then in case we desire to be
>   blessed, we ought to betake our selues to a course of pietie.
> But the godly man only is blessed.
> Therefore in case we desire to be blessed, we ought to betake
>   our selues to a course of pietie.   (p. 2)

Temple's analysis is detailed, establishing that the "*Proposition* is omitted, as a knowne and cleare description of a blessed man"; "The *Assumption* is vers. 3. in the end"; "the CONCLUSION is vers. 1. and 2. Of the said *Assumption* the Prophet yeeldeth vs an illustration, first from comparisons: and then from the efficient cause of the said prosperous successe. Of the comparisons the one is Similitude or a comparison of things like; the other a Dissimilitude or a comparison of things vnlike betwixt themselues" (p. 4.). The similitude is the comparison of the godly man with the tree planted by the waters; the dissimilitude is the condition of the wicked man contrasted with the condition of the godly man.

Temple's analysis, along with Bernard's, stresses the twofold character of the psalm. It reveals the condition of the godly as well as the condition of the wicked. The use of simile and contrast is further heightened by their analysis, with the twofold nature of the psalm clearly established. Neither Temple's nor Bernard's translation stylistically emphasizes the dichotomous nature of the psalm. However, both Milton's and Sidney's reveal the dichotomous nature of the psalm in several ways. First, both use a couplet form. Sidney's version is in three stanzas; the first establishes the condition of the blessed man, while the next two present us with the similitude and the dissimilitude: each segment of the psalm is given the equal attention of six lines. Milton's version offers six lines to establishing the condition of the blessed man, four for the simili-

tude, and four for the dissimilitude, with two lines for the efficient cause
of the blessed man's condition.

First Sidney's version:

> Hee blessed is who neither loosely treades
> The strayinge steppes, as wicked counsell leades
> Ne for bad mates in waie of Sinninge waiteth,
> Nor yett himself with idle Scorners seateth
> But on Gods lawe his hartes delight doth binde
> Which night and daie hee calls to marking minde.
>
> Hee shalbe like a freshly planted tree
> to which sweete Springes of waters Neighbours bee
> Whose braunches faile not timely fruit to nourish
> Nor withered leafe shall make it faile to flourish.
> So all the thinges wherto that man doth bend
> Shall prosper still with well-succeeding end.
>
> Not soe the wicked; But like chaff with wind
> Scatt'red, shall neither stay in Judgment find
> Nor with the just, been in their meetings placed:
> For good mens waies by God are knowne and graced.
> Butt who from Justice sinnfully doe stray,
> The way they goe, shall be their ruins way.[6]

Then Milton's version:

> Bless'd is the man who hath not walked astray
> In counsel of the wicked, and i'the way
> Of sinners hath not stood, and in the seat
> Of scorners hat not sat. But in the great
> Jehovah's law is ever his delight,
> And in his law he studies day and night.
> He shall be as a tree which planted grows
> By wat'ry streams, and in his season knows
> To yield his fruit, and his leaf shall not fall,
> And what he takes in hand shall prosper all.
> Not so the wicked, but as chaff which fanned
> The wind drives, so the wicked shall not stand
> In judgment, or abide their trial then,
> Nor sinners in the assembly of just men.
> For the Lord knows the upright way of the just,
> And the way of bad men to ruin must.
>
> (Carey and Fowler, p. 402)

The imagery of the psalm, which attracted Ramists because of its
capacity to convince in an argument, is essentially focused on horticul-

tural comparisons. The godly man is a tree planted on fertile land; therefore he gives forth his fruit and suffers no withering, a term chosen by many of the translators. Milton's choice of "fall," which agrees with Sternhold and Hopkins (1549) suggests the perfection of the godly man who remains upright and suffers no sin. The author of *Paradise Lost* may have signaled himself in lines nine and ten, linking a tree — the positive image of God's benison — with the idea of the fall; and the further imagery of "what he takes in hand" suggests the powerful hand imagery of *Paradise Lost*, especially that of Book IX.

Sternhold and Hopkins add a great deal to the psalm in order to satisfy their metrical needs, and their use of similar terms does not produce the same results that Milton achieves. Their lines are: "Whose leafe shall never fade nor fall, / but flourish still and stand: / Even so all things shall prosper well / that this man takes in hand." Naturally, our sensitivity to similar imagery in *Paradise Lost* makes us respond more immediately to it in the Psalm, but it is also true that Milton puts it to deeper and better use by compressing it. Other translators go to quite different lengths to make the psalmist's point. Francis Bacon's lines are: "Whose leaves continue always green, / And are no prey to winter's pow'r," and he makes no mention of taking action in hand. George Wither's lines are: "And his leaf shall never perish: / Ev'rie thing shall prosper to, / Which he undertakes to do." George Sandys's lines read: "His leaf shall never fall; the Lord shall bless / All his endeavours with desir'd success."

None of these translations has Milton's emphasis on imagery; in comparison, Milton is much more concrete and explicit (although one of Baldwin's early complaints was that Milton was continually too abstract in the Psalms). The temptation to link this psalm with the meeting of the Nominated Parliament hinges on the emphasis on "counsel" and the "assembly of just men." Ainsworth and Bacon refer to "the assembly of the just," while most of the translators refer to "the congregation of the rightuouse" (Calvin), or the "assembly of the righteous" (Bernard and Temple). Bacon has the interesting distinction of rhyming "just" with "must," although to quite different effect than Milton. Bacon's lines concerning the wicked man separated like chaff are: "And when he shall in judgment plead, / A casting sentence bide he must: / So shall he not lift up his head / In the assembly of the just." Milton repeats the word "just" much as other translators repeat "righteous." The connection with a new parliament may be alluded to in that choice, since the question of government and justice must be first. Justice is like a fruit of a proper plantation, and the curious rhyme of the final word, "must," may hide a horticultural reference. Coming as it does, it bears a certain ambiguity;

it has nothing to complete it, and thus seems almost a nominative rather than a verb. The echo of reference to crushed grape may be implied here, or, even more intriguing, it may be a reference to crushed apple used for apple cider in Hertfordshire in the seventeenth century.[7]

In comparison with Sidney's version, Milton's seems to have an urgency. To be sure, there is little urgency in other translations, but Sidney's is especially notable for its graceful periodicity and indirectness. Its language has a longeur and poise, a rhythmic swing that seems almost to elide accented words or terms. By contrast, Milton stresses, in the manner of Calvin, the key terms in the early verses: "walk," "stand," "sit," and "counsel," "way," and "seate" — taken from Bernard's Ramist chart. In that chart, such key elements are clearly highlighted. Milton's verbs — "walked," "stood," and "sat" — balance with his nouns — "counsel," "way," and "seat," — all in his first four lines. Each is stressed, and two nouns are rhyme words, while one verb ends a sentence. The polysyndeton of these lines echoes Calvin. Golding's translation stresses the parallelled "walketh not," "standeth not," and "sitteth not," whereas Milton's softening of the parallelism shifts emphasis from the verbs to the substantives.

Milton's rhyming of "delight" and "night" helps reinforce the joy with which the godly man contemplates religion, while his phrasing seems, to us at least, revealing of the poet of "Il Penseroso": "Jehovah's law is ever his delight, / And in his law he studies day and night." The stress on delight and the Miltonic form of meditation — study — is consonant with the affirmative exercise of God's law as revealed in Bernard's chart. Bernard's emphases on "plantation," "fruitfulnes," and "perpetuall flourishing" are all apparent in Milton's version, as they are in his own translation. Milton introduces a pleonasm, a favorite trope, in "but as chaff which fanned / The wind drives," since "fanned" is a synonym for winnowed — a separation of corn by the wind. Milton brings a subtle intensity to the concept of the separation of the good from the bad, the blessed from the sinners. This may link with the Nominated Parliament, which brought back a good number of the former Rump members, who, in a sense, had been twice winnowed.

Bernard follows the majority of translators in his line, "Therefore the wicked shall not stand in iudgement." Most versions, including Sidney's which substitutes "stay" for "stand," follow this phrasing. However, Milton amplifies it with a phrasing suggested in Bernard's Ramist chart: "being as chaffe, they shall not be able to endure the triall, to stand in iudgement." Milton adds "abide their trial then," emphasizing the extent to which the concept of humans as suffering appropriate trial was part of his world view.[8] Trial may appear particularly appropriate to

Samson Agonistes, of course; but, then, so are many of the concerns Milton addresses in the Psalms.

Milton's version of Psalm i further clarifies the logical implications or structure uncovered by Bernard, whose division of the psalm into two parts includes a description, the primary part of the psalm, and a "confirmation, shewing the cause," which is, in a sense, a kind of summation. Milton's final couplet neatly captures that structure; the first line implies the approval of the just (Bernard has "godly"), while the second implies the disapproval of "bad men." In this couplet lies the core of the psalm, since it is the knowledge of God that causes both approval and disapproval; the previous description is, then, a consequent of this proposition.

The extent to which Milton, as author of the *Art of Logic,* would be influenced by the logical commentaries and analyses of the Psalms is difficult to conjecture. However, as a logician versed in Ramist and Aristotelian procedure, Milton was in a position to be especially sensitive to such analyses and to qualify their value for the translator. His translation of Psalm i is distinctive for its introducing certain characteristically Miltonic features while relating positively to the logical analyses of Bernard and Temple.

While it is not my purpose here to discuss all Milton's metaphrases of 1653, I would like to point to some aspects of Psalm ii, which is analyzed by Temple and Bernard, who both emphasize its typology: "This Psalme contains an exhortation to all estates and degrees of men both Prince and people, to forbeare plotting and attempting against the kingdome of Christ, and consequently to doe worship and homage vnto him. For what *David* speaks here of himselfe, wee must take it spoken of him as he is a type and figure of Christ" (Temple, p. 7). Bernard's chart dichotomizes the psalm into "A two-folde narration" and "An exhortatory conclusion." The first part of the narration is "Of the attempts of the wicked against $\overset{e}{y}$ kingdome of Dauid, as the type, and of Christ as the antitype, set downe" (p. 48). Temple's translation goes so far as to substitute "Christ" for "Anointed," as it appears in the authorized version.

Milton does not go so far, although his terzetti rhymes may imply a trinitarian view, and for "Anointed" he chooses "Messiah dear." The divisions of the psalm respect the analysis of Bernard in that the first part of the psalm treats the narration of the rebels, to line seven, and the reaction of God to line twenty-one. As Bernard establishes the two-fold nature of God's maintaining David, he reveals God's power and mercy. Each of these has three, rather than two, parts: power, where

God "1. Scorneth their attempts, as not able to doe harme"; 2. Confound-eth them in his displeasure; 3. Annointeth his king and setteth him ouer Sion." Then there is mercy, in that God manifests "his decree, as if this might moue the [m] to obey, and that 1. Concerning the person of this King; 2. Concerning his kingdome and the amplitude thereof; Concern-ing the power and effects of it against such rebellious ones" (p. 48).

The remaining seven lines contain the exhortation, "And now be wise at length ye kings averse," following Bernard's three-part division to have wisdom to obey, to worship God, and to follow his king, as well as ending with Bernard's two-part division of the "Reasons to moue here-unto": God's displeasure "If once his wrath take fire like fuel sere," and the promise of happiness: "Happy all those who having in him their stay."

The authorized version is relatively similar in structure to the demands of Bernard, but that is to be expected because Bernard's and the authorized versions are closer to the original text than Milton's. The demands of Milton's stanza and rhyme are such that he must use more words than the authorized version (238 to 204 words). Temple's trans-lation is 194 words; Sidney's is 244. Milton's maintains the clear divisions of the psalm despite the needs of his form.

Milton's David is Oliver Cromwell. His opening with the term, "Gen-tiles," seems a reminder of the Puritan conception of England as Israel and the saints as the chosen people. If so, then the emphasis on military might, borrowing Sidney's "With Iron Scepter bruise," reminds England of threats from overseas, and acts as an encouragement to support his leadership. Because of the failure of Parliament to end its wrangling, Cromwell was forced to accept a leadership position virtually equiva-lent to that of the king before him. Milton could not have translated this psalm without being aware of its fittingness for the current situation.

Milton's translation of Psalm i reveals the habit of mind of the logi-cal analyst, while reflecting the anxieties and concerns of present poli-tics. Each of the Psalms can be made relevant to the current situation of Milton's England, which is why their political meanings have seemed to supply a motive for their translation. However, the fact that they are powerful arguments for adopting behavior has been much less appreci-ated. Milton's responsiveness to the Ramistic analyses of the structure of the Psalms demonstrates his awareness of the tradition of analysis rep-resented by Temple and Bernard. The logicians knew the Psalms were tightly reasoned arguments and were, therefore, powerful rhetorical weapons of Christianity. Milton knew it as well.

University of Connecticut

NOTES

1. The *Variorum* provides us with a useful overview of criticism up to 1971 (A.S.P. Woodhouse and Douglas Bush, eds., *A Variorum Commentary on the Poems of John Milton*, gen. ed. Merritt Y. Hughes [New York, 1972] vol. II, pt. III, pp. 991–1006). Carolyn P. Collette's "Milton's Translations: Petition and Praise," *ELR* II, (1972), 243–59, continues Margaret Boddy's work in "Milton's Translation of Psalms 80–88," *MP LXIV* (1966), 1–9, emphasizing a connection with Milton's "state of mind, the political events of the time, and, most important, the particular psalms he translated" (p. 248). She sees "Milton working within the context of his time, translating the psalms as private petitions or songs of praise" (p. 259). Mary Ann Radzinowicz in *Toward Samson Agonistes* (Princeton, 1978) accepts that Milton's 1648 translations derived from the Westminster Assembly's call for a new psalter. Discussing Psalm i, she points out a three part structure: "a conception of the ethically good man, given analytically or discursively in Milton's first six lines (verses 1 and 2 of the original Psalm), imagistically in his next five lines (verse 3), and dialectically by contrasts in his last six lines (verses 4–6)" (p. 202). The Psalms "were always fresh and interesting to Milton"; "the psalms as a sequence were crucial to his art" (p. 207) because of their ethical universality and because they teach with such delight.

2. Radzinowicz, *Toward Samson Agonistes*, pp. 200–01, summarizes the main views.

3. See the OED for "Metaphrasis." Dwalphintramis (John Bernard), *The Anatomy of the Service-book* (London, 1640), p. 30, says, "Now we come to the touch of *additions*, as the book adds three whole verses to the 14 *Psalme*, where a great difference is to be thought on, betweene a *Paraphraster* and a *Translater*. The former may amplifie; but yet in a *different letter* from the text; but the *Translater* may not adde, no not from other Texts of Scripture."

4. C. H. Firth and R. S. Rait, *Acts and Ordinances of the Interregnum*. (London, 1911), vol. I, p. 607.

5. I say this assuming, as Radzinowicz, *Toward Samson Agonistes, passim*, Boddy, *Milton's Translations*, pp. 1–9, and William B. Hunter, "The Sources of Milton's Prosody," *PQ XXVIII* (1949, pp. 125–44) do, that Milton intended to translate a segment of the Psalter for the Westminster Assembly.

6. J.C.A. Rathmell, *The Psalms of Sir Philip Sidney and the Countess of Pembroke* (Garden City, 1963), p. 3, prints from the Penshurst manuscript; William A. Ringler, Jr.'s version, *The Poems of Sir Philip Sidney*, pp. 270–71, based on the Woodford manuscript, is quite different.

7. See the OED, "Must," sb. 3.

8. The question of trial is raised in John Calvin's commentary on Psalm i, *The Psalmse of David and others with M. Iohn Calvins Commentaries*, trans. Arthur Golding (London, 1570), sig. 2v, "We see now how the Prophete auoucheth the vngodlye to be miserable, bycause happynesse is one of the inwarde goodes of the conscience. He denieth not but that before they be driuen to the tryal, al things go well with them: but he denieth them to be happye, onlesse they be founded upon sustantial and stedfast pureness. For by the tryall of the good, appeareth their true purenesse in the end."

PSALMS AND THE REPRESENTATION OF DEATH IN *PARADISE LOST*

Mary Ann Radzinowicz

DISCUSSING AN idea of death that he considers reasonable but heterodox and a matter of opinion not faith, Milton gathers together in *De doctrina Christiana* proof texts from eighteen psalms.[1] He makes out of that cluster of psalms a drama representing the process by which death comes to be understood in *Paradise Lost*, beginning with Semitic myth treated allegorically and ending with a demythologized rationality that the great metaphysical poets of death in his own century would have thought thoroughly unimpressive. Book I of the epic may be taken to show the whole course of the representation in little; the remaining eleven books then richly recapitulate that process. At every stage some of the eighteen death psalms supply idea, imagery, structure, and energy to the poet. With the possible exception of the Book of Job and Adam's death wish, no other part of the Bible could do or does do more for Milton as the poet of death. In particular, the personification allegories of the birth of Sin and Death and of their bridge to earth draw on Psalms xlix and lxxxix; the Father's version of their arrival on earth then displaces those personification allegories by a typology of death through Psalm xxii.

Milton opens Book I of *Paradise Lost* attributing to death an empire throughout all time and space; he closes it confining death's reign of terror to the kingdom of man's mind. At first the horror fills history, from "Mans first Disobedience" "till one greater Man / Restore us," and darkens "the world" with "all our woe." But both time and death are soon seen to pertain only to man and his way of thought. Fallen angels neither die nor fear death. Were they susceptible to dread of death, however, they would subject that irrational mood to the control of art, just as men may and often do. So the battalion of the fallen pass before their mighty chief:

> In perfect *Phalanx* to the *Dorian* mood
> Of Flutes and soft Recorders; such as rais'd
> To highth of noblest temper Hero's old
> Arming to Battel, and in stead of rage

Deliberate valour breath'd, firm and unmov'd
With dread of death to flight or foul retreat,
Nor wanting power to mitigate and swage
With solemn touches, troubl'd thoughts, and chase
Anguish and doubt and fear and sorrow and pain
From mortal or immortal minds. (I, 550–55)

Hence to "jocund Music," such as "some Belated Peasant" hears or dreams he hears, the angels reduce themselves and enter Pandaemonium, immortal in fact and in feeling. In Book I, Milton thus synechdochically rationalizes death — death, the very impetus in the creation of art — by the power of art. That control shown in Book I is the pattern Milton develops in the remainder of the poem.

Throughout his epic, Milton will show that death consumes the entire human being, body, mind, and soul; that death as the punishment of sin is transferred from mankind to his whole world of nature but that the knowledge of death is limited to human beings in their rationality; and that to understand death deprives it of power, on the physical level reducing it to a sleep, on the metaphysical converting it first to an instrumental good and then to a nullity. Death is shown encyclopedically in *Paradise Lost* as a physical and mental event. Milton represents it formally first by allegory, and then by history and typology. Death affords to rational men an intellectual test; when it is properly understood the patience of heroic martyrdom becomes possible. The synonymity of *human* and *mortal* is explored across the poem; that is, until a strictly human understanding arises about the uses of death. And throughout the whole course of the exploration, Milton calls upon the Psalter for figures and for themes.

Only human beings die in *Paradise Lost*. The decease of other created beings occurs everywhere but that cessation is never generalized by the use of the word "death." In Book X, for example, every order of creation from high to low meets destruction — from the "blasted Starrs" that "lookt wan" and the "Planets, Planet-strook" that "real Eclips / Then sufferd" down to the "graceful locks" of "fair spreading Trees" seen "shattering." They surrender to the inimical climate of man's doom; trees are blasted, boughs and vines lopped, beasts devour each other, but no creature save the human meets "death," "dies," or is found "dead." Those words are used only when a rational being on the scene registers his awareness of the moral and psychological significance of death as the punishment for man's sin.[2] Since death is an ethical state, the fate of subhuman creatures is not normally described as death. Milton actually writes that Sin and Death attack such creatures not to make them die but "to destroy, or *unimmortal* make / All kinds" (X, 611–12, my emphasis).

When death does come to the animal kingdom, Milton significantly amends the demography of his allegorical family of Sin and Death, introducing for the one and only time in the poem a female sibling for Death, a sister Discord, to give an ethical account of subhuman annihilation. And even then Adam is present to see and register ethical death, though not be seen:

> Discord first
> Daughter of Sin, among th' irrational,
> Death introduc'd, through fierce antipathie:
> Beast now with Beast gan war, & Fowle with Fowle,
> And Fish with Fish; to graze the Herb all leaving,
> Devourd each other; nor stood much in awe
> Of Man, but fled him, or with count'nance grim
> Glar'd on him passing: these were from without
> The growing miseries, which *Adam* saw
> Alreadie in part, though hid in gloomiest shade.   (X, 707–17)

The drama of death presented synechdochically in Book I is played across the remaining books of *Paradise Lost*. In Book II the universe of hell is drawn as a locale of spiritual nullity where Death lives personified. In Book III the Father and Son confirm the justice of death as a punishment for sin and then devise the mercy of death as a release from that punishment. In Book IV Adam and Eve ponder its meaning and vow the obedience that would prevent it. Its pointed absence in Books V and VI, when angels go to war, prepares for Raphael's instruction in Books VII and VIII that for disobedient humanity death is certain. In Book IX Satan lies about death and Adam and Eve experiment with it. In Book X Death himself steps in brief triumph onto earth before God predicts Death's death. In Book XI the Son pronounces the judgment of death on the human pair which His own death will cure; and in that book and the last Michael displays it, lectures on it, mentalizes it, moralizes it, and in the history of the Son expounds its final meaning. The lesson of death is a lesson of patience and temperance, contained within the large paideutic journey of Adam and Eve, developed like other lessons in the poem, in a pattern of increasing illumination and reasonableness.

In *De doctrina*, Milton argues his logic of death from scripture; psalms buttress each stage. Once that pool of reference has been established it is to be expected that he will use the same psalm material for the epic representation of death, and so he does. His study has given him a vocabulary of psalmic motifs, images, and concepts and a drama of psalmic growth in understanding. Both are so instinctive to Milton that the point of contact between the Psalms and the poem is not the verbal echo of a psalm formula, but rather the energy of the whole psalmic enterprise in the eighteen psalms taken together. Direct psalm references are copiously present in the epic. Milton clearly thought such density of reference valuable in itself. It has authorized a good deal of footnoting and more is possible. About the hellish universe of death, for example, it would be easy to show that the features Milton presents in Book II — its remoteness and distance from the land of the living; its dust, aridity, and darkness; the pestilence and unnatural corruption; the joylessness and silence of the region — all come from psalm proof texts Milton cited in the tractate to characterize stages of death.[3] But psalm copiousness is less interesting than the successive roles played by psalms in the "long days dying" of the poem. That progression shows two distinctive views of death, the first allegorical, the second literal. First the allegorical is presented from psalms; then the literal "single sense" of scripture, "a combination of the historical and the typological"[4] replaces it from psalms.

Two psalms in Milton's cluster personify death and scripturally authorize the allegory of Sin and Death in *Paradise Lost*. Metaphors of place — death as the pit from which a man does not return — are the most frequent resort of the psalmists in explaining death.[5] But they also define death as changed consciousness — sleep, amnesia, or oblivion[6] — and represent it as the decease resulting from divine or human violence — what God does through the instruments of fire, sword, plague, rod, and the like to those who displease or dishonor him, or what men do, God not preventing.[7] But only Psalms xlix and lxxxix personify death to draw attention in particular to its greedy mouth and rapacious hand.[8] The personification recollects an earlier Semitic religion of a dying god; for example, the Canaanite mythic struggle between Baal and Mot (Death), Baal's defeat, his resurrection, and his victory over Mot. That concept is unthinkable in Jewish faith where God is the "living God," not the god once dead and now alive again but precisely the being who cannot die. As Habakkuk puts it, "Art thou not from everlasting, O Lord my God, mine Holy One?" Hence the biblical personification of death is exceedingly rare, for to personify death is to recall the paganism of the dying god of vegetation. When it does occur, it ironizes that infidel concept. When Jeremiah, for example, denounces death to Jerusalem for reverting to the Canaanitish Baal worship, he appropriately does so by personifying death. "Because they have . . . walked after the imagination of their own heart, / And after Baalim, which their fathers taught them"(Jer. ix, 14), they will be destroyed by the death they and all Baal-worshippers idolatrously imagine. The Lord instructs mourning women how to lament that personified death. They are to sing (Jer. ix, 21–22): "For death is come up into our windows, / And is entered into our palaces, / To cut off the children from without, / And the young men from the streets."

The triumph of the Yahwist concept of the eternal God forbids the worshipper to represent unironically the eternal division of the universe between God and another being, Death, with whom he must at first unsuccessfully struggle though he may in the end enjoy an annual or even a final resurrection. But if to personify Death as God's enemy in the Old Testament is associated with unthinkable idolatries, not to envisage Death as God's enemy would create a problem in the New Testament period. Unless Death came into the world hostile to God, will not some consider that God made him? Hence some New Testament teachers devise obliquely allegorical parables of a crypto-Manichean bent. Of them, Milton particularly draws on James i, 13–15:

Let no man say when he is tempted, I am tempted of God: for God cannot be tempted with evil, neither tempteth he any man: But every man is tempted, when he is drawn away of his own lust, and enticed. Then when lust hath conceived, it bringeth forth sin; and sin, when it is finished, bringeth forth death.

James gives Milton an outline allegory of Sin. The allegory exonerates God by implicating his creature, responsible for death through an immortal act of mental evil. Milton fills James's sequence with content partly classical and partly biblical.

His classical sources allow Milton to represent in Satan's meeting with Sin and Death the epic hero's encounter with the guardians of the underworld and to ironize Satan's heroism as anti-heroic (evil) and unheroic (bathetic). Satan's grandeur is undermined when he learns from Sin how she and her son Death came to be assigned the guardianship of Hell's gates. He needs to hear her narrative, for he has somehow forgotten a vital part of his heavenly life: that he conceived and bore a daughter, Sin, in circumstances parallel to the myth of Athena springing full-formed from the head of Zeus. (That myth was interpreted by theologians as an allegory of the Father's generation of the Son; Milton treats the triad of Satan, Sin, and Death as an infernal parody of the Trinity.) She seduced her father Satan and bore a son Death who raped her, his mother. From that assault she continually bears a pack of dogs, who rekennel in her womb to eat her bowels, set on by the son; in bearing him, she was deformed. The story is news to Satan who has not only forgotten his only "love" but rejects and detests her and their child on sight. But he sees how Death can be turned against mankind, "the race of upstart creatures." His revulsion, concealment of it, and prudent rewooing of Sin so that she will unlock Hell's gate complete part one of the allegory.

The birth of Sin and Death allegorizes not only the force that "un-immortalizes" creation but also the dynamic that deforms the archetypal family. The relationship of the triad is not only a parody of the Trinity, as both Satan and Sin lusciously indicate in appropriating God's language to describe their own transactions — "Thyself in me thy perfect image viewing," "To reign / At thy right hand voluptuous"; it also contains every possible familial perversion. The attachments are all appetitive; the appetites are satisfied without pleasure; the sexuality is contaminated in every generation and bond. Satan unconsciously fathers Sin in consciously rebelling against his Father; his fatherhood is without love and his daughter without a mother — so much exclusive maleness counting for sterility, not potency. He is seduced into incest but his sexual feelings move through indifference to lust to repression to nausea and will never rise to more than voyeuristic envy. His daughter loathes and fears their son for he has raped her in hatred, would cannibalize her if it were safe, and intends parricide. Finally, her children-grandchildren are vicious dogs eating her entrails. The denunciation of "Death" on Adam and Eve prophesies the poisoning of the heart of human society.

Milton concludes the allegorical presentation of Sin and Death with the building of the bridge from Hell to Earth, a scene he gives from two perspectives. In the first, Sin, Death, and Satan proclaim the building of the bridge heroic work, "a Monument / Of merit high to all th'infernal Hosts." The celebration of a great architectural achievement is a conventional ingredient of epic; but the narrator shows that what Death builds with his "mace petrific" is a good deal less epic than what God created in building the universe. Theirs by a "wondrous art / Pontifical" is a "new wondrous Pontifice," both the tautology and the anticlerical pun fixing the triumph far below that by which chaos was divinely ordered, and not simply as here demonically over-built. Satan hails his family, by merit called the "Race of Satan," and returns to Hell to exult, "What remaines, ye Gods, / But up and enter now into full bliss," while Sin and Death commence to destroy the earth. And then the second perspective is expounded by God himself.

Between the birth allegory and the bridge allegory, Milton silently drops from *Paradise Lost* the hell hounds, the offspring of Death's rape of his mother. They entered the allegory by way of Ovid's Scylla and Spenser's Errour;[9] they leave it by way of God's displacement of Psalms xlix and lxxxix by Psalm xxii. Milton's hell hounds do not come with their parents to fallen Paradise; they were not separately real enough to Milton or to the reader to make the trip. Nonetheless they are present in name if not in fact, and so present because the poet draws an inspired confirmation for his allegorical fiction of death from within the psalm cluster we are examining. For Milton to render his ideas of death fully intelligible is not only to make them concrete in compelling allegory, but to argue them by reference to the highest intellectual authority of Holy Writ. As the Father and Son in heaven watch the destruction Sin and Death wreak on Eden, the Father applies to them the metaphor "Hell-hounds," which Milton had used allegorically for their incestuous children back in Book II:

> See with what heat these Dogs of Hell advance
> To waste and havoc yonder World, which I
> So fair and good created,
>
> . . . .
>
> I call'd and drew them thither,
> My *Hell-hounds*, to lick up the draff and filth
> Which mans polluting Sin with taint hath shed
> On what was pure, till cramm'd and gorg'd nigh burst
> With suckt and glutted offal, at one sling
> Of thy victorious Arm, well-pleasing Son,
> Both *Sin*, and *Death*, and yawning *Grave* at last
> Through *Chaos* hurld, obstruct the mouth of Hell
> For ever, and seal up his ravenous Jawes.   (X, 616–36)

Sin and Death remain "real" in God's speech but in it Milton modulates from a simple personification allegory into another mythic mode and commences his typologizing and historicizing of death. A more authoritative voice than Satan's gives a different interpretation of the same story we have just seen through Satan's eyes: Satan did not generate Sin and Death in despite of God any more than he is "self-made and self-begot." His imagined finalities are no more final than his pretended self-initiation was originary.[10] Nothing happens anywhere unbeknownst to or unpermitted by God; but permission is not sanction. By the birth allegory, Milton removes the onus of the creation of Sin and Death from God to the will of His creatures; he does so by this metaphor, redefining them as eschatological instruments. The horror of Sin and Death as allegorical persons is reduced by the new animal metaphor, "dogs of death," rendering them disgusting, followed by the merely material metaphor in which they gag the mouth or plug the door of hell.

The phrase "dogs of death" comes from Psalm xxii, 15–20. Milton refers to that psalm and calls it to the mind of his readers, since in Reformation exegesis Psalm xxii prefigures the Crucifixion, the one expiatory death that by ransoming mankind for immortality deals eternal death to death. The relevant verses read:

> And thou has brought me into the dust of death.
> For dogs have compassed me;
> The assembly of the wicked have inclosed me:
> They pierced my hands and my feet.
> I may tell all my bones:
> They look and stare upon me.
> They part my garments among them,
> And cast lots upon my vesture.
> But be not thou far from me, O Lord;
> O my strength, haste thee to help me.
> Deliver my soul from the sword;
> My darling from the power of the dog.

Milton glosses the psalm as typological in *De doctrina*, in the normal Reformation way. To gloss it literally would be to see in it vestiges of the rejected pagan ritual, commemorating the humiliation and rebirth of the vegetation god who dies but lives again. This god was commemorated by the annual offering of blood sacrifice to be consumed by him in fire. Milton uses that literalistic paganism in the conclusion of his falsely heroic or Luciferian epic in *Paradise Lost*. Milton contrasts Christ's understanding of Psalm xxii, expounded as the prefiguring of his Incarnation and Passion back in Book III, with Satan's experience when he returns to hell to glory at his heroic destruction of mankind. As Satan exults, he is "punisht in the shape he sin'd, / According to his doom." He and his followers are physically changed into serpents; they slither from Pandaemonium into the fields of hell, and there eat bitter ashy fruit. Then Milton tells us how to respond to the serpent epic of false heroism opposed to the true heroism of Christianity.[11] He treats the story of Satan as simply too paganly fictional to finish decisively, let alone interpret. In the end who knows what becomes of Lucifer and the fallen, changed into their ideal shape? Some tell one kind of story about their fate, some tell another. The carnal reading of Psalm xxii would suppose them

> Yearly enjoynd, some say, to undergo
> This annual humbling certain number'd days,
> To dash thir pride, and joy for Man seduc't.   (X, 575–77)

Other pagans, however,

>   tradition they dispers'd
> Among the Heathen of thir purchase got
> And Fabled how the Serpent

>   .   .   .   .

> had first the rule
> Of high Olympus, thence by Saturn driv'n.   (X, 578–83)

Milton demythologizes the allegory of death by establishing God's version of it and by leaving Satan's to end in indeterminacy. Milton then sees the true and psalm-validated version of death's meaning to its conclusion by means of the remaining psalms of his cluster. That we can encompass very briefly. On the one hand, Milton examines all human death; on the other, Christ's salvatory death. In treating the first, man's mortality, Milton draws on the conviction of the Psalter that all men and all *of* men die and yet that God is just and good to man. He shows Adam's education toward an understanding of how those propositions fit together. First Adam fears death and longs to escape from his sense of guilt. Milton uses the Psalms proving total mortality in *De doctrina Christiana* to weave together those two feelings in Adam's long night of self-examination after the judgment. From some of the rhetorical questions of Psalm lxxxviii, for example—"Shall thy wonders be known in the dark? / And thy righteousness in the land of forgetfulness?" and "Lord, why castest thou off my soul? / Why hidest thou thy face from me?"—he derives expressions of both fear and longing—"did I sollicite thee / From darkness to promote me?"; "why delays his hand?"; "no fear of worse / To mee and to my offspring would torment me." From this oscillation between fear and longing, as God explains in preface to his charge to Michael, man is released only by the mercifulness of death:

> I at first with two fair gifts
> Created him endowd, with Happiness
> And Immortalitie: that fondly lost,
> This other serv'd but to eternize woe;
> Till I provided Death; so Death becomes
> His final remedie, and after Life
>   · · · · · · · · ·
> Resignes him up with Heav'n and Earth renewd.   (XI, 57–66)

Psalm civ of the cluster—"Thou takest away their breath, they die / And return to their dust. / Thou sendest forth thy spirit, they are created"—expresses God's secure control as well as any.

In answer to God's charge, Michael teaches Adam an indifference to dying, first by showing him how to distinguish the morbid pathology of distempered death from the ripened mortality of well-tempered death. All of the faces of death are shown him and what he sees is gradually cleansed of the revulsion Milton drew from the psalms of lament in sickness.

Michael's principal lesson, however, nullifies death in treating the Son's voluntary sacrifice of himself as the instument of man's redemption. That lesson Michael teaches through the specifically Protestant concepts of imputation and vicarious satisfaction in language increasingly theological and hence decreasingly psalmic. Nonetheless, in *De doctrina* Milton argued from psalms that the resurrection of the dead was believed before the birth of Jesus. He returns for a brief moment to two of those psalms in Michael's full exposition of the atonement, crowned by Adam's confession of faith. He alludes to Psalms xvi and xvii in the only figurative passage in Michael's whole last lesson:

> so he dies,
> But soon revives, Death over him no power
> Shall long usurp; ere the third dawning light,
> Returne, the Starres of Morn shall see him rise
> Out of his grave, fresh as the dawning light.   (XII, 419–23)

To which may be compared:

> For thou wilt not leave my soul in hell;
> Neither wilt thou suffer thine Holy One to see corruption.
> Thou wilt show me the path of life.   (Psalm xvi, 10–11)

> Hide me under the shadow of thy wings
> . . . from my deadly enemies, who compass me about.
>   .   .   .   .
>   I will behold thy face in righteousness:
> I shall be satisfied, when I awake, with thy likeness.
>   (Psalm xvii, 8–9, 15)

As personification allegory is authorized in Milton by the Psalms, so is its correction into metaphor. While the displacement of allegory into typology is authorized by the New Testament, the moment at which the language of poetry yields to the language of theology in *Paradise Lost* is the last moment in which death is represented psalmically.

Cornell University

NOTES

1. The chapters are XII, "Of the Punishment of Sin"; XIII, "Of the Death which is called the Death of the Body," and XXXIII, "Of Complete Glorification, also of Christ's Second Coming, the Resurrection of the Dead, and the Conflagration of the World." I

shall quote *De doctrina Christiana* from *The Complete Prose Works of John Milton*, 8 vols., ed. Maurice Kelley (New Haven, 1973), vol. VI. I shall quote *Paradise Lost* from *The Works of John Milton*, 15 vols, ed. Frank Allen Patterson (New York, 1931), vol. I, part 1. All references to these volumes will be hereafter cited in the text. All references to the Bible will be to *The Westminster Study Edition of the Holy Bible* (Philadelphia, 1948).

2. What may look like the single exception, the line "Cattel must of Rot and Murren die" (XII, 179), turns out to register the punishment on Pharoah for his sin, visited on his property. Milton's conviction that purification comes through choice and trial and his belief that even death is an experience to be controlled by reason causes him to restrict his use of the word to its ethical bearing.

3. Distance from the land of the living, is shown in Psalms vi, 5; xvi, 10; xxxix, 13; dust, aridity, darkness in Psalms xxii, 15; lxxxviii, 10; civ, 29; pestilence and unnatural corruption in Psalms xlix, 9; lxxviii, 50; lxxxviii, 10; and joylessness and silence in Psalms xciv, 17; cxlvi, 4.

4. YP VI, p. 581.

5. Death as a place characterized by dust, darkness, silence, and solitude is represented in Psalms vi, xvi, xxii, lxxxviii, xciv, cxv, and cxlvi of the Miltonic cluster. For example, Psalm xxii, 15, "Thou hast brought me into the dust of death"; Psalm lxxxviii, 10, "shall thy wonders be known in the dark"; or Psalm xciv, 17, "Unless the Lord had been my help, my soul had almost dwelt in silence."

6. See Psalms xvii, 14, "I shall be satisfied when I awake with thy likeness," and xxxix, 13, "O spare me, that I may recover strength before I go hence, and be no more," for example, in the cluster of *De doctrina Christiana* Psalms concerning death.

7. See Psalms ii, xxxi, lxxviii, and xciv. For example, Psalm lxxviii, 94 "He spared not their soul from death, but gave their life over to the pestilence."

8. Psalm xlix, 14, in the Authorized Version reads "Man abideth not: he is like the beasts that perish. Like sheep they are laid in the grave; Death shall feed on them"; in the Coverdale version it reads, "They lie in the grave like sheep; death is their shepherd." Psalm lxxxix, 48 in the Authorized Version reads "What man is he that liveth, and shall not see death? / Shall he deliver his soul from the hand of the grave?" In the Coverdale version it reads, more evasively, "What man is he that liveth and shall not see death? and shall he deliver his soul from the power of the grave?" Milton's translation of Psalm lxxxviii — for our purposes it is a pity he did not translate Psalm lxxxix, of course — shows a general responsiveness to the possibilities of personifying death:

> Wilt thou do wonders on the dead,
>   Shall the deceas'd arise
> And praise thee from their loathsom bed
>   With pale and hollow eyes?
> Shall they thy loving kindness tell
>   On whom the grave *hath hold*
> Or they who in perdition dwell
>   Thy faithfulness unfold?

9. We have already suggested that Milton's dedication to consistent Spenserian allegory is weak in noting the surprising appearance of Death's younger sister, Discord. As we did not note, however, Milton had already written an allegorical entity named Discord into the poem in Book II, line 967, where she accompanied other noisy personifications around the throne of Chaos and Night, her apparent parents. She had there only one significant at-

tribute, her noisiness — such great noisiness that Milton made her an icon difficult to imagine concretely — she has "a thousand various mouths." When he needed an Ate figure, however, to account for a rising viciousness in animals that cause them to turn against each other and experience death as well as unimmortality, Milton either forgot or didn't bother to cancel the previous appearance or give one of the girls another name, Rupture or Fury. The fundamental readjustment, by which allegory is replaced by typology and demystification, however, relies a good deal more on the deletion of the hound-shaped children-grandchildren and their reconstitution as metaphors of the allowed bacteria-eating bacteria than it does on the brief introduction of an extra child.

10. For the likening of Satan's sense of an ending to his sense of a beginning, I am indebted to Maureen Quilligan, *Milton's Spenser: The Politics of Reading* (Ithaca, 1983) pp. 84–91. I do not read Sin's story as she does, however, as a story about the sexual origin of perverse creation in a poem about every sort of creation. Some elements of my analysis similarly draw on the work of John Broadbent, *"Paradise Lost": Books I and II, The Cambridge Milton for Schools and Colleges*, Cambridge, England, 1972, pp. 44–46; Alastair Fowler, *The Poems of John Milton*, London, 1968, 538–48; William Kerrigan, *The Sacred Complex: The Psychogenesis of "Paradise Lost,"* Cambridge, Mass., 1982, pp. 263–98 and Michael Lieb, *Poetics of the Holy: A Reading of "Paradise Lost,"* Chapel Hill, 1981, especially pp. 89–118.

11. Fowler, *The Poems of John Milton,* is right to attribute the introduction of the concept of the opposing satanic epic to Dennis Burden in *The Logical Epic* (London, 1967), p. 950, but could not have known how thoroughly it would become the orthodox reading and remain so even today. See, for example, the particularly interesting discussion in Richard DuRocher, *Milton and Ovid* (Ithaca, 1985), *passim.*

THE LYRIC DIMENSION
OF *PARADISE LOST*

John R. Mulder

SCHOLARS MAY agree to differ about Chaucer, or Spenser, or Shakespeare, but about Milton they differ passionately. *Paradise Lost*, in particular, has been, and will continue to be, a battleground in the strife of refutation. The Romantics found the poem riddled with contradictions.[1] Readers in our century have been of three minds on this. To some, the alleged contradictions are merely the inventions of the modern intellect, unwilling to accept the consequences of the principles Milton adopted.[2] Others argue that Milton exposed the ideological contradictions of his time without being aware that he was doing this.[3] A third party is of the opinion that Milton understood the deconstructive possibilities of the arguments in his poem and used apparent contradictions for a purpose.[4] This essay will support the last position, but it intends neither to disprove other readings nor to prove its own. Believing that an authentic interpretation is unattainable, it does no more than recommend a perspective — that of modern liberal theology[5] — for making access to the poem easier for readers in our time. *Paradise Lost* is a classic in the strict sense: a work that most readers now come to know because a syllabus requires that it be read. I should like to facilitate its first reading by tracing in it the curvature of a design that may help the reader to set the poem spatially in the mind and to experience it, not as a dated rationale in defense of the just logic of God's ways, but as the picture of a great poet's tentative and faltering search for certitude.

Most readers have a preconception of Milton — one might call it his public image — before they have come to know him.[6] He has a reputation for didacticism as a poet with a "palpable design" upon his audience: he would have them better than they are. Hence, readers often expect not to find Milton congenial, for the modern aesthetic creed does not favor the didactic tone; rather, it requires that the artist should refine himself out of existence and should *present* rather than *tell*. To readers who have been taught to admire the poem that dramatizes a speaker, Donne, not Milton, is the preferred seventeenth-century poet. Donne is a lover of many postures; each of his poems is a speaking picture that tests the reader's powers of observation, skill in inference, and capacity for empathy. It often happens, therefore, that readers who are unsure of "what Donne really means" do not hesitate over Milton's meaning. Relying on Milton's public image, they are sure that they are listening to an author who is certain of his convictions and who, in *Paradise Lost*, delivers his story by way of illustrative confirmation. They are not inclined to observe in that poem a *persona* in the process of articulating a gradually unfolding experience. To them, the voice of the poem's narrator is the voice of Milton, and they take him immediately at his word; they isolate the principles of his justification of God's ways, and endorse them with parallels from Milton's earlier poems, his pamphlets, and his *Christian Doctrine*.

Neither time nor skill suffices to examine here the complex origin of this approach to Milton, but several reasons may be urged against it. The matching of parts — mixing poetry and prose, early works and late — slights differences in Milton's age and circumstances and in the genres he uses; it assumes that Milton's career declares a consistency of outlook and feeling that is rarely, if ever, found in other writers. Milton is perhaps the least intimate of English poets; he habitually expresses himself indirectly, screened by a masterly adaptation of known genres, models, and rules of decorum. The difficulty of catching the private man behind his rhetorical poses is, however, insufficient warrant for turning him into a marmoreal monolith. "Long choosing, and beginning late" (IX, 26), Milton completed *Paradise Lost* during the years following the Restoration. He was then an aging man, stricken with blindness, exiled from public life, having suffered the loss of cherished aspirations and the defeat of all the causes for which he had fought and for which he suffered persecution and imprisonment. He had buried two wives and a son, and he was dependent for every comfort on his third wife and his daughters. He must have been very different from the young man who, twenty-odd years earlier, had returned from his continental tour to lend his talents to revolutionary causes. The changed circumstances of his later years are one reason for dislodging the marmoreal effigy of a Milton fixed in his certitudes.

The assumption of fixed consistency of principles throughout Milton's oeuvre and its corollary — the method of interpreting *Paradise Lost* by matching parts of it with parts of other works — also risk violating the integrity of the epic. Although there is no known hermeneutical principle that allows us to draw a line between poetry and prose, a great poem invariably illustrates the deliberate and artful play of the strategies of ordinary speech. The meaning of the simplest statement depends on the context of its utterance, but a poem is extraordinarily specific in its context(s) and depends for the possibilities of its meaning on antecedents of diction, arrangement, genre, and theme. *Paradise Lost* involves its readers in an intricate interplay of perspectives. The poet's narrative voice is often prominent: he announces and arranges characters and action, anticipates and postpones the outcome at will, and comments on motives and moral lessons. Much, however, of the poem is dramatic in construction. For nearly two-thirds of this epic, the reader listens, not to the narrator, but to a cast of characters who, although they are of the narrator's making, diffuse the narrative point of view so that the reader must, as in drama, judge by inferences from the relations between the conduct, speech, and situation of the characters. (Milton's use of a dramatic mode of presentation has led some of his best readers to remark on the discrepancy between the characters and events so presented and the narrator's comment on them.) *Paradise Lost* forces us to approach its most crucial issues through circles of design. When, in Book VIII, the poem takes up the question of the origin and role of gender, sex, and love, we listen at one point to a dramatic exchange between God and Adam that Adam introduces as part of his exchange with Raphael, which in turn forms part of the narrator's address to his readers. We must, similarly, catch the reasons for Lucifer's rebellion at three removes: the poet reports to us Raphael's report to Adam of Lucifer's report to his cohorts. Milton's reputation for directness is surprising in view of his indirection in framing the narrative perspective. Indirection is also a feature of his style. He complicates his diction with ambiguities and his sentence structure with amphibologies. A poem that so entangles its readers leaves us with choices — choice is, after all, the subject and center of *Paradise Lost*. Moreover, the recent reformation in literary theory undermines the authority of received interpretation by its stress on the indeterminacy of texts and thus, like the Reformation of the sixteenth century, prompts new conjectures.[7] The sketch of *Paradise Lost* that follows is therefore admittedly and inevitably sectarian. The motive that prompts it is to show that *Paradise Lost* need not be read as the *product* of Miltonic certitude; one may also experience the poem as a *process* of surrendering to the absence of human certainties.

Focusing on the prologues to Books I, III, VII, and IX, this essay traces in *Paradise Lost* a double pattern of affirmation and denial and renders the action of the poem as the recantation of an overweening aspiration through the reenactment of that aspiration. This recantation through reenactment may be seen as Milton's simultaneous avowal and disavowal of his character, his aims, and his achievements.[8] The visual analogue of this baroque design is the spiraling column, the thrust of which also combines a double motion, one up and one down. The closest analogue, however, is the pattern of *Lycidas*. In *Lycidas*, a young singer searches for an understanding of providential design. The contrapuntal development of the elegy is a series of movements; in each, the poet's human need for a place in this world meets with a religious correction until, at last, mortal anxiety finds relief in the faith in a world to come. *Paradise Lost* seems to me analogous to *Lycidas* in being — though far larger — a composition of incremental movements originating in the character of the poet singer whose attempts to explicate the thought of God are checked and redirected in the course of his epic song. Although *Lycidas* pictures the younger Milton's own concerns, he clearly sees himself from a distance, as is evident from the way he frames his elegy at the end: "Thus sang the uncouth swain." I see *Paradise Lost* as an analogous instance of self-portraiture. The portrait, of course, is not the sitter, and I therefore use the old "new critical" device of the *persona* and distinguish between Milton and his *alter ego*, the narrator of *Paradise Lost*. Since the writing of the poem is the narrator's declared reason for being, I shall henceforth refer to this *persona* as the poet.[9]

He plots meticulously all the stratagems we use to outwit despair, and shows how each necessarily fails. On the positive side he leaves only the unredeemed promissory note that in some inexplicable fashion Christian faith will overcome despair by grounding the self "transparently in the power which constituted it."[10]

Milton's great poem begins by beginning twice. The opening invocation consists of two apostrophes and so introduces two motifs. The first apostrophe (I, 1–16) addresses a heavenly Muse, the second (I, 17–26) addresses a Spirit.[11] The Muse has no certain habitation; she is the Muse of Oreb, or of Sinai, or of Sion and Siloa's brook. The Spirit chooses to reside in the pure and upright heart. The Muse is asked to sing the poem, but the Spirit is invited to instruct and illumine the poet. The Muse inspired Moses to write "how the Heav'ns and Earth / Rose out of *Chaos*," but the Spirit is God's creating power itself. In the first apostrophe the poem is an "advent'rous Song," but in the second it becomes "this great Argument." The statement of purpose also differs in each apostrophe: the poet's song "with no middle flight intends to soar / Above th' Aonian mount," in pursuit of "Things unattempted yet," but the poet's great argument will seek to "assert Eternal Providence, / And justify the ways of God to men." In the first apostrophe the poet longs for the deliverance of mankind from death, woe, and loss, but in the second he asks for his own restoration as he admits that his heart is dark and low.

The double pattern of this invocation separates the poet from the poem; it also separates the poet from mankind, for it asks for two acts of restoration: one for mankind and one for the poet.

The poet's variations on the source, substance, and purpose of his undertaking prohibit a summary of the invocation, for it is not a single statement; it gradually delineates an initiative, a motive, and a disposition. As line follows line, the invocation grows elusive, for the sense hovers between possibilities. Who makes this poem? Is it the poet, the Muse, or the Spirit? Is the poet himself or another's instrument? Does he teach or is he being taught? Does his matter have a source beyond him or does he find it within himself?

Here, meaning is draped in allusions to other texts. The poet presents himself as the latest and last arrival, heir to a tradition that he desires not only to continue but also to complete. Interpreting *Paradise Lost* thus entails interpreting the texts this poem incorporates; these in turn depend on other texts, so that the point of origin constantly recedes as we approach it.

The poet traces two ancestral lines, one classical, the other biblical, but the latter in turn is a double cable: Old Testament and New Testament. The text interweaves references to mountains, waters, and temples as inspirational origins of pagan myth, of Old Testament history, and of New Testament faith. How do we restrict the resonance of these allusions? The theoretical distinction between text and context collapses in practice, for allusions are both text and context. Allusion, like metaphor, symbol, or indeed any other element of style, begets a potentially endless series of redescriptions because we determine what is said by including what is left unsaid. When the poet "intends to soar / Above th' Aonian mount," do we think only of Mount Helicon or also of Pegasus, the mount who stamped his hoof there and so created the Hippocrene spring? Does Pegasus perhaps recall Bellerophon, who presumed to ride this mount to heaven, and whose fatal flight is fearfully remembered as we reach the halfway mark of *Paradise Lost*? The poet intends "no middle flight"; do we take this phrase as a reference to the region of the middle air, or to the middle style, or does it bring in its wake the fate, not only of Bellerophon but also of Icarus, who ignored Daedalus's advice to fly the middle way and so came to a great fall? Does this first prologue then infer an analogy between the high fliers of antiquity and a biblical motif, illustrated in the flight and fall of Satan: the danger of ambitious pride? If so, then "advent'rous" becomes ominous, for then the poet's song is not merely a song of many adventures, a song that comes by chance, but also one that entails a risk, an enterprise undertaken at one's great peril.

The layered biblical allusions increase the possibilities of meanings veiled in the text. God gave the law to Moses on Oreb, established his temple and ark on Sion's hill, and Christ healed the blind man near Siloa's brook. The invocation therefore embraces the span of redemptive history, from Adam through Moses and David to Christ, but it never raises the latter's heroic name. The poet speaks in types and shadows, another double-dealing, for the types and shadows of biblical narrative describe historical events that foreshadow and make way for spiritual facts. In this invocation they evoke, but never name, the sacred antitype; "till one greater Man / Restore us" is the poet's future optative. It asks the reader to fill in an identity, to redescribe the text. In an invocation that aspires to oracular utterance, we might hesitate at the phrase "the Oracle of God." The oracle on Sion's hill foreshadowed a yet absent oracle; in the poet's present, however, the last and lasting oracle ought to be the Savior who rendered all oracles dumb.

The word "Argument" too gives us pause. Does it mean "subject" or "theme"? May we translate it as "summary," since the poem will sum up all of human history? It may also mean "proof," or a process of reasoning in support of a proposition, such as the justification of God's ways. But justification may itself mean a process of reasoning to vindicate, defend, or exculpate. The use of the word "justify" is provocative in this context, for it reverses the theological tradition that it inevitably recalls. Theologians sought to explain how man was justified in the sight of God, not how God might be justified in the eyes of man for, indeed, God is beyond human ken. Justification was the central issue in the Reformation debate over salvation by works, or by faith, or by predestination. All parties in the debate agreed, however, that Christ was the only justifier; his death abrogated the justice of the old Law and made way for mercy. Justice is no longer at issue in the New Testament; mankind is at peace with God; the kingdom of Heaven, as Milton says elsewhere, is "at hand."[12] Does the poet here presume to act as mediator and to assume Christ's office? In my redescription of the first prologue, the poem becomes an adventurous, risky, and proud undertaking by a poet of awesome ambition.

The two apostrophes that distinguish between the poem and the poet introduce a double perspective or a double moral. One is the moral that the poet assigns to his tale, the other is the moral that he illustrates in his way of telling the tale. He recounts an action but his way of recounting it is itself an action, initiated by the apostrophic opening. Addressing himself to Muse and Spirit, the poet turns his back on the reader. He addresses his own poetic power and dramatizes his presence by dividing it into two, himself and another aegis, the personification of his power raised to the status of an independent agency. Thus, the great narrative of *Paradise Lost* has a lyric frame and the later apostrophic prologues, in Books III and VII, reestablish this lyric dimension. The apostrophic, lyric opening calls attention to the writing of the poem itself; it makes the act of writing the poem its first great event and enables the apparently arbitrary leaps and bounds in the narration that have irked so many of Milton's readers. The very process of composition is the poem's great happening that contains all its other happenings. The apostrophic frame suspends the usual narrative conventions, for it announces that the poem will take the shape of a series of impromptu, unpremeditated revelations.

Unlike Dante in the *Divine Comedy*, Milton does not lay down a plot structure beforehand. The *Comedy* opens without a lyric apostrophe; the narrator simply starts talking about his past experience and tells the reader what to expect: the story of all that befell the poet on a miraculous journey. In Dante's hereafter, the reader's needs are accommodated: things happen for a reason, event succeeds event in sequence, and we follow the passage of time. *Paradise Lost* has no such order. The narration begins with apparent arbitrariness: "Say first" — the starting point is the poet's choice and/or the Muse's bidding. The great event of writing determines the poem's unfolding and overrides mere chronological sequence; past and future are rearranged to fit the needs of the poet's present; the only sequential span of time is the time of writing. (This feature gives special prominence to Milton's use of the present tense, not only in the prologues but also in the poet's editorial comments and epic similes: it continually returns us to the present of reading.)[13] Milton's focus on the present event of writing accounts for the major structural difference between the *Divine Comedy* and *Paradise Lost*. Dante's poem reenacts a *journey* toward understanding — the reader asks: What happened next? Milton's poem reenacts a *search* for understanding — the reader can only ask: What will the poet think of next? In spite of this important difference, the two poems also share a significant feature.

Milton professed an affection, rare in his time, for Dante. The noble poet of medieval Catholicism and the grand spokesman for the Reformation interpreted their desire to instruct their societies as a duty owed to God; both pursued a vision of life in which the motives of conduct, private and public, should cohere with a higher wisdom, biblically revealed and confirmed in the course of history. After 1660, the likeness between Milton's career and Dante's became obvious: Milton had, like Dante, become an outcast, a poet in exile. Milton's references and allusions to Dante are numerous,[14] but Milton may owe to Dante more than details.

I suggest that Milton found in the *Comedy* a warrant for the prominence of the poet's "I." This emphasis on self-portraiture is one of the main features that distinguish Dante from his avowed exemplar, Vergil. All the levels of God's creation serve as the stage and setting for the spectacle of the salvation of Dante's *alter ego*, who moves from the encounter with evil, through the purification of motive, to an understanding of divine love. *Paradise Lost* combines the generic features of Vergilian epic with a Dantean dramatization of a poet-protagonist. If the action of *Paradise Lost* is the process of writing, then the plot of that action is the transformation of the poet. Aspiring at first to oracular utterance, he is forced by the process of inspiration—the gift of the Spirit he invokes at the beginning—to submit to the liabilities of human reason and the limits of its rationales; he is converted from ambition to humility, from active to passive, from wishing to speak for God to repeating (in the closing books) God's biblical lessons. We may see in *Paradise Lost*, as in the *Divine Comedy*, the story of the salvation of a poet.[15]

Given the poet's aim and condition at the opening of *Paradise Lost*, his search for justification begins with the fall of Satan not merely because the rules of epic require a start *in medias res* but also because the narrator's condition in part resembles Satan's: both poet and Satan are laid low and in the dark; both have aspiring minds. The first justifying principle for the developing action—Satan's rise from stupor, his energy in revitalizing his cohorts, his success in council and in his voyage through chaos—is a summary adaptation of theological ethics: whatever God wills is good because he wills it: anything that opposes this will is, for that reason, evil. Satan is the first to introduce that argument and the first to set in motion the alternating metamorphosis of good into evil and vice versa:

> To do aught good never will be our task,
> But ever to do ill our sole delight,
> As being the contrary to his high will
> Whom we resist. If then his Providence
> Out of our evil seek to bring forth good,
> Our labor must be to pervert that end,
> And out of good still to find means of evil.   (I, 159–65)

The poet shortly thereafter (210–20) endorses that argument and pattern. Throughout the first two Books, the poet stays with Satan and plots Satan's plotting. As Satan reaches the end of Chaos and takes off for the distant light of creation, the poet takes off for the light of God. Their actions are joined in one continued aspiration as the poet links the last line of Book II to the first of Book III: "in a cursed hour he hies. / Hail holy Light."

The apostrophic prologue of Book III is a prayer in which alternating moods of desperation and aspiration intensify each other. In the prologue to Book I, the poet admitted that his heart was yet low and dark; now he sketches his portrait in more detail. His elation at having escaped from hell is followed by the first admission of his blindness:

> thee I revisit safe,
> And feel thy sovran vital Lamp; but thou
> Revisit'st not these eyes, that roll in vain
> To find thy piercing ray, and find no dawn.   (III, 21–24)

The poet feels a light that he cannot see; this increases his pain. He compensates for that — "Yet not the more / Cease I to wander" (26–27) — by haunting the gardens of the Muse, a world of peaceful pastoral delight, in hope of immortal fame — a hope Milton, in *Lycidas*, called "That last infirmity of Noble mind" (71). The world of imagination will not suffice, for it makes way again for the poet's real experience in a bitter catalogue of his privations:

> Thus with the Year
> Seasons return, but not to me returns
> Day, or the sweet approach of Ev'n or Morn,
> Or sight of vernal bloom, or Summer's Rose,
> Or flocks, or herds, or human face divine.   (III, 40–44)

He is an old man, on a new day, in a new season; he is a shepherd without flock, a man without the comforts of human society, shut off from others, and shut in upon himself:

> But cloud instead, and ever-during dark
> Surrounds me, from the cheerful ways of men
> Cut off.   (44–46)

The poet gradually reveals his condition; the address to light is prompted by a need for light. Like the old man in Yeats's "Sailing to Byzantium," the poet sets sail for eternity because he suffers a mortal burden as a transient in a transitory world that offers him nothing. He seeks compensation for being so bereft: "So much the rather thou Celestial Light / Shine inward" (III, 51–52). The poet who sings and searches in *Paradise Lost* is not a disembodied, oracular voice. He lives in this time, in this world, in known circumstances.

With the doubling of moods in this prologue goes a doubling of every attempt to articulate the vision he hopes to achieve. The first lines ask: Shall I incur a fault if I call thee "offspring" or "coeternal"? His attempt to mediate divinity in language ends up in the formless void where all categories collapse: "Bright effluence of bright essence increate" (III, 6). There follows another stuggle for expression: Shall I liken thee to water? But tracing that "pure Ethereal stream" (7) to its secret origin discovers only a cloak for the numinous (9–12). The opening rhetorical questions are inherently a doubling device, for they can be answered in two ways. "May I express thee unblam'd?" (3) is an ominous question since, as the poet goes on to say, God dwells "in unapproached Light" (3–4). The next question repeats this pattern: "Or hear'st thou rather pure Ethereal stream, / Whose Fountain who shall tell?" (7–8). The second half of the question forbids this line of questioning altogether.

As in the prologue to Book I, the allusions in Book III have contrasting effects. As the poet hopes for immortal fame, he remembers the examples of Thamyris, Maeonides, Tiresias, and Phineus. Except for Maeonides, meaning Homer, the names introduce dubious precedents. In several classical sources, the prophets Tiresias and Phineus were stricken with blindness as punishment for divulging the secrets of the gods.[16] Thamyris was a byword for the folly of aspiring beyond one's talents, for he challenged the muses to a contest in which he lost both sight and lyre. The poet's prayer seems to me to hint throughout at a double blindness, in which the poet's bereavement drives him to claim the loss of eyesight as the privileged condition that allows him to tell of things that I/eye cannot see. His wish, in any case, is father to his deed. He next leaps up into the throne of God. The poet's lyric longing and the poem's narrative line match perfectly as the poet's eye and God's eye coincide. The Almighty Father, looking down, surveys a theatrical scene exactly like the one the poet has staged in the first two books. God sounds like a human theologian because he knows only the theology the poet knows; God expands a doctrine the poet first announced in Book I and then denounced in Book II as a vain pursuit when the fallen angels

> reason'd high
> Of Providence, Foreknowledge, Will, and Fate,
> Fixt Fate, Free will, Foreknowledge absolute,
> And found no end, in wand'ring mazes lost.   (II, 558–61)

How does the vanity of hell become the wisdom of heaven? If we regard the *search* for a justification as the soul of the poem's plot, the apparent contradictions of the arguments and the obvious manipulation of the plot acquire a cogent and consistent frame. The poet's justification is necessarily an ex post facto explanation. We know the narrative: the Fall is a foregone conclusion and must inevitably happen; it has already happened. Yet the poem is woven out of incidents, moves, and characters that try to forestall its happening. The consequence of beginning with Satan is that the initiative is Satan's; the poet's God must catch up with the poet's Satan. Hence Uriel, expressly placed in the sun to keep an eye out for Satan, fails to recognize him in the guise of a devout cherub, for only God can discern the evil of hypocrisy. All the protective devices must therefore fail. As Satan swoops down upon the earth at the beginning of Book IV, the poet asks for a "warning voice" against an evil that even angels cannot discern. The angelic squadrons under Gabriel's command, set about for the protection of the garden, do not see Satan entering. When, at the end of Book IV, they discover him, a verbal contest threatens to become physical violence. As the angels hem Satan in "With ported Spears" (980), the poet likens them to ripe ears of grain at harvest time, swaying in the wind, "the careful Plowman doubting stands / Lest on the threshing floor his hopeful sheaves / Prove chaff" (983–85). As the doubting ploughman is uncertain of his harvest, so the poet is uncertain of the course of his poem. The fray that might ensue is clearly embarrassing to the plot which requires that the angels fail in their appointed task and that Satan gain access to Eve. The poet therefore again makes God his easy instrument by having him execute a balancing act with the scales of Libra. God weighs "The sequel each of parting and of fight" (1003) and finds parting preferable. This outcome cuts off the developing action, gets Satan off the stage, and allows the poet to make another start by having God send Raphael as the "warning voice" that the poet has asked for (IV, 1).

In Book V, Raphael starts on a mission that he knows will be fruitless. He must prepare Adam to withstand an attack against which, it is foretold, Adam will fail. Part of Raphael's warning is the story of Satan's rebellion and defeat. Adam may find joy in Satan's overthrow, but the reader's joy is tempered by the knowledge that Satan is on the move again. The battle in heaven shadows a limitless potential for violence, including the ingenuity required to explode the world into a universal wrack. The heavenly tumult is the pattern for events here below for, in the poet's rationale, human history is a continued skirmish between two battles; the first was fought in heaven before the world began; the last shall be that battle in which the world will be consumed.[17] The agents of this ruin, God and Satan, are locked into an irreconcilable conflict of wills, each interminably engaged in the undoing of the other's purpose until the end of time. The battle in heaven, serving as the "shad-owed" lesson of the history of the world, exhausts the rationale of theo-logical ethics. At the end of Book VI, as Satan is thrown into hell, we are back at the beginning with Satan in the pit, from which we have seen him rise to take possession of the world we know. It is appropriate that anguish is again counterpoint to confidence in the poet's next apos-trophe, the invocation of Book VII.

Again the poet struggles to find an adequate language. He invokes Urania but calls that name into question; he must speak through nega-tions to affirm what he cannot directly express. As in the first invoca-tion, we are not sure who is responsible for the epic undertaking:

> Up led by thee,
> Into the Heav'n of Heav'ns I have presum'd,
> An Earthly Guest, and drawn Empyreal Air,
> Thy temp'ring.   (VII, 12–15)

The poet's high flight is the Muse's doing and his own; it is both privilege and presumption. Again he soars higher than Olympus, "Above the flight of Pegasean wing." His apostrophe develops a patterned contrast between classical antecedents and his own inspiration. Urania was the classical muse of astronomy, the knowledge of which tempted Bellerophon to use Athena's bridle to ride Pegasus into the sky; angered by Bellerophon's presumption, Jove sent a gadfly that stung Pegasus, whereupon the horse bolted and flung the rider from his back. Thereafter Bellerophon spent his life wandering, lame, alone, and embittered. The Urania of the poet's apostrophe is beyond mere astronomy; she is a secret and sacred spirit who plays with her sister, Wisdom, in the eternal presence of the Al-mighty Father. Her tempering enabled the poet to breathe the air of the heaven above the heavens, a sacred precinct Bellerophon could not even dream of. Although the poet prays that Bellerophon's fate may not be-fall him, the subsequent description of his condition resembles Bellero-phon's plight.

The first half of the invocation (VII, 1–20) glorifies the poet's endeavor, but the recall of Bellerophon begins the modulation of the song from grandeur to misery. The first part ends with the suggestion of fear in the reference to Bellerophon's presumption; the second closes with im-plied terror in the extended recall of the cruel death of Orpheus. The first part *invokes* the Muse, the second *implores* her. The language in the description of the poet's woeful condition is often ironic. The circu-lar movement around the chiasmus of "though fall'n on evil days / On evil dayes though fall'n" (25–26) verbally illustrates a life in bondage. The emphatic "Standing on Earth" (23) is undercut by the repetition of "though fall'n." In view of the poet's admissions about himself, it is a grim paradox that his "mortal voice" should make him feel "More safe" (24), especially since every allusion in this invocation conjures up fearful incidents. The poet who has cast himself as greater than Bellerophon has become, like Bellerophon, a lonely outcast; he hopes that his song may find a small audience, but he fears that the sound of human voices will drown him out.

Although the circumscription of the poet's elusive Muse echoes the language of Proverbs and the book of Wisdom, the tone of this prologue has a pagan ring because of the prominence of its classical prototypes: Urania, Bellerophon, and Orpheus. In the recollection of Orpheus (VII, 32–39), the poet associates himself with a suffering hero whom Christians had come to regard as a type of Christ. Here, Orpheus has no such halo. Instead, the poet embraces his own misery, associates himself with a savior figure, a poet-mediator, and raises the possibility that he too may become a sacrificial victim.

The poet next addresses his Muse as his Goddess (40) and embarks on another beginning: the creation of the world, the destruction of which has already been foretold. The magnificent celebration of God's creative power and of the beauty of his creation (Book VII) has a tragic setting since it follows immediately upon the picture of an apocalyptic battle that foreshadows the final undoing of God's creative purpose (Book VI).[18] In Book VIII, Adam questions apparent disproportions, first in God's great world and then in his own experience of love. He is doubtfully answered, and the dialogue between man and angel ends inconclusively. Adam's view of holy matrimony is at odds with Raphael's, who leaves Adam finally in "the thick shade" (653).[19] In spite of all the schemes of order that Raphael expounds to Adam — the degrees of knowledge, the chain of being, the hierarchy of created life — Adam can find no analogy or pattern for his experience of love.

The Fall, it is clear, is intimately linked with the experience of love, but how love leads to the Fall is not clear, for on this great question the poem diffuses the focus. The angle of perspective is refracted on three levels, those of action, of discourse, and of figurative language: Adam and Eve enact the turns and counterturns of love; Raphael and Adam discourse about it; the poet, in his late time of writing, embroiders it with image, allegory, and symbol, and with multiple allusions to the metamorphoses of love in myth, legend, and history. From action, to discourse, to figure, the perception of the relationship between Adam and Eve becomes more complex. The picture of their happy innocence in the garden (Book IV) is altered by the argument between Raphael and Adam (Book VIII). Adam presents a recognizably Petrarchan idealization of love in his picture of Eve as his *donna angelicata;* Raphael hews to the older Pauline and Patristic suspicion of eros and warns against the tumult of desire. (The two disputants divide between them Sidney's argument with himself in *Astrophil and Stella.*) The views of man and angel fail to coincide. When Adam at last questions the experience of his tutor and asks Raphael how angels make love, he learns that their immediate and total union is unlike his with Eve, for he and Eve must live with the obstacle of "membrane, joint, or limb" (625). Adam is caught in a paradoxical union — Eve is his *other* self, and the schemes of order and reason that he has been examining cannot accommodate the reasons of his heart. The poet's discourses in *Paradise Lost* are, to borrow Wallace Stevens's phrase, "the compass and curriculum / Of introspective exiles, lecturing."[20] They are postlapsarian schemes, prompted by the desire to correct the deficiencies of fallen understanding, and are therefore flawed in their origins; the descriptions of the ideal orders of nature, of knowing, and of loving are redescriptions of what might have been, if only the fall had not happened. These explanatory schemes had become a traditional part of the subject Milton takes up in his epic; he incorporates them, as he incorporates theological arguments, not as definitive answers but as part of the habitual human search for such answers. After the discourse between Raphael and Adam has reached a dilemma, Milton shifts to a mythical perspective and delivers the cause of evil in Paradise under the guise of a teasing allegory: Satan effects his reentry into Paradise unseen by the angelic watch; he dives into the river of Eden and emerges involved in the rising mist that waters the Tree of Life (IX, 69–76). The very source of life, the union of man and woman, is also the occasion of distance, separation, and otherness. The allegorical rendering softens the focus, dilutes previous arguments, and leaves the reader, in its indeterminacy, with a sense of the mystery of iniquity.

The prologue that introduces the fall in Book IX is not an invocation but an argument, not an apostrophe to the poet's power but a commentary on the modulations of his song. It constitutes another beginning of the subject postponed since Book I: man's first disobedience. "I now must change / Those Notes to Tragic" (IX, 5–6). All that has passed in the poem is prologue to this moment. Interrupting the narrative that has oscillated between past and future, the poet's *now* reminds us of the poem's only continuity: the event of writing. He must modulate from epic to tragedy and fragment his song into notes; he has no choice but obeys necessity: he must begin *da capo*. His recapitulation of the fall (6–13) returns us to the opening of Book I, to the mortal taste and its consequences, but now without mention of a redeemer to come.

One striking rhetorical difference between this and the other three prologues lies in the change from apostrophe to exposition. The poet's argument now addresses neither the Muse nor the reader; it is as if we overhear the poet talking to himself. He no longer calls upon the Muse; she comes to him uninvited; he merely copies her nocturnal dictation (IX, 21–23). The visionary gleam has gone; he is an old man, living in a late age and cold climate (44–45), listening to a private whisper (47). He is now a passive medium, no longer responsible for the remainder: he may well fail, "if all be mine / Not Hers who brings it nightly to my ear." The poet's role has changed from active to passive; no longer in pursuit of the Muse, he suffers the Muse's pursuit of him.

This prologue, in contrast to earlier apostrophes, has an almost embarrassingly narrow focus. The "Great Argument" that was to justify God's ways is now justified by invidious comparisons between this poem and its antecedents. As the poet devalues the great epics of antiquity, he implicitly recants the themes he has himself taken up: wrath, rage, and ire have been his subjects too. Although he professes himself "Not sedulous by Nature to indite / Wars" (IX, 27–28), his own poem includes "the long and tedious havoc" of a feigned battle; and although he dismisses the motifs of romance, his own earlier song has adapted many of the details he now has no use for. The poet can only advance his claim by disclaiming and circumscribing his "Sad task" by negation: "No more of talk" (1); "Not less but more Heroic" (111) "Not sedulous by Nature" (27) "Not that which justly gives Heroic name" (40) "Nor skill'd nor studious" (42) "If all be mine / Not Hers" (47–48).

None of the precedents the poet rehearses has justified the heroic name given to a person or a poem (IX, 40–41). As he confesses himself to be inadequate by nature, talent, and training to the mean task of fiction, a "higher Argument" remains to him. The description of that argument is enclosed in the parenthetical aside in the middle of a denunciation of his predecessors who neglected to sing of "the better fortitude / Of Patience and Heroic Martyrdom" (31–32). But the poet now disclaims any responsibility for his having to justify a heroic name: the argument, which the Muse brings him, will be "sufficient of itself to raise / That name" (43–44). The poet's refusal to name his hero may remind us of the debate that has, for generations now, circled around the question:

Who is the hero of *Paradise Lost?* Although Christ is the hero of redemptive history, he is never so named in the poem; *Paradise Lost* is no *Christiad*. Christ is both present in, and absent from, the biblical allusions in the first two prologues; in sequence, the prologues become less instead of more religious. The last one is an argument *pro domo*, an entirely secular defense of the style and subject of the poet's song in comparison to its precedents. Avoidance of Christ is a necessary condition for the development of the poem's action. If the action is a reenactment of the search for a justification, it cannot begin with Christ, for that would eliminate the search. The continuity of the action is centered in the poet who, in the first invocation, prayed that his great argument might rise, by divine instruction, out of his own heart. The poet who, in earlier apostrophes, complained of suffering but interpreted his pain as a privileged condition and as a mark of his election, now concludes that the suffering he cannot escape is the very instruction he asked for, and thus suffering must become the argument of his poem. In each of the prologues, the revelation of the poet's experience *now* coincides with what must *now* happen in his narration of what happened *then*.

After the poet's defense, or self-defense, Book IX dramatizes the Fall, arranged in five acts, the narrator providing choric commentary and stage directions. Book X elaborates the consequences of the mortal taste of the fruit. No book of *Paradise Lost* changes its setting so often as it builds a bridge across the entire span of the narrative, covering in succession God's verdict in heaven, the judgment of the guilty in Paradise, the ascent of Sin and Death, the descent of Satan and his punishment, the conquest of the earth by Sin and Death, the mutability of the universe ordered by an angry God, the mortal grief of Adam and Eve, and, finally, the tears of their repentance. With that we are back again at the beginning, the human condition in the world we know now, longing for deliverance.

In the last two books, the song that attempted "the unattempted yet" becomes instead an adaptation of biblical history, tracing a promise of deliverance in types and shadows until the coming of the Messiah, whose coming, however, will effect no visible change; the world will go on "To good malignant, to bad men benign" (XII, 538), so long as time shall be. The poem that began so audaciously ends without triumph — we hear no music at the close; the poet falls silent. Finally, *Paradise Lost*, like *Paradise Regained*, rejects all human historical achievement and leaves but one stark historical fact, the coming of the only mediator, the Messiah, whose life, death, and resurrection take up less than a hundred lines of Book XII.

The poet's original aim to justify the ways of God is only the necessary starting point of the poem's action. That action may be seen as the reenactment, in the character and conduct of the poet, of the conflict between hell and heaven. The performance of the poet tells a story in the attempt at justification and teaches that the attempt must ultimately fail. Proud and ambitious, the justifying poet begins in covert and unacknowledged kinship with Satan but, taught by failure, he ends in kinship with Adam, moving through clouds, types, and shadows, waiting for deliverance. Throughout the retelling of biblical history the poet portrays a series of figures (from Abel to Moses) who are reminiscent of Abdiel in Books V and VI. The steadfast Abdiel hopes to report to God what he later discovers is already known (VI, 19–21); he is sent into battle with God's promise of victory (VI, 37–43), only to discover that God's triumph does not need the strength of angels. The biblical figures of the closing books are likewise steadfast in faith, but their virtue also is unavailing in the fight against evil; they bear witness to God's design but their place in the latter is unknown to themselves. (Milton takes up this theme again in *Samson Agonistes*.) At the end of *Paradise Lost*, the poet has become such a figure; his blindness is no longer a sign of privilege but an image of the human condition. The change he has undergone in the course of his writing of the poem is both a decline and an ascent, for it justifies God in a manner that the poet did not intend when he asked, in the first invocation, for the Spirit to instruct him; his transformation illustrates what religion has always taught: that God subdues human reason by working upon the human heart.

The reading of *Paradise Lost* suggested in these pages is no more than a sketch. In the process of contriving it, I have recast the image of Milton after the model of Kierkegaard. The poet-narrator of *Paradise Lost* has become a *persona* "whose dramatizations of existential alternatives may spur the reader to personal reflection and appropriation." Milton the author has become a "maieutic trickster who lures his reader into the kind of 'double reflection' that will permit him to discover his own 'subjective truth.'"[21] Supporting analogues and argument introduced along the way serve only to invite the reader to share two anterior dispositions: one is that any text manipulates the reader's subjective response; the other is that, when religious doctrine changes in the course of time, a religious poem of the past may be reread so as to render a religious message in the present.

Drew University

NOTES

1. James Holly Hanford concludes his survey of nineteenth-century commentary on *Paradise Lost* with the statement that the "unresolved contradictions" in the poem "have persistently suggested that he [Milton] was divided against himself on the fundamental issues which the poem presents." *John Milton, Englishman* (New York, 1949), p. 174.

2. "Thus the special features of *Paradise Lost* can be explained as the consequences, positive and negative, of what has long been seen to be Milton's unique formal intention." Ralph W. Rader, "Fact, Theory, and Literary Explanation," *Critical Inquiry* I (1974), 150.

3. This is the position taken by Jackie DiSalvo, "Blake Encountering Milton," in *Milton and the Line of Vision*, ed. J. A. Wittreich, Jr. (Madison, 1975), p. 150, who argues, e.g., that when it comes to sexual love, "the schizophrenic, fallen consciousness of Adam and Eve reflects that of Milton himself."

4. "He may have meant the poem for a dimly envisaged 'fit audience though few' of extreme radicals, with the dominant (orthodox) ideology displayed sufficiently to allay the suspicions of those many unfit conformists, whose heirs are Lewis, Fish, Patrides, and others." David Aers and Bob Hodge, "Milton on Sex and Marriage," in *Milton Studies*, vol. XIII, ed. James D. Simmonds (Pittsburgh, 1979), p. 29.

5. For a description of the modern liberal consensus in theology, see Thomas Sheehan, "Revolution in the Church," *New York Review of Books*, 14 June 1984, pp. 35–39. Sheehan describes the changes in the historical evolution of dogma and doctrinal explanations, the contemporary surrender to the absence of certainty in matters of faith, and the return to Pascal's wager.

6. The features of this public, marmoreal Milton were roughly chiseled by Samuel Johnson and refined by some eminent Victorians (Arnold and Meredith). Passing references to Milton in historical surveys, college outlines, and journalistic writings draw upon and reconfirm this traditional image of Milton as a reserved youth, a stern husband and severe father, a man who was partisan in politics, zealous in matters of faith and morals, and always intellectually certain of his grounds.

7. Among writers on Milton, Stanley Fish most clearly illustrates the recent change of assumptions in interpretation. In *Surprised by Sin* (New York, 1967), Fish extrapolated Milton's intention from the context of seventeenth-century experience. He describes his radical transformation in *Is There a Text in this Class?* (Cambridge, Mass., 1980): "Whereas I had once agreed with my predecessors on the need to control interpretation lest it overwhelm and obscure texts, facts, authors, and intentions, I now believe that interpretation is the source of texts, facts, authors, and intentions" (p. 16).

8. I owe the formula "recantation through reenactment" to Mark Musa, *Dante's Vita Nuova: A Translation and an Essay* (Bloomington, 1973), pp. 160–74, who argues that it describes the "design of Dante's *Vita Nuova*."

9. The first extended treatment of the persona of *Paradise Lost* was Ann Davidson Ferry's *Milton's Epic Voice: The Narrator in "Paradise Lost"* (Cambridge, Mass., 1967). The relationship between Milton and the persona of the epic, as illustrated in the prologues, has been a continuing preoccupation among Miltonists. In Fish's *Surprised by Sin*, the persona serves Milton's magisterial purpose to provoke and correct the reader's fallen responses. In William Kerrigan's *The Prophetic Milton* (Charlottesville, Va., 1974), Milton and the persona of *Paradise Lost* virtually coincide, the latter directly expressing Milton's belief in his prophetic power and function. My own reading of the relationship between Milton and his persona was stimulated by William G. Riggs's observation in *The Christian Poet in "Paradise Lost"* (Berkeley, 1972), p. 17: "In his epic he [Milton] antici-

pates the Satanist response repeatedly by asking us to compare the portrait of the poet with the portrait of Satan; the similarities are not hidden; the differences are consciously defined." I commented on the prologues to Books I and VII in "'Ambiguous Words and Jealousies': A Secular Reading of *Paradise Lost*," in *Milton Studies*, vol. XIII, ed. James D. Simmonds (Pittsburgh, 1979), pp. 145–80. The present essay is, in part, intended to correct my "secular reading" of 1979. In that year Roger H. Sundell published "The Prologues of *Paradise Lost*," in *Milton and the Art of Sacred Song*, ed. J. Max Patrick and Roger H. Sundell (Madison, 1979), pp. 65–80. Sundell and I read the prologues as the sequential illustration of changes in the poem's persona, but we differ in our extrapolations of what these changes signify. For Sundell, the poet's "stance . . . is proper at the outset, flawed during the process of creation, and finally modified appropriately at the end" (p. 71).

10. Josiah Thompson, *Kierkegaard* (New York, 1973), pp. 201–02.

11. Quotations from *Paradise Lost* are taken from John Milton, *Complete Poems and Major Prose*, ed. Merritt Y. Hughes (New York, 1957), hereafter cited in the text.

12. *Christian Doctrine*, in *The Works of John Milton*, ed. Frank Allen Patterson et al. (New York, 1931–38), vol. XV, pp. 300–01.

13. I owe my understanding of the function and effects of apostrophe to Jonathan Culler's analysis of that rhetorical figure in his *The Pursuit of Signs: Semiotic, Literature, Deconstruction* (Ithaca, 1981), pp. 135–54.

14. For the echoes of, allusions to, and quotations from Dante in Milton's writings, see Irene Samuel's admirable compendium, *Dante and Milton* (Ithaca, 1966).

15. The poetry of Dante and Petrarch furnishes the earliest examples of poetry as theurgy, illustrating divine grace at work in the *pattern* of the poet's experience. The sequence of Herbert's *The Temple* reflects God's guidance in the experience of living. See my "*The Temple* as Picture," in *Too Rich to Clothe the Sunne: Essays on George Herbert*, ed. Claude J. Summers and Ted-Larry Pebworth (Pittsburgh, 1980), pp. 3–14. In *Paradise Lost*, the Spirit invoked at the outset presides over the experience of writing.

16. Milton was aware of the ambiguity inherent in these allusions. In the passage on his blindness in *A Second Defense of the English People*, in *Complete Prose Works of John Milton*, 8 vols., ed. Don M. Wolfe et al. (New Haven, 1953–82), vol. IV, pp. 584–85, he refers to Tiresias and Phineus as visionaries and refuses "to impute their blindness to them as a crime."

17. Joseph H. Summers's central chapter, "The Pattern at the Centre," in *The Muse's Method* (Cambridge, Mass., 1970), pp. 112–46, explains the conclusion of the battle in heaven as the "image and anticipation" of the Last Judgment (p. 135).

18. See again Summers's "The Pattern" on the effects of "the sequence of the major actions as they are presented to the reader" (p. 114).

19. For a more detailed, deconstructive reading of Book VIII, see my "'Ambiguous Words and Jealousies,'" pp. 170–75.

20. Wallace Stevens, "Le monocle de mon oncle," *Collected Poems* (New York, 1954), p. 15.

21. Thompson, *Kierkegaard*, p. 184.

CITIZEN ANGELS: CIVIL SOCIETY AND THE ABSTRACT INDIVIDUAL IN *PARADISE LOST*

Carrol B. Cox

WAR, OR at least civil war, implies a social order of sufficient internal complexity to generate those antagonisms which only force can resolve. So much is tautological. But heaven being (as Raphael informs Adam) more like to earth than we might assume, we would do well to explore not only the theological or moral meaning of Milton's angelic actors but to ask what earthly social relationships are the shadow of those which we see angels enact in heaven. Two episodes in particular offer windows onto those relations—that is, exhibit angels acting outside the presence of divine or human agents. The first is that of Uriel and the "cherub"; the second, Abdiel's challenge to Satan's rebellion. Milton's immediate concern in each of these episodes, of course, was hardly to elaborate a "heavenly sociology." But for that very reason they may exhibit Milton's spontaneous assumptions—assumptions which would be more immediately grounded in his own tacit social experience rather than in any self-conscious theology. And what we find, I believe, is neither a monarchy nor a feudal hierarchy, but something much closer to Dickens's London or Austen's bourgeois gentry than to either Dante's heaven or Homer's Olympus.

A.S.P. Woodhouse flatly rejected the label "bourgeois" for Milton. The "*bourgeois* tradition" in literature, he argued, began with Defoe, while Milton "proudly takes his place in the humanistic, the predominantly aristocratic, tradition of Sidney and Spenser."[1] If by "bourgeois" we mean not Eliot's "small house agent's clerk" but that class which, beginning with rioting artisans in twelfth-century France,[2] had by the end of the nineteenth century brought about a transformation in human relations without parallel since neolithic times—if *that* is the bourgeoisie, then what had Defoe to do, more than marginally, with *the* bourgeois tradition in literature? Rather than attending to life-styles or political principles, what we might first seek out are those works which created the forms of perceiving that made and make it possible for "bourgeois man" and "bourgeois woman" to imagine the conditions of their lives in capitalist society.

Although the explosive burst of commodity production in classical Greece gave such foreshadowings of the modern hero as Aeschylus's Orestes, Sophocles's Oedipus, and Plato's Er, in Milton's epics we see the "abstract — *isolated* — human individual" for the first time fully separated from tribal ties or feudal hierarchy.[3] And directly or indirectly most critics of Milton honor this achievement. John Arthos, for example, seeing Dante as featuring the "immediacy of experience," and Milton as providing "the long view of the journey through yet undetermined tracts of time," suggests that "One of the great advantages of Milton's manner is that it largely frees the Christian view from the limited contexts of contemporary society and draws us instead to think of Adam and Eve as ourselves at any moment in history and at any place entering upon an unknown life."[4] "The individual" in abstraction from such a "limited context" of concrete social relations is an ideological illusion, but one grounded in and drawing historical reality from the actual conditions of capitalist society — and the great task of modern literature has been to make imaginable this unreal reality which is both fundamental to experience in capitalist society *and* wholly beyond the reach of human sense.

As Arthos notes, Adam and Eve are separated from any historical context, any web of social relations, "entering upon an unknown life" from without. Arthos presumably sees this as reflecting a basic reality, corresponding to the human condition or the permanent (ahistorical) nature of man, rather than a powerful and necessary illusion grounded in historically determinate social relations. This latter assumption, however, would have the advantage of freeing the critic from either engaging in ideological quarrels with Milton *or* from attempting to defend Milton or any other poet for his moral or political profundity, as Barbara Lewalski, for example, does when, embroiled in the conflict over Milton's male supremacy, she finds it necessary to argue that the great poets "are gloriously and supremely right about the most essential things, presenting us with a vision of the human condition which astonishes by its profundity."[5] The greatness of Milton's epic should be more, not less, visible when its "ideas" (or "vision") are indeed dead — as unfortunately they are not yet. *Paradise Lost* does, in Lewalski's phrase, present a vision which can astonish by its "profundity," but the content of that vision is historically specific rather than generically "human."

In denying that a "Marxist interpretation" of Milton is possible, Woodhouse assumes that such an interpretation must be tied to a particular construal of the poem's meaning. A "Marxist" interpretation, he argued,

fails for utter lack of evidence. It is true that he in general concurred with the political policy of the grandees of the army . . . [and] that behind their policy the initiated have found the motives of the class struggle. . . . But Milton manifests no concern with these matters, and no real interest in the parties of the left save as they espouse with him the cause of religious toleration. Nor is his outlook distinctively *bourgeois* despite his conviction that "the most prudent men and most skilful in affairs are generally found" in "the middle sort" (*Pro Populo Anglicano Defensio*, Col. 7: 392). Education and his subsequent pursuits largely cancelled out the influence of his social class.[6]

More recently critcs (particularly Christopher Hill) have insisted on a closer and more overt connection than Woodhouse allows between Milton's fundamental concerns and his participation in revolutionary politics. But Woodhouse himself in this passage pointed to how Milton's experience could have prepared him to write the prototypical works of the capitalist era: "Education and his subsequent pursuits largely cancelled out the influence of his social class." Precisely the *lack* of such a profoundly revolutionary experience would partly explain the ambiguous mixture of old and new elements in the consciousness of the great Elizabethan writers, for they did not live so fully the fundamental modern experience of being compelled to a consciously free choice of career.

Since so profound a historical change as the rise of capitalism covers centuries and proceeds unevenly, with the new incorporating much of the old, to name any one author or period as *founding* the capitalist tradition in literature is absurd. Nevertheless, in Milton's epic we have, I think for the first time in such completeness, a developed vision of what by the late eighteenth century had become a spontaneous assumption, the abstract individual existing prior to and autonomously of concrete social relations. Though to create this individual and his (or her) modes of perception could hardly have been Milton's intention (conscious or unconscious), he could and did effect such a creation insofar as he found himself living in a world in which social relations were in material reality no longer given but created by the acts of isolated individuals acting independently — in necessary and imposed independence — of the material and social conditions which gave meaning to their actions. Though a London scrivener might well escape the influence of the particular interests of scriveners, the experience of that escape — the experience, that is, of having to choose to be a scrivener, a lawyer, a clergyman, a poet — could be profoundly radical in its results. The very process of escaping a particular background through the repeated choice of pursuits (none of which imposed itself as visibly necessary) would fix and deepen a view of the world as a field of necessary free choices by the isolated individual.

Milton consistently introduces his characters from nowhere, in isolation from all social relations. By the choices they make they then create new social relations within which their action can take on meaning not inherent in the action itself. The characters, rather, create that meaning through grounding their motive in a principle which operates in abstraction from the visible actuality which it explains or controls. This freedom of characters from prior social relations is the material content of the freedom to choose which the poem endlessly reiterates. This separation (freedom) of an act's meaning from its visible consequences is the precondition for such freedom, and whenever in *Paradise Lost* characters ascribe meaning (including analogical meaning) to an act's visible consequences or to the act itself, they fall, cutting themselves off from all possible social relations. But when they base their choice on correct principle, in abstraction from all visible or analogical meaning, then their free choice enacts a society in which the coherence of motive and act and of act and result is guaranteed by the Providence to which they have freely submitted themselves.

The compulsion here lies not in the submission of the will to Providence (which is the condition of their freedom) but in the total freedom of choice itself, in the freedom inherent in the separation of action from result which *compels* the individual to choose freely the action which will embody her motive. In *Paradise Lost* we can see this compulsory freedom most simply in the episode of Uriel and the cherub, particularly if we view the latter (as Uriel must) *as* a cherub rather than as Satan in disguise, for the whole dialogue makes clear that there was nothing in the direct "cherubic" experience of the cherub or in his hierarchical place to initiate his action. This cherub has received from most critics the cruelest possible treatment, that of ignoring his very existence. Seeing him only as *Satan* in the guise of a cherub, they seldom explore the fact that for Uriel he is only a cherub. Milton is as explicit as possible on this point: "So spake the false dissembler unperceived; / For neither man nor angel can discern / Hypocrisy" (III, 681–83).[7] If Satan's hypocrisy is perceivable only to God, then the overt narrative, a meeting of two angels, merits consideration in its own right, uncolored by the knowledge that it is Satan who speaks. So considered the scene introduces us to social relations in Milton's heaven, the poem's one example of the everyday life of the unfallen angels. The premise of Satan's ruse, the possibility that all *might* be as it seems to be, reveals the most radical distinction between Milton's heaven and Dante's to be that in Milton's anything can happen, including an angel on a solitary sight-seeing tour. Both Uriel and the cherub exhibit what Marx called the "dot-like isolation"[8] of the agent in capitalist society, and no sooner does Uriel appear than he is confronted with an imposed free choice under conditions which, in themselves, give no indication of the meaning of that choice.

Uriel's judgment may be incorrect, but the text seems to insist that he was correct in assuming the cherub's declared mission a possible one in itself, its legitimacy depending only on the legitimacy of the motive and understanding that inspired it. Merritt Hughes, recognizing that independently of the cherub's motives the situation requires some explanation, notes that "Like the writer of Job (ii.1), Milton calls the angels Sons of God and thinks of them as living scattered through the provinces of heaven, except on the days when they must 'present themselves before the Lord.'"[9] Biblical precedent or not, the scene would be unimaginable in Dante's world, in which agents do not appear from nowhere, with their roles (or relationships) undefined until by an abstractly free choice they enact a role. In Homer the contrast is perhaps sharper yet, for Odysseus separated from his *oikos* is "no man" in simple reality and not merely as a clever ruse.

Jon Lawry, however, has challenged Uriel's choice, seeing the episode as a temptation bearing some similarity to the temptation of Eve herself:

Nearly as foolish as Limbo's refusal to choose is the credulity that chooses blindly:

> oft though wisdom wake, suspicion sleeps
> At wisdom's Gate, and to simplicity
> Resigns her charge, while goodness thinks no ill
> Where no ill seems. (III, 686–89)

Uriel is such an unguarded sleeper, for he takes Satan's professed desire for knowledge to be praiseworthy. The wiser Raphael later will have some properly "suspicious" words when such a wish is voiced by Adam.[10]

The "professed desire" is *not* Satan's but that of a wandering cherub, one a complete stranger to Uriel, and even Lawry does not condemn Uriel's failure to be suspicious of that material fact itself, nor does he even find the basic situation, the encounter of strangers, to require remark. His concern is the legitimacy of the cherub's abstract motive. The random encounter of strangers, it seems, is as unremarkable in Milton's heaven as it is in the everyday experience of his modern interpreters. Lawry further underlines the centrality of abstract principle in Uriel's judgment when he draws a comparison to Raphael and Adam, for the question is not who the cherub or Adam *is* but only the invisible motive which controls their desire for knowledge. Raphael, of course, knows both who Adam is and what he will be, but Uriel has no prior reason to suspect a cherub, it being a tacit premise of the poem that no further defections will occur among the loyal angels, though they may still make mistakes of judgment. Uriel simply examines the cherub's judgment, not his will.

This cherub is perhaps Milton's most remarkable presentation of the "abstract — *isolated* — individual human" concretely imagined and made imaginable. By the poem's implicit premises it is possible for him to be wandering through space and to have had no prior or given relationship to Uriel, that relationship having to be created or enacted through a wholly indirect grounding in the abstract will of God rather than in terms of any shared visible actuality. Uriel judges that the cherub's declared motive is in harmony with the will of Providence (or abstract law), and on the basis of that assumed harmony they can enter into one of those "inevitable relationships which," according to Desmond Hamlet, "all men are required to establish and vigilantly to pursue."[11] This bourgeois reality of a world of invisible relationships and motives judgeable only on the basis of abstract principle is the material basis for seeing hypocrisy as the one sin visible only to God.

The episode has generated its own train of conflicting interpretations, all of which serve equally to underline how it dramatizes the plight of the isolated individual forced to choose freely on abstract principle. William Empson, no less moralistic than Lawry, focuses on Satan's motive for choosing his particular disguise: "Uriel finds it natural for a promoted proletarian to be a busybody, trying to curry favour no doubt." Alastair Fowler, rejecting this construal, suggests the motive "would be that the order of cherubim was supposed to excel in knowledge; so that in asking questions [Satan] is pursuing his proper vocation." Stanley Fish brings in the episode to gloss his commentary on Eve's willingness to follow the serpent: "*At this point*" (Fish's italics), "Eve is in Uriel's position, involved in an evil which cannot be imputed to her without distorting the facts." That, Fish argues, would be to deny "the spontaneousness of the Fall."[12] Many critics *do* find Eve virtually fallen already when she follows the serpent, but however that may be, the very disagreement among critics reveals that the *occasion* (whether the appearance of a wandering cherub or of a talking serpent) bears no necessary or visible relationship to its meaning. When Lawry reprimands Uriel or when J. M. Evans claims that Eve's quarrel with Adam has prepared her "to listen sympathetically to tributes to her dignity,"[13] both critics must appeal to the very same grounds for their arguments as do Uriel and Eve: some abstract principle which is argued or assumed both to be the will of God *and* to be knowable to the isolated individual prior to and independently of the occasion (the particular social relationship) that instances it. The disagreement between Lawry and Uriel is grounded in their differing interpretations of the *principle* which the cherub's request for knowledge expresses and whether that principle is or is not in harmony with divine will.

The episode tells two stories simultaneously (that of Satan and that of the cherub), as in allegorical fictions, but it is wholly unallegorical in that the two stories bear no necessary relationship, analogical or otherwise, to each other. If we are to link them, it is only by appealing to a principle which is abstractly valid independent of any particular visible manifestation, for the meaning of Satan's story does not express the meaning of the cherub's, nor does that visible narrative express the meaning of the real story. The principle that hypocrisy is visible only to God (or that, temperature remaining constant, the volume of gases varies inversely with the pressure) explains but neither causes nor is caused by the phenomena to which it refers.[14] The "law of gravity," for example, does not cause an object to fall; it is a theoretical formulation which explains (makes intelligible and sometimes controllable) the material relations involved in that falling.

What all critics describe in the Uriel episode is the encounter of two social monads, who must enact or create a social relationship where none existed before, under conditions which do not in their visible actuality impose any given form of action. And in describing that encounter they also link *Paradise Lost* to the later tradition of the bourgeois novel. Whether or not Lawry correctly construes the episode, his judgment of Uriel happens to be nearly a paraphrase of the self-judgment of a famous heroine of the novel, Elizabeth Bennet, as she reviews her earlier willingness to believe Wickham: "She was *now* struck with the impropriety of such communications to a stranger, and wondered it had escaped her before. She saw the indelicacy of putting himself forward as he had done, and the inconsistency of his professions with his conduct."[15] Elizabeth sees that she ought not to have required the facts of Wickham's history, since a grasp of *principle* would have led to correct judgment of his immediate conduct. Lawry, similarly, claims that Uriel did not need the fact provided by seeing Satan on Mount Niphates but could have judged the "impropriety" of the cherub's request through a wiser grasp of the principle of proper and improper knowledge.

Though Lawry's specific construal of the episode is strained, he is correct in posing the kind of question appropriate to the classical bourgeois novel, a principle-obsessed literary form. In both *Paradise Lost* and the novel the motive of action is necessarily abstracted from the action itself since there is no direct relation between act and intended results. The cobbler in bourgeois society makes shoes not to wear them (and hence his own reality is not analogically present in his visible action) but on the faith or calculation that through sale he will realize their exchange value—a purely spiritual attribute not detectable by an examination of the shoes' material reality. Separated in time and space from all the human activities which must constitute an equilibrium if his activity is to have meaning, he trusts to abstract principle to give that meaning—he can only stand and wait. Similarly, there is nothing in the material actuality of the cherub's request which allows Uriel to judge it. Not even Lawry faults Uriel for failing to raise the kind of challenge which Virgil and Dante regularly encounter even in purgatory: Why are you out of your "place"? Clearly the cherub is not out of place, that place being wherever his knowledge of divine will leads him to be, and only the validity of that knowledge is in question either in Uriel's reply or in Lawry's commentary.

No other critic has taken up Lawry's suggestion that Uriel himself is being tempted, and indeed that construal clutters reading of the episode. Uriel, Lawry says, is an "ethical meaning," but to define that meaning as consisting in showing the ill effects of "dewy innocence and credulousness" as opposed to "exacting skill and caution" undercuts the ethical meaning Milton explicitly attaches to the episode, that hypocrisy is the only evil that is invisible to created beings (III, 683–84). The *choice* the episode poses is the correctness or incorrectness of the principle the cherub offers to explain his desire. The choice is only obscured by seeing Uriel as tempted to place himself before Christ: "he [Satan] temptingly nominates Uriel as 'first' in doing God's will (displacing Christ) and as 'interpreter through highest Heav'n' (ignoring Christ as Word [III, 657])."[16] If "exacting skill and caution" were sufficient to unmask Satan here, the hypocrisy would not be visible to God alone but to any unfallen creature. The temptation Lawry names, of displacing Christ, is the temptation to assert a direct connection, bypassing Providence, between act and result, and it is that possibility to which Uriel does, with "exacting skill and caution," attend, concluding that the cherub's motive is sound. Each temptation in both *Paradise Lost* and *Paradise Regained* urges such a direct route to some goal, bypassing the divine will which alone can connect act to result. In Milton's eyes Satan's naturalism or empiricism is indistinguishable from Catholic sacramentalism, being merely a different form of the same error: that of finding meaning somehow to inhere in the visible itself.

Lawry's interpretation of the episode makes doubtfully legitimate use of the reader's knowledge that the cherub is in fact Satan. The episode is enriched, not impoverished, by abstracting from that fact and seeing only two angels who, through recourse to shared knowledge of providential intent, create between them a set of social relations where none had existed before. So viewed, the scene has a possible connection to the later temptation of Eve more interesting than Lawry's suggestion that Satan is staging an "aerial temptation . . . foretelling those on earth."[17] From this premise, Lawry can only see Uriel as misguided in declaring the cherub's desire to see the new creation to be not only praiseworthy but to reveal, by contrast, something like *lesser* merit on the part of those who "Contented with report hear only in heaven" (III, 701). There are, it seems, degrees of merit and not simply hierarchical places in heaven, and, if so, Empson does reflect part of the episode's tone when he calls the cherub a "promoted proletarian." Only it is Uriel himself who confirms by his words what is, in effect, the cherub's self-promotion through merit. Achievement of that higher level of merit depends on the recognition of the divine will in the abstract, independent of any visible embodiment of that will. If Satan as a cherub has successfully mimicked a higher virtue (recognition of the divine will in abstraction from experience of it), the cherub then provides a foreshadowing not of the serpent's temptation but of what might have been Eve's response to that temptation. The question one critical tradition insistently raises is whether Eve possessed the necessary defenses to resist Satan's arguments. John Armstrong is typical:

Might not the jealous overlord indeed have arbitrarily withheld from man some vast new potential? One safeguard might conceivably have availed at this point: an immediate knowledge of God. But this Eve lacks. Seventeenth-century Humanism has made him a distant absentee landlord of whom she knows only by hearsay, so that there is nothing inherently absurd in Satan's suggestion that the idea of divine creation is an imposture. . . . Her loyalty to her maker has no basis in personal intercourse or affection and thus her decision resolves itself into a calculation of probable risks.[18]

Armstrong, like Lewalski, wishes to find the great poets "right about the most essential things" and is willing to dismember their poems to adjust their vision to his own. In particular, he is among those who see a split between the poem's real and official themes because Eve must ground her choice on adherence to an abstract principle rather than a concretely experienced relationship.[19] He thus takes direct issue with those critics who see such adherence as nearly *the* unifying pattern of the poem, shown centrally in the Son's offer of sacrifice, reflected in the actions of the loyal angels, and providing a model for Adam and Eve. A recent assertion of this view is Stella Revard's comparison of the trials of Abdiel and Eve:

> Abdiel faces his trial alone and succeeds, winning the favor of God. . . . On earth the drama of confrontation, which Abdiel acted triumphantly, is reenacted with fatal consequences. Thus this brief episode that Raphael relates not only serves to illuminate the kind of service God's creatures may choose, it testifies how Eve's encounter with Satan might have been different. Free will can have its triumphs as well as its tragedies.[20]

Abdiel, Eve, *and the cherub* must make decisions in isolation, separated from direct knowledge or experience of the grounds of their decision. (The cherub is explicit that his knowledge of God's "wondrous works," like Eve's knowledge of her "absentee landlord," is only by hearsay.) The lines Lawry quotes as tempting Uriel to displace Christ can have the different thrust of exhibiting the isolated individuality of the angels, their abstract relationship to the divine will. He addresses Uriel as one who is "wont his great authentic will / Interpreter through highest heaven to bring, / Where all his sons thy embassy attend" (III, 656–58). This asserts a fact of Uriel's own practice, and if it is false Uriel's failure to challenge it reveals him as more obtuse or more sorely tempted than even Lawry suggests. If true, then even for the angels God is indeed a sort of "absentee landlord," and if the cherub's mission is valid it will be because he honors the divine will in abstraction from direct knowledge of its content in the instance at hand.

Uriel's reply takes the factual accuracy of the cherub's statements as given and comments on motive, giving praise to the desire

> that led thee hither
> From thy empyreal mansion thus alone,
> To witness with thine eyes what some perhaps
> Contented with report hear only in heaven.   (III, 698–701)

This is not Eve succumbing to temptation but the Father himself greeting Abdiel:

> Servant of God, well done, well hast thou fought
> The better fight, who single has maintained
> Against revolted multitudes the cause
> Of truth.   (VI, 29–32)

Armstrong and Revard disagree not in their construal of the Fall but in their ideological judgment of whether or not life ought to be that way. If, however, we abstract from that quarrel, accepting the poem's premises without concerning ourselves with their existential validity, we can see in the cherub's lonely decision to view the "wondrous works" of God a first foreshadowing of the imitation of the Son which Abdiel achieved and which Eve could not maintain. The common kernel in all is precisely that of honoring (or of not honoring) a divine will known only as abstract principle. Writing in an age of capitalist collapse, Armstrong attempts to extract from myth and art a refurbished version of the abstract individual's inner paradise; Revard construes what she takes to be Milton's version and implicitly reaffirms it as valid for "us." Milton, however, held to a sturdier version of that bourgeois ideal than Armstrong (and perhaps than Revard) and could demand of Eve a faith not based on "personal intercourse or affection."

The confrontation of the cherub and Uriel, then, can be construed as exemplifying Satan's capacity to mimic true virtue rather than merely to make a vicious principle seem virtuous. But suppose Lawry's construal is correct. As already pointed out, to support his judgment he must, like Uriel and the cherub themselves, appeal to an abstract principle not inherent in the occasion. That action is purely neutral — empty of concrete content — unless we suppose that the cherub has no business on *any* grounds to have left his proper place among the cherubim, an assumption which not even Lawry makes. Satan's hypocrisy would consist of his putting forth a vicious principle which is made to seem legitimate in part by its appeal to the vanity or weakness of his victim, in part because the victim naively assumes that the deceiver's role, being proper in itself, thereby authenticates the rightness of his motive. Again, the novel offers the best parallels for Uriel's error: Osmond's deception of Isabel in *Portrait of a Lady*, Mrs. Norris's of Sir Thomas in *Mansfield Park*, and Prince Vasíli's of Pierre in *War and Peace*. In each case interpretation hinges on judgment of whether or not the victim had potential access to the correct principles on which to base choice. In the case of Isabel, some critics have seen her as "involved in an evil which cannot be imputed" to her, while others have judged her as Lawry judges Uriel, or Elizabeth Bennet herself.

On Lawry's interpretation or on any of those which, like his, ignore the reality of the cherub as cherub, the episode still remains an instance of two abstract and isolated individuals groping to find the principle through which they can form a social relationship, though the material content of the relation be as trivial as the passing on of some navigational data. Lawry, construing the episode to be one of temptation and thereby narrowing its range of connections, has only underlined the extent to which Milton consistently creates actions which do not express their own meaning for either the characters involved or the reader. The reader, too, as so much recent criticism has insisted, is radically individualized by being compelled freely to judge the propriety of the cherub's declared motive. In contrast, any attempt to exercise a free judgment of motive in most prebourgeois literature tends to make reading a nearly impossible act. As soon as the reader feels called upon to judge why or whether Odysseus should choose home over immortality, for example, the *Odyssey* loses coherence. The question cannot be asked, and because it cannot be asked no new social relationship is created between author and reader as abstract individuals.

In Abdiel's confrontation with Satan we see a feudal hierarchy, claiming to be the analogical expression of its own inner reality, transformed by Abdiel's abstractly free act into a civil society of autonomous individuals, each in his own isolation responsible for his action. In opposition to the inherent validity of the angelic order which Satan claims, Abdiel dissolves that order by subordinating it to abstract law or principle. To make place depend on merit empties hierarchy of real content, creating in its stead an empirical chaos of phenomena which must then be made to exhibit order by appeal to law existing independently of the chaos it explains. Abdiel's courage is the very opposite of that courage which Allen Tate thought needed to "face the spiritual truth in its physical body."[21] On the contrary, Abdiel seems to insist that it requires extraordinary courage to accept that "spiritual truth" has no physical body. Abdiel appears abruptly, like Uriel and the cherub, one of the sheer inventions of the poem:

> when among the seraphim
> Abdiel, than whom none with more zeal adored
> The Deity, and divine commands obeyed,
> Stood up.   (V, 804–07)

The powerful abstractness of this contrasts sharply with the careful placing of characters in most or all precapitalist narrative. A minor detail from Boccaccio instances the practice: "In Messina there were three young brothers, all of them merchants, who became very rich after the death of their father (*who was from San Gimagno*)."[22] The italicized detail is not novelistic but feudal. It places the father rather than contributes to developing plot or character. Milton, in contrast, provides only the principle which explains Abdiel's action, his zeal and obedience.

Abdiel's only preexisting relationship (expressed in his zeal) is the un-mediated relationship to an abstract divine will. Until he stands up the other angels are not individuals but places in a hierarchy to which Satan ascribes autonomous reality; "Thrones, dominations, princedoms, vir-tues, powers" (V, 772). They have, according to Satan, a given and un-challengeable existence within that fixed order of visible social relations:

> Who can in reason then or right assume
> Monarchy over such as live by right
> His equals, if in power or splendour less
> In freedom equal? Or can introduce
> Law and edict on us, who without law
> Err not.   (V, 794–99)

Satan objects not to superior "power and splendour" (which do not chal-lenge the hierarchical freedom and equality he defends) but rather to the claim to rule by merit or law, the leveling power of which dissolves all distinctions based on hierarchical position. Satan's rhetoric appeals to his followers to defend those places, to resist the tyranny of imposed free choice, of having their status dissolved in their abstract individual-ity. Abdiel's shifting of the debate to a question of the son's merit and the justice of law dissolves that hierarchical stability.

Milton himself may or may not have distinguished sharply between feudal dominion and corrupt republican tyranny. William Empson as-sumes that Satan does express republican sentiments much like Milton's own, arguing that the poem's first readers "would not be at all sure how far the author meant the devil's remarks to be wrong." Hughes is close to Empson in substance in his note to Book V, line 799: "*to be* cannot be definitely related to any verb; *much less* seems to compare the idea of a lord, or law-giver with the only less obnoxious idea of laws."[23] In practice, "lord" and "law-giver" are more apt to be contrary than synony-mous, and from a true feudal perspective laws are not less but more ob-noxious than a lord. Theognis of Megara was clear on this: "Shame has perished; pride and insolence have conquered justice and possess the earth. . . . The city is still a city but the populace is changed: once they knew nothing of laws."[24] Alastair Fowler, citing Balachandra Rajan's claim that Satan's appeal is a "perfectly orthodox version of the claim that monarchy is not grounded on the law of Nature," responds that "Satan omits altogether the value of obedience or discipline, which M. regarded as the essential condition of republican freedom."[25] Rajan, Fowler, and Empson all substantially agree that Satan's argument is somehow a republican one, disagreeing only as to how complete a statement of that position it is or how the reader is to construe Milton's judgment of it. The fundamental coherence of Milton's poem does not, however, depend on its analytical consistency in terms of any imposed theoretical framework (including Milton's own, however that is construed). As a feudal aristocrat, Satan repudiates the subordination of hierarchy to merit or law; as *also* an enterprising individualist he repudiates the "value of obedience and discipline" (which in their feudal forms of order and degree or "power and splendour" he honors). Nevertheless, critics of Milton who fail to recognize the objective distinction between a feudal hierarchy or aristocracy and a capitalist elite are apt not only to ignore the poem's historical significance but even to misconstrue its intentions. A feudal aristocracy is a true hierarchy; capitalist elites presuppose the *ideal* egalitarianism of a bourgeois civil society of abstract, isolated individuals.

In his last soliloquy before imbruiting himself in the serpent, Satan will return to his outrage at the subordination of place to merit:

> man he made, and for him built
> Magnificent this world, and earth his seat,
> Him lord pronounced, and, O, indignity!
> Subjected to his service angel wings.   (IX, 152–55)

Whether or not Satan by this point is trapped in self-deception does not affect the significance of his overt stand: still denying the abstract individuality of the angels, he repudiates their subjection to any measure of abstract merit, simply refusing to acknowledge the legitimacy of any principle operating independently of visible actuality but giving meaning to it. Satan's opening speech to the angels, then, defends feudal order with a polemic against bourgeois civil society and its unifying principle of abstract law — abstract because it is not embodied in or drawing sanction from a visible reality but rather invoked as the sanction for the exercise of power: "Messiah, who by right of merit reigns" (VI, 43). For Satan, the angels without law "Err not" because they possess by status a right not subject to abstract judgment. It is an indignity for "angel *wings*," an attribute of their angelhood, to be subjected to human service, for such subjection has no basis in any visible hierarchy of degrees of being.

Abdiel's free act, dissolving that visible hierarchy of fixed relations and transforming the angels into isolated individuals who *must* freely choose, calls into being a whole social microcosm in the remaining hundred lines of Book V. But the relationships which characterize that society are all after the fact, emerging from the action of wills existing independently of and prior to the society which they enact. Satan despite

himself becomes a demogogue rather than a feudal lord and his followers citizens of a modern republic (however totalitarian). Rejoicing at
Abdiel's failure to gain adherents, Satan replies "more haughty." Presumably this show of support emboldens him, but that very need is a
sign of the usurper (or *caudillo*) who must depend on the abstractly (and
therefore *freely*) offered assent of his followers. And his reply, beginning
with the accusation of newness, ends with the threat of overt violence.
Milton fuses feudal violence with the terrorism of the modern capitalist
state, but in this scene at least Satan seems primarily the feudal lord,
intolerant of any appeal to law not embodied in a visible hierarchy. A
critical commonplace is that in hell Satan establishes a parody of heaven —
but it should be added more often that the heaven he parodies is one
which exists only in his own perception. For Satan, heaven is a hierarchy, and it is a hierarchy modeled after that illusory heavenly one that
he tries to establish in hell. A certain irony, then, enters into that modern criticism of Milton which makes hierarchy Milton's *own* principle.
"The hierarchic principle of order and degree," Douglas Bush wrote in
1945, gave "hierarchic order to man's own faculties and values. Thus while
the doctrine provided a metaphysical philosophy, it was far more religious and ethical than scientific."[26] If I understand this at all, Bush claims
that hierarchy is the grounds of true freedom. Satan would seemingly
have agreed: "and if not equal all, yet free; / Equally free; for orders
and degrees / Jar not with liberty, but well consist" (V, 791–93). "Order"
frees the person from the intolerable tyranny of compulsory free choice
in a world in which no relationships are fixed, in which no act contains
its own meaning, and in which all relations must be continually recreated through new and equally free (unattached, isolated) choices.

Critics who construe Satan as a rebel against rather than a defender
of hierarchy see as pure hypocrisy the lines in which he defends "order
and degree." Harold Toliver is typical in arguing that "Satan obviously
cannot have it both ways . . . if all angels are equal, Satan has no inherited right to his position; and if hierarchy prevails, he should not have
rebelled."[27] In fact, Satan nowhere claims that all angels are equal; rather
he consistently denies equality in order to assert that (aristocratic) "freedom" which consists in the secure possession of one's appointed *place* in
a hierarchy not subject to either challenge or "reform." Michael Lieb
is equally confident: "In his rebellious attitude, Satan equates freedom
and equality with reference to God in order to reveal the supposed injustice of God's dominion over the angels, but he does not in the least
equate these terms with reference to his own assumed omnipotence."[28]
Milton may have intended Satan's argument to be so interpreted, but

both Toliver and Lieb assume that it is inherently inconsistent in abstraction from Milton's intentions—that one can, in fact, read Milton's intentions from the fact of the inherent inconsistency of Satan's position rather than having, first, to determine Milton's intentions in order to judge Satan's consistency. This is not true, for in itself Satan's position is quite consistent. (Moreover, since Milton seems to give something like historical location for the granting of power to the Son, which occasioned Satan's rebellion, it is at least debatable whether Satan had always viewed "God's dominion over the angels" as unjust.)

Satan's speech, taken by itself, is consistent in terms of the most common understanding of freedom from at least the time of Plato, who was insistent on the point that the artisan and the guardian in his republic were "equally free" precisely because they acknowledged the rightness of their places in a hierarchy. But that acknowledgement, as Socrates's proposed lie of the three metals reveals, was grounded ultimately in the sheer givenness of the social order. And Plato would have been as appalled as Satan at the concept of hierarchy being dissolved by the tyrannical imposition of an abstract principle of merit. Though the decay of virtue (merit?) in the guardians leads to the decay of the ideal state, Plato simply could not have conceived of that decay being countered by replacing hierarchy with an endlessly shifting "meritocracy." No more could Satan. Satan's speech, therefore, is contradictory if (and only if) Milton intended Satan to represent a corrupt republican leader or demagogue; if, on the other hand, Satan's position is a feudal or royalist one, his speech is perfectly consistent; and, finally, out of context the speech can be *either* a consistent expression of feudal outlook *or* an instance of bourgeois demagoguery.

Joan Webber assumes Milton intended Satan's argument to be a consistent expression of the royalist outlook:

the parallel between Satan and Charles I as eclipsed sun-kings enables a true Miltonic perspective on both the English Revolution and the war in heaven. In announcing the begetting of the Son, God reveals himself as a creative, active, living force, while Satan, unwilling to risk his own status, attempts to freeze the hierarchy by replacing God.[29]

Toliver is simply wrong, *in the abstract*, in arguing that "if hierarchy prevails, he should not have rebelled." God's begetting of the Son overturned (or dissolved from within) an established hierarchy which guaranteed the *freedom* of each of its members. Satan launches a counterrevolution in defense of that hierarchy. Just *because* he believes that hierarchy prevails Satan finds not only justification for rebellion but hopes of success. Lieb is on equally shaky ground in speaking of Satan's "own presumed omnipotence," for at least as likely a construal of the text is that Satan based his hopes for power not on his own claim to omnipotence but on the denial of omnipotence as such; he did not overestimate his own power but underestimated that of God. Toliver and Lieb may still be concretely correct, wrong only in what they believe to be sufficient validation. Critics of the last decade (such as Webber) have been as overly anxious to see in Milton a poet of growth and life as those of the preceding decades were to see in him a poet of stasis and hierarchy. However, these interpretive puzzles need not be resolved to perceive Milton's epics, independently of their concrete meaning or intention, to be epics of capitalist individualism. Since the vision of a hierarchy grounded in the acts of free (isolated) individuals, absurd as it would be in reality, has been a major strand in some bourgeois thought from the beginning of capitalism, the presence of this contradition in the epic of capitalism would be a real possibility, consistent with the tendency, not uncommon even today, to individualize precapitalist history. Support for this possibility can be found precisely in the arguments of those critics who have construed *Paradise Lost* as a poem either grounded in or distorted by hierarchic symbolism. Balachandra Rajan saw Milton as having self-consciously chosen a hierarchical world view. Malcolm Ross saw him as having been unable to escape such a view. The two critics were less far apart than appears at first sight.

Rajan's account of hierachy as the informing principle of *Paradise Lost* has, in fact, a curious twist. After quickly summarizing Renaissance conceptions of "order," "degree," and "harmony," and noting the disintegration of the tradition in the mid-seventeenth century, he poses what he calls the "problem" of why Milton should have chosen a "symbolism so evidently dying" for a poem which was to be a "unifying and permanent embodiment of the consciousness and culture of his age." The twist comes in the solution to this problem: "There are times when a man can only preach effectively by preaching in the wilderness." Milton abstractly *chose* a tradition, a "massive, unchallengeable synthesis of knowledge," which was, Rajan adds, "far richer and far more reassuring than the fragile, limited substitutes which have replaced it."[30] This could be correct, for Milton as well as Rajan could have shared the idealist assumption of "ideas as autonomous entities which develop independently and are subject only to their own laws"[31] — from which it follows that such autonomous ideas can (in Pound's phrase) "go into action" independently of real historical conditions. Given such an assumption, one could as an "abstract — *isolated* — human individual" abstractly and magnificently reassert a "massive, unchallengeable synthesis of knowledge" originally grounded in material social relations within which such abstract acts of will would have been simply unintelligible.

Neither Homer nor Dante chose abstractly among alternative world views or traditions the one which his poem would express, but this, according to Rajan, was precisely Milton's practice. And Rajan's own commentary on crucial elements of that expression brings out the strangeness inherent in an individualist affirmation of a hierarchical world. He relates the angelic dance (V, 618–27) to the symbolism of degree, primarily because "the cosmic dance is made an analogue of the celestial," construes "references to Satan's 'hierarchical standard' and to triple hierarchies of angels" as "evocations of degree," and then claims "an ironical climax in Satan's treatment of the Son's exaltation as a violation of the hierarchical principle." Here Rajan, in the comment Fowler quoted, finds Satan to be expressing standard republican theory and describes Abdiel's reply as not a challenge to Satan's logic, but rather a shifting of the grounds of judgment to the facts of Satan's creation and to the principle that "obedience to a hierarchic superior is a confirmation, not a denial, of freedom."[32] But the relationship between celestial and cosmic dances is not analogical—it is a simple ("modern") comparison. The irony is there only if one accepts the conclusion to be proved. And as to the last point, Rajan cannot have it both ways: *both* Abdiel and Satan cannot be defenders *both* of republican theory and of the rightness of hierarchic obedience (and, in hierarchical terms, Satan is Abdiel's hierarchic superior). By any reading of the text, the confrontation contains evocations of "degree," but Rajan along with Satan assumes "degree" to be self-explanatory and self-justifying rather than a fact requiring explanation and justification. Abdiel, not Satan, offers such a justification—the abstract principle of merit.

Both Satan and Abdiel, according to Rajan, assert that hierarchy is a confirmation rather than a denial of freedom—but when Satan says it Milton is "ironic"—and besides, "To Milton's reader . . . he [Satan] was wrong because he was the devil, and doubly damned by quoting Scripture for his purpose."[33] Robert Adams was to note how Rajan, attempting to identify Milton's "reader," reached the "discouraging" conclusion "that such a person scarcely existed after 1660," a conclusion which, Adams said, failed to solve the problem of audience "except by the indirect device of admitting that none actually existed." Accordingly, it would seem that Milton "created his audience out of his own fantasy."[34] Rajan could not follow up on his discovery that the poem had no actual audience while remaining so anxious to present it as "keeping alive" a given cultural synthesis — and one which, moreover, made no sense except in terms of an audience which already not only accepted but lived that synthesis. Rajan solved this problem with the brute-force device of refusing to follow up the implications of his characterization of Milton as a "voice preaching in the wilderness" by exploring the historical content of that wilderness and the preacher's relationships to it. Malcolm Ross had already discovered essentially the same "problem," but his solution was to deny that *Milton* had discovered a solution. The problem for Ross was the question of the relationship of divine to secular monarchy:

the vanity and evil of earthly monarchies are suggested in poetic terms indistinguishable from those which suggest the splendor of Heaven. By inserting signposts, by telling us when to feel "This is vain" and "This is glorious," Milton seeks to keep his distinctions clear, to keep God innocent of associations with British royalism. That he fails is evident, and that he is conscious of the dilemma in which he finds himself is equally evident.[35]

The crucial assumption Rajan and Ross share is that the world view a poem expresses is abstractable from the relationship of the author to that world view and to the real social relations which ground it — or, at least, that the relationship is always essentially a passive one. And yet both recognize that the relationship may be, and in the case of Milton was, an active one, for every page of both studies honors the fact that Milton self-consciously "chose" his world view as prebourgeois writers typically did not. To say, as Rajan does, that Milton chose a symbolism which no longer reflected the "consciousness or culture of his time" or, as Ross does, that Milton was conscious of the "dilemma" posed by his royalist imagery, is to say that *Paradise Lost* does not assume a preexisting relationship between author and reader — *or* between reader and the poem's world view. Those relationships must be created by the free acts or choices of author and reader.

The absence of any preexisting relationship between author and reader is the essential burden of Stanley Fish's *Surprised by Sin*, for independently of the correctness or incorrectness of his interpretations, Fish is certainly correct in seeing that the relationship between writer and reader must be continuously recreated at almost every step throughout the poem: it is *never* given. And when Malcolm Ross focuses on Milton's "signposts," what he brings out is simply that on the occurrence of each such signal the reader is *compelled* to judge freely the rightness or wrongness of the signpost. What each critic looks for, and finds, in his or her examination of the confrontation of Abdiel and Satan is either confirmation of his own values or evidence that Milton failed to express properly the correct values. Rajan looks for reaffirmation of the medieval synthesis (finding subsequent syntheses "fragile," in fact, because capitalism has failed to deliver on its early utopian promises at the same time that it has developed its own actual potential so much more rapidly and explosively than had earlier modes of production). Ross looks for a revolutionary purism (defined as coherence of image and idea according to some abstract criterion of such coherence) and finds Milton lacking. Neither can entertain the possibility that the Abdiel-Satan clash, by imposing free choice upon the reader, was profoundly revolutionary in its enactment of the characteristic social relationship of bourgeois civil society.

Satan's arguments on order and liberty, then, can be either contradictory or consistent, depending on whether they express feudal or bourgeois relations. Moreover, either reading leads the reader to acknowledge the compulsion exercised on him or her to judge — to judge on the basis of some abstract principle which he or she either brings to the text or accepts, as abstractly stated, from the narrator. The action never carries its own meaning. If the narrator has invoked the right principle, and if the reader in turn accepts that principle as the correct basis for judgment of the narrated event, then a social relationship of writer and reader — a miniature bourgeois civil society — will have been created where none existed before. These "ifs" can be qualified in various ways. Stanley Fish argues that in the final book the reader who has successfully navigated all its "good temptations" receives as a reward something like a mystical experience. "If he has done his part, the reader is raised to an imaginative, almost mystical apprehension of what the poem has continually asserted from a thousand varying perspectives — salvation is through Christ." All the conditions, that is, for establishing, *temporarily*, a society of writer and reader have been met. Fish stresses the impermanence of the relationship: "And as Adam must descend from the mount of speculation to take up his new life on the subjected plain, so must we descend . . . from this total and self-annihilating union with the Divine, to re-enter the race of time." Reading the poem reunites for the reader the "shattered visage of truth," but such "direct apprehension cannot be prolonged," only its "memory" can be "a source of energy."[36] Fish's claim is that together author and reader have established a social relationship grounded in a shared recognition of and obedience to an abstract principle of social unity, that of "salvation through Christ."

Fish's "direct apprehension" is, however, misleading, because it obscures Milton's powerful abstractness. The anti-Miltonists of the 1930s were in one way more perceptive than many of his defenders in their insistence that Milton's narrative and imagery did not visibly embody his meaning — that, in Ross's version, they required "signposts" for their proper interpretation. The error lay only in dogmatic insistence that such organic unity of action and meaning was a sensible literary criterion. We can contrast to almost any passage in *Paradise Lost* part of the passage from Saint Catherine of Siena that Allen Tate quotes in his essay, "The Symbolic Imagination." Catherine is recounting her experience in comforting a young man unjustly convicted of treason, and she tells of his execution:

I stretched out his neck; and bowed me down, and recalled to him the Blood of the Lamb. His lips said naught save Jesus! and Catherine! And so saying, I received his head in my hands, closing my eyes in the divine goodness and saying, "I will."

When he was at rest my soul rested in peace and quiet, and in so great fragrance of blood that I could not bear to remove the blood which had fallen on me from him.

Tate comments, "It is deeply shocking, as all proximate incarnations are shocking," going on to argue that only those "of extraordinary courage . . . can face the spiritual truth in its physical body." However that may be, it is clear that for Saint Catherine, but *not* for Milton, truth was available only in its "physical body." She "does not," Tate claims, "report it [the "Blood"]; she recreates it, so that its analogical meaning is confirmed again in blood that she has seen."[37]

The rise of capitalism (in its usual oligarchic as well as in its occasionally democratic forms) liberated humanity forever from the fetters of analogical thought and from subservience to visible social relations or physical appearances as embodying their own meaning. The most reactionary aspect of much twentieth-century criticism was its effort (as in Tate's essay) to reimpose those fetters on criticism and literature. Boyd Berry, contrasting the "Establishment" to the Puritans and Milton, almost inadvertently reveals how reactionary even attenuated expressions of analogical thinking could be. According to Berry, the Establishment "conceived of God's immutable plan as incorporating within itself elements of historical change; the plan itself was unchanging, but the contents were occasional, temporary, and fluid." Milton and the Puritans, on the other hand, "before they turned their attention to this world . . . first pursued an eternal vision. Only after that vision did they descend to reform this world"[38] Recognizing that for the seventeenth-century conservatives "God's plan" was knowable only through the "physical body," as exhibited in visible social relations, Berry fails to recognize that the new social reality of the seventeenth century could be understood and controlled only by those who searched for its reality in principles existing independently of the visible.

Both positions are ahistorical in their reduction of history to a manifestation in time of a reality (or *telos*) which is beyond history. The sense of history or recognition of "elements of historical change" which Berry ascribes to the Establishment acted in practice to conserve an order in which change was only an incarnation of unchanging reality. The problem for the Puritan revolutionaries was to change the world without denying God's "immutable plan," a premise they shared with their adversaries. How difficult that task was is still evident in the glibness with which too many of Milton's modern critics can declare (as Joan Webber does) that the execution of Charles I was neither "right [nor] legal . . . despite all Milton's claims."[39] Michael Fixler, exploring the same question, quotes from a letter of Cromwell's canvassing grounds on which the army might impose its will on Parliament. Fixler notes approvingly that even Cromwell dropped his third reason as too ambiguous; nevertheless it clearly provided the real grounds that made the execution not only right and legal but necessary. "Thirdly," Cromwell wrote, "whether this Army be not a lawful power, called by God to oppose and fight against the King upon some stated ground, and being in power to such ends, may not oppose one name of authority, for those ends, as well as another, the outward authority which called them, not by their [the Parliament's] power making the quarrel lawful, but it being so in itself."[40] However torturously, what Cromwell was articulating is that necessary premise of every revolution, whatever its class basis, the premise which Plato incorrectly associated with despotism: Justice is the interest of the stronger. Between two fundamentally opposed social orders, the only higher authority is force.

The Puritans were, in practice, transforming history, and to do so they had to subvert not only feudal ideology but that earliest form of capitalist ideology, the divine right of kings. Whereas feudal ideology conceived history as narrowly cyclic, the Puritans went outside it to appeal to an eternal ground or larger cycle (*their* version of "God's immutable plan") to subvert the given of the established order. Tested against that "eternal vision" the actualities of recorded history proved to be a usurpation (on earth) of divine omnipotence; justice was, in metaphysical terms, indeed the interests of the stronger, of divine Providence itself, and injustice was that rebellion which accused others of rebellion. Abdiel's own final argument (V, 892–95) is also an appeal to force.

Satan sees the Son as rebel, from outside the given hierarchy, and presents himself as defending the old order.

> Thrones, dominations, princedoms, virtues, powers,
> If these magnific titles yet remain
> Not merely titular, since by decree
> Another now hath to himself engrossed
> All power, and us eclipsed under the name
> Of king anointed. (V, 772–77)

Milton and other revolutionaries through the eighteenth century saw their enemies as precisely such a fraudulent authority as Satan here claims to defend. True authority in the bourgeois view (whether embodied in an absolute monarch, a parliament, a revolutionary committee, a Muslim clergy, or a military junta) is described by Abdiel in his reply:

> Canst thou with impious obloquy condemn
> The just decree of God pronounced and sworn,
> That to his only Son by right endued
> With regal sceptre, every soul in heaven
> Shall bend the knee . . . ? (V, 813–17)

This is an instance of the kind which so disturbed Ross and led him to ascribe to the poem a "conflict of symbol and idea." But Ross was too mechanical. Liberal democracy is not even the most characteristic mode of rule in capitalist societies but an exceptional case maintained only so long as the working class accepts capitalism as not only the best but, essentially, the only possible form of society. Abdiel's reply vigorously evokes the abstract egalitarianism of bourgeois civil society, which he captures in the substitution of "every soul" for Satan's thrones and dominations. This *ideal* egalitarianism of capitalist society creates and justifies rather than contradicts the material inequality of such societies. That material inequality seems imposed by the working of abstract law rather than direct personal power, and though liberal bourgeois consciousness finds obedience to personal power intolerable, it honors power or authority embodied in law rather than a person—or even embodied in a person in material fact so long as, ideologically, that power can be viewed as the expression of some abstract principle (such, for example, as German "nationhood" or "authoritarianism" as opposed to "totalitarianism").

Even the divine right of kings was ideologically a transitional form to the bourgeois rule of law, and it was contradictory to medieval royalism as was parliamentary rule or Cromwell's military dictatorship. Bruce Coggin has drawn the distinction nicely in his essay, "Sir John Fortescue on Organic Politics." Coggin begins with a distinction which, though he himself admits it is "perhaps . . . too fine," is important ideologically, however detached from reality. "A constitutional monarch," he says, "is limited by statute," while in Fortescue's theory the king is limited "only by essence and role." The history to be found in a one-volume desk encyclopedia could reveal that the reality of that limitation was the economic and military power of the feudal nobility and that both Fortescue in 1476 and Coggin in 1979 were spinning fairy tales. Coggin concludes by contrasting Fortescue to all "modern" political theory:

There is no question of rights surrendered or powers usurped, only the matter of a proper stewardship of a set of given political facts, facts that were fairly commonplace in medieval political thought. The king ruled according to law, checked by the authority which dwelt thickset in the fabric of the body politic of which he, as king, was part. It was a conservative view, really, despite its later expansion and exploitation at the hands of revolutionaries. Its very strangeness is a clear indicator how far the Western experience is now removed from its reassuring synthesis.[41]

Both constitutional monarchs and those who ruled by "divine right" were, ideologically, above rather than part of the "body politic," and the one's ideal subordination to an abstract divine will was as opposed to medieval experience as the subordination of the other to statute. But that "set of given political facts" and that "fabric of the body politic" in which Coggin finds such a "reassuring synthesis" were simply the relations of personal dominion and servitude which characterized precapitalist modes of production.

Abdiel, in defending God's "just decree," recognizes that obedience to the Son is obedience to law rather than a person, as is implicit in the astounding line, "Messiah, who by right of merit reigns" (VI, 43). Abdiel himself incessantly returns to the theme of abstractly just law (V, 819, 822, 844, 883), particularly in the lines:

> since he the head
> One of our number thus reduced becomes,
> His laws our laws, all honour to him done
> Returns our own.   (V, 842–45)

These lines provide perspective on the carping of those critics who, though recognizing Milton as a revolutionary, tend to regret that he was not a consistent forerunner of (say) John Stuart Mill or Bertrand Russell. Boyd Berry is again representative:

it would be foolish to forget that there were severe limits to what changes did occur and blithely to glorify the Puritans for having developed fullblown religious toleration as well as modern democracy and physical science. . . . The Puritans seldom tolerated atheists and Catholics, they most frequently feared democracy, and they almost always set their scientific pursuits within the old hierarchy, subordinate to theology.[42]

Leaving aside the fact that what Berry calls "modern democracy" has so tenuous a material content, the simple and very nearly sufficient answer to his complaint is "Why should it have been otherwise?" The objective content of the rise of capitalism (however Milton subjectively defined it) was the smashing of "status" (Bruce Coggin's "set of given political facts") and its replacement with abstract "merit" (or power not limited by tradition or any visible actuality) — that is, with bourgeois egalitarianism. In historical context Abdiel's "One of our number thus reduced" is an extreme expression of that ideology.

A monarch who claims to rule by merit thereby dissolves the grounds of royalism and feudal hierarchy, the differences between such a monarch and a parliament or a military junta being techical, not fundamental. This holds especially if merit is primarily an ideological expression of strength. The person or class that rules on the basis of greater strength (however expressed ideologically) being subject to tests of that strength, God's reliance on his omnipotence in *Paradise Lost* is an expression, ultimately, of democratic ideology. However Milton in the poem or in his theology might have worked out the doctrinal implications, to assert that the Son rules by right of merit is indeed to reduce him, in principle, to "One of our number" — and, translated into secular terms, the doctrine of rule by merit provides full justification for the execution of a king should he fail of that merit. Abdiel has transformed not only the fallen angels but the whole of Milton's heaven into a bourgeois civil society of "abstract — *isolated*" citizens.

Modern reactionaries, attempting to reassert feudal values on a basis of capitalist commodity production, are as outraged as Satan by this state of affairs. Jacques Maritain fulminates against theodicies which, "setting out to comprehend the divine ways in order to render them acceptable, will religiously prepare the way for atheism."[43] But, nostalgia for the lost medieval harmony or synthesis apart, the attempt to justify God's law was indeed, as Abdiel saw, a historically liberating force; by smashing the fetters of direct personal dominion and isolating the individual from all visibly determining social relations it creates the world of abstractly and compulsorily free choice which *Paradise Lost* celebrates. Satan sees law as the destruction of legitimate authority and true liberty. Abdiel sees it as the very principle of freedom since only abstract law can sanction and maintain the autonomous choices of the free and isolated — free *because* isolated — individual.

The characters in Milton's poems, emerging suddenly from nowhere, and immediately facing the imposed necessity of a free choice which determines their possible relations, must then confront an unending series of such choices, continuously recreating new social relations which in turn never become fixed or visibly given. This endless recreating of relations as though all relations — all choices — were yet to be made is part of the substance both of the classical novel and of the great romantic poets. Each act and each subsequent set of relations are as new as the responses of the newly created Adam because the relations formed are never direct; they are never direct because the action which they constitute does not materially embody its own motive. Motive and action are linked, rather, only through forces or principles which are beyond the direct experience of the agents — and often beyond their possible knowledge. Adam at the moment of his creation becomes the model for all human action. Because no relationship is ever given, humans must endlessly rediscover that principle ("God"), which makes relationships always a new and unaccomplished obligation.

This is only to paraphrase, in abstraction from theology, a repeated perception in criticism of Milton. Stanley Fish remarks near the end of *Surprised by Sin:*

Since all agents maintain their positions and their identities by virtue of their relation to God, selfhood, too, is preserved through obedience. When an agent "breaks union" (V, 612) he voluntarily cuts himself off from a fixed point of reference and moves from a dependence that preserves his dignity to an independence that destroys it. The responsibility of keeping union belongs to the agent and continuity of character is merely persevering in this holding action. Apart from God there can be no stability and no true, that is internally consistent, self.[44]

Fish offers here an account of the abstract or separated individual's entrapment in a world of compulsory free choice — choice the agent exercises without knowledge of his act's meaning. And though the Father's phrase is "*breaking* union," the material content of this is *failing to establish union*. The phrase is from the Father's decree of the Son's power:

> Under his great vicegerent reign abide
> United as one individual soul
> For ever happy: him who disobeys
> Me disobeys, breaks union.   (V, 609–12)

The abstract individual is isolated (without "identity") until by a new choice he or she recreates a new union (or set of social relations). Joseph Summers's comment on an earlier passage applies equally to the dance in Book V:

It is in Heaven that we experience harmonious action, with no perversion and no frustration; and it is in the speech of the Father (III. 80 ff.) that we learn . . . what constitutes the divine ideal: it is the result of a multiplicity of wills and motions, truly free, yet moving either in unison or harmony. There is no necessity (III. 110), for necessity's supposed functions are resolved in spontaneously willed action (cf. III. 370–371). Within such "concord," the question of the immediate origin of the wills, like the question of the origin of the motions of the sun and constellations, is finally irrelevant as well as unknown.[45]

And Summers quotes the lines on the cosmic dance (III, 579–86). He defines a "society" — a term which does not usefully designate feudal and prefeudal social orders in which social relations were visible (however fetishized), and the "origin of the wills" was the given place the agent held within those visible social relations.

The origin of the concord was an intuitive recognition of divine will. When the angels lose or repudiate that recognition, concord collapses into chaos, and then (this is the burden of Desmond Hamlet's argument) the mercy of God is expressed in the justice of God.[46] In the world of *Paradise Lost* order does not depend on anything like Coggin's "set of given political facts" or "authority which dwelt thickset in the fabric of the body politic" — those are satanic notions. Society, an invisible abstraction, had come into existence when, with the triumph of commodity production and the progressive individuation of all social relations, the consequences of human acts escaped the agent's direct control: "The contrast between the power, based on the personal relations of dominion and servitude, that is conferred by landed property," Marx writes, "and the impersonal power that is given by money, is well expressed by the two French proverbs, 'Nulle terre sans seigneur' and 'L'argent n'a pas de maître.'"[47] A "society" is a social order in which agents are freed from personal relations of dominion and servitude and in which, accordingly, there is no longer "a set of given political facts" in which authority can "dwell."

As Summers implicitly recognizes (even while denying its relevance), the origin of the wills in such a social order is wholly problematic. Coggin describes that new world (though this is hardly his intention) when he describes what he regards as a perversion of Fortescue's political theory by later "Whig" theoreticians: "The integrity-in-separation between power and authority collapses into a fusion, both functions passing to a state with limitless police power and erastian religion."[48] That is, in a society of abstractly free individuals, in which action is separated from its consequences, order can emerge only from the (invisibly) willed adherence of each social monad to some (invisible) principle of harmony. In the unfallen state there is "no necessity" but only "spontaneously willed action" — or so it *seems*, for among the participants in the angelic dance is that Lucifer who immediately thereafter will launch his rebellion with, as we know, extraordinarily violent consequences. In the utopian civil society of Milton's heaven, disruption of harmony comes only from feudal attempts to usurp power. There is even a suggestion that the motive of Eve's fall is to gain something like the independence of a feudal barony: she will achieve status (overcome Adam's "merit") by a usurpation of power paralleling Nimrod's usurpation in Book XII. Abstracting from all particular construals either of the revolt in heaven or of the Fall itself, however, in both Milton's fallen and unfallen worlds the guarantee of order is the "limitless police power" (freed from implicit hierarchical restraints) to which Coggin objects.

Though Coggin fetishizes both feudal and capitalist states, he does offer an abstractly accurate account of the relationships of Milton's God to his creatures. His objections to the modern state are precisely those of John Armstrong to the unfair conditions imposed on Eve at her temptation. She has recourse only to an "absentee landlord" of a God rather than (in Coggin's terms) to a "given set of political facts" as grounds of her choice. The authority of Milton's God neither dwells "thickset in the fabric of the body politic" nor is it in any "separation" from his power — *and therefore it had to be justified by its goodness*, by having attributed to it a complex of abstract principles not even analogically available to "human sense." Under such conditions of "fair equality, fraternal state" (XII, 26) society exists as the whole web of invisible relations which are continuously created and recreated by the objectively free choices of individuals who are, ideally, prior to the society ("concord") which they create by the continual exercise of their free choice. Such individuals experience themselves as well as others as coming from nowhere, as being able to enter into social relations only through submitting to the necessity of freely choosing among alternatives not dictated by the visible reality of the dance in which they perform. The angelic dance *seems* "irregular" because each angel acts independently of the visible pattern of the dance, in both ignorance and independence of the intentions of others. It *is* "regular" because each, independently, incorporates the divine will (or abstract principle) which gives that regularity.

"And the faithful," Malcolm Ross wrote in 1954, offering to summarize Milton's world, "enter this invisible fellowship, if at all, by equally invisible means. The old lines of communication between the visible and the invisible are discarded. The Mystical Body is retained as a thoroughly bodiless concept."[49] Ross and Armstrong (however opposed otherwise) make essentially the same point, and again the proper answer to the complaint is not to deny, with many of Milton's medievalizing defenders, that he breaks "the lines of communications between the visible and the invisible," but rather to insist that he does indeed discard them, and that that bold divorce constitutes precisely the greatness of the poem.

Illinois State University

NOTES

1. A.S.P. Woodhouse, *The Heavenly Muse: A Preface to Milton*, ed. Hugh Mac-Callum (Toronto, 1972), p. 102.

2. See Michael E. Tagar and Madeleine Levy, *Law and the Rise of Capitalism* (New York, 1977), pp. 3–4.

3. Karl Marx, *Theses on Feuerbach*, in Frederick Engels, *Ludwig Feuerbach and the End of Classical German Philosophy* (Peking, 1976), pp. 63–64. A basic (explicit or implicit) premise of contemporary "ultra-left" theory in the academy is that revolutionary action is dependent on elaborating a prior critique of "capitalist culture" of something like the degree of sophistication and completeness of Marx's own analysis of the economy — a premise which may but need not depend on an argument that to be "historical" one must recognize the existence of fundamental transformations *within* the capitalist epoch. From the latter standpoint this essay is hopelessly "ahistorical," focusing as it does on what has *not* changed from Milton's day to our own.

4. John Arthos, "Milton, Andreini, and Galileo: Some Considerations on the Manner and Form of *Paradise Lost*," in *Approaches to "Paradise Lost": The York Tercentenary Lectures*, ed. C. A. Patrides (Toronto, 1968), pp. 163–64.

5. Barbara Lewalski, "Milton on Women — Yet Once More," in *Milton Studies*, vol. VI, ed. James D. Simmonds (Pittsburgh, 1974), p. 5.

6. Woodhouse, *Heavenly Muse*, p. 101.

7. *The Poems of John Milton*, ed. John Carey and Alastair Fowler (London, 1968). All further book and line references to *Paradise Lost* are to this edition, as are references to annotations by Fowler.

8. Karl Marx, *Grundrisse: Foundations of the Critique of Political Economy (Rough Draft)*, trans. Martin Nicolaus (Harmondsworth, England, 1973), p. 485. The whole context illuminates the revolutionary nature of bourgeois individualism. Marx is speaking of precapitalist communities based on the production of use-values: "An isolated individual could no more have property in land and soil than he could speak. . . . The relation to the earth as property is always mediated through the occupation of the land and soil, peacefully or violently, by the tribe, the commune, in some more or less naturally arisen

or already historically developed form. The individual can never appear here in the dot-like isolation [*Punktualität*] in which he appears as mere free worker."

9. John Milton, *Complete Poems and Major Prose*, ed. Merritt Y. Hughes (New York, 1957), p. 274, note to Book III, line 658.

10. John Lawry, *The Shadow of Heaven: Matter and Stance in Milton's Poetry* (Ithaca, 1969), p. 167.

11. Desmond Hamlet, "Recalcitrance, Damnation, and the Justice of God," in *Milton Studies*, vol. VIII, ed. James D. Simmonds (Pittsburgh, 1975), p. 286: "the poet appears indeed to be suggesting that it is only such a recognition ["of the reprehensible nature of evil and of the possibility of still exercising one's rational liberty"] on the part of the reader . . . that will correctly define the heinousness of evil, egoism, and injustice and simultaneously, the desirability of good, altruism, and true liberty in the inevitable relationships which all men are required to establish and vigilantly to pursue." Hamlet's essay is invaluable for raising to the level of inspired cliché the tautology implicit in most efforts to stress the "relevance" to "us" of *Paradise Lost*.

12. William Empson, *Milton's God* (London, 1961), p. 61; Fowler, *Poems*, p. 601, note to Book III, lines 636–37; Stanley Fish, *Surprised by Sin: The Reader in "Paradise Lost"* (London, 1967), p. 139.

13. J.M. Evans, *"Paradise Lost" and the Genesis Tradition* (London, 1968), p. 275.

14. I use Boyle's law in its original (uncorrected) form. See *Anti-Dühring*, pp. 114–15. Engels makes it clear that when a "law" is conceived as having other than mental existence the result is idealism. Milton of course ascribes some sort of metaphysical reality to law, but he has carried the process of separating law from the phenomena it explains so far that it is only a slight step further to the world of Diderot.

15. Jane Austen, *Pride and Prejudice*, 3rd ed., ed. R. W. Chapman (London, 1959), p. 207.

16. Lawry, *Shadow of Heaven*, p. 166.

17. Ibid., p. 166.

18. John Armstrong, *The Paradise Myth* (London, 1969), p. 117. In *Paradise Lost* God, or the principle of intelligibility, offers no less a basis for "personal intercourse or affection" than do any of the abstract principles (more or less consciously recognized) that explain or express social relations in capitalist society. Armstrong prefers to call that principle a "calculation of probable risks"; Milton preferred to call it faith in Providence. The quarrel is between two particular forms of individualism, to which Armstrong himself, with some help from Jung and anthropology, merely adds a third.

19. If we abstract from theology, what Armstrong calls "Seventeenth-century Humanism" had made a permanent contribution to human knowledge; cf. Marx, *Grundrisse*, p. 143: "In order to determine what amount of bread I need in order to exchange it for a yard of linen, I first equate the yard of linen with its exchange value. . . . I equate each of the commodities with a third; i.e. not with themselves. This third, which differs from them both, exists initially only in the head, as a conception, since it expresses a relation; just as, in general, relations can be established as existing only by being *thought*, as distinct from the subjects which are in these relations with each other." The notion that any relationship can be "experienced" is a form of fetishism nicely illustrated by Marx in explaining what Hegel called "reflex categories": "For instance, one man is king only because other men stand in the relations of subjects to him. They, on the contrary, imagine that they are subjects because he is king." See Karl Marx, *Capital: A Critical Analysis of Capitalist Production*, ed. Frederick Engels, trans. Samuel Moore and Edward Aveling (Moscow, n.d.), vol. I, p. 63 n.1.

20. Stella Revard, *The War in Heaven: "Paradise Lost" and the Tradition of Satan's Rebellion* (Ithaca, 1980), p. 281.

21. Allen Tate, *The Man of Letters in the Modern World: Selected Essays: 1928–1955* (New York, 1955), p. 99.

22. *The Decameron*, selected and trans. Mark Musa and Peter Bondanella (New York, 1977), p. 95. The sentence begins the fifth story of the fourth day.

23. Empson, *Milton's God*, p. 82; John Milton, *Paradise Lost*, ed. Merritt Y. Hughes (New York, 1935), p. 177, note to Book V, line 799. Hughes does not annotate the line in *Complete Poems*.

24. Quoted in George Thomson, *Aeschylus and Athens: A Study in the Social Origins of Drama* (New York, 1968), p. 87; no source cited.

25. Fowler, *Poems*, p. 724, note to Book V, lines 787–802, citing B. Rajan, *"Paradise Lost" and the Seventeenth Century Reader* (London, 1962), p. 63.

26. Douglas Bush, *"Paradise Lost" in Our Times: Some Comments* (Ithaca, 1945), p. 42.

27. Harold Toliver, "The Splinter Coalition," in *New Essays on "Paradise Lost"*, ed. Thomas Kranidas (Berkeley, 1969), pp. 50–51.

28. Michael Lieb, *The Dialectics of Creation: Patterns of Birth and Regeneration in "Paradise Lost"* (Amherst, 1970), p. 100.

29. Joan Webber, *Milton and His Epic Tradition* (Seattle, 1979), p. 120.

30. Balachandra Rajan, *Seventeenth Century Reader* (London, 1947), pp. 58–59.

31. Engels, *Feuerbach*, p. 55.

32. Rajan, *Seventeenth Century Reader*, pp. 62–64.

33. Ibid., pp. 62–64.

34. Robert Adams, *Ikon: John Milton and the Modern Critics* (Westport, 1972), p. 200.

35. Malcolm Ross, *Milton's Royalism: A Study of the Conflict of Symbol and Idea in the Poems* (Ithaca, 1943), p. 110.

36. Fish, *Surprised by Sin*, pp. 328, 330–31.

37. Tate, *Man of Letters*, pp. 99, 98.

38. Boyd Berry, *Process of Speech: Puritan Religious Writing and "Paradise Lost"* (Baltimore, 1976), pp. 71, 41.

39. Webber, *Epic Tradition*, p. 106. Webber does honor an essential point, for she writes that "By an act of illegality and violence, the country irrevocably committed itself to the primacy of law and individual conscience" (p. 106). But Webber failed to recognize that since under feudalism (or even the Tudor and Stuart monarchies, however subversive they were of feudal independence) the primacy of law was itself "illegal," *only* through illegality and violence could that primacy be achieved. Hopes for a peaceful or legal transition to socialism involve a similar contradiction. (The history of the twentieth century might have suggested to Webber that the phrase "law and individual conscience" is something of an oxymoron.)

Milton also shared the view, common among many later revolutionaries, that the revolution was in fact a restoration, that the "Establishment" was a usurping power: "And from rebellion shall derive his name, / Though of rebellion others he accuse" (XII, 36–37). The fullest argument that Milton intended a specific parallel between Charles I and Satan is Joan S. Bennett, "God, Satan, and King Charles: Milton's Royal Portraits," *PMLA* XCI (1977), 441–57. My own presentation of Satan as feudal lord and counterrevolutionary does not depend on the validity of such attempts to construe the poem's intentional historical references. William Empson (*Milton's God*, p. 77) seems, curiously to believe that he is offering some sort of extenuation of Satan when he calls him a "rippingly grand aristocrat" and argues that a "Norman lord in England did not entertain the modern idea of a nation; his obligations of loyalty were often complicated, and his main view of the English throne was that he would only let one of his cousins have it." Fowler (*Poems*, p. 22, note to Book V, line 756) is certainly correct in pointing out that the "analogy would hardly have seemed creditable to M." Baronial autonomy, or aspiration to it, must have seemed to Milton to be close to the heart of human evil.

40. Michael Fixler, *Milton and the Kingdoms of God* (London, 1964), pp. 145–46. Fixler describes Cromwell's (and Milton's) considerations as "based . . . on two distinct grounds," the first being "justification under natural law" and the second, finally conclusive, being "the argument that an immediate, objective, self-evident divine sanction existed" (p. 146). What both reasons amounted to was an assertion of justice as the interest of the stronger, the new rising class; that is the only possible legitimization for human action which transforms history. Cf. Marx, *Capital*, p. 225: "The capitalist maintains his rights as a purchaser when he tries to make the working-day as long as possible. . . . And the labourer maintains his right as a seller when he wishes to reduce the working day to one of definite normal duration. There is here, therefore, an antinomy, right against right, both equally bearing the seal of the law of exchanges. Between equal rights force decides. Hence it is that . . . the determination of what is a working-day, presents itself as the result of a struggle, a struggle between collective captial, *i.e.*, the class of capitalists, and collective labour, *i.e.*, the working class." See also Frederick Engels, "On Authority," in Marx and Engels, *Selected Works* (Moscow, 1969), vol. II, pp. 376–79 and Engels, *The Role of Force in History*, in Marx and Engels, *Selected Works* (Moscow, 1970), vol. III, pp. 377–428.

41. Bruce Coggin, "Sir John Fortescue on Organic Politics," *Modern Age: A Quarterly Review* XXIII (1979), 270, 271.

42. Berry, *Process of Speech*, p. 149.

43. Jacques Maritain, *Distinguish to Unite, or The Degrees of Knowledge*, trans. Gerald B. Phelan (London, 1959), p. 226.

44. Fish, *Surprised by Sin*, p. 337.

45. Summers, *Muse's Method*, pp. 72–73.

46. Hamlet, "Recalcitrance, Damnation, and the Justice of God," *passim*.

47. Marx, *Capital*, 145n.

48. Coggin, "Sir John Fortescue on Organic Politics" p. 270.

49. Malcolm Ross, *Poetry and Dogma: The Transfiguration of Eucharistic Symbols in Seventeenth-Century English Poetry* (New Brunswick, 1954), p. 189.

BEAUTY AND THE BEAST: A SINUOUS REFLECTION OF MILTON'S EVE[1]

King-Kok Cheung

T HE MUSE of *Paradise Lost* answers promptly and unambiguously
the question of what first caused human disobedience: "Th' infernal Serpent; hee it was, whose guile . . . deceiv'd / The Mother of Mankind."[2] Although the answer accords well with Genesis, it raises the
knotty issue of responsibility by implying that neither God nor humankind caused the original sin, that it was brought about by the subtle beast
inspired by Satan. A literal reading of Genesis, moreover, contradicts
the New Testament passage which declares that every person is self-
tempted (James i,13–14) and renders our first parents as unwitting victims. As a fervent believer in human liberty, Milton takes great pains
to resolve the contradiction — largely at the expense of our First Mother.
Despite the assertion that Eve is deceived, her potential for — if not disposition to — evil is hinted at throughout the epic by her affinities with
the serpent. Just as "Adam is tempted by Eve and Eve is part of himself,"
as Arnold Stein has observed,[3] the serpent in *Paradise Lost* is to some
extent, I believe, the image of Eve: she is at once deceived and self-
deceived. Availing himself of the traditional association between the serpent and Eve, Milton persistently intertwines the two in his poem to
convey his idea of human responsibility: the Fall occurs when the Serpent without beckons to a shadowy serpent within, when human desire
answers to beastly provocation.[4]

I

The alleged resemblance between Eve and the Eden serpent dates
back to the biblical exegesis of the Middle Ages. Henry Ansgar Kelly
notes that the tradition of the maiden-faced serpent emerged around
1170, thanks to Peter Comestor, who explicated the story of Genesis as
follows:

Because [Lucifer] was afraid of being found out by the man, he approached the
woman, who had less foresight and was "wax to be twisted into vice" and this by
means of the serpent. . . . He also chose a certain kind of serpent . . . which had
the countenance of a virgin, because *like favors like*. (Emphasis added)[5]

The last three words quoted suggest that the serpent chosen by Satan resembles Eve, and that Eve is attracted by the serpent because of the resemblance. It is tempting to apply Comestor's psychological explanation to Milton's Eve, who falls in love with her own countenance as soon as she is created. Furthermore, in the context of *Paradise Lost*, "like favors like" has a sinister significance: with the exceptions of the divine Father and the Son, and of God and Man, doting on one's image (whether literally as Eve on her reflection or metaphorically as Satan on Sin, and Adam on Eve) invariably presages mischief.[6]

Besides appearing in numerous literary sources, versions of the maiden-headed serpent abound in the visual arts — the most famous being Michelangelo's painting of the temptation on the ceiling of the Sistine Chapel.[7] While Milton might not have had access to some of the literary sources, he was certainly familiar with Giambattista Andreini's *L'Adamo* (the oft-mentioned "source" for *Paradise Lost*), in which the Satanic serpent is represented as a woman — serpentine only from the waist down (II.iii).[8] He was also familiar with the iconographic tradition of the maiden-headed serpent, as suggested by J. B. Trapp and Roland M. Frye. Frye, however, thinks that the poet chooses to ignore this tradition: "he was not an antifeminist and could scarcely have put a 'lady visage' on his Tempter without seeming to some readers to invite an identification of the devil with woman"; but the argument is disputable on two grounds.[9] First, the devil does not demonize creatures by disguising himself as these creatures. Although Satan at one point disguises himself as a cherub, cherubs are not henceforth diabolical. Second, the womanized serpent was not in itself an expression of antifeminism. Diane McColley, for instance, has noted that the context of Raphael's fresco *Adam and Eve,* wherein the "the Serpent . . . is a shadowed Eve," is the Stanza della Segnatura's "magnificent tribute to divine and humane learning." Yet McColley goes even further than Frye in justifying the ways of Milton to Eve. Milton, McColley insists, works against the iconographic tradition that links Eve and the serpent: his Eve is sensuous without being wanton, whereas Raphael's, "surrounded by monuments to humanity and divinity, seems the wanton portress at the gates of divine mercy and human achievement."[10]

Despite the arguments by Frye and McColley to the contrary, I submit that Milton's Eve does have affinities with the serpent. Whether or not the poet is antifeminist, he does not scruple to ferret out a serpentine root to the name of Eve. His etymological awareness of her name is discussed in D. C. Allen's analysis of Adam's vituperative speech to Eve:

> Out of my sight, thou Serpent, that name best
> Befits thee with him leagu'd, thyself as false
> And hateful; nothing wants, but that thy shape,
> Like his, and color Serpentine may show
> Thy inward fraud, to warn all Creatures from thee
> Henceforth.   (X, 867–72)

Although according to Genesis Eve was so named "because she was the mother of all living" (iii, 20), Allen points out that this correct meaning was not unanimously accepted by Milton's generation, that some mistook a Hebrew form of Eve as meaning serpent. He traces the erroneous interpretation to the *Protrepticus* of Clement of Alexandria, an author well known to Milton: "In the Hebrew, says Clement, if the name of Eve is aspirated it is the same as the feminine of serpent." A similar account is found in Eusebius, another known authority for Milton: "according to the exact Hebrew pronunciation, the name Heva with an aspirate is interpreted as a female serpent." "So when Adam tells his wife that the name of serpent befits her best, neither he nor Milton is talking off the top of the head," Allen concludes. "A little tradition and some bad Hebrew stood behind the remark."[11] With the tradition of the maiden-headed serpent still in mind, I suspect that more stands behind that remark than even Allen realizes. While Milton does not explicitly use that tradition, he consciously incorporates parallels between Eve and the serpent. While he does not feminize the Eden serpent, he imbues his Eve with "color Serpentine"; he blurs the line between tempter and tempted to accentuate the woman's moral responsibility and culpability.[12]

II

Both Eve and the serpent in *Paradise Lost* are remarkable for their physical charm and potential danger. Portentous shadows hover over the very first portrait of Eve:

> For softness shee and sweet attractive Grace
> . . . .
> Shee as a veil down to the slender waist
> Her unadorned golden tresses wore
> Dishevell'd, but in wanton ringlets wav'd
> As the Vine curls her tendrils, which impli'd
> Subjection, but requir'd with gentle sway,
> And by her yielded, by him best receiv'd,
> Yielded with coy submission, modest pride,
> And sweet reluctant amorous delay.   (IV, 298, 304–11)

As several critics have noted, many words in this passage are discomfiting.[13] Adjectives such as "wanton" and "amorous" anticipate their post-lapsarian use — as when describing the "lustful" daughters of Eve in Book XI: "A Bevy of fair Women, richly gay / In Gems and wanton dress; to the Harp they sung / Soft amorous Ditties" (582–84). Similes also insinuate. The "veil" of hair that hides Eve implies modesty but also suggests guile and disguise, a suggestion reinforced by the use of similes: "as a veil" and "as the vine." Her hair looks like something it is not;[14] such "seeming" anticipates Adam's denunciation of the discrepancy between Eve's outward form and inner substance (X, 872–73).

Even her disarming attributes take on foreboding implications. While "softness" conveys femininity, and "yielded with coy submission" conveys docility, "softness" and the tendency to "yield" are put forward by the author of *The Cave of Treasures* as the actual *reasons* why the serpent chooses the woman as target; "soft" for that author implies "easily swayed by specious argument" and "yield" implies "being liable to succumb."[15] Milton's Eve will likewise be swayed and will succumb to the serpent's temptation. Her "sweet attractive Grace" also strikes a warning note, for we have heard Sin boast of *her* "attractive graces" (II, 762). Eve's "pride," despite its various positive connotations and despite its "modest" qualification, furnishes yet another caveat, for hitherto pride has been associated solely and persistently with Satan — so persistently that it is called "his wonted pride" (I, 527).

More disconcerting, Milton repeats many of the words and images that describe Eve when portraying the satanic serpent — he that

> toward *Eve*
> Address'd his way, not with indented wave,
> Prone on the ground, as since, but on his rear,
> Circular base of rising folds, that tow'r'd
> Fold above fold a surging Maze, his Head
> Crested aloft, and Carbuncle his Eyes;
> With burnisht Neck of verdant Gold, erect
> Amidst his circling Spires, that on the grass
> Floated redundant
> . . . .
> his tortuous Train
> Curl'd many a wanton wreath in sight of *Eve*,
> To lure her Eye.   (IX, 495–503, 516–18)

Words indicating similar shape and color — "wave / wav'd" and "gold / golden" — inform both passages quoted above.[16] In one we see waves of "golden tresses" covering Eve's nape, described again as "the flowing gold of her loose tresses" (IV, 497); in the other we see the serpent's "burnisht Neck of verdant Gold." The "wanton ringlets" of Eve, which "wav'd / As the Vine curls her tendrils," are suggestive of the "circling Spires" of the serpent, of his "tortuous Traine" which "Curl'd many a wanton wreath."[17] As a result of the insistent suggestions, it is difficult to read "ringlets" without thinking about the lascivious "wreaths"; to aggravate matters, the two alliterating words are both modified by "wanton," surely a provocative adjective. The provocation comes specifically from a certain bewitching disorder common to Eve and the serpent: her flowing, luxuriant hair is "dishevell'd"; the "rising folds" of the serpent, that "roll'd / In tangles" (IX, 631–32), move in a "surging Maze." Both the hair and the folds are difficult to untangle; both are resplendent, mesmeric. And the sibilants in the two passages are enough to form a "contrapuntal serpent hiss." The details seem to cause Eve's "soft" and "slender" body to follow serpentine contours, her sensuousness insinuating sensuality.[18]

Associations between Satan/serpent and Eve creep up again and again — in scenes depicting her awakening, her demonic dream, her separation from Adam, her temptation, and her postlapsarian cunning. They become inescapable as the epic unfolds, culminating in the *meeting* of the woman and the serpent.

Warning signals can be detected from the moment Eve awakes into life, an awakening that differs markedly from Adam's. Waking in direct sunlight, Adam instinctively turns his eye and mind heavenward in the hope of knowing and adoring his creator (VIII, 253–82). By contrast, Eve awakens in the shade — where snakes slumber. She too wonders about her creation, but instead of looking up to the sky, she bends over a pool, seeing the sky only as a shadow and herself as an image:

> I thither went
> With unexperienc't thought, and laid me down
> On the green bank, to look into the clear
> Smooth Lake, that to me seem'd another Sky.
> As I *bent* down to look, just opposite,
> A Shape within the wat'ry gleam appear'd
> *Bending* to look on me, I started back,
> It started back, but pleas'd I soon return'd,
> Pleas'd it return'd as soon with answering looks
> Of sympathy and love; there I had fixt
> Mine eyes till now, and pin'd with vain desire.
>
> (IV, 456–66, emphasis added)

D. C. Allen points out the ominous significance of Eve's posture by paraphrasing St. Augustine: "When the angels were created they looked first at themselves, surprised at their own existence. Then some looked upward and found the source of creation in the Word. Others fell in love with themselves and sank in their own darkness."[19] Ominous analogues are found within the epic itself, for we have already been introduced to Mammon, whose "looks and thoughts / Were always downward *Bent*" (I, 680–81, emphasis added), and to Satan, who fell in love with Sin, his "perfect image" (II, 764). So when Eve looks down at her image in the pool, we sense trouble.

We are further troubled by the analogous reactions of Eve and Satan to their respective images. "Starting" to and fro, Eve conveys dread and longing, a response Satan has exemplified with Sin: recoiling from Sin at first, he then becomes "familiar" with his "perfect image" (II, 761, 764). Innocent Eve, to be sure, does not know that she is looking at herself, but her gesture foreshadows her less innocent encounter with the serpent, which I will suggest is yet another "fair image" of her.

Eve's description of her reaction to the watery image stirs up in the reader the first troubling reflections — now of Satan, now of his serpentine incarnation. Other water images are conjured up — those associated with the serpent that moves "not with indented *wave*," but like "a *surging* Maze . . . that on the grass / *Floated* redundant" (IX, 496, 499, 502–03; emphasis added). Both Eve and the serpent are set off against a green background, the former "on the green bank," the latter "on the grass." Just as Eve is enamored of her image, so will she be enchanted by the serpent. Just as she is fooled by appearances at the pool, mistaking the lake for the sky and her reflection for a sympathetic being, she will be fooled by Satan's disguise.

Her very shape and movement appear ophidian. Her sinuous contours contrast sharply with the rugged lineaments of Adam, whom she will find "Less winning soft, less amiably mild" (IV, 479). The words "bent" and "bending" used by Eve to describe herself and her image evoke an arched back with flexible spine — a languid, S-shaped creature. And if we visualize the image in the pool as extending from the figure by pool, we have the configuration of an erect serpent. It wriggles insidiously: "I started back, / It started back, but pleas'd I soon return'd." The back-and-forth movement is both reminiscent of a serpent's spasmodic motions and emblematic of a human reaction upon seeing a serpent: being lithe, graceful, but possibly venomous, a serpent often both fascinates and frightens.

Also fascinating and fearsome is the serpent's steady glance, which is perhaps hinted at in Eve's wistful fixation on her image. "I had fixt Mine eyes till now" anticipates Satan's "gaze admiring" (IX, 524) and "gaze / Insatiate" (IX, 535–36); Eve hankers after herself much as Satan will hanker after her. She will, moreover, receive "looks / Of sympathy and love" from the serpent, who will tell her that she should be worshipped universally, not just by beasts and Adam, and that she should be seen a "Goddess among Gods" (IX, 547). Finally, her pining "with vain desire" recalls Satan's "fierce desire . . . / Still unfulfill'd with pain of longing pines" (IV, 509, 511), a "vain" desire insofar as Satan can feel "neither joy nor love" (509).

Eve's vain desire is checked for the moment by a divine voice, which warns her against self-love. But we encounter the words "vain" and "desire" again in the dream episode when Satan attempts to raise in Eve "Vain hopes, vain aims, inordinate desires / Blown up with high conceits ingend'ring pride" (IV, 808–09). Since "vain," "desire," and "pride" echo words that have been used earlier to describe Eve, recalling her "modest pride," her "pining with vain desire," the question remains whether these qualities are demonically induced or self-engendered.

Satan's adulation of Eve in the dream similarly reflects her own musings. Just before she retires, she has asked an abrupt question regarding nocturnal beauty: "But wherefore *all* night long shine these, for whom / This glorious sight, when sleep hath shut *all* eyes?" (IV, 657–58, emphasis added). Adam answers by explaining order; Satan, pandering to Eve's curiosity and vanity, answers by perverting order:

> Heav'n wakes with *all* his eyes,
> Whom to behold but thee, Nature's desire,
> In whose sight *all* things joy, with ravishment
> Attracted by thy beauty still to gaze.
>
> (V, 44–47, emphasis added)

These lines hark back to the scene at the pool. The wakeful heaven brings to mind the lake that has seemed to Eve another sky, and both the watery and the nocturnal skies arouse narcissistic longings in her. More immediately, Satan's repetition of "all" parallels Eve's repetition of the same in her question to Adam just before retiring. The question perhaps conceals a desire for the answer which the voice in her dream supplies: Satan's repetition echoes and compounds the self-love latent in the question. As Arnold Stein observes, the voice in the dream may be construed as Eve's very own — "assumed, projected, and heightened by the tempter who is external, but who cannot effectively tempt except internally" (87). The tempter's voice approximates the dreamer's.

More approximations can be heard, notably during the separation scene. Eve suggests to Adam that by gardening separately they might more efficiently fulfill their responsibilities. Her wish accords well with that of the satanic serpent, who hopes to find "*Eve* separate . . . when to his wish, / Beyond his hope, *Eve* separate he spies" (IX, 422–24). Adam tries to dissuade Eve from working alone by pointing out that her reason may be misguided by "some fair appearing good" (354). The distinction between fair and good not only looks forward to Satan's disguise as the beautiful serpent but also looks back to Adam's own evaluation of Eve: "in outward show / Elaborate, of inward less exact" (VIII, 538–39). Hence Adam's warning to Eve should also be his self-warning against being dazzled by his fair spouse. The beast and the beauty are enmeshed yet once more.

Furthermore, Eve's argument for separation strongly anticipates the serpent's argument for a perilous venture; both paraphrase and distort *Areopagitica*.[20] Eve seeks to prove her worth through personal experience: "What is Faith, Love, Virtue unassay'd / Alone, without exterior help sustain'd?" (IX, 335–36). The serpent urges her to know through personal experience: "if what is evil / Be real, why not known, since easier shunn'd?" (IX, 698–99). Eve disparages untried virtue; the serpent encourages tried virtue.

Eve seems to be in the grip of a desire to leap into the unknown, a desire reinforced by dread. That an attraction can sometimes be made more, not less, irresistible by fear has been suggested in the demonic dream of Eve: when she sees that Satan has eaten the forbidden fruit, "damp horror chill'd" her (V, 65), yet she thinks she "Could not but taste" (86). Similar dual responses of fear and fascination run through the temptation scene, where one finds striking correspondences between Eve and the satanic serpent. He has arrived at the garden:

> Spot more delicious than those Gardens feign'd
> Or of reviv'd *Adonis*, or renown'd
> *Alcinoüs*, host of old *Laertes'* Son,
> Or that, not Mystic, where the Sapient King
> Held dalliance with his fair *Egyptian* Spouse.
> Much hee the Place admir'd, the Person more.
> . . . .
> What pleasing seem'd, for her now pleases more,
> She most, and in her look sums all Delight.
> Such Pleasure took the Serpent to behold
> This Flow'ry Plat, the sweet recess of *Eve*
> Thus early, thus alone; her Heav'nly form

Angelic, but more soft, and Feminine,
Her graceful Innocence, her every Air
Of gesture or least action overaw'd
His Malice, and with rapine sweet bereav'd
His fierceness of the fierce intent it brought:
That space the Evil one abstracted stood
From his own evil, and for the time remain'd
Stupidly good, of enmity disarm'd.   (IX, 439–44, 453–65)

The garden of Eden never seems more beautiful than when it is about
to be lost; Eve never seems more delightful than just before her fall. The
beauty and the delight are due in part to the poetic description, but also
in part to the reader's awareness of their imminent loss, of their tran-
sience. By a similar token, Satan is never more pitiful than when he is
"stupidly good," for we know how rare that moment is for the Evil one,
and how fleeting. Coming to seduce, Satan is seduced. Satan, against
his worse instincts, is momentarily charmed, immobilized by his victim.
Taken aback by his own susceptibility, he remonstrates against himself,
"Thoughts, whither have ye led me, with what sweet / Compulsion thus
transported to forget / What hither brought us, hate, not love" (473–75).
Thus he counters love with "Fierce hate," which he "recollects" with an
effort of will (471). Satan's panegyrical description of Eve reveals her
strong attraction — so strong that his malice is "overaw'd," that he finds
in love and beauty "terror" (490) which he can overcome only with
"stronger hate" (491).

We are puzzled for a moment. Who is the one being seduced? The
allusions to the gardens of Adonis, of Alcinoüs, and of Solomon evoke
a temptress more than a tempter; it is "female charm" that predominates
in those gardens.[21] The last allusion — "where the Sapient King / Held
dalliance with his fair *Egyptian* Spouse" — in particular nudges our
thoughts toward Eve, who has twice been described as Adam's "fair
Spouse" (IV, 742, V, 129).[22] And "dalliance" is reminiscent of her "sweet
reluctant amorous delay" (IV, 311). In the light of the allusion, Eve seems
not so much the innocent victim of the satanic serpent as his match.

That the satanic serpent tries to seduce Eve is quite obvious. Wolfgang E. H. Rudat, for instance, has observed that "Satan as serpent . . .
jealously attempts to usurp Adam's place and seduce Eve, *sexually*." The
seduction is, however, complicated by the Circean allusion just before
Eve notices the serpent. The poet tells us that the serpent's ingratiating
overture fails to gain her attention immediately because she is used to
receiving homage "From every Beast, more duteous at her call / Than
at *Circean* call the Herd disguised" (IX, 521–22). At first glance the

analogy seems misaligned, for we would normally expect Satan, about to enchant Eve, to be likened to Circe, and Eve, about to be ensnared, to be likened to Circe's victims—"the Herd disguised." But instead the allusion points to a Circean Eve and a bewitched serpent. Noting the curious analogy, Rudat argues that "Milton endows Eve with the Circean power to transform Satan into a *phallic serpent*," thereby suggesting that "Eve is indirectly reponsible for her own pursuit by the Serpent."[23]

To me this suggests something else: Circean Eve and the satanic serpent *reflect* each other. While Eve is as yet unaware of Satan's presence, the reference to Circe implicates her and foreshadows her transformation into a "snare" (X, 873, XI, 165), the kind of "mortal snare" (IV, 8) that Satan himself personifies.

The reciprocal seductiveness of Eve and the serpent finds potent expression in their provocative eyes. The serpent, "Carbuncle his Eyes" (IX, 500), flaunts his voluptuous body "in sight of *Eve*, / To lure her Eye" (517–18). As Edward Sichi, Jr. has noted, "Carbuncle," in its sense of "lantern," "closely resembles that time-honored image used by Courtly Love poets of 'eyes darting contageous fire.'"[24] But one need not look outside *Paradise Lost* for such an image. Even before the Fall Eve "shot Darts of desire / Into all eyes" (VIII, 62–63), and Adam confessed his weakness "Against the charm of Beauty's powerful glance" (VIII, 533). The metaphor from archery, connoting passion and violence, seems out of place in the prelapsarian world. But we will no longer find the metaphor obtrusive after the Fall, when Eve's "Eye darted contagious Fire" (IX, 1036). The emphasis in the temptation scene on her eyes, objects which the serpent is trying to "lure," evokes prior and subsequent descriptions of Eve's luring eyes, no less flashy, aggressive, and dangerous than the serpent's "Carbuncle." And just as the serpent, by virtue of his beauty, turns the "Eye of Eve to mark his play" (IX, 528) and is "glad / Of her attention gain'd" (528–29), beautiful Eve at that moment is, according to Adam, also "longing to be seen" (X, 877) and, according to Milton, "desirous to make trial of her strength" (IX, Argument). She is apparently no less eager than Satan for their prospective confrontation.

Eve and the serpent continue to reflect and inspect each other during their meeting. Eve's encounter with the serpent recalls her encounter with her image upon first awakening into life. In both scenes, curiosity is aroused through the auditory faculty: in the earlier one she is aroused by "a murmuring sound / Of waters" (IV, 453–54); in the latter it is the "sound / Of rustling leaves" (IX, 518–19) produced by the serpent, who has been likened to a "surging Maze." In the earlier instance she encounters her image in the pool; in the latter, the serpent. Because her image and the serpent share similar physical attributes, as illustrated earlier, the temptation scene brings to mind the reason Comestor imputed to Satan for choosing the serpent — "like favors like."

The likeness is, however, more than physical. The serpent has regarded Eve earlier with love and terror; Eve's reaction to the serpent is a mixture of fascination and *amazement*. Tracking various "mazy" words in the poem, Giamatti notices "a movement whereby physical characteristics cease only to signify and simply become mental states."[25] Thus the serpent's "mazy folds" (IX, 161) and "surging Maze" (499) make way into Eve, who listens (to the beast) "Not unamaz'd" (552) and "Yet more amaz'd" (614). But Giamatti does not explain why it is the *serpent's* physical characteristics that become *Eve's* mental states. I believe these words provide another verbal mirror whereby the serpent is made to reflect Eve. Just as the serpent "Misleads th' amaz'd Night-wanderer from his way" (640), Eve will adopt tortuous expression to mislead Adam, though at this point the serpent's physical tangles may reflect no more than her mental confusion, "in wand'ring mazes lost."

The movement of starting back and forth, reminiscent of the figure at the pool and of "Serpent error wand'ring" (VII, 302), is repeated here, though again psychologically rather than literally. Eve is enticed by the serpent's flattery but wary of its excess; yet notwithstanding her awareness that his "overpraising leaves in doubt / The virtue of that Fruit" (IX, 615–16), she asks to be led to the tree. Recognizing the forbidden tree for what it is, she again draws back, recalling God's command, "Ye shall not eat . . . lest ye die" (662–63); but being "more soft" than angels (458), she will "yield" to the serpent's guileful arguments which, as previously mentioned, echo her own in the separation scene.

The subtle beast both elicits and replicates her wavering response. He begins the temptation by dazzling Eve with his voluptuous body and human speech, the one to attract, the other to amaze. The voluptuous body, the flashing colors, and the wanton dance are sensuous baits designed to lure Eve's eye. But the visual allurement is only an overture to the miracle of language, which takes the form of an amorist's serenade:

> *Wonder* not, sovran Mistress, if perhaps
> Thou canst, who are sole *Wonder*, much less arm
> Thy looks, the Heav'n of mildness, with disdain,
> Displeas'd that I approach thee thus, and *gaze*
> Insatiate, I thus single, nor have fear'd
> Thy *awful* brow, more *awful* thus retir'd.
> Fairest resemblance of thy Maker fair,

> Thee *all things* living *gaze* on, *all things* thine
> By gift, and thy Celestial Beauty adore
> With ravishment beheld.   (IX, 532–41, emphasis added)

Echoing the voice in the dream, the speech once more sets up a symmetry between Eve and the serpent. They regard, or claim to regard, each other with mingled fear and fondness. Eve is asked not to "wonder," a word which connotes both amazement and fascination and which Eve will reiterate when she says with respect to the talking serpent that "such wonder claims attention due" (IX, 566). And they indeed give each other due attention. In words that again convey fear and appreciation, the serpent claims to "adore" Eve despite her "awful brow," to behold her "with ravishment."

The several pairs of identical words in the speech constitute a verbal mirror. The repetitions of "wonder" and "awful" blur the distinctions of Eve as the subject, and as an object of veneration. In "Wonder not," Eve is the implied subject and the serpent is the implied object; the serpent is saying, "Eve, do not wonder at me." But in "sole Wonder," Eve becomes the object of the serpent's admiration. (The serpent is again the object of wonder in line 566.) The first "awful" modifies her brow, but the second "awful" calls attention to the serpent's perception: it is the serpent that judges Eve to be "more awful thus retir'd." Similarly, Eve, the object of the serpent's "gaze" and of universal "gaze" ("Thee all things living gaze on"), is also the "mistress" of the gazers ("all things thine"). Their gazes answer her "looks." The shifts in personal focus which the pairs of identical words effect produce a ventriloquistic effect.

Other echoes reinforce the symmetry between Eve and the serpent. His emphasis on being "single" reminds us of Eve's single state, having separated from Adam for the moment. As the serpent begs Eve not to arm her look with disdain, one remembers that he has just armed himself with disdain (473–93) so as not to be "disarm'd" (465) by her beauty. His flattering compliment of Eve — "Fairest resemblance of thy Maker fair" — chimes in with the narrator's description of the serpent as "lovely, never since of Serpent kind / Lovelier" (IX, 504–05). The serpent, that description continues, is lovelier than "those that in *Illyria* chang'd / *Hermione* and *Cadmus*, or the God / In *Epidaurus*." (505–07). Given the fearful symmetry between fair Eve and the lovely beast, William Empson's view (dismissed by Hughes) that these classical allusions imply that "Eve turned into a snake and became Satan's consort" may not be as far-fetched as it sounds.[26]

Whether she literally turns into a snake or not, Eve wants to *copy* the serpent. Admiring both his gorgeous shape and his gift of tongue, she inquires how he comes to possess the faculties of speech and reason. When the serpent answers that he has acquired both by eating the fair apples of a goodly tree, Eve assumes that she may by the same means ascend the scale of being. Such an assumption requires a twist of thought, for as Fish points out, "What holds for serpent, if it did hold, may not hold for man."[27] By thinking that she may improve herself by eating the apple, Eve tacitly identifies with the serpent, imputing a parallel between herself and the animal. As though the parallel were not transparent enough, Milton has Eve echo the serpent's argument before eating the fruit. Like the serpent, she pays tribute to the knowledge of good and evil, disparages the threat of death, questions God's motive in imposing the prohibition, and uses empirical evidence to evaluate the forbidden fruit (IX, 745–79). Even without her reiteration, one can assume from her act that the serpent's argument works. By making her rehearse the argument — reflecting the serpent verbally — Milton seems to insist that the serpent's argument is also Eve's own.

But Eve does not voice what is probably her strongest motive in wanting to taste the fruit: divine aspiration. "Nor was Godhead from her thought" (IX, 790), the narrator divulges; and we can infer from his remark that Eve succumbs to the desire to be seen a "Goddess among Gods, ador'd and serv'd / By angels numberless" (IX, 547–48). Like her tempter, Eve "trusted to have equal'd the most high" (I, 40). Like her tempter, who disdains submission (IV, 81–82), Eve wants to be equal or superior to Adam: "for inferior who is free?" (IX, 825). The "modest pride" she displayed at her first appearance now distends into the "considerate Pride" of Satan (I, 603); the cause of his fall is now hers.

When the poet has Eve parrot the serpent, and links the reason of her fall with that of Satan's, he goes far beyond the author of Genesis in stressing her culpability. In Genesis, "the serpent beguiled [Eve]" (iii, 13). Milton's Eve, by contrast, is hardly beguiled by the serpent; rather, she *concurs* with him.

After the Fall her wiles continue to bring Satan — the "wily Adder" (IX, 625) — to mind. Just as the Devil turns aside in envy upon witnessing the embrace of Adam and Eve, Eve cannot bear the thought (should only she die) of Adam in the company of another Eve. Both Eve and the serpent hide their dark motives "under show of Love well feign'd" (IX, 492) by pretending that they want to share their enlightenment with their victims. The speech with which Eve persuades Adam to eat the fruit is, as Fish observes, "a tissue of Satanic echoes."[28] Both the serpent and Eve offer themselves as proofs of the fruit's benign effects. The serpent urged Eve, "reach then, and freely taste" (IX, 732); Eve, having eaten the fruit and acknowledged the serpent's "Experience" as her "Best guide" (IX, 807–09), urges Adam, "On my experience . . . freely taste" (IX, 988). After his fall Adam will openly link Eve and the serpent and wish that Eve would emit "color Serpentine" (X, 870) as a warning, "lest that too heav'nly form, pretended / To hellish falsehood, snare [men]" (X, 872–73).[29] What some earlier artists made explicit in paintings Milton has woven into poetry; he has blended the contours of Eve into those of the Eden serpent.

III

Milton's Eve is certainly not an innocent victim, whether or not she is "crooked" from the start, or "bent . . . / More to the part sinister" from her inception (X, 885–86). That she appreciates her beauty as much as does anyone else, that she dreams an alarming dream, that she enjoys spending time alone and receiving attention from beings other than Adam, and even that she shares certain physical characteristics with the serpent and admires the talking animal, are attributes sinless in themselves. But guided by Milton's warning voice, which importunately aligns Eve with Satan through reverberating verbal echoes, we cannot help seeing them as indicative of the "liability to fall with which man was created."[30] More importantly, when Eve finally crosses the boundary from innocence to sin by eating the fruit — an act putatively instigated by the satanic serpent — we must see her as at least collusive, and not merely deceived.

We can also see her as guilty at large. In the light of the persistent liaison between Eve and the serpent, it is tempting to view the serpent as a psychological projection, though Milton's Satan — like the Homeric gods — may seem far too convincing a presence to be treated allegorically. But just as the alleged god-abetted transgressions in Homer are often consistent with what one would expect from the human culprit (so that never would a Hector abduct Helen or a Penelope elope with Paris because of divine intervention), the serpent in *Paradise Lost* may be seen as "an external agent who presses home the self-temptation," to use Stein's perception in another context.[31]

It is the attempt to dramatize this dual aspect of sin rather than any conscious attempt on Milton's part to stigmatize woman, as some feminist critics (e.g. Gilbert and Landy) claim, that chiefly accounts for the many parallels between Eve and the serpent. Nevertheless, these persistent parallels do, to some extent, give away the poet's attitude toward the opposite sex.[32] Whereas Genesis merely records that the serpent beguiled Eve and Comestor merely suggests that the serpent resembled Eve, not vice versa, Milton takes pains to entwine the two. Notwithstanding that the serpent as a phallic symbol lends itself more readily to association with Adam,[33] it is Adam who calls Eve a serpent, who hammers the homology while reproaching Eve: "with the Serpent meeting / Fool'd and beguil'd, by him thou, I by thee" (X, 879-80). The pronouns "thou" and "thee" conflate Eve as the beguiled victim and as the beguiling agent.

Although critics often cite this passage to demonstrate Milton's misogyny, a detailed examination of the homology — developed by the poet all along — suggests that his attitude toward women is rather one of sympathetic antipathy: they enchant him as much as the serpent enchants Eve; but unlike Eve, Milton is more than wary and all too mindful. He likens Eve to Pandora, "whom the Gods / Endow'd with all thir gifts" (IV, 714-15), yet "O too like / In sad event," when "she ensnar'd / Mankind with her fair looks" (715-16, 717-18). Like Satan, Milton seems to find terror in love and beauty. Hence he sees in the captivating serpent a fit emblem for the First Mother. Both Eve and the serpent in *Paradise Lost* charm, ensnare; indeed both use their charm to ensnare. In both, to use Adam's words, a "too heav'nly form" is "pretended to hellish falsehood" (X, 872-73). But if Eve serves as a satanic agent by ushering sin and death into the world, and all our woe, it is also "by" her that "the Promis'd Seed shall all restore"; it is "her seed" that shall bruise the serpent's head (XII, 623, X, 181). The poet's aversion to women is so involved and interwoven with attraction that they are as inseparable as the knowledge of evil and good.

We will find no end to disentangling Milton's attitudes toward the first woman, or toward women in general, but will find ourselves lost in wandering mazes. Far less intricate, however, is his attitude toward human responsibility. In stressing the affinities between the serpent and Eve, the poet implies that external persuasion corresponds to personal desire. Cautioning Eve against separation because of the subtle foe, Adam no less insists that it is "within [herself] / The danger lies" (IX, 348-49). To cause human disobedience, the serpent that stalks Eden must worm his way into the "paradise within."

University of California, Los Angeles

NOTES

1. In writing this paper I have invoked the aid of John Anson, who first taught me how to read Milton, and of Henry Kelly, who illumined what in me is dark with his formidable scholarship; to both, my endless gratitude.

2. I, 34–36. Quotations of the poem are from *Paradise Lost: A Poem in Twelve Books*, ed. Merritt Y. Hughes (New York, 1962).

3. Arnold Stein, *Answerable Style: Essays on "Paradise Lost"* (Minneapolis, 1953), p. 75.

4. Cf. Carl Jung's description of the "shadow" — one of the three components of the psyche — as "the invisible saurian tail that man still drags behind him," in *Psychological Reflections* (London, 1945), p. 217. Sandra Gilbert, in "Patriarchal Poetry and Women Readers: Reflections on Milton's Bogey," *PMLA* XCIII (1978), enumerates some of the parallels between Satan and Eve in order to show Milton's misogyny (372). I offer not only a more comprehensive study of the parallels but also a different interpretation of their significance, viewing the poet's attitude toward women (in my opinion an ambivalent rather than a downright misogynous one) as only a secondary cause for the parallels.

5. "Timens vero deprehendi a viro, mulierem minus providam et certam [sic; *lege* ceream] in vitium flecti aggressus est, et hoc per serpentem. . . . Elegit etiam quoddam genus serpentis . . . virgineum vultum habens, quia similia similibus applaudunt" (*Historia Scholastica, Liber Genesis*, in *Patrologia latina*, ed. J. P. Migne vol. CXCVIII [1855], col. 1072; quoted in Kelly, "The Metamorphoses of the Eden Serpent During the Middle Ages and Renaissance," in *Viator* II (1971), 308).

6. The notion that the serpent resembles Eve also appears in an ancient Syrian biblical history, *The Book of the Cave of Treasures: A History of the Patriarchs and the Kings their Successors from the Creation to the Crucifixion of Christ*, trans. E. A. Wallis Budge (London, 1927), pp. 63–64: "And when she turned round towards him, she saw her own form [reflected] in him, and she talked to him; and Satan led her astray with his lying words, because the nature of woman is soft (or, yielding)." Kelly rightly concludes from this account "either that Eve looked like a serpent or that the serpent looked like a woman" ("The Metamorphoses," 310). Though the Syrian text is unlikely to have influenced *Paradise Lost*, the epithets chosen by the ancient author to describe "the nature of woman" — "soft (or, yielding)" — are also used by Milton repeatedly to describe Eve (IV, 298; IV, 309; IV, 310; IV, 471; IV, 489; VIII, 254; IX, 386; IX, 458; X, 865). Some forms of the female-headed serpent appear also in the *Chester Plays*, William Langland's *Piers the Plowman*, Arnoul Gréban's *Le mystére de la passion*, Saint Bonaventure's commentary on Peter Lombard's *Sentences*, Guido delle Colonne's *Historia destructionis troiae*, Vincent of Beauvais's *Mirror of Nature*, Thomas of Cantimpré's *De natura rerum*, and Giambattista Andreini's *L'Adamo*. See Kelly, "The Metamorphoses," 319–22, and John K. Bonnell, "The Serpent with a Human Head in Art and in Mystery Play," *American Journal of Archaeology*, 2nd series, XXI (1917), 258–78.

7. Bonnell, "The Serpent," 257–78, hypothesizes that the woman-headed serpent originates in literary sources (i.e. Peter Comestor, Vincent de Beauvais, Guido delle Colonne, and the *Speculum Humanae Salvationis*), which then influence the dramatic form, and that in turn influences the art form. Hence Michelangelo was following a tradition that was by his time two hundred years old. Kelly, however, points out to me that the hybrid figure appears in art before it appears in drama. For the divergent interpretations of the woman-headed serpent, see Alice Kemp-Welch, "The Woman-headed Serpent in Art," *Nineteenth Century and After* LII (1902), 983–91.

8. Watson Kirkconnell, *The Celestial Cycle: The Theme of "Paradise Lost" in World Literature with Translations of the Major Analogues* (Toronto, 1952), p. 242. Hughes, p. 213 n. 14, believes that Milton *consciously* departs from Andreini by introducing the satanic serpent as "Mere Serpent in appearance" (IX, 413).

9. J. B. Trapp, "The Iconography of the Fall of Man," in *Approaches to "Paradise*

Lost," ed. C. A. Patrides (London, 1968), pp. 223–65; Roland M. Frye, *Milton's Imagery and the Visual Arts: Iconographic Tradition in the Epic Poems* (Princeton, 1978), p. 104. Kelly alerts me to the dubiety in Frye's argument.

10. Diane McColley, *Milton's Eve* (Urbana, 1983), p. 8.

11. D. C. Allen, "Milton and the Name of Eve," *MLN* LXXIV (1959), 682, 683.

12. Milton's inspiration may also have come from art. In a fourteenth-century French painting at the Louvre, entitled "Virgin and Child, with Eve (?) Beneath," and reproduced in Jeffrey M. Hoffeld, "Adam's Two Wives," *The Metropolitan Museum of Art Bulletin* XXVI (1968), 435, the female figure underneath the Virgin has a distinctive serpentine profile. Especially suggestive of a serpent are her mouth and her seemingly legless body. That she is Eve is suggested by her eating an apple. Hoffeld thinks that the woman is a conflation of Eve and Lilith (436). However, Bonnell, "The Serpent," 290 n.2, points out that there is no proof of Lilith's influence, and Kelly, "The Metamorphoses," 302 n.8, observes that Hoffeld has offered none.

13. Ann Davidson Ferry, *Milton's Epic Voice: The Narrator in "Paradise Lost"* (Cambridge, Mass., 1963), pp. 112–15; Stanley Fish, *Surprised by Sin: The Reader in "Paradise Lost"* (1967; rpt. Berkeley, 1971), pp. 92–93; Christopher Ricks, *Milton's Grand Style* (Oxford, 1963), p. 110.

14. I owe this and several other valuable insights to my colleague Susan Brienza.

15. See note 6 above.

16. Though aware of the negative construction — "not with indented wave" — in the second passage, I believe that the negative qualifies "indented" rather than "wave"; the serpent is still wavy, though the wave moves vertically — in "rising folds" — not horizontally. A. Bartlett Giamatti notes that Milton's serpent is modeled on the seamonsters of Virgil: "pectora quorum inter fluctus arrecta iubaeque / sanguineae superant undas; pars cetera pontum / pone legit sinuatque immensa volumine terga" ("Their bosoms rise amid the surge, and their crests, blood-red, overtop the waves; the rest of them skims the main behind and their huge backs curve in many a fold") (*Aeneid* II, 206–08; quoted and translated in Giamatti, *The Earthly Paradise and the Renaissance Epic* [Princeton, 1966], p. 304 n.13).

17. Philip E. Slater, *The Glory of Hera: Greek Mythology and Greek Family* (Boston, 1968), p. 81, observes that "clinging vine" is traditionally a "serpentine perception of femininity" and that Ovid explicitly links vines and serpentine curls in describing how Salmacis pursues Hermaphroditus,

> Surrounding him with arms, legs, lips, and hands
> As though she were a snake caught by an eagle,
> Who leaping from his claws wound her tall body
> Around his head, and lashed his wings with her
> Long tail, as though she were quick ivy tossing
> Her vines round the thick body of a tree.
>
> (*Metamorphoses* IV, 357–62; quoted in Slater)

18. Fish, *Surprised by Sin*, p. 102, also notes that Eve "seems to curl, even coil, in the manner, perhaps, of a serpent."

19. D. C. Allen, "Milton's Eve and the Evening Angels," *MLN* LXXV (1959), 108–09. See also *Hermetica: The Ancient Greek and Latin Writings which Contain Religious or Philosophic Teachings Ascribed to Hermes Trismegistus*, vol. I, trans. Walter Scott (Oxford, 1924), pp. 121–23. Like the Ovidian story of Narcissus, the *Hermetica* episode underlines the relation between self-love and the Fall of Man.

20. John S. Diekhoff, "Eve, the Devil, and *Areopagitica*," *MLQ* V (1944), 429–34; Diekhoff analyzes the similarity and fallacy of the arguments used by Eve and Satan in the light of *Areopagitica*.

21. Nausicäa, the daughter of Alcinoüs, is in search of a husband; the ardent goddess woos the reluctant Adonis; Solomon, referred to elsewhere as "that uxorious King . . . Beguile'd by fair Idolatresses" (I, 444–45), extols the beauty of his spouse in the garden. For other allusions to temptresses in Milton's garden, see Giamatti, *The Earthly Paradise*, pp. 318–34.

22. Ricks, *Milton's Grand Style*, p. 135.

23. Wolfgang E. H. Rudat, "'Thy Beauty's Heav'nly Ray': Milton's Satan and the Circean Eve," *MQ* XIX (March 1985), 17, 18.

24. Edward Sichi, Jr., "The Serpent with Carbuncle Eyes: Milton's Use of 'Carbuncle' in *Paradise Lost*," *MQ* XIV (1980), 126.

25. Giamatti, *The Earthly Paradise*, p. 306.

26. William Empson, *Some Versions of Pastoral* (1935; rpt. New York, 1974), p. 175.

27. Fish, *Surprised by Sin*, p. 250.

28. Fish, *Surprised by Sin*, p. 253.

29. Gilbert, "Patriarchal Poetry and Women Readers," 372, believes that the hostility God sets between the woman and the serpent is "the discord necessary to divide those who are . . . too much alike, too much attracted to each other."

30. John Milton, *De doctrina Christiana*, trans. Charles R. Sumner, ed. James H. Hanford and W. H. Dunn, *The Complete Works of John Milton* (New York, 1933), vol. XV, p. 181.

31. Stein, *Answerable Style*, p. 75; there Stein is commenting on Adam's Fall.

32. In addition to the works by Gilbert and McColley cited above, see David Aers and Bob Hodge, "'Rational Burning': Milton on Sex and Marriage," in *Milton Studies*, vol. XIII, ed. James D. Simmonds (Pittsburgh, 1979), pp. 3–33; S. A. Demetrakopoulos, "Eve as a Circean and Courtly Fatal Woman," *MQ* IX (1975), 99–107; Marilyn R. Farwell, "Eve, the Separation Scene, and the Renaissance Idea of Androgyny," in *Milton Studies*, vol. XVI, ed. James D. Simmonds (Pittsburgh, 1982), pp. 3–20; Christine Froula, "When Eve Reads Milton: Undoing the Canonical Economy," *Critical Inquiry* X (1983), 321–47; Marcia Landy, "'A Free and Open Encounter': Milton and the Modern Reader," in *Milton Studies*, vol. IX, ed. James D. Simmonds (Pittsburgh, 1976), pp. 3–36 and "Kinship and the Role of Women in *Paradise Lost*," in *Milton Studies*, vol. IV, ed. James D. Simmonds (Pittsburgh, 1972), pp. 3–18; Barbara K. Lewalski, "Milton on Women — Yet Once More," in *Milton Studies*, vol. VI, ed. James D. Simmonds (Pittsburgh, 1974), pp. 3–20; Joan Malory Webber, "The Politics of Poetry: Feminism and *Paradise Lost*," in *Milton Studies*, vol. XIV, ed. James D. Simmonds (Pittsburgh, 1980), pp. 3–24.

33. However, Slater, *The Glory of Hera*, pp. 80–83, 111–15, contends that the serpent has always been a bisexual symbol.

MILTON'S "DRAMATICK CONSTITUTION": THE CELESTIAL DIALOGUE IN *PARADISE LOST*, BOOK III

Michael Lieb

I

I N   H I S   criticism of *Paradise Lost*, a deservedly obscure eighteenth-century schoolmaster by the name of John Clarke once took Milton to task for introducing God and the Son as "Actors in his Poem." "A Poet," observed Clarke, "may contrive Scenes of Action, and find speeches for his Fellow Mortals of the highest Degree," but that poet dare not "bring down the most High into a Scene of Diversion, and assign him his Part of Acting and Speaking."[1] Although Clarke made no mention of specifically what "Scene of Diversion" he had in mind, we may safely assume that the dialogue in heaven in Book III is an excellent candidate. Few scenes in *Paradise Lost* have occasioned as much difficulty as that one.[2]

Responding to the scene, critics have traditionally objected not only to Milton's handling of character delineation but to his treatment of theological doctrine. In both respects, they have taken issue with Milton's attempt to render God and the Son dramatically. Those troubled by character delineation have customarily leveled their barbs at the figure of God. Pope's quip that "God the Father turns a School-Divine"[3] implies as much the failure of drama as the impropriety of attempting drama under such circumstances in the first place. These are exactly the issues that underlie more recent criticism of the scene. William Empson's charge that Milton's God is reminiscent of Uncle Joe Stalin represents the crude extreme to which a criticism of Milton's dramaturgy is liable to extend.[4] Complementing the criticism of Milton's delineation of God is that which calls into question the theology his deity espouses. This criticism faults Milton for his failure to make his theology palatable. That failure, argue the proponents of such a view, is the result not just of the theology itself but of the manner in which it is transmitted. For these critics, the theology is transmitted in a way that suggests nothing more than the flat presentation of dogma by an unpleasant and pedantic figure who has his "Yes Man" sitting at his right-hand side ready to assent to anything his Father might hand down.[5] What results for those

who hold this view is a scene that is decidedly undramatic in its trans-
mission of theology. For them, dogma has usurped drama.

In response to such an outlook, critics like Irene Samuel have attempted to reclaim the integrity of the scene by arguing that it is incorrect to "read the scene as a mere presentation of doctrinal assertions con-
veniently divided between Father and Son." Reacting to the scene in that
way, readers "have incautiously misconstrued as dogma what Milton intended as drama."[6] This emphasis upon drama invites an interpretation
of Father and Son not as mouthpieces for the expression of an unpalatable
theology but as fully conceived characters participating in a dramatic
interchange. As perceptive as Samuel's argument is, however, her insights
have not won as many converts as might be expected. Jackson Cope, for
example, maintains that the so-called drama Samuel discovers is really
not drama at all. Rather, what she misconstrues as drama is actually
a kind of ritual enactment of dogma reinforced through the employment
of rhetorical schemes from one set speech to the next.[7] Such a view is
in keeping with J. B. Broadbent's observation that the scene is founded
upon an "impregnable rhetoric of dogma" through which "corridors of
verbal mirrors" do nothing but reflect "unbodied concepts."[8]

One does not need either Cope or Broadbent, however, to call into
question the dramatic point of view that Samuel endorses. Samuel ironically does that herself. Precisely as she argues for a dramatic reading
of the dialogue in heaven, she compromises her own point of view by
maintaining that Milton's God as Transcendent Being speaks tonelessly
and dispassionately. Representing "the toneless voice of the moral law,"
Milton's God, avers Samuel, "speaks simply what is." In other words,
one finds a curious turn-about in Samuel's essay. While maintaining
that the scene must be read dramatically, she deprives the dialogue of
just that drama which would otherwise bring it to life. She does so because the moment it is conceived as true drama, those characters who
participate in it become liable to the very judgments that prompted critics like William Empson to level his charges in the first place. If God
is removed from the arena of drama, then such charges no longer obtain. God is conceived not as character but as principle: "Total Being,"
"Primal Energy," the "Voice of Reason," to invoke Samuel's epithets.[9]
One cannot have it both ways: either the scene is conceived dramatically, or it is not. The decision to interpret the scene one way or the
other makes all the difference in the world for an understanding of Milton's epic and the theology it embodies.

In his reading of the scene, Stanley Fish, for example, opts to interpret it totally as nondrama. Transforming the scene from dialogue into

monologue, Fish conceives of Milton's God as a being who makes logical, accurate, and objective pronouncements in a kind of divine vacuum. This being, says Fish, "does not argue, he asserts, disposing a series of self-evident axioms in an objective order, 'not talking to anyone in particular but meditating on objects.'" If the reader takes exception to what God says, "the fault (quite literally)" is his own, not God's. Almost as an afterthought, Fish does concede, albeit parenthetically, that God is "technically address[ing] the Son"; nonetheless, God "is not in any sense . . . initiating a discussion."[10] Like the God of Irene Samuel, the God of Stanley Fish is relieved of any of the responsibilities that constitute dramatic verisimilitude. Totally removed and fully aloof, he effectively assumes the role of an abstraction void of dimensionality. He is cleansed of the taint of drama: He simply *is*.

In effect, what Fish does is to argue for a Ramistic interpretation of Milton's God, which, considering the profound influence of Ramism upon Milton, is quite understandable. As Fish documents, the phrase "not talking to anyone in particular but meditating on objects" comes from Walter J. Ong's pioneering study *Ramus, Method, and the Decay of Dialogue*.[11] According to Ong, the Ramist mentality is fundamentally antidialogic: "in the characteristic outlook fostered by the Ramist rhetoric," observes Ong, "speaking is directed to a world where even persons respond only as objects — that is, say nothing back." Markedly hostile toward drama, Ramus supported an educational reform that included the abolishing of plays.[12] Ramus's attitude, in turn, was particularly congenial to the English Puritans. In its own way, the closing of the theaters in 1642 represents ample testimony to the influence of this outlook in the political sphere. From the aesthetic perspective, the outlook is equally as compelling. So Ong observes that "when the Puritan mentality, which is here the Ramist mentality, produces poetry, it is at first blatantly didatic, but shades gradually into reflective poetry which does not talk to anyone in particular but meditates on objects."[13]

The statement returns us once again to Stanley Fish, who says of Milton's God that "the tonal qualities usually ascribed to his voice are accidental, the result of what the reader reads *into* the speech rather than what is there. The form of his discourse is determined by the nature of the thing he contemplates rather than by the desire to project a personality (*ethos*) or please a specific audience (*pathos*); its mode is exfoliation; that is, the speech does not build, it *unfolds* according to the rules of method."[14] As far as I am concerned, nothing could be further from the truth. To remove Milton's God to a realm of abstraction void of dimensionality, to cleanse him of the taint of drama, to conceive him simply as that which *is* denies him those essential characteristics that constitute Milton's rendering of God as a fully realized being in *Paradise Lost*.

This is a being who may disturb us, who may even repel us. But he is a being nonetheless. His proper environment is that of drama; his proper discourse that of dialogue, not monologue. As such, Milton's conception of God is in harmony with what Mikhail Bakhtin implies is "the dialogic imagination," according to which the word as uttered "encounters an alien word . . . in a living, tension-filled interaction."[15] It is this "living, tension-filled interaction" that underscores the celestial dialogue in *Paradise Lost*. If Milton's rendering of God causes us discomfort, so be it. The answer to this discomfort is not to consign the deity to the realm of abstraction. The appropriate response, paradoxically, is that of God's critics who are inclined to argue with him, to impugn his motives, to be offended by what he says and how he says it, to engage him in debate, to struggle with him, to see him struggling with himself.[16] It is the critics of Milton's God who provide the greatest insight into how the deity of *Paradise Lost* is to be understand. For, knowingly or not, these critics at the very least credit Milton with the courage, if not the audacity, to have conceived God dramatically. This, as I shall argue, is how Milton did conceive God and, along with him, the Son in Book III of *Paradise Lost*. There, Milton provides a full account of what he terms in *De doctrina christiana* "the drama of the personalities in the Godhead" ("*et personalitatum illud totum drama advocem*").[17] Although disinclined to discuss that drama in his theological tract, Milton gave it full play in the epic.

If one examines the dialogue in heaven closely, he will discover there what amounts in fact to a five-act drama. In act 1 (80–134), the Father foretells the fall of man but promises grace; in act 2 (144–66), the Son responds to his Father's promise in a way that causes the Father in act 3 (167–217) to delineate his intentions further by calling for a volunteer to sacrifice himself on behalf of man. That request, in turn, sets the stage for the Son's act of accepting his sacrificial vocation in act 4 (227–65). This gesture is followed by the Father's praise of the Son and prognostication of the future in act 5 (274–343).[18] The action, of course, is essentially comedic: although it begins tragically, it resolves itself in an assertion of the *felix culpa* upon which the epic as a whole is based.[19] From the comedic perspective, the Son's *anagnorisis* or recognition concerning the nature of redemption and his role in becoming the means by which God brings it about is followed by a *peripeteia* or reversal in the action: "So Heav'nly love shall outdo Hellish hate, / Giving to death, and dying to redeem, / So dearly to redeem what Hellish hate / So easily destroy'd"

(III, 298–301).[20] The five-act structure of the dialogue that encompasses this *mimesis*, furthermore, is framed by a prologue and an epilogue. If the prologue is represented by the poet's "Hail" that inaugurates Book III (1–55), the epilogue is represented by the "Hail" of the assembled hosts that surround the throne as witnesses to the dialogue (372–415). As such, both prologue and epilogue embody their own doxologies, one human, the other angelic. To the angelic "Hail" that closes the dialogue, the poet joins his own voice: "Hail Son of God, Saviour of Men, thy Name / Shall be the copious matter of my Song / Henceforth, and never shall my Harp thy praise / Forget, nor from thy Fathers praise disjoin" (III, 412–15). Framed by prologue and epilogue, the five-act drama is thereby brought full circle in its course.

If Milton found a discussion of "the drama of the personalities in the Godhead" unsuitable to his theological tract, then, the recreation of the drama as epic event became entirely appropriate to the action of *Paradise Lost*. Such is only natural given Milton's predisposition to accommodate sacred matter to the demands of secular form. *Pace* John Clarke, Milton saw nothing amiss in "bring[ing] down the most High into a Scene of Diversion, and assign[ing] him his Part of Acting and Speaking." Doing so, in fact, was entirely in accord with his interpretation of the biblical text, which for Milton represented a veritable storehouse for dramatic reenactment. All one need do is glance at Milton's plans for dramas in the Cambridge manuscript to verify this fact. If those plans provide insight into the dramatic underpinnings of Milton's epics, they suggest the extent to which his closet drama is a fully realized product of this dramaturgical perspective. Defending that perspective in the preface to *Samson Agonistes*, Milton accordingly found himself in agreement with those who viewed the Book of Revelation as a tragedy, divisible into "Acts distinguisht each by a Chorus of Heavenly Harpings and Song between."

The idea is one enunciated as early as *The Reason of Church-government*, in which Milton revealed his inclination to view the events of Scripture in dramatic terms. Ranging over the entire field of literary precedent available to him in the fulfillment of his own future endeavors, he enthusiastically endorsed a reading of Scripture consistent with the practice of conceiving the biblical text as the highest form of drama, one comparable even to the "Dramatick constitutions" of Sophocles and Euripides. Embedded in Scripture could be found drama of all kinds. So Milton observed that "Scripture affords us a divine pastoral Drama in the Song of *Salomon* consisting of two persons and a double *Chorus* . . . and [that] the Apocalyps of Saint *John* is the majestick image of a high and stately Tragedy, shutting up and intermingling her solemn Scenes and Acts with a sevenfold *Chorus* of halleluja's and harping symphonies" (III, pp. 237–38). In keeping with such views, Milton proposed in *The Reason of Church-government* "to celebrate in glorious and lofty Hymns the throne and equipage of Gods Almightiness" (III, p. 238).[21]

By the time Milton came to formulate the celestial drama through which this would be made possible, he was prepared to stage an event that would represent the culmination of all those dramatic plans earlier set down in the Cambridge manuscript. He was prepared, that is, to fulfill his role as dramatist by writing what John Demaray has so aptly called the "theatrical epic."[22] In its own way, the dialogue in heaven in *Paradise Lost* is as much a fully conceived drama within that "theatrical framework" as any Milton ever wrote.[23] "Shutting up and intermingling her solemn Scenes and Acts," the dialogue in heaven is a "Dramatick constitution," to use Milton's phrase, that portrays as vividly as one can possibly imagine the conflicts, the struggles, the passionate interchanges, and the reconciliations of "the drama of the personalities in the Godhead." To gain a fuller appreciation of how the dialogue was originally conceived and how it is to be understood, then, one might well begin with Milton's early plans for a drama on the Fall. An examination of those plans will suggest something of the literary bearing that the dialogue would come to assume in *Paradise Lost*. This understanding, in turn, will provide a greater awareness of how Milton fashioned God and the Son as dramatic characters.

II

As the plans in the Cambridge manuscript make clear, Milton definitely had in mind some sort of celestial dialogue as part of his projected dramas. Although a dialogue between Father and Son is not specifically mentioned, a debate among the figures of Justice, Mercy, and Wisdom certainly is. In the second draft of his plans, for example, Milton included "Justice, Mercie, and Wisdome" among the "Persons" of his proposed drama, and in the third draft, he fleshed out his intentions by conceiving Justice, Mercy, and Wisdom as "debating what should become of man if he fall." The third draft is particularly apposite, for it not only projects a debate among Justice, Mercy, and Wisdom but subscribes to a five-act structure framed by a prologue and a choric epilogue. As outlined in the fourth draft, Justice and Mercy reappear to admonish man and to comfort him after he falls (XVIII, pp. 229–32).

The inclusion of Justice, Mercy, and Wisdom in his dramatic plans suggests Milton's indebtedness to the medieval tradition that allegorizes Psalm liiiv, 10: "Mercy and truth are met together; righteousness and peace have kissed each other."[24] Dating back at least as early as the twelfth century, the allegory depicts Mercy, Truth, Righteousness (or Justice), and Peace as the Four Daughters of God debating over the soul of man in the dramatic setting of a celestial parliament. Although the occasion of the various parliaments ranged in time from the Creation to the Last Judgment, the debates among the Daughters consistently focused upon what would become of the soul of man. Presided over by God, these debates normally resolved themselves in the offer of the Son to atone for man's sins as an expression of divine grace. As a result of that offer, the Four Daughters were reconciled. If the allegory of the Four Daughters of God enjoyed wide currency during the Middle Ages, it left its mark on the Renaissance as well.[25] For our purposes, the importance of the allegory lies in the uniquely dramatic character it bestows upon the conception of the celestial parliament. Because of the way in which the allegory was traditionally formulated, the celestial parliament was transformed into an arena of emotionally charged conflict with the future of the human race at stake. Even a cursory overview of medieval and Renaissance renderings of the allegory will suggest how fully it lent itself to drama of the most spirited sort.

In what is probably its earliest Christianized form, Hugo of St. Victor's *Annotations* on the Psalms (ca. 1120 A.D.) depicted Truth and Mercy not simply meeting but, in effect, contending with one another over the soul of man. According to Hope Traver, Hugo might have been influenced in this regard by a tenth-century midrash, which has Mercy and Truth not just meeting but "thrusting" at one another, and Justice and Peace not kissing but "fighting" together.[26] The spirit of contentiousness underscores the allegory from the very beginning. The drama implicit in this contentiousness informs the debates to a greater or lesser degree throughout the Middle Ages and the Renaissance. So in the play of the Salutation and Conception from the *Ludus Coventriae* (ca. 1468), there is a parliament in heaven in which the Four Daughters debate over the salvation of man. "Should he be saved?" asks Justitia, and then responds to her own question with "Nay! nay! nay!" Following this harsh and emotional judgment, Misericordia observes, "Sister Righteousness, you are too vengeable!" The debate is not resolved until Filius offers himself as a sacrifice for man in a Council of the Trinity, after which the virtues are finally reconciled.[27] The emotionally charged atmosphere discernible here extends into the celestial parliaments portrayed in such Renaissance works as Giles Fletcher's *Christ's Victory and Triumph* (1610) and Joseph Fletcher's *The History of the Perfect-Cursed-Blessed Man* (1628).

As one greatly influenced by this tradition, Milton might well be expected to be responsive to its dramatic implications. Accordingly, the concept of debate that one finds so much a part of the plans in the Cambridge manuscript is likewise present in the dialogue in heaven in *Paradise Lost*. So pervasive is its presence, in fact, that Barbara Lewalski sees it as the means by which Milton structures the drama as a whole. For Lewalski, each of the speeches in the drama accords with the office of one of the Four Daughters: "God's first speech . . . sets forth the *truth* of things — Satan's escape, his impending success in the temptation, man's Fall, the doctrines of free will, sufficient grace, and personal responsibility for choice"; the Son's response, in turn, "pleads the case for *mercy* to mankind, but appeals also to God's justice to prevent the triumph of Satanic evil"; the Father's next speech voices "the stern demands of *justice*" but, at the same time, restates his intention to renew and save mankind and ends with a call for charity; the Son's response emphasizes the "*peace* assured, / And reconcilement" he will achieve for man, along with an affirmation that he will "satisfy God's justice by his death and so allow the divine mercy to flow to man." These four speeches (each represented by one of the Four Daughters) culminate in the Father's concluding speech which "celebrates the Son for reconciling all these elements in love."[28] What we have seen as the five-act structure of the drama, then, subscribes for Lewalski to the tradition of the Daughters of God. Although this reading might strike some as a bit too paradigmatic, it does suggest the extent to which Milton assimilates the concept of the Daughters into his dramaturgical outlook. More telling for our purpose, however, is the way in which Milton appropriates the sense of emotionally charged conflict so characteristic of the Four Daughters tradition in order to delineate the figures of Father and Son as fully conceived characters.

In the triumphant song of jubilee that fills the eternal regions after the completion of the dialogue, the angelic hosts provide their own dramatic cue to the intensity of this conflict. Hymning both Father and Son, the angels declare: "No sooner did thy dear and onely Son / Perceive thee purpos'd not to doom frail Man / So strictly, but much more to pitie enclin'd, / *He to appease thy wrauth, and end the strife / Of Mercy and Justice in thy face discern'd*, . . . offerd himself to die / For mans offence" (III, 403–10; my italics). These lines are revealing not simply because of the way in which they acknowledge the tradition of the Four Daughters but because of the way in which they suggest how the dialogue is to be read. What they suggest is that this conflict occurs not just *between* characters: it occurs *within* characters as well. What Milton offers us, in short, is a kind of psychodrama through which inner turmoil comes to the surface in rather disturbing and unsettling ways.[29] When applied to the figure of man as a character, such psychodrama is perfectly acceptable. We witness it, for example, in the figure of Adam when, after he has fallen, he is tossed "in a troubl'd Sea of passion" (X, 718). When applied to the figure of God as a character, however, such psychodrama tends to make us uncomfortable. We don't like to see God struggling with himself: it is somehow unbecoming, ungodlike, as it were. Milton, of course, was perfectly aware of the chances he was taking in portraying God in this manner. Doing so, however, represented for him not just a testimony to his own powers as a poet but an assertion of his faith in the kind of God he felt called upon to portray.

In order to support so radical an outlook, Milton sought justification once again in the Holy Scriptures. On the basis of his reading of those Scriptures, he maintained in *De Doctrina christiana* that "our safest way is to form in our minds such a conception of God, as shall correspond with his own delineation and representation of himself in the sacred writings. For granting that both in the literal and figurative descriptions of God, he is exhibited not as he really is, but in such a manner as may be within the scope of our comprehensions, yet we ought to entertain such a conception of him, as he, in condescending to accommodate himself to our capacities, has shown that he desires we should conceive." We may be certain, Milton assures us, "that sufficient care has been taken that the Holy Scriptures should contain nothing unsuitable to the character or dignity of God, and that God should say nothing of himself which could derogate from his own majesty." Nonetheless, if the Scriptures indicate that "it repented Jehovah," "let us believe that it did repent him." Moreover, if the Scriptures say that "it grieved the Lord at his heart," "let us believe that it did grieve him." Finally, if it be said that "he feared the wrath of the enemy," "let us not believe that it is beneath the dignity of God . . . to fear in that he feareth." So Milton concludes: "For however we may attempt to soften down such expressions by a latitude of interpretation, when applied to the Deity, it comes in the end to precisely the same" (XIV, pp. 33–35).[30] Far from attempting to "soften down such expressions," Milton affords them full play in the dialogue in heaven in *Paradise Lost*. An analysis of the first two speeches in that dialogue should suggest the extent to which the dialogue as a whole embodies "the drama of the personalities in the Godhead."

III

A sense of conflict is present from the very outset of the dialogue. It is, in fact, what distinguishes the Father's opening speech and underscores his character. If the Father's speech culminates in the assurance that his glory shall excel "in Mercy and Justice both" but that "Mercy first and last shall brightest shine" (III, 132–34), it is not so much the reconciliation of the two as it is the struggle through which that reconciliation is achieved that distinguishes the divine presence from the beginning and throughout the speech as a whole. The speech itself begins from the perspective of observation. "High Thron'd above all highth," God "ben[ds] down his eyes, / His own works, and their works at once to view" (III, 56–59). Surrounded by "the Sanctities of Heav'n" and accompanied "on his right" by His "onely Son," He beholds "from his prospect high" past, present, and future (III, 77–78). His address to his Son is in response to the foreknowledge that such a prospect affords. It is with the nature of this response that the present analysis will be concerned.

The address begins dispassionately enough. Commenting upon Satan's act of presuming to break the bounds of his captivity, God traces the course of the Adversary from hell, through Chaos, to the "Precincts of light," as he heads "Directly towards the new created World," there "with purpose to assay / If him by force he can destroy or worse, / By som false guile pervert" (III, 80–92). Such attempts at "desperate revenge," God has already assured his audience, shall do nothing but "redound / Upon his [Satan's] rebellious head." Despite these assurances, however, the tone of detachment with which God's speech begins undergoes a transformation as the deity moves from the present prospect to the immediate future in the exercise of his foreknowledge. What follows an introductory section of dispassionate observation and commentary is a passage of righteous indignation, moral outrage, and self-justification. In Satan's attempt to pervert man, God proclaims, the Adversary will be successful:

> For man will heark'n to his glozing lyes,
> And easily transgress the sole Command,
> Sole pledge of his obedience: So will fall
> Hee and his faithless Progenie: whose fault?
> Whose but his own? ingrate, he had of mee
> All he could have; I made him just and right,
> Sufficient to have stood, though free to fall.   (III, 92–99)

Far from being a passage in which a "toneless" deity speaks "simply what is" or disposes "a series of self-evident axioms in an objective order," this is an impassioned, emotionally charged utterance underscored by a sense of genuine conflict (or, to use the telling word of the angelic hosts, "strife").

The language in which that utterance is cast is harsh and uncompromising: it grates, it repels, it provokes. The word "ingrate" itself is enough to cause any reader to bristle. The discomfort we feel in response to the use of that word is intensified, moreover, by our awareness that "ingrate" is applied to unfallen beings who have not even had the opportunity to be ungrateful yet, just as the word "faithless" is applied to offspring who have not even had the opportunity to be born yet. If God beholds "past, present, and future" in a timeless realm of "foreknowledge absolute," his utterance treats future events as if they had already transpired. Collapsing temporal distinctions in this manner intensifies the severity of the pronouncements and thereby causes the distress that a foreseeing deity experiences to be that much more disturbing. Verbal repetition ("*sole* Command," "*sole* pledge"), followed by verbal variation ("*so* will fall," "whose *fault?*") does nothing to alleviate the harshness of this impression. Nor is that harshness confined to the first speech alone: "He with his whole posteritie must die, / Die hee or Justice must" (III, 209–10) is one of a number of examples that might be cited to suggest the presence of such harshness in later utterances as well.

If we find God's language sharp and cutting, however, we must remember that it proceeds from a deity who has already been betrayed once by reprobate "Ethereal Powers" and "Spirits" (III, 100–01) and who knows that he is soon to be betrayed again by his new terrestrial creations. "He had of me all he could have" is as applicable to what has already transpired as it is to what will yet once more transpire in the near future. Portrayed as one who "foreseeing spake" (III, 79), God is thereby dramatized as a wrathful and aggrieved parent who looks before and after only to find betrayal. The result of this knowledge is an ire, a defensiveness, an anguish that gives rise to a language at once tortuous and torturous: "Not free, what proof could they have givn," "What pleasure I from such obedience paid?," "nor can justly accuse / Thir maker," "As if Predestination overrul'd / Thir will," "they themselves decreed / Thir own revolt, not I," etc. (III, 100–19). This is hardly a language of detachment, of equanimity. It is rather troubled speech, a language of pain. If Milton was courageous enough, even audacious enough to dramatize his deity in this manner, we as readers should not attempt to tone down what the dramatist has taken such great pains to portray according to his understanding of that which constitutes the *ira Dei*.[31] It is no accident that Milton has his own God refer to himself later in the dialogue as "th'incensed Deitie" (III, 187). If God refers to himself as "incensed," we ought at the very least acknowledge that Milton's God knows what he is about.

It is in this spirit, then, that we are to read the concluding portion of the speech. In these lines, we find a full expression of God's attitude toward his creations, their behavior, and the decrees that he has issued to govern their behavior:

> So without least impulse or shadow of Fate,
> Or aught by me immutablie foreseen,
> They trespass, Authors to themselves in all
> Both what they judge and what they choose; for so
> I formd them free, and free they must remain,
> Till they enthrall themselves; I else must change
> Thir nature, and revoke the high Decree
> Unchangeable, Eternal, which ordain'd
> Their freedom, they themselves ordain'd their fall. (III, 120–28)

What Milton presents us with here and throughout the speech as a whole is a deity who undergoes the "strife" of one fully aware of the demands that his own decrees have placed both upon himself and his creations. As a result of that awareness, we behold a deity at pains to justify those demands and unwilling to compromise them. Knowing what the past has brought and the future will bring, this is a deity who is put to the expense of attempting to justify the ways of God not only to his creations but, by virtue of the setting in which that justification is rendered, to himself as a dramatically conceived character. *Paradise Lost* is an epic in which God justifies the ways of God to God. It is an epic in which God talks to himself, that is, in which God responds as Accommodated Being to what he as Absolute Being *is*.[32] In this respect, he, like his own creations, is "Author to Himself in all / Both what He judges and what He chooses." As "Author to Himself," he not only accepts the responsibility of abiding by his own decrees but assumes the *role* of one fully conscious of what those decrees entail both for himself and for his creations. Having become "Author to Himself" in this manner, he appears to us as Accommodated Being. By its very nature, his presence in that role is dramatic: it embodies that personality, that *ethos*, through which Accommodated Being makes itself known. If Absolute Being is beyond perception, Accommodated Being is manifested in that dramatic portrayal called "God." It is this portrayal which we as audience witness in the dialogue in heaven in *Paradise Lost*. What we witness in this portrayal is nothing less than an *agon* through which Milton's God as *Deus agonistes* struggles with his own theology.

If we find the fact of that struggle unsettling and disturbing, Milton would maintain that such is exactly as it should be. An encounter with *Paradise Lost* and the theology it embodies is not meant to be a comforting experience, one that encourages the sort of complacency which Milton decries in *Areopagitica* as the mark of "a fugitive and cloister'd vertue, unexercis'd & unbreath'd" (IV, p. 311). "A man may be a heretick in the truth," Milton observes in that same tract, "and if he beleeve things only because his Pastor sayes so, or the Assembly so determins, without knowing other reason, though his belief be true, yet the very truth he holds, becomes his heresie" (IV, p. 333). So in an encounter with *Paradise Lost:* conflict is at the heart of it; conflict is its very soul, the very source of its being. To encounter Milton's epic is to grapple with it. It is the drama of that combat which Milton portrays through his delineation of God in Book III of *Paradise Lost.* If such is true of Milton's delineation of God, it is no less true of his delineation of the Son. In that delineation, we come to appreciate as never before what Milton means by "the drama of the personalities in the Godhead." To understand that drama, however, one must come to terms as fully as possible with the Son's response to his Father's first speech.

Despite this fact, one of the pronounced curiosities of Milton criticism is its unwillingness to give that response its due. Readers have almost invariably made hash of what the Son says. Those critical of the Son's response misread with a certain perverseness. Excising the first ten lines or so from the response as a whole, J. B. Broadbent accuses the Son of simply "weav[ing] lyrical patterns" with his Father's speech "as if to beautify brutality."[33] John Peter blames the Son for being guilty of "tactful bribery."[34] Those who defend the Son, on the other hand, do him more harm than good. Almost as if afraid to give the Son his due, Allan Gilbert, for example, sees the Son as "a prudent courtier, beginning with deference his speech to the monarch . . . and then endeavoring to persuade him [the monarch] not to go too far in his punishment of disloyal man."[35] At the very least, these assessments have the virtue of crediting the Son with some kind of dramatic presence, an alternative Stanley Fish, we recall, deprives him of almost entirely. Not only does the Son enjoy a dramatic presence, however: he infuses the scene with a sense of energy and excitement previously unknown to the traditions of celestial debate through which Milton fashioned his dialogue in heaven.

The Son's rejoinder to his Father begins courteously enough. It praises his Father for concluding his "sovran sentence" with the promise that "Man should find grace" (III, 144), the means by which the conflict between Justice and Mercy will finally be reconciled. As the embodiment of divine compassion, infinite love, and immeasurable grace (III, 141–42), the Son is understandably joyful at the prospect that "mercy first and last shall brightest shine." He communicates that feeling of joy in a language of assent that runs over six lines:

> O Father, gracious was that word which clos'd
> Thy sovran sentence, that Man should find grace;
> For which both Heav'n and Earth shall high extoll
> Thy praises, with th'innumerable sound
> Of Hymns and sacred Songs, wherewith thy Throne
> Encompass'd shall resound thee ever blest.   (III, 144–49)

Were his response to conclude at this point, then the sense of conflict that so underscores the Father's speech would remain confined to that speech alone. This is not the case: that sense of conflict becomes part of the Son's rejoinder as well.

Six lines of praise are followed by seventeen lines of challenge that call into question the very promise of grace that the first six lines made a point of extolling. In effect, the first six lines perform the task finally not of extolling but of anticipating what amounts to a series of animadversions that are as extreme in their implied censure as any that Milton himself ever marshaled during his polemical career:

> For should Man finally be lost, should Man
> Thy creature late so lov'd, thy youngest Son
> Fall circumvented thus by fraud, though joynd
> With his own folly? that be from thee farr,
> That farr be from thee, Father, who art Judge
> Of all things made, and judgest onely right.
> Or shall the Adversarie thus obtain
> His end and frustrate thine, shall he fulfill
> His malice, and thy goodness bring to naught,
> Or proud return though to his heavier doom,
> Yet with revenge accomplish't and to Hell
> Draw after him the whole Race of mankind,
> By him corrupted? or wilt thou thy self
> Abolish thy Creation, and unmake,
> For him, what for thy glorie thou hast made?
> So should thy goodness and thy greatness both
> Be questiond and blaspheam'd without defence.   (III, 150–66)

Rhetorically, the animadversions assume the form of two sets of questions (III, 150–53, 156–64), the first set of which is followed by an answer (III, 153–55) that serves as much to admonish as to affirm and the second set of which is followed by an answer (III, 165–66) that serves at once to challenge and to warn. In outline, the first set of questions looks like this:

> Should man "finally be lost"?
> Should man "fall circumvented thus by fraud"?

Answer: "That be from thee farr, / That farr be from thee, Father." Implication: If that be far from one who "judgest onely right," why do God's judgments provoke the kinds of questions that cause his own Son to raise the possibility that these judgments might lead to the loss of God's "creature late so lov'd" in the first place?[36] Rather than settling the matter, the answer provides a transition into the second set of questions. This set is potentially even more damaging (certainly more unrelenting) than the first. In outline, the second set of questions looks like this:

> Shall Satan triumph?
> Shall Satan obtain his end?
> Shall Satan fulfill his malice?
> Shall Satan accomplish his revenge?
> Will you allow yourself to be frustrated, Father?
> Will you allow your goodness to be undermined?
> Will you abolish your creation?

Unlike the answer to the first set of questions, the answer to the second set is an assertion not of the unlikelihood that the answer might possibly be "yes" but a warning that if the answer is indeed "yes" (the very real possibility is implied here), then God's "goodness and . . . greatness both" would be justifiably "questiond" and, what is even more devastating, "blaspheam'd without defence" (III, 165–66). Consider the implications of the Son's challenge. Warning that if his Father's decree is not executed in a manner consistent with his promise of mercy, the Son charges that his Father's actions would render him defenseless against whatever justifiable accusations (either in the form of questioning or outright blasphemy) his actions might provoke. One senses in the challenge that the Son himself would be foremost among the reprobate in excoriating the Father, should the father fail to heed his Son's warning.

The intensity of the drama at this point could not be greater, an intensity that the language of the challenge does much to reinforce: "So should thy goodness and thy greatness both / Be questioned and blaspheam'd without defence." Recalling the whole series of questions that build to a crescendo in the Son's response, the word "questiond" encapsulates the response as a whole. The Son in effect has been questioning

God's goodness and greatness all along. At the same time, the word "questiond" threatens future acts of questioning in response to which any claims of divine goodness and greatness would be rendered totally ineffectual.

Moving from the word "questiond," the challenge culminates in the astounding word "blaspheam'd." To have the Son proclaim that his Father's actions might be justifiably "questiond" is one thing. To have him proclaim that his Father's actions might be "blaspheam'd without defence" is quite another. Blasphemy, as Milton was quick to point out in *De doctrina christiana*, runs counter to the spirit of the Ten Commandments ("thou shalt not take the name of the Lord thy God in vain"[Exod. xx, 7]). As an "impious or reproachful mention of God," blasphemy for Milton is a sin of the greatest magnitude.[37] Milton knew from the Gospel of Matthew that, whereas "all manner of sin shall be forgiven," blasphemy against the Spirit of God is absolutely unforgivable: "Whoever speaketh a word against the Son of Man," says Jesus, "it shall be forgiven him: but whosoever speaketh against the Holy Ghost, it shall not be forgiven him, neither in this world, neither in the world to come" (Matt. xi, 31–32). In Revelation, blasphemy is the sin of the Beast, which carries the name of blasphemy upon its heads: "And he opened his mouth in blasphemy against God, to blaspheme his name, and his tabernacle, and them that dwell in heaven" (Rev. xii, 1, 6). Closer to his own time, Milton no doubt remembered the figure of Capaneus in the inferno of Dante's *Commedia*. Railing ceaselessly against God, this most disdainful and scowling of blasphemers is doomed to an eternity of fire and burning sand (I, xiv, 43–75).

In *Paradise Lost*, blasphemy, of course, is what Satan is charged with: "O argument blasphemous, false and proud!" exclaims Abdiel upon hearing the rebellious words of the Adversary; "Words which no ear ever to hear in Heav'n / Expected, least of all from thee, ingrate / In place thy self so high above thy Peers. / Canst thou with impious obloquie condemn / The just Decree of God [?]" (V, 809–14). If one recalls this charge in the context of the Son's response to his Father's decree after the defeat of the impious rebels, one cannot help but be struck by the dramatic irony that Abdiel's words elicit. Assuming that the fiery and zealous servant of God is among the assembled host when not Satan but the Son of God has uttered his challenge, one is prompted to ask: "What must Abdiel be thinking now?" "Who is the ingrate, after all?" "Will the real adversary please step forward?"

"So should thy goodness and thy greatness both / Be questiond and blaspheam'd without defence." In an epic that purports to justify the ways of God to men, Milton creates a circumstance in which the very theology upon which that justification is founded threatens to undermine its own cause. I know of no other instance in the history of either dramatic or epic poetry in which a poet has undertaken such risks. When Milton referred to his "adventrous Song" as one that "pursues / Things unattempted yet in prose or Rime" (I, 13–16), he knew only too well whereof he spoke. By having the Son challenge the Father in these terms, Milton deliberately placed himself in a situation "compasst round" with all kinds of dangers. His purpose, however, was not to be provocative simply for the sake of being provocative. If Milton writes incendiary drama, it is because the theology of his poem must be constantly testing itself, constantly subjecting itself to challenges of the most extreme sort. Through the dramatization of his theology, Milton gives us his own version of Jacob's combating with God. In this respect, Milton conceives of God's own Son as a figure who is not afraid to wrestle with his Father "until the breaking of the day." Embodied in the Son is the name that God bestowed upon Jacob after their combat: "Thy name," says God to Jacob, "shall be called no more Jacob, but Israel: for as a prince hast thou power [lit. 'have you contended'] with God . . . and hast prevailed" (Gen. xxxii, 24–30).

IV

As startling as the Son's defiance of the Father appears to be, the spirit of contentiousness is accordingly not without biblical precedence. When the God of Isaiah declares, "Come now, and let us reason together" (Isa. i, 18), his use of the word "reason" is derived from a Hebrew term (*yachach*) that suggests the idea of arguing, debating, and contending, as much as it does the act of reasoning. What is true for Isaiah is similarly true for the Old Testament in general. In fact, the idea of contending with one's God is part of the fabric of Old Testament theology. God's faithful are forever engaged in controversy with him, whether in the form of Job who wishes to arraign God in a court of law (Job xiii, 6; xl, 2), or Jeremiah who is prompted to dispute with God concerning the nature of God's ways (Jer. xii, 1).[38] As Merritt Y. Hughes has shown, the psalmist himself is hardly reluctant to reprimand God when the occasion calls for such chastisement. Significantly, this act of chastisement in the Psalms occurs within the context of the reconciliation of mercy and truth, righteousness and peace of Psalm lxxxv that is the basis of the allegory of the celestial debate we have been exploring. In the very next Psalm, comments Hughes, "'David strengthens his prayer' for divine mercy in a public calamity by reminding God of his vaunted pre-eminence among all gods. Later, in the same tone of reverence and intimacy, he praises God because justice, mercy, and truth share his throne. But he also warns God that Israel's reverses destroy confidence in his will and power to keep his covenant to preserve it as a kingdom forever, and that the sneers of its enemies threaten his prestige in the world."[39]

Psalm lxxxvi, of course, is part of the earlier group of Milton's Psalm translations (Psalms lxxx–lxxxviii), rendered in 1648 during the civil wars. As a group, these Psalms shed a good deal of light not only upon the concept of a debate within a celestial council but upon the idea of the faithful servant's act of admonishing his Lord. So Psalm lxxxii, a *locus classicus* in its own right,[40] depicts God within "the great assembly" of celestial beings (1–3). There, according to Milton's rendering, God "judges and debates" (4). Significantly, the word "debates" is not in the original: it is Milton's own interpolation. In Psalm lxxxvii, Milton envisions God within his holy mountain and provides a rendering of the Psalm that suggests the posture of one who not only praises his Lord but admonishes him as well: "City of God, most glorious things / Of thee *abroad* are spoke; / I mention Egypt, *where proud Kings / Did our forefathers yoke,* / I mention Babel to my friends, / Philistia *full of scorn,* / And Tyre with Ethiops *utmost ends*" (9–15).[41] None of this implied bitterness is in the original: one can only imagine what "glorious things" are said of the City of God by its various enemies, who either yoked the psalmist's forefathers or are full of scorn in reaction to the psalmist's God and his city. Certainly, as a political document, Milton's translation admonishes those in authority during the civil wars to remember the enemy, particularly to avoid coming once again under the power of "proud Kings." But as a personal document in a time of trouble, Milton's rendering contains an implicit call to God to recognize the adherence of his faithful, a recognition that is fulfilled in the promise that Sion shall be established eternally.

If the Psalms (especially as portrayed through Milton's own translations) suggest something of the biblical background that underlies the Son's rejoinder to the Father in Book III of *Paradise Lost*, the most immediate source for that rejoinder is to be found in three crucial biblical passages, drawn respectively from Genesis, Exodus, and Numbers. Whereas in Genesis, chapter xviii, Abraham argues against the wholesale destruction of the Sodomites, Moses in Exodus, chapter xxxii, and Numbers, chapter xiv, argues against the wholesale destruction of the Israelites. As John E. Parish, Merritt Y. Hughes, and I have respectively argued, the language through which the dialogue in heaven (and in particular the Son's first speech) is formulated alludes directly to these biblical passages.[42] Thus, the Son's locution, "that be from thee farr, / That farr be from thee, Father, who art Judge / Of all things made, and judgest onely right" (III, 153–55), derives from Abraham's statement to God: "That be far from thee to do after this manner, to slay the righteous with the wicked: and that the righteous should be as the wicked, that be far from thee: Shall not the Judge of all the earth do right?" (Gen. xviii, 25). Moreover, the questions that follow upon the Son's "that be from thee farr," namely "Or shall the Adversarie thus obtain / His end . . . shall he fulfill / His malice [?]," etc. — these questions find their counterpart in Moses' words to God both in Exodus and in Numbers. So in Exodus, Moses admonishes God: "Lord, why doth thy wrath wax hot against thy people, which thou hast brought forth out of the land of Egypt with great power, and with a mighty hand? Wherefore should the Egyptians speak, and say, For mischief did he bring them out to slay them in the mountains, and to consume them from the face of the earth? Turn from thy fierce wrath and repent of this evil against thy people" (Exod. xxxii, 11–12). In Numbers, Moses' words are likewise to the point: "Now *if* thou shalt kill *all* this people as one man, then the nations which have heard the fame of thee will speak, saying, Because the Lord was not able to bring this people into the land which he sware unto them, therefore he hath slain them in the wilderness" (Num. xiv, 15–16).

It is in the spirit of such challenges to authority that Milton in *The Doctrine and Discipline of Divorce* invokes the Genesis, chapter xviii, account of Abraham's confrontation with God: "Therefore *Abraham* ev'n to the face of God himselfe, seem'd to doubt of divine justice if it should swerve from the irradiation wherewith it had enlight'ned the mind of man, and bound it selfe to observe its own rule" (II, p. 445). When it appears not "to observe its own rule," Milton counsels the kind of healthy defiance reflected in Moses' challenge to God. For that purpose, Milton calls upon Exodus xxxii, 10 to support the following statement that appears in *De Doctrina christiana:* "Hence our knowledge of God's will, or of His providence in the government of the world ought not to render us less earnest in deprecating evil and desiring good, but the contrary" (XVII, p. 102). The kind of "evil" Milton would have us "deprecate" is none other than God's own desire to consume the Israelites, a desire that Moses persuades God to overcome.[43] Indeed, the effect of Moses' challenge to divine authority is to cause the deity to reconsider his original intentions. In Exodus, God goes so far as to "repent . . . of the evil which he thought to do to the people" (Exod. xxxii, 14). Having already indicated that he will be merciful, Milton's God does not need to repent.[44] Nonetheless, the spirit of contentiousness that pervades the Old Testament is still very much a part of the way in which Milton conceived the

dialogue in heaven in *Paradise Lost*. The high drama of that dialogue
finds its antecedents in the various biblical encounters that call into question God's ways, that challenge those ways, and upon occasion even cause
God to repent of his anger and alter his intentions.

If the foregoing suggests something of the biblical background that
Milton drew upon to fashion his dialogue, this background should not
blind us to the radical tenor of the dialogue as Milton conceived it. In
fact, an awareness of the background bespeaks as much the failure as
it does the success of biblical precedent to illuminate the text in question.
For no amount of digging into backgrounds of various kinds will produce a source for the Son's challenge: "So should thy goodness and thy
greatness both / Be questiond and blaspheam'd without defence." Nowhere does Abraham, Moses, or David venture such an affront to God.
This is Milton's doing, and Milton only must stand accountable for it.

Once we realize the extent to which Milton radicalizes dialogue at
this point, we shall have gained an invaluable insight not only into the
character of his dramaturgy but into the nature of his theology. The
character of his dramaturgy is clear enough. As we have discussed, Milton is content with no middle flights; he pursues only "things unattempted
yet in Prose or Rime" (I, 16), and those "things unattempted" include
the contents not just of secular literature but the most sacred of books
as well. When Andrew Marvell, in his commendatory poem, "On Paradise Lost," wrote, "the Argument / Held me a while misdoubting his
[Milton's] Intent, / That he would ruin . . . / The sacred Truths to Fable
and old Song," Marvell included among his list of "sacred Truths" *Messiah* Crown'd, Gods Reconcil'd Decree" (3–8), just the subjects that engage us here.[45] In his poetic reformulation of those subjects, Milton did
not hesitate to take chances, even at the risk of undermining sacred truths.
Although he held the Bible as the repository of these truths in the highest
esteem, his ultimate guide was the Spirit of God within him. So he maintained in *De Doctrina christiana*: "the Spirit which is given to us is a
more certain guide than Scripture, whom therefore it is our duty to follow" (XVI, p. 279). This is as much a declaration of aesthetic independence as it is of doctrinal independence. It accounts in part for the dramaturgical extremes to which he is willing to go when the occasion calls
for such extremes.

His radicalizing of dialogue, however, is not confined just to his
dramaturgy. It likewise extends to (and is an expression of) his theology.
The *Logos* for Milton contains a quality that is essentially combative.
The Son may be God's "word . . . [his] wisdom, and effectual might"
(III, 170), but the Son's personality (his *essentia*, to use Milton's theologi-

cal terminology) is his own. It is this quality that renders the dialogue in heaven so compelling, for, when all is said and done, the purpose of the dialogue is the proving of the Son, the establishing of his identity, an event that cannot occur before the Son has been given the opportunity to manifest his true nature. If that event involves the act of issuing the most extreme of challenges, it also implies a willingness to accept the most awesome of responsibilities: that of offering oneself as a sacrifice for man. In light of this offer, the act of issuing the challenge moves inexorably to the point at which the acceptance of such a responsibility is the one possible course for one who is the embodiment of "Love without end, and without measure Grace" (III, 142). This fact accounts for the nature of the Son's response to his Father's own challenge regarding the ultimate future of man. So, we recall, the Father proclaims: "He with his whole posteritie must die, / Die hee or Justice must," but then concludes: "unless for him / Som other able, and as willing pay / The rigid satisfaction, death for death. / Say Heav'nly Powers, where shall we find such love, / Which of ye will be mortal to redeem / Mans mortal crime . . . / Dwels in all Heaven charitie so dear?" (III, 209–16). Breaking the awesome silence that follows hard upon this challenge, the Son responds according to his nature: "Behold mee then, mee for him, life for life / I offer, on mee let thine anger fall; / Account mee man" (III, 236–38). With this offer, this *ecce* (cf. John xix, 5), the Son proves himself "By Merit more then Birthright Son of God" (III, 309).

Viewed in the context of the interchange between Father and Son, the dialogue in heaven that graces Book III of *Paradise Lost*, then, represents a moment of high drama in Milton's epic. It is a drama of fully delineated characters engaged in the kind of dialogue that Milton no doubt had in mind when he endorsed a reading of Scripture consistent with the practice of conceiving the biblical text as the highest form of drama, one comparable even to the "Dramatick constitutions" of Sophocles and Euripides. The dialogue in heaven is just this sort of "Dramatick constitution." As a "drama of the personalities in the Godhead," that dialogue draws upon all the resources available to it in its portrayal of the divine interchange. Resorting to the traditions of the celestial parliament made evident in the Middle Ages and the Renaissance, it derives its spirit from the combativeness and contentiousness implicit in the biblical models. But it ventures beyond these models to fashion for itself an event that extends the frontiers of drama to a point at which the very theology upon which *Paradise Lost* is founded threatens to undermine its own cause. In the jargon of contemporary critical parlance, one might say that the dialogue in heaven provides the occasion by which Milton's epic threatens to deconstruct itself. Whether or not such an occurrence actually takes place — and I would argue that it does not — the dialogue offers ample evidence of Milton's willingness to push drama to its limits. Doing so, Milton succeeds in pursuing "things unattempted yet in Prose or Rime." As one of the most compelling of "Dramatick constitutions," the dialogue in heaven in Book III of *Paradise Lost* fulfills this intention admirably.

University of Illinois at Chicago

NOTES

1. John Clarke, *An Essay Upon Study* (1731) in *Milton: The Critical Heritage*, 2 vols., ed. John T. Shawcross (London, 1970–72), vol. I, pp. 263–64. Earlier versions of this paper were presented at the University of Kentucky and at the NEH funded Milton Institute, Arizona State University. I would like to thank the faculty and staff of both the universities for the opportunity to present the results of my research.

2. References to Milton's poetry in my text are to *The Complete Poetry of John Milton*, 2nd rev. ed., ed. John T. Shawcross (Garden City, 1971).

3. Alexander Pope, "The First Epistle to the Second Book of *Horace*," in *Poems of Alexander Pope*, 11 vols., 2nd ed., ed. John Butt (New Haven, 1953), vol. IV, p. 203, line 102.

4. *Milton's God* (1961; rev. ed., Cambridge, England, 1981), p. 146. For a counterstatement to the premises underlying the Empsonian conception, see Denis Danielson, *Milton's Good God: A Study in Literary Theodicy* (Cambridge, England, 1982).

5. See, among other works, J. B. Broadbent's *Some Graver Subject: An Essay on "Paradise Lost"* (New York, 1967), pp. 144–57.

6. Irene Samuel, "The Dialogue in Heaven: A Reconsideration of *Paradise Lost*, III, 1–417," in *Milton: Modern Essays in Criticism*, ed. Arthur E. Barker (New York; 1965), pp. 233–245. Reprinted from *PMLA* LXXII (1957), 601–11. See also Merritt Y. Hughes "The Filiations of Milton's Celestial Dialogue (*Paradise Lost*, III, 80–343)," in *Ten Perspectives on Milton* (New Haven, 1965), pp. 104–35. More recently, Albert C. Labriola has explored the deliberative and iconographical contexts of the dialogue in heaven in an excellent study entitled "'God Speaks': Milton's Dialogue in Heaven and the Tradition of Divine Deliberation," *Cithara* XXV (1986), 5–30. Labriola's views are very much in accord with my own.

7. Jackson Cope, *The Metaphoric Structure of "Paradise Lost"* (Baltimore, 1962). pp. 170–73.

8. J. B. Broadbent, *Some Graver Subject*, pp. 146–48.

9. Samuel, "The Dialogue in Heaven," pp. 234–35. Compare Hughes, *The Filiations of Milton's Celestial Dialogue*, p. 105.

10. Stanley Fish, *Surprised by Sin: The Reader in "Paradise Lost"* (New York, 1967), p. 86.

11. Fish, *Surprised by Sin*, p. 62. See Walter J. Ong's *Ramus, Method, and the Decay of Dialogue: From the Art of Discourse to the Art of Reason* (Cambridge, Mass., 1958), pp. 287–88.

12. Ong, *Ramus, Method, and the Decay of Dialogue*, p. 287.

13. Ibid., pp. 287–88.

14. Fish, *Surprised by Sin*, p. 62. In this regard, see Francis C. Blessington, "Autotheodicy: The Father as Orator in *Paradise Lost*," *Cithara* XIV (1975), 49–60; and Blessington's *"Paradise Lost" and the Classical Epic* (London, 1979), pp. 39–49. See also Anthony Low, "Milton's God: Authority in *Paradise Lost*," in *Milton Studies*, vol. IV, ed. James D. Simmonds (Pittsburgh, 1972), pp. 19–38.

15. Mikhail Bakhtin, *The Dialogic Imagination: Four Essays by M. M. Bakhtin*, ed. Michael Holquist, trans. Caryl Emerson and Michael Holquist (Austin, 1981), p. 279. According to Bakhtin, "every word is directed toward an *answer* and cannot escape the profound influence of the answering word that it anticipates" (p. 280). Barbara Lewalski, *"Paradise Lost" and the Rhetoric of Literary Forms* (Princeton, 1985), p. 17, has recently commented that *Paradise Lost* "manifests many of the characteristics . . . that Bakhtin finds in the emerging Renaissance novel." For additional study of dialogue in Milton, see Joseph Stuart Moag, "Traditional Patterns of Dialogue and Debate in Milton's Poetry," Ph.D. diss., Northwestern University, 1964.

16. In short, I actually find myself closer to A.J.A. Waldock, *"Paradise Lost" and Its Critics* (Cambridge, England, 1966), pp. 102–04, who responds to God's first speech by saying that Milton has taken "the supreme risk . . . of permitting a theoretically perfect character to dilate on his own impeccability." Waldock is right for all the wrong reasons, as I shall attempt to show.

17. *The Works of John Milton*, ed. Frank Allen Patterson et al. (New York, 1931–38), vol. XIV, pp. 196–97. I prefer the Sumner translation of this passage to the Carey translation in the *Complete Prose Works of John Milton*, 8 vols., ed. Don M. Wolfe et al. (New Haven, 1953–82), vol. VI, p. 213: "all that play-acting of the persons of the godhead." Hereafter cited in the notes as YP. References to Milton's prose in my text are to the Columbia edition, hereafter cited as CM in the notes.

18. Milton's own prose summary of the dialogue in the "Argument" to Book III suggests something of the five-act structure into which the dialogue might be divided:

Act 1 (80–134)

God sitting on his Throne sees *Satan* flying towards this world, then newly created; shews him to the Son who sat at his right hand; foretells the success of *Satan* in perverting mankind; clears his own Justice and Wisdom from all imputation, having created Man free and able enough to have withstood his Tempter; yet declares his purpose of grace towards him, in regard he fell not of his own malice, as did *Satan*, but by him seduc't.

Act 2 (144–66)

The Son of God renders praises to his Father for the manifestation of his gracious purpose towards Man.

Act 3 (167–217)

God again declares, that Grace cannot be extended toward Man without the satisfaction of divine Justice; Man hath offended the majesty of God by aspiring to Godhead, and therefore with all his Progeny devoted to death must dye, unless some one can be found sufficient to answer for his offense, and undergo his Punishment.

Act 4 (227–65)

The Son of God freely offers himself a Ransom for Man.

Act 5 (274–343)

The Father accepts him, ordains his incarnation, pronounces his exaltation above all Names in Heaven and Earth; commands all the Angels to adore him.

19. In this regard, see Arthur O. Lovejoy's classic essay, "Milton and the Paradox of the Fortunate Fall," *ELH* IV (1937), 161–79.

20. The terms *anagnorisis* and *peripeteia*, of course, are derived from Aristotle's *Poetics* (XI, 1–5). See further, Martin Mueller, *Children of Oedipus and Other Essays on the Imitation of Greek Tragedy 1500–1800* (Toronto, 1980), esp. p. 217: "The central action of *Paradise Lost* is in Aristotle's words a *mythos dramatikos*." Although "the term *dramatic*, as Aristotle uses it, does not primarily refer to drama" but to "composition of the action," *Paradise Lost*, as Mueller observes, embodies both this strict Aristotelian definition and a "more conventional sense" of drama as heightened action as well.

21. To this end, he viewed himself as having assumed the prophetic role. In that role, Milton prayed "to that eternal Spirit who can enrich with all utterance and knowledge, and sends out his Seraphim with the hallow'd fire of his Altar to touch and purify the lips of whom he pleases" (III, p. 241; Isa. vi, 1–8). As a result of this inspiration, Milton saw himself not only as recreating the drama of Scripture but as veritably participating in that drama.

22. John Demaray, *Milton's Theatrical Epic: The Invention and Design of "Paradise Lost"* (Cambridge, Mass., 1980).

23. The "theatricality" of the celestial council scene in Book III must, of course, be compared with the "theatricality" of the infernal council scene in Book II. The one is true drama, the other a put-up job "devis'd" by Satan (II, 379–80). If the "drama of the personalities in the Godhead" is drama at its most intense, the drama of the personalities among the devils is drama at its most parodic. As such, it serves to heighten the true drama that is created by the interchange between Father and Son.

24. This is Psalm lxxxiv in the Vulgate. As Milton's Cambridge manuscript plans attest, the debate among the Daughters of God in one form or another was to assume an important part in his projected drama on the Fall. Scholars such as Robert L. Ramsay, "Morality Themes in Milton's Poetry," *SP* XV (1918), 123–59, esp. pp. 133–53, have already documented Milton's interest in and indebtedness to the allegory in the *Fair Infant* elegy, the *Nativity* ode, *On Time*, *Upon the Circumcision*, and Milton's own translation of Psalm lxxxv, which elaborates upon the allegory. Most recently, John T. Shawcross, "Milton and the Covenant: The Christian View of Old Testament Theology," in *Milton and Scriptural Tradition: The Bible into Poetry*, ed. James H. Sims and Leland Ryken (Columbia, Mo., 1984), pp. 160–91, esp. pp. 181–83, has shown how significantly the allegory underscores Milton's concept of covenant. What has not been sufficiently emphasized, however, is the degree to which the sense of heightened drama implicit in the conflict among the Daughters underscores the celestial parliament in Book III of *Paradise Lost*.

25. See Hope Traver's *The Four Daughters of God: A Study of the Versions of this Allegory with Especial Reference to those in Latin, French, and English* (Philadelphia, 1907), and Samuel Chew, *The Virtues Reconciled: An Iconographic Study* (Toronto, 1947).

26. Traver, *The Four Daughters*, pp. 12–15.

27. *The Corpus Christi Play of the English Middle Ages*, ed. R. T. Davis (Totowa, N.J., 1972), pp. 123–29. For the most extensive morality rendering of the scene, see *The Castle of Perseverance* (ca. 1425).

28. Lewalski, *"Paradise Lost" and the Rhetoric of Literary Forms*, p. 119. Lewalski quite correctly sees other literary forms underlying the dialogue as well. She traces the scene, for example, to the tradition of the *Concilia Deorum*, made evident in the *Odyssey* I, 31–98, as well as to such interchanges as that between Apollo and Phaethon in Ovid's

Metamorphoses II, 1–152 (pp. 114–17). God's first speech she sees as a mode of forensic or judicial oratory in which God argues a case publicly before an angelic court (pp. 120–21).

29. In this regard, see Joseph A. Wittreich, Jr., "'All Angelic Natures Joined in One': Epic Convention and Prophetic Interiority in the Council Scenes of *Paradise Lost*," *Composite Orders: The Genres of Milton's Last Poems*, ed. Richard S. Ide and Joseph A. Wittreich, Jr. (Pittsburgh, 1983), pp. 43–74, esp. p. 48: The council scenes in *Paradise Lost* are "objectifications of inner turmoil and emblems of mental divisions."

30. Milton's statement here raises the vexed question of *anthropopatheia*, the attribution of human emotions to God. Although Milton is opposed to this notion, his commentary draws upon the language of those who endorse the idea. See the full and helpful annotations in YP VI, pp. 134–37.

31. In this respect, the divine anger of God (what Milton in *Upon the Circumcision* had earlier called "the full wrath" of "vengefull Justice" [22–31] offers fit contrast to the diabolic anger of Satan, that is, what God himself in *Paradise Lost* refers to as the "rage" that "transports our adversarie" (III, 80–81). Whereas the first is justified and finally resolved in the assertion of mercy (III, 134), the second is unjustified and self-defeating (III, 85–86). *Paradise Lost* implicitly contrasts the *ira Dei* with the *ira diaboli*. For appropriate background, see Lactantius, "On the Anger of God," in *The Works of Lactantius*, 2 vols., trans. William Fletcher (Edinburgh, 1871), vol. I, p. 32 and *passim*.

32. The distinction is implicit in the interchange between God and Adam in Book VIII of *Paradise Lost*. God refers to himself as one who is "alone / From all Eternitie" (405–06). In that state, God, as Adam comments, is "accompanied" with himself, that is, the "self" with whom he converses. When he does converse with others, he raises his creatures to what "highth" he wishes "Of Union or Communion, deifi'd" (427–31).

33. Broadbent, *Some Graver Subject*, p. 148.

34. John Peter, *A Critique of "Paradise Lost"* (1960; rpt. Hamden, Conn., 1970), p. 12.

35. Allan Gilbert, "Form and Matter in *Paradise Lost*, Book III," in *Milton Studies in Honor of Harris Francis Fletcher* (Urbana, 1961), p. 52.

36. The phrase "creature late so lov'd" (III, 151) contains its own criticism: it implies that he who was loved of late is perhaps not loved now. The word "late" might also modify "creature" and thereby suggest the idea of one who has died. (According to the OED, such usage was commonplace in the seventeenth century. Compare Milton's own usage in "late espoused saint" [*Sonnet XXIII*, 1].)

37. Milton provides a full discussion of "blasphemy" in *De doctrina christiana* (XVII, pp. 154–61).

38. For a detailed analysis of this biblical motif, see Sylvia Scholnick's important study "Lawsuit Drama in the Book of Job, " Ph.D. diss., Brandeis University, 1976. The technical term for such a lawsuit in Job is *rîv*, but there are also a number of other such terms that suggest the idea of litigation, among them, *yachach*. In this regard, see also William Holladay, "Jeremiah's Lawsuit with God," *Interpretation* XVII (1963), 280–87; Herbert Huffmon, "The Covenant Lawsuit in the Prophets," *Journal of Biblical Literature*, LXXVIII (1959), 285–95; James Limburg, "The Lawsuit of God in the Eighth-Century Prophets," Ph.D. thesis, Union Theological Seminary, 1969, among others.

39. Hughes, "The Filiations of Milton's Celestial Dialogue," p. 116.

40. In this regard, see H. Wheeler Robinson, "The Council of Yahweh," *Journal of Theological Studies* XLV (1944), 151–57; G. Ernest Wright, *The Old Testament Against Its Background* (Chicago, 1950), pp. 30–41; and Frank M. Cross, Jr., "The Council of

Jahweh in Second Isaiah," *Journal of Near Eastern Studies* XII (1953), 274–77. For these references, I am indebted to Sister M. Christopher Pecheux's excellent article, "The Council Scenes in *Paradise Lost,* " in Sims and Ryken, eds., *Milton and Scriptural Tradition*, pp. 82–103.

41. For a discussion of the concept of the holy mountain, see my *Poetics of the Holy: A Reading of "Paradise Lost"* (Chapel Hill, 1981), pp. 140–70.

42. See Parish, "Milton and an Anthropomorphic God," *SP* LVI (1959), 619–25; Hughes, "The Filiations of Milton's Celestial Dialogue," pp. 114–18; and my *"Paradise Lost,"* Book III: The Dialogue in Heaven Reconsidered," in *Renaissance Papers 1974* (Valencia, 1975), pp. 39–50. See also Kitty Cohen, *The Throne and the Chariot* (The Hague, 1975), pp. 103–16.

43. In *Paradise Lost,* such an outlook gives rise to parody as much as it does to high drama. Satan tempts Eve by appealing to and ironically distorting those very terms that the Son himself employs (IX, 700–701). The sense of parody appears full blown in Adam's rationalization for disobeying God (IX, 938–51).

44. God even suggests in his omniscience tht he has known all along what the Son was going to say and that the Son's words have corresponded with God's own frame of mind (III, 171–72). Nonetheless, the Son's challenge does bring the Father to the point of clarifying the nature of his merciful intentions (III, 173–202). For additional discussion of the Abrahamic and Mosaic backgrounds, see my earlier essay in *Renaissance Papers*, esp. pp. 43–48.

45. Marvell's poem can be found, among other places, in CM, II, pp. 3–5.

THE VERBAL PLOT OF *SAMSON AGONISTES*

Leonard Mustazza

I N A N article on *Paradise Regained,* Stanley Fish observes that in much of Milton's poetry there are two plots, one narrative or dramatic, the other verbal. "On the verbal level," he goes on, "there is a progressive diminishing first of the complexity of language and then its volubility, until finally, as the relationship between the self and God is specified, there is only silence. In other words, there is a perfect and inevitable correspondence between the conceptual thrust of the poem and the progress (or anti-progress) of its language"[1] This "verbal plot," this movement from volubility to silence and the poet's concern with the implications of speech generally, are clearly discernible in *Samson Agonistes,* but the concept operates somewhat differently in the drama than it does in the brief epic or in *Paradise Lost.* This difference is predicated upon the fact that *Samson Agonsites* does not really provide a direct and complete narrative line as do Milton's other major poems. Rather, the narrative details of the biblical account are used for the most part as background material, and the play essentially elaborates upon the deliberate process that occurs prior to Samson's final conflict with the Philistines. Indeed, Milton's Samson, so vastly different in effect than the character in Judges, is largely invented by the poet and then placed in a context where the biblical narrative is reticent — in the interval between Samson's imprisonment in Gaza and his summons to entertain the Philistines (Judg. xvi, 21–25). Since the narrative details are thus subordinated to character development and since the protagonist of Milton's drama is, as we shall see, so concerned with his lack of wisdom in the past — specifically his ignorance of the potency of language and the prudence of silence — it follows that, of the two plots Fish perceptively identifies, the verbal takes precedence over the dramatic. (In *Paradise Lost* and Paradise Regained, on the contrary, the narrative line is more obvious and the verbal plot more subtle.)

In this essay, I would like to consider this verbal plot in *Samson Agonistes,* the movement from Samson's "shameful garrulity" precedent to the action, to his heroic silence at the end. Milton presents Samson's preparation for his heroic role almost exclusively in terms of language, and so, in effect, language *is* action in the play. As I see it, the movement of this word-action plot is tripartite,[2] corresponding to the order of Samson's visitors: (1) Samson's verbal encounter with domestic figures (the Chorus and Manoa), with whom he assesses, for the most part, the errors of the past; (2) his verbal duels with Dalila and Harapha, the former demonstrating his acquired resistence to verbal assault, the latter concerned with the relationship between words and deeds; and (3) his final conflict with the Philistines which firmly synthesizes the verbal and narrative plots, moving rapidly from his internal divine summons,[3] to prudent speech, to deeds, to the noise that such deeds beget, and ultimately to silence and posthumous praise for the hero. In this scheme, as Fish notes, language decreases in complexity and volubility, and the right relationship between self and God is betokened by silence, albeit, in Samson's case, silence of a different kind than that of Adam and Eve and of the Son in Milton's epics.

I

"Prior to his humiliation," Robert Entzminger writes, "the biblical Samson is a bully who plays crude practical jokes and takes an unmerited pride in his verbal dexterity. As with the riddle his wedding guests solve, however, his reliance upon his wit and tongue to forestall Dalila's curiosity leads to disaster. Milton's Samson suffers the consequences of his scriptural heritage. . . . Samson becomes distrustful of words, fearful of their power, and reluctant to credit their apparent meaning."[4] Indeed, it would not be excessive to assert that, prior to his encounter with Dalila, Samson is downright confused about the potency of words, like a maturing child who suddenly realizes that life is not so simple as it had seemed, like a Hamlet who, at a relatively advanced age, finds it necessary to record in his tables the fact that "one may smile, and smile, and be a villain." Although the Israelite champion acknowledges certain aphoristic truths (e.g. "wisdom bears command" over physical might), and rightly assesses the specific reasons for his predicament, he nevertheless reveals himself to be confused, uncertain about the entire situation. This bewilderment often takes a verbal form, as seen in his continual wavering between questioning God's ways acquittal of God's plans, and self-blame:

> Yet stay, let me not rashly call in doubt
> Divine Prediction; what if all foretold
> Had been fulfill'd but through mine own default,
> Whom have I to complain of but myself?   (43–46)[5]

The breaking of his "Seal of silence," he realizes, is the "default" he has committed, and he is here forced to acknowledge, as Marcia Landy observes, his own lack of awareness of the nature of words.[6]

At the same time, however, Samson's blindness necessitates his increased reliance upon language, since his perception of the external world depends almost exclusively upon the ear. Hence, when, at the Chorus' approach, Samson says, "I hear the sound of words, thir sense the air / Dissolves unjointed ere it reach my ear" (176–77), there is not only literal truth in the statement but a figurative or extended meaning as well. The struggle with language, the need to ascertain the reliability of speakers, the healthy suspicion of "unjointed" utterance or sound in the metaphoric sense, and the awareness of the strength that silence confers all become, if anything, more dire despite his ruinous condition.

Moreover, Milton underscores Samson's pressing need to know about language and his emergent awareness of its power — an awareness which will serve to advance the verbal and narrative plots of the drama — by means of numerous figurative references to speech as balm, as weapon, as counterfeit coin, as fortress. To begin with, the Chorus comments upon the healing power of language, its corrective function. They bring to Samson only words, "Counsel or Consolation," to salve his sores, for, they proverbially note, "apt words have power to swage / The tumors of a troubl'd mind, / And are as Balm to fester'd wounds" (183–86). In turn, Samson pursues the somatic metaphor, acknowledging that their coming does "revive" him but not fully subscribing to their proverb. Rather, he notes that he appreciates the *action* of their coming and not so much their words, since "talking friends" can be like counterfeit coins that only appear genuine (187–91). This is a subtle indication that he has learned by "experience, not of talk" what true friends are, and this admission suggests the advent of beneficial change in the defeated champion. Words by themselves are as soon damaging or misleading as they are good or useful, and the action of his friends' visit speaks to him more eloquently than mere words. After all, Samson goes on, was it not "a word, a tear" that made him foolishly divulge "the secret gift of God / To a deceitful Woman" (200–02)? And as for the wisdom of proverbs, was he not at this very moment being "sung and proverb'd for a Fool / In every street" (203–04)?

Such considerations lead Samson to comment upon the verbal assaults that have made for his predicament, and, as further evidence that action and experience have taught him about the treachery of words, he blames himself (significantly, in marital terms) for his defeat:

> of what now I suffer
> [Dalila] was not the prime cause, but I myself,
> Who vanquisht with a peal of words (O weakness!)
> Gave up my fort of silence to a Woman.   (233–36)

Anthony Low is right to see this admission as a "regroupment, a preparation for more effective action and communication."[7] Though Samson is
surely unaware that he is preparing himself in this way since his despair
and pessimism are far from dispelled at this point, the reader must recognize that it is so, that the knowledge of verbal aggression and prudent
silence has taken shape in his mind.

Samson's retrospective movement from acknowledging the gesture
(rather than the words) of his friends, to his questions about the Philistines' proverbial assaults upon his name, to the "fort" he lost to Dalila's
verbal assault leads him yet further back in time. He then censures Israel's governors and heads of tribes for not supporting him when he demonstrated his might to the Philistines. At that time, the Israelites' "deafness" prevented them from hearing what his deeds bespoke: "The deeds
themselves, though mute, spoke loud the doer" (248).[8] Again, Samson's
emergent knowledge of the dichotomous relationship that sometimes obtains between words and deeds, his ability to interpret incident and apply
his newly acquired knowledge, becomes clear. Such is wisdom that one
cannot imagine the biblical Samson at Etham ever applying to the situation, ever extrapolating from his experience.

And then this retrospective application of wisdom proceeds even further back chronologically, this time with the Chorus picking up Samson's complaint against the ingratitude of the Israelite elders and applying it to the experiences of Gideon and Jephtha. The latter becomes
especially significant in light of the play's verbal plot generally and Samson's assertion that deeds speak loud the doer specifically. Jephtha's successful defense and delivery of his fellow Israelites from their Ammonite
oppressors, the Chorus says, was effected "by argument / Not worse than
by his shield and spear," an allusion to the cogent case Jephtha makes,
through messengers, to the king of Ammon concerning the Israelite occupation of what the latter considers Ammonite lands (Judg. xi, 12–28).
When such reasonable argument fails to persuade the king, Jephtha attacks and conquers the Ammonites. Then, when the Ephraimites show
their ingratitude for Jephtha's efforts, his martial prowess is turned toward civil war, the identification and subsequent slaughter of the Ephraimites dependent upon their inability to pronounce "Shibboleth." The
Chorus finds in this story about one of Samson's predecessors an illustration not only of the past ingratitude of Israel's tribal heads, but also
of Samson's claim concerning the eloquence of action — indeed, with regard to the latter, a very literal-minded illustration. For both the Ammonites' and Ephraimites' fate depended upon language and prudence,
and unreasonable, imprudent utterance leads in such cases almost inevi-

tably to violence.[9] In this sense, Samson shares qualities of both Jephtha, insofar as he is wronged by his allies, and Jephtha's enemies, insofar as *his* imprudent speech led to his own defeat.

This movement from the present circumstances to the tribal past, from the personal to the societal, also occurs in Samson's encounter with Manoa, with whom Samson further analyzes, in specifically verbal terms, the mistakes of his life and, more significantly, considers what the future holds at the personal and societal levels. However, there is also a difference to be noted. The Chorus' movement into the tribal past to illustrate the justice of Samson's complaint about the Hebrew elders' disloyalty to their heroes has the effect of diffusing the burden of culpability. We are made to see the justice of Samson's claim that Israel's continued servitude is due in large measure to "deafness" and lack of action on the part of its governors; we are also made to appreciate the Chorus' further illustrations of these tendencies since it is easy to see how such mistaken action (or inaction) can lead to servitude. And yet, we must also question the justice of Samson's "transfer" (241) of the blame for this servitude and the real utility of the Chorus' recalling of the past. The expanded context provided by these observations turns out to be a useful palliative to Samson's suffering, an indication that others must share in his failings, and, in this respect, the Chorus does provide verbal "balm" to Samson's wounded mind. But how effective will this kind of "balm" be in the long run?

Of course, such comfort does not endure long, as we see when Samson hears of his father's approach. Manoa's name alone reawakens Samson's "inward grief" and "renews th' assault" (330–31), and, in keeping with his "assailing" name, Manoa will effectively (though unintentionally) assail his son's mind with more relevant considerations than the Chorus engaged in. He, too, will analyze the past and the present, and he will add to these analyses the future implications of Samson's tragic capture, but, unlike the Chorus, he will focus unrelentingly upon Samson's life, a focus which, though more distressing to the champion than the Chorus' diffusion of guilt, will compel Samson to prepare for his future role.

On the personal level, Manoa's primary concern is with his son's immediate future, specifically his liberation and homecoming. Ironically, this paternal attempt to rescue him occasions only pain in the defeated champion, for it prompts him to imagine himself "a burdenous drone; to visitants a gaze, / Or pitied object" (567–68). To him, returning home would be harsher prison than the one in which he finds himself, and his jailers, his thoughts, would be worse than the Philistines, more brutal and assailing. Nevertheless, Manoa, claiming a "Father's timely care" and a sense of optimism, persists in his object of ransoming Samson, and he invites his son to be calm and "healing words from these thy friends admit" (605).

The reader, of course, knows that Manoa's plans are not to be realized, and I think Milton, depending upon the reader's awareness of that fact, prompts us to look elsewhere for the beneficial function of Manoa's discourse. This function lies, ironically, in the old man's reminders of his son's past errors and in his predictions about the future of Israel and of God's name. To begin with, his calling into question God's "gifts," which appear desirable but which really "draw a Scorpion's tail behind" (360), compel Samson to reassert his faith in God and to focus upon his own culpability, his vulnerability to feminine verbal assault. Manoa here inadvertently encourages Samson to acknowledge the fact that his favored status as a Nazirite was not without its responsibilities; its preservation and defense depended upon, among other things, human action, in this case silence being one such action. But to maintain in silence the "holy secret" was an act that required inner fortitude, which, Samson now realizes, he lacked. On a less significant scale, he yielded to the verbal entreaties of the woman of Timna, who "wrested" from him the secret of the marriage riddle and carried it to Samson's enemies in the bet. Then, having learned nothing from this experience, Samson yielded his capital secret to Dalila, the agent of his and his nation's true enemies. Samson admits to his father that he perceived "How openly, and with what impudence / She purpos'd to betray [him]" (398–99); he also admits his imprudent and misguided attempts to turn her importunity to sport (396), a contest she ultimately wins by means of little else besides words: "With blandisht parleys, feminine assaults, / Tongue batteries, she surceas'd not day nor night / To storm me over-watch't, and wearied out" (403–05). What was to him "sport" was to her war, and it is therefore not surprising that she beat him. All of these admissions—that he did not learn from experience, that he was not prudent enough to resist verbal battery because he did not take it seriously, that words can be used as weapons—are significant not only in themselves, but, more importantly, insofar as it will soon become necessary for Samson to use this newly acquired information (though he has no way of knowing that yet). In short, by working through these issues, he is really preparing himself, with Manoa's unwitting support, for future action, and we will not have to wait long to see the forms that action will take.

Our first glimpse of it occurs when Manoa, like the Chorus, expands the context of the exchange. However, whereas the Chorus moved into the tribal past with its consideration of Gideon and Jephtha, Manoa moves forward in time. He reminds Samson that his greatest shame is the honor he has brought to Dagon, who will be glorified at the upcoming Philistine feast, and the blasphemy he has brought to God. In keeping with the verbal plot that runs through these exchanges, Samson's response, his admission of guilt, is very much concerned with words. He acknowledges that he has "advanc'd [Dagon's] praises high / Among the Heathen round" (450–51), brought obloquy to God and scandal to Israel, and "op't the mouths / Of Idolists, and Atheists" (452–53). But Samson does not leave the matter there. Rather, he asserts his faith in God, who, he predicts, will soon break silence, assert his great name, and despoil Dagon "Of all these boasted Trophies won on me, / And with confusion blank his Worshippers" (470–71). Of course, Samson cannot know that he, the instrument of Dagon's victory, will also be the instrument of God's, yet that lack of awareness is unimportant at this point. What is important is his newly acquired understanding of the power of words, his humility, his willingness to accept blame for his actions, his firm belief that God will prevail, despite Samson's dark fate. Such understanding is, to be sure, the first major step in his preparation for heroic action.

Nevertheless, in the immediate context, Samson himself feels no heroic stirrings. To the contrary, he feels despair, shame for his crime of "Shameful garrulity," fear that he is considered "a blab, / The mark of fool set on his front" (495–96), guilt over "publishing impiously" God's holy secret. Thus, he asks his father not to ransom him, and, in what seems to be a deliberate ironic reversal of the Chorus' offer of consoling words as "balm" (186), he now prays for death, which will bring the "close of all my miseries, and the balm" (651). On the surface, then, his encounter with Manoa has effected no change, has moved him nowhere; Samson begins and ends in despair, and, to judge by this fact alone, the beneficial influence of the Chorus' and Manoa's words are negligible. Yet, below that emotional surface much change has occurred in Samson's attitude toward himself, his nation, and God.

II

This change becomes evident in Samson's encounter with Dalila; their exchange is in tone, focus, volubility, and theme much different from the prior one. It is, as several critics have noted,[10] a word-duel which will end not with Samson's rhetorical defeat of Dalila (the only defeat she suffers is the frustration of her plan to take him back with her) but with something more important: a *demonstration* that Samson has learned the potency of words and silence, that he is now able to withstand feminine verbal assault, that he can use words, silence, and even voluntary deafness to maintain integrity. It is with this encounter that the verbal plot is thrown into sharp relief, and we see the new Samson emerge.

Dalila's appearance, as described for Samson by the Chorus, is semicomical. The Chorus isn't quite sure what it is that approaches ("Female of sex it seems" [711], and they liken what they see to "a stately Ship / Of *Tarsus* . . . With all her bravery on, and tackle trim" (714–17) – and all of this for a blind man. But, for the reader, a more ominous note is sounded when they describe her attempts to speak:

> Like a fair flower surcharg'd with dew, she weeps
> And words addrest seem into tears dissolv'd,
> Wetting the borders of her silk'n veil;
> But now again she makes address to speak. (728–31)

For readers of *Paradise Lost*, there is a resonance to be heard in these lines. Compare the narrator's description of Satan about to address his troops after their expulsion from Heaven: "Thrice he assay'd, and thrice in spite of scorn, / Tears such as Angels weep, burst forth: at that / Words interwove with sighs found out thir way" (*PL* I, 619–21). Like Dalila's appeal to Samson, Satan's speech to the defeated angels is highly ambiguous. On the other hand, both may actually feel the stings of remorse; but, on the other, both also have selfish motives for action, both want to maintain the affections of those whom they have led into disaster, both want to maintain control. The primary difference between speakers lies in the effect of their words. Beelzebub proves to be right when he advises Satan to call the vanquished troops, who lay prostrate in hell after their defeat by the Son. Satan's voice alone, Beelzebub declares, will be "thir liveliest pledge / Of hope in fears and dangers," "Thir surest signal [to] resume / New courage and revive" (*PL* I, 274–79).

By contrast, the sound of Dalila's voice does not achieve its desired effect, although, ironically, it does cause Samson to reveal that he is reviving. He calls her "Hyaena, " the "wilde beaste that counterfaiteth the voyce of men" (Gloss of Geneva Bible to Ecclesiasticus xiii, 18, quoted in Hughes, pp. 569, 748n.), and rejects her specious repentance and entrapping offers. She is not repentant, he says, but seeks merely to "assail" his weakness, to "beguile" him, to entangle him with "a poisonous bosom snake," to further destroy his reputation, which is already "to Ages an example" of weakness and uxoriousness (748–65). Lacking a clear indication of authorial intent, we cannot know precisely how Milton would have liked to hear these lines spoken (or read), but I think Samson, though angry and despairing, though his pain is enkindled by her very presence, speaks these words like a person who is in control of himself, who has learned important lessons about love and life and language. If he were out of control, then we must conclude that his words are motivated by vindictive anger rather than informed with wisdom, and I believe that the overall evidence of the play suggests the latter. Hence, when Dalila presents her "reasons" for betraying him — that women are wont to publish secrets, that he should have known this and not revealed his to her, that the jealousy of love made her want to keep him with her, that the Philistines importuned her and promised that no harm would come to him — the champion can respond calmly, identifying with crystal clarity his own errors, her lies and evasions, and the equivocation that he used in the past and she continues to use. "All wickedness is weakness (834)," he can now declare categorically.

Dalila surely recognizes the change in Samson's attitude toward words, as seen in his unambiguous insistence upon his weakness and her treachery and his recognition of her seductive verbal urgings. And so, though she does not desist, she sees the need to change arguments, this time maintaining that she herself has been the victim of verbal assault:

> Hear what assaults I had, what snares besides,
> What sieges girt me round, ere I consented;
> Which might have aw'd the best resolv'd of men,
> The constantest to have yielded without blame.
> It was not gold, as to my charge thou lay'st,
> That wrought with me: thou knowst the Magistrates
> And Princes of my country came in person,
> Solicited, commanded, threat'n'd, urg'd,
> Adjur'd by all the bonds of civil Duty
> And of Religion
>
> . . . .
>
>   and the Priest
> Was not behind, but ever at my ear,
> Preaching how meritorious with the gods
> It would be to ensnare an irreligious
> Dishonorer of *Dagon:* what had I
> To oppose against such powerful arguments?   (845–62)

In the midst of this verbal barrage by Philistine civil and religious authorities — a battle in which she unconvincingly claims to have been without weapons — Dalila yielded to the public good over "private respects" (867–68), an argument reminiscent of Satan's claim that he will destroy Eden for "public reason," which compels him to do things that "else though damn'd I should abhor" (*PL* IV, 389–92).

Again Dalila is confronted with an unexpectedly altered Samson. Not only does he refute her arguments, indicating that love of her husband should have taken precedence over the public good, but, even more revealing, he claims to have presupposed her argument: "I thought where all thy circling wiles would end; / In feign'd Religion, smooth hypocrisy" (871–72). Such forethought is not a quality that one easily associates with the earlier Samson, who, though always claiming to be doing God's work in his marriage choices, has proven to be something of an Epimethean figure, one who considers the ramifications of words and actions only after they have led to disaster. A subtle but unmistakable shift occurs at this point: Samson moves from defensive to offensive verbal attack, and this shift is most clearly seen when, following her weak argument that women always lose to men in argument, he declares sarcastically, "For want of words no doubt, or lack of breath, / Witness when I was worried with thy peals" (905–06). A further suggestion of this change in Samson's role in the verbal war, moreover, is his claim to have learned the "Adder's wisdom" with which he can "fence [his] ear against [her] sorceries" (936–37). This shift in snake imagery from Samson's calling Dalila a "pois'nous bosom snake" (763) earlier to his assuming the wisdom of the Adder, which is deaf to the charmer's voice (an allusion to Psalm lviii) is quite significant. Samson is now both an active rhetorical defendant and assailant, and we see the latter role when Dalila censures him for being "deaf" to her prayers (960), which deafness she interprets as aggressive action. It is for this reason that I cannot agree with Northrop Frye's argument that Samson's self-imposed deafness is symbolically akin to his blindness. "Samson lives in a kind of seance-world of disembodied voices," Frye writes. "Everyone who speaks to Samson, including Manoa and the Chorus, has something to add in the way of reproach, something to suggest distrust or uncertainty. . . . Even Samson's hearing has to be mortified: he can only break from Dalila by, so to speak, putting out his ears."[11] On the contrary, I think that if Samson's blindness and deafness are akin, it is by contrast, the former being symbolic of his victimization wrought by his own ignorance, the latter of his self-protective and assailing action as a result of all that he has learned.

Recognition of Samson's inner strength then prompts Dalila to attempt a reestablishment of her role as verbal warrior. She revels in the fame she has gained as a result of her victory over the Philistines' prime adversary — in effect, a restatement of her claim to have performed a public good. But somehow her reiteration of that claim now seems a rationalization for her failure to bring him back with her. What she says may be true for the moment (of course, Samson's imminent destruction of the Philistines will render her fame short-lived), but she must also acknowledge the failure of her immediate objective, and that fact must rankle. On the other hand, her arguments have served to advance the verbal plot considerably. "The power of her appeal," writes Louis Martz, "has certainly accomplished a remarkable change in Samson; she has stirred him out of his sense of loss, stung him into more positive mental responses."[12] In addition, her stirrings have, I think, led him to reveal the inner changes wrought by the realizations he has reached during his encounters with the domestic figures. Now, in turn, his militant attitude toward words and deeds is ready to be fully exhibited in his confrontation with Harapha.

"With the approach of Harapha," George Muldrow notes, "the drama begins to move from its spiritual level of action to that of a drama of event."[13] Indeed, this is a movement that grows directly out of the internal struggles that Samson has undergone to this point in the drama, and Milton has subtly and carefully prepared the way for the emergence of the renewed and new Samson — the *renewed* seen in the return of his physical strength and his willingness to use it against the giant,[14] the *new* seen in his attitude toward words, notably his rejection of deceptive words and his disdain for boasting. The new Samson has learned a great deal, has changed and been changed, and his true strength now grows out of the lessons of experience, as well as, to use John Steadman's words, his manifest *fiducia in Deo* rather than his erstwhile *fiducia carnalis*.[15]

Milton underscores Samson's growing prudence with respect to language when the Chorus announces the approach of Harapha, referring to him figuratively as a coming storm. When Samson realizes that he has been misled by their metaphor into thinking a real storm was coming, he demands clarity in their speech; "Be less abstruse, my riddling days are past" (1064). If they are acting for the moment as his eyes, Samson suggests, they must report phenomena as they are and not use potentially misleading verbal devices. In keeping with Samson's concern with speech, the Chorus responds in kind, emphasizing the kind of language the approaching giant is likely to use with the Israelite champion:

> Look now for no enchanting voice, nor fear
> The bait of honied words; a rougher tongue
> Draws hitherward, I know him by his stride,
> The Giant *Harapha* of *Gath*, his look
> Haughty as is his pile high-built and proud.
> Comes he in peace? what wind hath blown him hither
> I less conjecture than when I first saw
> The sumptuous *Dalila* floating this way:
> His habit carries peace, his brow defiance. (1065–73)

The Chorus' synechdoches related to language ("no enchanted voice," "a rougher voice") are revealing of their preoccupations with speech. Interestingly, though, while their prediction to Samson of what he is about to hear from the giant is accurate enough, their reliability as visual interpreters is weakened by their inability to "read" Harapha's intentions based upon his appearance. And even more revealing is Samson's unemotional, laconic response to their uncertainty: "Or peace or not, alike to me he comes" (1074). A subtle and significant turning point in the verbal plot occurs here. In practical terms, the work of the bringers of verbal balm is over. Samson, having learned the true relationship between words and deeds and having placed his confidence in God, is now prepared to meet whoever approaches, whatever their intentions. He demands clarity of expression from his friends, he feels the alignment of inner and physical strength, and he is prepared to meet his enemies in either verbal or martial combat (or, as is the case with Harapha, both).

What is more, Milton provides in Harapha a convenient index of how much Samson's attitude has changed, for the giant resembles in many ways the type of person Samson likely was before his change — proud, boastful, secure in his might and reputation, and slightly ridiculous. Harapha's principal concern in his initial address to Samson is also with language, specifically with fame, his own and Samson's. It is clear that he does not see the defeated hero as a threat to him in any way. Thus, in his introduction, he does not merely announce who he is, but also boasts of his fame, which, he claims, Samson must have heard of if Samson himself is known at all (1081–82). (Compare Satan's boastful response to Ithuriel and Zephon, who, finding Satan in Eden near the sleeping Eve, ask who he is: "Not to know mee argues yourselves unknown" [*PL* IV, 830].) Then, having asserted his own fame, Harapha attempts to diminish Samson's:

> Much I have heard
> Of thy prodigious might and feats perform'd
> Incredible to me, in this displeas'd,
> That I was never present on the place
> Of those encounters, where we might have tried
> Each other's force in camp or listed field;
> And now am come to see of whom such noise
> Hath walk'd about, and each limb to survey,
> If thy appearance answer loud report.   (1082–90)

Harapha's words here are themselves concerned with words, and he wishes to leave his superiority over Samson at that verbal level, as seen in his claim that the opportunity to prove the reports ("noise") is obviated by Samson's wretched condition. The intent of Harapha's inflammatory assertions is to humiliate the fallen champion and to place him on the verbal defensive, to engage in a verbal contest that he is sure Samson must lose.

But, to his surprise, Samson has something else in mind. Refusing to contend in words, implicitly diminishing the importance of fame (and his earlier concern with his name is meant to be recalled here), and denying that Harapha's opportunity to try his might is now past, Samson issues a terse and direct challenge: "The way to know were not to see but taste" (1091). I cannot agree with those critics who argue that this challenge betokens a kind of spiritual backsliding on Samson's part.[16] To the contrary, in light of all that precedes it, the challenge is a measure of how far he has come. No longer bewailing his condition or defending his disastrous actions or concerned with the ill repute he has gained among his countrymen, Samson's internal renovation and spiritual consolation enable him to resume action, to fuse word and deed, to disdain mere words, and to become a militant champion of God again. This is not the erstwhile Samson; it is the new Samson, who will before long liberate his nation and bring glory to God.

In his initial speech, Harapha expressed incredulity over Samson's reputed might (whether he really doubts the reports or merely says so to humiliate Samson is disputable), but now his sense of disbelief is really enkindled. And, significantly, he chooses to evade the issue Samson raises and to cling to his prior wish that he could have met Samson in battle. But Samson will not let the cowardly giant take refuge in the past. Rather, he censures Harapha's boasting and reissues the challenge, to which Harapha's only response is bathetic rationalization: he disdains to fight a blind man and, besides, Samson is unwashed.

This ludicrous claim provokes Samson into making a fuller statement of his philosophy, as Mary Ann Radzinowicz has observed:

These exchanges [i.e. to this point] are brief and stichomythic, for no points of issue have emerged. But Harapha's disdainful comparison of himself, clean and elegantly armed, with Samson, unwashed, incapable, and blind, prompts Samson to make his own contrast, to compare his type of championship with Harapha's in a fuller description ending in a clear challenge: he "only with an Oak'n staff" will defeat "all thy gorgeous arms." The contempt Samson expresses for the accouterments of chivalric tourney is a contempt for the vanity of all military glory compared with spiritual dedication.[17]

What follows is a series of provocative (in terms of Samson's pride) and evasive (in terms of the challenges Samson issues) statements by the "Tongue-doughty Giant," Samson's responses to which clearly show the champion's spiritual fortitude, "trust in the living God," and awareness of how words, silence, and action can be used in the cause of God — hence, the terse challenges, the decreasing volubility in his speeches, the admissions of blame matched with the faith that Providence will not let matters rest as they are.

In effect, Samson does fight Harapha, who has come "armed" with more words than his opponent, just as he possesses the "glorious arms" that Samson lacks. Harapha came merely to observe Samson's "boist'rous locks" and to shame the Israelite strongman, but the giant is himself revealed to be foolish and boisterous; he came to remind Samson of what he was, but he discovers what Samson is. His defeat is so sweeping, in fact, that even the Chorus, who feared his approach, take the liberty of using a disparaging epithet, "His Giantship" (1244) to describe the "baffl'd coward." Rudrum is right to argue that the episode with Harapha "is only 'inconclusive' at the level of external event; for we now learn that Samson is ready to be 'God's champion' once more."[18] Indeed, not only is he "once more" God's champion, but also something he has not hitherto been: a verbal strategist who uses words to his advantage and who is also able to instruct others in such strategies. The latter is seen when the Chorus expresses fear that Harapha will "with malicious counsel" (1251) stir up the Philistine lords, to which Samson confidently asserts that, if the giant does so, he will have to "allege some cause, and offer'd fight / Will not dare mention, lest a question rise / Whether he durst accept the offer or not" (1253–55). In short, Samson has come a long way from the figure who was in need of verbal "balm" at the beginning of the play.

III

Robert Entzminger has argued that "we measure the protagonist's recovery in part by his growing control over language and reason, and he acquires the opportunity to fulfill God's promise not by renouncing words but by recovering his ability to exploit verbal ambiguity. Where before he had employed riddles as a means of flaunting his superiority over his enemies, however, by the end of his ordeal he adopts a metaphoric, ironic language that expresses both self-deprecation and faith in God."[19] The development of this "metaphoric, ironic language" is an immensely important aspect of the verbal plot of the drama, for Samson's ability to employ guilefully aggressive language turns out to be the prelude to direct heroic action — action which Steadman correctly calls "the logical culmination of a spiritual process rather than as the effect of purely external causes."[20] Divine inspiration ("Some rousing motions") and his own redefinition of heroism come together and he acts, first in words and then in deeds.[21]

The verbal "action" involves his studied prevarication with the officer during the latter's second visit and then his use of a grand ironic metaphor to the assembled Philistines. In the first instance here, Samson reveals his newly acquired skill at verbal assault as he uses half-truths against the enemy. He is, he claims, content to go with the officer because "Masters' commands come with a power resistless / To such as owe them absolute subjection" (1404–05), but he adds that he will do nothing to violate Israelite law. Nothing Samson says here is, strictly speaking, false, though he does not specify in his general statement which master's command he means to follow. "This is the first moment in the play that Samson speaks not to communicate or enlighten, but instead to mislead," Anthony Low observes.[22] I would like to take this idea one step further. Not only does he wish to mislead strategically, but this display of verbal strategy is meant to remind us subtly of the inept rhetorician Samson used to be. The earlier Samson did not even know enough to conceal his secrets from his lovers, whereas this Samson conceals his plans even from his friends, the Chorus. All he admits to them is that they may "expect to hear / Nothing dishonorable, impure, unworthy / Our God, our Law, my Nation, or myself" (1423–25), an assertion that reveals his humility, his respect for his nation and its laws, his recovered strength and his acquired inner strength, and his abandonment of concern over his current reputation, over being "proverb'd for a Fool" (202).

Finally, in Samson's defeat of the Philistines, the movement from volubility to silence that Fish observed at work in *Paradise Regained* is completed, but with a difference here. What we see in the play is both the steady tapering off of language use where Samson is concerned and an abrupt cessation of the Philistines' boasts and jeers with, appropriately enough, noise.[23] The first noise, which seems to Manoa to tear the sky (1472), is the shout of the Philistines when they observe the captive strongman. The second, as the Chorus comments to Manoa, turns out to be more dire and more glorious:

> Noise call you it or universal groan
> As if the whole inhabitation perish'd?
> Blood, death, and deathful deeds are in that noise,
> Ruin, destruction at the utmost point.   (1511–14)

The manifold ironies and reversals of this last scene soon become clear in Manoa's conversation with the Chorus and then in the Hebrew messenger's report of what has taken place. The defeat and death of Samson turn into his greatest victory over the adversary; the man who sought to retire from the "popular noise" (16) near the beginning of the play comes to operate amidst the noise and then creates noise of a different kind; the man for whom language has been a source of entrapment and torment ends his career with silent deeds preceded only by one last pun as he promises the Philistines a show of strength that "as with amaze shall strike all who behold" (1645).

In the end, Samson's fears that he would live out his days as a "burdenous drone," a pitied object with "redundant locks," the vain monument of strength serving no purpose, a proverbed fool, turn out to be unfounded. Interestingly, Manoa, in effect, literalizes his son's figurative complaint and vows to build him a monument "With all his Trophies hung, and Acts enroll'd / In copious Legend, or sweet Lyric Song" (1736–37). Hence, he will be celebrated in ceremonial language for an act that, to a large extent, language enabled him to perform. Words, in Milton's estimation, are dangerous forces, a fact that he reminds us of even late in the play when the Hebrew messenger fears to report the death of Samson to Manoa "Lest evil tidings with too rude irruption / Hitting thy aged ear should pierce too deep" (1567–68). And yet, words can also provide the means to true wisdom, to fortitude, to self-defense, and to glory.

Pennsylvania State University

NOTES

1. Stanley E. Fish, "Inaction and Silence: The Reader in *Paradise Regained*," in *Calm of Mind*, ed. Joseph Anthony Wittreich, Jr. (Cleveland, 1971), p. 27. In her article "Language and the Seal of Silence in *Samson Agonistes*," in *Milton Studies*, vol. II, ed. James D. Simmonds (Pittsburgh, 1970), Marcia Landy makes a similar point: "Samson passes through and then beyond the limits of speech into the final noise and then into silence" (p. 176).

2. In her article "Rhetoric Agonistic in *Samson Agonistes*" *MQ* XI (1977), 1, Heather Asals also describes a tripartite division, which she relates to the three types of Aristotelian debate rhetoric: Manoa as epideictic, Dalila as deliberative, and Harapha as forensic.

3. With regard to Samson's patient waiting and his divine vocation, he resembles the speaker of *Sonnet XIX*, as Joseph Pequigney, "Milton's Sonnet XIX Reconsidered," *TSLL* VIII (1967), 497, points out, but again a difference obtains: "The hero of the tragedy at first reacts to blindness with frustration and despondency much like that of the hero of the lyric. But out of his capacity and loss of sight, Samson ultimately gains his supreme triumph. . . . His 'waite' turns out to consist not of mere quiescent acceptance

of tribulation but to eventuate in the fulfillment of his own vocation through the heavenly assignment of massive action."

4. Robert L. Entzminger, "*Samson Agonistes* and the Recovery of Metaphor," *SEL* 22 (1982), 137.

5. All quotations are from *John Milton: Complete Poems and Major Prose*, ed. Merritt Y. Hughes (Indianapolis, 1957).

6. Landy, "Language and the Seal of Silence," p. 184.

7. Anthony Low, *The Blaze of Noon: A Reading of "Samson Agonistes"* (New York, 1974), p. 108.

8. Commenting on this line, Landy, "Language and the Seal of Silence," p. 184, writes, "Milton seems to be working with a favorite Spenserian and Shakespearean distinction between words and deeds, and Samson's preoccupation with words is therefore a painful reminder of misdirected actions. For all these writers, reality is conceived of as efficacious action rather than verbalization dissociated from gesture." Landy makes a good point, but I cannot agree completely that Milton's Samson considers his past actions (specifically at Etham) "misdirected." Rather, he admits that he and the Israelite governors failed to apply the idea that his actions were more efficacious than mere words.

9. Ironically, though, Jephtha also becomes the victim of his own words in his vow to the Lord that, if God grants him victory over the Ammonites, he would offer as a burnt offering the first person to issue from his home (Judg. xi, 30–31). This turns out to be his only daughter, whom he eventually sacrifices since he cannot revoke his promise to God.

10. In "Vocation and Spiritual Renovation in *Samson Agonistes*," in *Milton Studies*, vol. II, ed. James D. Simmonds (Pittsburgh, 1970), pp. 161–62, John S. Hill notes, "the encounter here. . . . is to be fought not with cannon but with rhetoric. Dalila's temptation is that of *concupiscentia oculorum* (Temptation by fraud or persuasion)." Marcia Landy, "Language and the Seal of Silence," p. 185, sees the presentation of Dalila's words in the context of martial behavior as an indication that Milton conceives of language as a form of aggression. And Robert Entzminger, "The Recovery of Metaphor," p. 146, argues that language, "the instrument with which [Dalila] had earlier defeated him, now becomes the 'trivial weapon' he uses to withstand her renewed verbal barrage."

11. Northrop Frye, "Agon and Logos: Revolution and Revelation," in *The Prison and the Pinnacle*, ed. Balachandra Rajan (Toronto, 1973), p. 149.

12. Louis L. Martz, "Chorus and Character in *Samson Agonistes*," in *Milton Studies*, vol. I, ed. James D. Simmonds (Pittsburgh, 1969), p. 128.

13. George M. Muldrow, *Milton and the Drama of the Soul* (The Hague: Mouton, 1970), p. 201.

14. In *Heroic Knowledge* (1957; rpt. Hamden, Conn., Archon Books, 1965), p. 180, Arnold Stein notes that "the challenge of muscles is easy and welcome, a gift of refreshment after the torture of mind. And Samson's answer rises like a gift of lyric simplicity out of the long, torturing struggle with the inner self."

15. John M. Steadman, *Milton and the Renaissance Hero* (Oxford, 1967), pp. 30–31.

16. Citing the apparent similarity between the old Samson's actions and his challenges to Harapha, Joan Bennett, "'A Person Rais'd': Public and Private Cause in *Samson Agonistes*," *SEL* XVIII (1978), 161, argues that "Samson does not reach immediately for a full Miltonic solution to the challenge posed, but answers the Philistine warrior in his own terms. . . . Since Harapha assumes the strongest should rule, Samson demands a duel to see . . . whose God is strongest." John S. Hill, "Vocation and Spiritual Renovation," p. 166, maintains that, although Samson's intention in wanting to fight Harapha is good, "his defiant and almost selfish challenge to Harapha puts him on the verge of committing

another act of presumption, of sacrificing all the spiritual headway he has made through one negligent, though well-meaning act. . . . His spiritual renovation is not yet complete. He must still learn that, as God's champion, patience is a necessary virtue."

17. Mary Ann Radzinowicz, *Toward "Samson Agonistes": The Growth of Milton's Mind* (Princeton, 1978), p. 50.

18. Alan Rudrum, *A Critical Commentary on Milton's "Samson Agonistes"* (London, 1969), pp. 50–51.

19. Entzminger, "The Recovery of Metaphor," p. 138. Likewise, Anthony Low, *The Blaze of Noon*, p. 109, asserts, "neither in fact nor in spirit is Samson a man who abandons language as a means of communication or persuasion."

20. John M. Steadman, "'Faithful Champion': The Theological Basis of Milton's Hero of Faith," in *Milton: Modern Essays in Criticism*, ed. Arthur E. Barker (New York, 1965), p. 480.

21. Joseph Summers, "The Movements of the Drama," in *The Lyric and Dramatic Milton*, ed. Joseph H. Summers (New York, 1965), p. 174, rightly observes that this spiritual renewal is intimately bound with his destiny: "All the significant movements of the drama are centered in the destiny of Samson. But the destiny of a chosen and fallen hero of God involves not merely the 'recognition' but the re-creation of the self; and it must be manifested in action which, making evident the will of God, transforms the hero's world."

22. Low, *The Blaze of Noon*, p. 75.

23. A similar progression from volubility to noise finally to silence occurs in *Paradise Regained*. For a discussion of this idea, see Fish's "Inaction and Silence," and my "Language as Weapon in Milton's *Paradise Regained*," in *Milton Studies*, vol. XVIII, ed. James D. Simmonds (Pittsburgh, 1983), pp. 195–216.

SAMSON AGONISTES:
THE DELIVERER AS JUDGE

Hugh MacCallum

THE ANSWER to Dr. Johnson's well-known objection that *Samson Agonistes* lacks a middle lies in the proposition that the inner struggle of the hero provides a suitable middle. So much modern criticism seems agreed upon. But whether the middle so defined is securely integrated in the conflict that leads to the catastrophe is still questioned, and even those who conclude that it is fully integrated do not always agree on the significance of the resulting design. One path of investigation — perhaps still the main path of modern commentary — assumes that Samson recovers in order to serve God in a final act of self-sacrifice. Such an approach frequently leads to an exploration of motifs which have special connotations for a Christian audience, such as the phoenix and its symbolism of resurrection. A dissenting path of interpretation, only slightly less traveled, emphasizes tragic loss and the thwarting of spiritual aspiration by violence and revenge. Frequently, however, critical effort is directed toward reconciling tragic insight and tragic waste by giving full weight to the suffering of Samson and his friends while yet recognizing the restorative elements which also appear to be comprehended in Milton's conception of catharsis.[1]

The limited goal of the present essay is to suggest a way of looking at the pattern of loss and recovery which is consistent with the conviction that the play's middle is causally integrated with its tragic denouement. My central thesis has two parts: first, that *Samson Agonistes* is deeply concerned throughout with the contrast between the Mosaic law as external prescription and the inner, rational freedom best fulfilled in the gospel;[2] and second, that this antinomy receives only a partial resolution and that the process of discovery thus remains tragically imperfect. In Samson's growth to freedom can be seen the lineaments of heroic and spiritual endeavor; in the absence of love, the ground of tragedy. This approach views Samson as judge or interpreter as well as deliverer,[3] and seeks to put in perspective the elements of tragic loss and tragic insight by stressing the incompleteness of the judgment and consequently also of the deliverance.

As a preliminary to discussion of the play it will be useful to comment on the treatment of law and freedom in Milton's late prose, especially *De doctrina christiana*. This will provide the context for a consideration of the way in which *Samson Agonistes* represents the religious culture of the age of Samson. Attention will next be turned to the treatment of law and freedom throughout the five acts of the play; and, finally, an effort will be made to show how the failure to achieve a full resolution of the problem contributes to the tragic effect.

I

At the outset it is worth stressing that Milton's view of the Mosaic Law is distinctive and in some repects departs from Protestant orthodoxy. An unusual feature of his handling of the Mosaic law is his assertion that its promise of life referred only to temporal life, not to life eternal. Milton does not deny to the Israelites all knowledge of eternal life, but holds that this concept did not properly belong to the law, which justified those who kept its commandments only by enabling them to spend this present life happily (YP VI, p. 519–20). Milton differs here from the main line of Reformed thought, for that stresses the connection between the fulfillment of the law and eternal life. John Calvin, for example, interprets the law in terms of a promise of eternal life to those who are obedient, and belittles the idea that the Jews were looking for earthly happiness.[4]

Wherever we turn, we find Milton restricting and downplaying the value of the Mosaic law and ignoring the devices used by Calvin to unify the Old and New Testaments. He separates the law from the promise of the gospel, refrains from employing interpretation based on synecdoche, and shows no interest in seeking the positive hidden under the negative (compare Calvin's *Institutes* Book II, chapter vii). He stresses the artificiality of the law and its cumbersome use of prescription. A written code, it contains many stipulations intended for the Israelites alone, and its discipline is slavish and childish, serving merely to make them recognize their depravity, as Paul notes (Romans iii, 20), and thus to turn them to the righteousness of the promised Christ. Its chief function is thus propaedeutic. Calvin warned against exaggerating the contrast of law and gospel, but Milton seems determined to highlight their differences (*Institutes*, p. 426; YP VI, pp. 517–20).

Milton introduces the gospel as "MUCH MORE EXCELLENT AND PERFECT THAN THE LAW" (YP VI, p. 521). The proof of this excellence is found in the internal character of the gospel, for it is written in the hearts of believers rather than on tablets of stone (YP VI, pp. 523–24). With the introduction of the gospel, the new covenant through faith in Christ, the old covenant, the entire Mosaic law, is abolished (YP VI, pp. 525–26). This view is central to Milton's position, and he clearly considers it to be distinctive and original; to its defense he devotes what he calls a "huge array" of scriptural authority (YP VI, p. 533). His point is that the gospel abolishes not only the ceremonial law, with its types and figures of Christ, but the moral part of the Mosaic law also, so that Christians are released from the entire Decalogue (YP VI, p. 526).

Milton accepts the view that historically the law served to make the Israelites turn to the righteousness of the promised Christ. But the principal reasons for its enactment were retributive or corrective (see YP VI, p. 528), and most or all of these have become obsolete. In this area, at least, Milton is not eager to move from the example of the ancient Jewish people to the experience of the modern Christian. He concedes, rather sardonically, that those who need to be forced to come to Christ may find some use in the law, but those who are already believers, he insists, are firmly attached to Christ. They do not need the law because they have a better teacher. Like certain books, the law may serve to scout into sin, but only as an intellectual venture, for any attempt to live by the law makes us wander further away from Christ (YP VI, pp. 534–35). He thus repudiates the view affirmed by Calvin that the law is not only a mirror in which we can see our sins, but also has as its end perfect righteousness, inward and spiritual, and that its precepts have perpetual validity (*Institutes*, p. 371). For Milton the law can only disturb believers, and make them waver; it even tempts God if we try to fulfill it (YP VI, p. 529–30).

The radical principle in Milton's view of Scripture is that the law is fulfilled in love. The two great commands of the gospel, love God and love your neighbor, sum up the essence of law. Contrary to Calvin, he concludes that these two commandments are not clearly implied by the Decalogue, for the first appears initially in Deuteronomy vi, 5 and the second in Leviticus xix, 18 (YP VI p. 532). They contain the inner law which is expressed in Christian liberty, and which frees us from the authority of sin, of the outward law, and of men: "SO THAT, BEING MADE SONS INSTEAD OF SERVANTS AND GROWN MEN INSTEAD OF BOYS, WE MAY SERVE GOD IN CHARITY THROUGH THE GUIDANCE OF THE SPIRIT OF TRUTH" (YP VI, p. 537; see also YP II, pp. 262–65). The spirit, Milton holds, renews the law of nature in the hearts of the regenerate. This law was given to Adam in his state of perfection, but was obscured by the Fall, even though some gleams remain in the hearts of all mankind. With its renewal, the regenerate

are restored to a condition of freedom analogous to that enjoyed by unfallen Adam before the introduction of a covenant of works. Unlike the
law written on the tablets of stone, this inner law operates through regenerate reason and will rather than through a multitude of stipulations
requiring servile obedience. As the metaphor of the heart makes clear
(YP VI, pp. 523–24), it represents the possibility of an inner motivation
which combines obedience and liberty.[5]

All this is far from Calvin's view that the law can be smoothly as-
similated to the gospel by considering it to be the same substance appre-
hended under a diverse but complementary form (*Institutes*, pp. 449–50,
454, 462–63). For Milton, substance and form cannot be so easily
discriminated. The outward form of legal codification represents bondage
and servility, and in this sense the Mosaic law obscured rather than expressed the real meaning of the law in the heart. Drawing the contrast
between outward law and inner gospel becomes a form of praise for the
latter, and a way of energizing Christian liberty. Filial obedience, on
the other hand, is both form and substance of the gospel; present but
imperfectly realized in the Old Testament, it shines forth in the New
(YP VI, pp. 536–37).

Calvin, it is true, acknowledges an antithesis between the law as
literal doctrine which creates fear and bondage and the spiritual testament of freedom found in the gospel (*Institutes*, pp. 456–60). In the *Institutes*, however, Calvin seems anxious to restrict the implications of this
Pauline doctrine and to dissolve antithesis and opposition into a series
of distinctions and differences.[6] Only in the commentaries does Calvin
show a lively sense of the creative tension between law and gospel (see,
e.g., II Corinthians iii, 6ff and Romans viii, 15). His restraint in the *Institutes* is no doubt related to his search for the underlying unity of scriptural revelation, but it also is relevant to his opposition to antinomianism.

Milton's position respecting the Mosaic law is technically antinomian,
although he is not indebted to any particular school of antinomian teaching. Certainly the temper of his thought is quite different from that of
the antinomianism which flourished in England and New England during the thirties and forties through the teaching of John Eaton, Tobias
Crisp, or John Cotton. Yet if we turn to such English critics of the antinomian school as Henry Burton, Thomas Taylor, or William Ames,
we find that Milton holds the principal tenet of the position which they
considered heterodox.[7] Burton, for example, maintains that the Decalogue provides both an image by which we may see our sins and a guide
to sanctification. He reprimands those who allow the law "no further
use, then as to bee a Schoolmaster to bring us to Christ, and then fare-

well law."[8] By this seventeenth-century criterion, Milton stands convicted of antinomianism.

Milton, of course, does not mean that the Christian, now exempt from moral responsibility, can act in a lawless manner (neither, to be fair, did other antinomians usually mean this, but they consistently received a bad press). From a modern standpoint it can be maintained, as by A.S.P. Woodhouse, that Milton escapes antinomianism by replacing the outward with the inward law, the latter "conceived as ethical and rational in character, and identified with the law of nature."[9] Yet we must remember that the law of nature is itself not a collection of prescriptions or commandments, or a kind of synthesis combining Moses and the wisdom of Athens. It is only realized through the exercise of interpretation and rational choice carried out under the direction of the spirit. The firmness of Milton's antinomian rejection of the Mosaic law as a guide to the love of God and man is evident in his refusal to use the Decalogue as a basis for Book II of *De doctrina christiana:* "Some theologians insist the form of good works is their conformity with the ten commandments. . . . But I do not see how this can possibly be true under the gospel" (YP VI, p. 639; see also editor's note 1, pp. 637–38).

II

It is in the light of Milton's critical view of the law that we should try to understand his choice of a subject from the Book of Judges. The age of Samson precedes the great prophets of the New Dispensation who clarified the relation between the law written on stone and the law written on the heart (see, for example, Isaiah li, 7; lxvi, 1–2; Jeremiah xxxi, 33; Ezekiel xi, 19). Yet it is also an age when men have begun to neglect the heroic story which was the original setting of the law. History seems now to have truly descended from the heights to the subjected plain. In the time of the patriarchs, the chosen people had a purpose and cohesiveness which allowed them to keep their identity in the face of frequent trials and much back-sliding. After Joshua, however, a kind of demoralization sets in as a new generation appears which forgets what the Lord did for Israel and turns from the ways in which their fathers walked (Judges ii, 10). From time to time the Lord sends judges or deliverers and "saves them penitent," as Milton summarizes this age in *Paradise Lost* (XII, 319). Thus there is in Judges a new sense of discord and failure; society seems to have lost touch with the truth, for the law is neglected and faith and worship are stripped down to the barest essentials.

This is an age, then, when the process of educating men in order to lead them from the works of the law into the works of faith has only begun. Here Milton can place a biblical hero who learns from experience without frequently resorting in an explicit manner to Scripture. *Samson Agonistes* gives the distinct impression that the characters normally draw on memory and tradition rather than on the written word. When the members of the Chorus wish to compare Samson with past deliverers, for example, they say "Thy words to my remembrance bring" (277). Their sense of the past seems in large measure to depend on the spoken word. Their only reference to books (653), which is apparently concerned not with Scripture itself but with humanistic and philosophical literature, is belittling in the manner of Jesus in *Paradise Regained* (IV, 321). The great events of sacred history are of course known to Samson and his friends. Thus Samson can refer to light as the "prime decree" of God (85), recalling the creation scene in Genesis, or to "the God of *Abraham*" (465), implying some knowledge of Israel's history. And of course he knows the law. The Chorus, too, can refer to the great events wrought by God "for his people of old" (1533), in this way recalling the events of Exodus which were so often rehearsed by singers and prophets, and they seem to have some knowledge of the scene of judgment subsequent to the Fall (1053). Even Dalila knows the song of Deborah and Barak, while Harapha can mention the giants of the Pentateuch. But these allusions are not very detailed or specific, and seldom imply direct quotation of a text. (Samson's "Let there be light" is a notable exception — but this is such a memorable phrase!)

The historical awareness of these people, moreover, is highly selective and omits much. Moses and his leadership, for example, are never overtly recalled. Milton is presenting a society in which the sacred texts are locked up in the ark of the covenant, and the past is kept alive primarily by oral tradition. In this respect the play provides a striking contrast with the companion poem, *Paradise Regained*, where "it is written" is a phrase of power and authority, and where Jesus reads the law as a child and later revolves in his mind the law and prophets, searching "what was writ / Concerning the Messiah" (I, 260–61). Samson never refers to Scripture as a written document, and for him the promises of God are expressed in the events which preceded his birth and which have been remembered by his family.

The contrast with the handling of God's promises in *Paradise Lost* is instructive. In the last two books of the epic, Milton weaves the *protevangelium* into his history of the world, discovering the progressive revelation of the seed of the woman who will bruise the serpent's head. Samson's calling as deliverer clearly has a relation to the promise made first in the scene of judgment after man's fall, and repeated with increasing clarity through the types and prophecies of the Old Testament. This being so, it is surprising that Samson fails to interpret the prophecy made by the angel at his birth in terms, if not of the *protevangelium*, at least of the larger scheme for making all nations blessed in the seed of Abraham. He and the Chorus appear to be suffering from a kind of historical and cultural amnesia, and they are unable to place the vivid and absorbing events of their own age in relation to the great revelations of the past. Their view of history thus lacks the sweep and integration found in the reflections of Milton's Adam or of his Jesus.

While the characters do not give the impression that they consult and meditate upon cultural and literary documents, they display a lively sense of the way history is in the process of being made into literature, whether into legend, song, or drama. When the Chorus speaks of Gideon and Jeptha, Samson responds, "Of such examples adde mee to the roul" (290). The characters share the sense that their lives are being recorded: "The rarer thy example stands" (166), "to Ages an example" (765). Dalila, taking comfort in the thought that she will be "renown'd" among her own people and "sung at solemn festivals" (983), recalls how the fame achieved by Jael and others was preserved by the song of Deborah. Manoa imagines that his son's acts will be "enroll'd / In copious Legend, or sweet Lyric Song" (1736–37). His remark suggests how the literature of the people contributes to the growth of Scripture, particularly at a time before the establishment of official custodians to oversee and tend sacred writ. Milton observes that in this period the law of Moses was kept in the ark of the covenant, and that it passed into the care of its pledged protectors, "the priests and prophets and other divinely instructed men" (YP VI, p. 588), only after the captivity in Babylon.

Another suggestive way of looking at the time of Samson is to see it as precursor to the great age of the Psalms. Milton is remarkably successful in using allusion, echo, image, and theme to place Samson in a world like that of the Psalms. Normally, however, "psalmic texture" seems a more accurate phrase to describe this element than "psalmic citation."[10] There are few direct quotations, and frequently passages echo two or three Psalms at once. Often the connection is a matter of thought rather than language. The method thus differs from the use of rich clusters of specific references to the Bible found in such sections of *Paradise Lost* as the council in heaven in Book III.

It is of course obvious that while Samson and his friends can recall Genesis or the Mosaic law, they cannot cite the Psalms without a kind of anachronism. Milton's keen sense of historical and cultural evolution is evident here, for he implies that the experience of the servants of God in the early books of scripture lies behind the psalmist's treatment of the human condition. Samson clearly lives at a time when lyric flourishes. The choral odes and the other passages of heightened speech in *Samson Agonistes* show how the servants of God in the earlier books of Scripture developed the modes of expression which later found fulfillment in the Psalms. In this way the play suggests the historical growth of religious consciousness.

The tradition of interpreting the Psalms typologically received an infusion of new vigor with the Reformers. As Barbara Lewalski points out, the Psalms provided an important illustration of the continuity of religious experience, so that Luther could identify with the faith of the Old Testament people, the "Faithful Synagogue," and Calvin could emphasize the recapitulation of David's experience by the Christian.[11] While Milton explores the relevance of the Psalms to Christian experience in *Paradise Regained*,[12] he is, as we have already seen, more inclined than Calvin to stress the limitations in outlook of those who lived under the law. In *Samson Agonistes* those limitations are prominent, and become evident in the selective way in which the Psalms are put to use. Psalmic motifs which are rich in Christian implication are sometimes noted, but their potential is left undeveloped. At the same time, certain distinctive elements in the Psalms are downplayed or ignored altogether.

There is, for example, no stress on those Psalms employed in Hebrews to present the nature and priesthood of the Son of God, an omission which is of particular interest when we remember the importance of this material (especially Psalm ii, 7, cited in Hebrews i, 5; v, 5) to Milton in *Paradise Regained* and *De doctrina christiana*. The Pauline view of salvation, which the "Paul" of the Epistles supports by frequent references to the Psalms, is present only indirectly in the play. As Samson has no perception of the Son of God, so he is unable to apply to himself the language of sonship which is so important to the Pauline conception of freedom (Galatians iv, 7) and which finds an anticipation in the son and servant language of the Psalms (e.g., lxxxvi, 16; lxxx, 17). The closest we come to such language is in Manoa's remark that God is "Best pleas'd with humble and filial submission" (511), but characteristically Samson's father uses such a potent formula only when arguing for a fruitless course of action. The repeated references to Samson as Manoa's son, and to the sons of Israel, are also suggestive, and sometimes this language has a messianic or christological flavor, as when the Chorus says that Samson is "with might endu'd / Above the Sons of men" (1293–94). But the important thing about these intimations is that they are muted, fugitive, and unrecognized by the characters themselves. Samson moves toward freedom, but lacks the language of sonship to express it.

Manoa's concern to ransom his son is suggestive in a similar way, and has been seen as alluding to the doctrine of atonement as ransom discussed by Paul in I Timothy ii, 6. But this language simply highlights the absence from the world of the play of a divine mediator. The primary reference of "ransom" is to Psalm xlix, 7, where it is said that the wealthy man cannot "redeem his brother, nor give to God a ransom for him," a saying which Manoa, to his grief, finds to be true. This Psalm is one of the few that hints (in verse 15) at survival after death; but the play does not introduce belief in the afterlife as a feature of Hebrew thought, and in this respect it adopts the usual viewpoint of the psalmist.[13] What intimations of life after death the play contains are in any case not comprehended by its Hebrew characters and thus serve to draw attention to the absence of this belief from the culture of the time.

The play thus understates or suppresses a number of gospel and Pauline themes which could have been introduced through the language of the Psalms, such as sonship, the Messiah, ransom and salvation. The downplaying of such elements is even more striking when we remember their prominence elsewhere in Milton's writing. Of particular importance to the present argument, however, is the restrained and selective handling of the psalmist's comments on law and on love. As Milton observed (YP II, p. 301), the law is repeatedly celebrated by the psalmist who characteristically presents himself as one who seeks to fulfill it: "O how love I thy law! it *is* my meditation all the day" (Psalm cxix, 97). Sometimes in the Psalms this law is treated as prescriptive and eternal, at others it is linked to the heart and the word. While sacrificial worship following the ceremonial code seems to be regarded as normal, there are a few passages repudiating such sacrifices ("burnt offering and sin offering hast thou not required") and calling for a more spiritual worship to realize the law in the heart (xl, 6–7; li, 16–17). In the play it is Manoa who imagines, perhaps recalling the visit of the angel (26), that "off'rings" may avert God's anger (519), while Samson comes to understand that the best sacrifice is a contrite heart. The reflections on the law by the Chorus and Samson are troubled and critical, however, and eschew panegyric. As we have seen, the stress falls on the difficulty of the task of interpreting the law in the freedom granted by the spirit. Unlike Paul, who in Romans, Chapter iii, uses the Psalms to define the limits of the law, they do not have the guidance of faith in Christ.

Mercy or loving kindness is a pervasive theme running through the Psalms and providing a touchstone essential to the understanding of God and his laws. As W.O.E. Osterley observes, in the revised version "mercy" is normally used as the equivalent of the Hebrew *chesed*, a word which includes much more than mercy since it has connotations of compassion, graciousness, long suffering, and truth: "If there were any one word in English which could express the meaning of this word it would be love."[14] On occasion it is translated as "lovingkindness." In the New English Bible the normal translation is simply "love." Milton in his translations of the Psalms frequently uses "mercy" instead of "love," but also freely employs "love" and "lovingkindness." He would clearly have accepted the view that the God of the Psalms is a God of love. In the play, however, none of the characters, not even Samson, manages to express the idea of divine love.

The word itself appears almost exclusively in relation to erotic love in the parodic arguments of Dalila. The Chorus refers once to the paternal love of Manoa, and when linked to the efforts of the old man to ransom his son the term is certainly resonant with implications. Yet the Chorus is not aware of these, and uses other terms to describe the relations of Samson to his family and people, terms such as duty and honor. The closest we come to the conception of a merciful God of lovingkindness is in Samson's words to Harapha when he says that he despairs not of God's gracious pardon (1171–73), and in the final words of Manoa and the Chorus concerning the God who "unexpectedly returns." Connected with the muted treatment of the language of mercy and love is the absense of that sense of joy in communion with God that is so characteristic of the Psalms. Neither Samson in the prayer before his death, nor the Chorus at the close, is in a position to say "in thy presence *is* fulness of joy" (Psalm xvi, 11).

III

The so-called five acts of *Samson Agonistes* provide a searching treatment of the evolution of the idea of freedom in a society shaped by law and limited in its view of God. At the outset of his career, the prescriptions which particularly concern Samson are those of the ceremonial, rather than the moral, law, for he grew to manhood under the special rules governing the behavior of the Nazarite which are set out in Numbers, chapter vi. Chosen by God before his birth, he obeys the vow to avoid wine and strong drink and his hair clusters beneath the shoulders. But Samson discovers that it is not a simple matter to be separate to God. The hero who acts for God at the play's climax is a Nazarite only in some metaphoric sense. He is no longer concerned with outward ritual, but rather with spiritual impulse, and he knows that the heart of his dedication is his faith in God, not the secret of his hair. Each act leading to that climax can be interpreted in terms of the hero's struggle with the idea of law and his gradual progress toward an understanding of freedom.

The play opens with a suggestion of hope. The blind hero, led by an attendant, expresses relief at his temporary escape from toil and prison. Diction and imagery at once contrive to suggest the change from bondage to freedom. But in the long soliloquy that develops when he is left alone, we find that bodily relief has not been matched by ease of mind. His tormenting thoughts lead him to seek an excuse for himself, and twice he must check his rebellious mood and struggle to accept God's will. Remorseful but not yet truly repentant, he next gives up the effort to understand and plunges into anguished lamentation bewailing his loss of sight and imprisonment.

If we ask whether this initial position is determined by the Mosaic law, the answer is clearly negative. Samson is not preoccupied with the law but with the promises of God. The pain in the first part of the soliloquy springs from his realization that he has failed in the role of deliverer: "Promise was that I / Should *Israel* from *Philistian* yoke deliver" (38–39). There will be several references of this kind to the words of the angel at Samson's conception. That prophesy, however, stated only that Samson would "begin to deliver Israel out of the hand of the Philistines" (Judges xiii, 5). Samson will eventually recognize that he is a forerunner, one of those who initiate the process of national renewal, but his opening assumption of the whole responsibility serves to intensify his distress.

In the latter part of this great soliloquy Samson is preoccupied with light, the prime decree of God: "Let there be light, and light was over all" (84). Samson apparently knows Genesis, and is able to cite the commandment that marks the beginning of the work of creation.[15] His words recall the Psalms of lament, and especially those which praise God as the fountain of being and the source of joy and meaning in the life of man: "in thy light shall we see light" (Psalm xlvi). He does not make the direct association of light with grace in the heart found in the New Testament (2 Corinthians iv, 6), but he does associate physical light with life and with the soul, and his loss of physical sight includes a sense of alienation from God's word and his grace.

Samson as we meet him at the outset, then, is not a man broken by the law. His primary concern is to understand his relation to God and interpret the apparent failure of God's promise. There is, however, one aspect of the problem which does bear on law, and it involves an issue of importance throughout the play. Samson first defines his sin as "impotence of mind" (52) for he broke the "Seal of silence" (49) and revealed to Dalila the secret of his strength. This is to define his sin as the breaking of a prohibition, and the reader is likely to draw a comparison with the prohibition on the fruit of the tree of knowledge in *Paradise*

Lost. Samson's first description of his error is legalistic and superstitious. He speaks as if his strength were a magical gift, something extraneous to his physical nature, and thus bitterly observes that God "to shew withal / How slight the gift was, hung it in my Hair" (58–59). Repeatedly he speaks of his guilt as arising from a single act of sacrilege. Thus he tells his father that he has profaned "The mystery of God" (378) and revealed his "capital secret" (394). Manoa agrees that he has violated "the sacred trust of silence" (428).

Yet in what sense is the connection between Samson's strength and his hair a secret? The biblical idea requires interpretation. In Numbers there is no suggestion that the unshorn locks of the Nazarite are the seal of a secret; rather they bear public witness to vows of self-dedication. Presumably the same is true of Samson. Is the significance of the locks then a matter hidden from Dalila only because she is a Philistine, not privy to the ritual law and state secrets of the Hebrews? But this seems too general an explanation; all Nazarites are dedicated to God, yet no others have received the gift of such immense strength. The specific meaning of Samson's vocation as Nazarite goes back to the words of the angel, in which his role as deliverer is made to seem dependent on obedience to the code of the Nazarite. In Judges, this is the explanation he gives Dalila at the moment of his failure (Judges xvi, 17): Samson assumes that his special strength is dependent on the special calling sealed by his vows, and he reveals this "secret" to Dalila just as he revealed the riddle's answer to the woman of Timna.

In Milton's treatment of the issue, as we have seen, it is Samson who first espouses the secrecy theory. Yet as he develops, his position changes. When he speaks of having published God's holy secret "impiously, / Weakly at least" (498–99), he moves from the idea of ritual impurity to that of moral failure, and his identification of the secret with "Gods counsel" (497) gives it a more comprehensive significance. Shortly thereafter he stresses the way his disloyalty found expression in action as well as words when he allowed Dalila to shear him "Like a tame Weather" (538). Samson gives Dalila not only information but the opportunity to put it to use. He thus surrenders to the enemy. The idea of a secret, with its suggestion of the warrior's magical purity, has given way to a more adequate conception of human responsibility and divine providence. Samson's sin was moral and spiritual rather than ritual, and consisted in abandoning his vocation and surrendering to the enemy.

It is during the exchange with Harapha that Samson gives the most satifying expression to the terms of the trial. God, he says,

> gave me
> At my Nativity this strength, diffus'd
> No less through all my sinews, joints and bones,
> Then thine, while I preserv'd these locks unshorn,
> The pledge of my unviolated vow.   (1140–44)

Here there is no recourse at all to the notion of a secret. The unshorn locks are simply the pledge or symbol of his vow; they did not contain his strength any more than the forbidden fruit contained knowledge. The vow, moreover, was not a commitment to silence, but an act of self-dedication to God's service accompanied by visible signs. His failure was rooted not merely in garrulousness, as he once thought, nor even in uxoriousness, although that also made a contribution, but in loss of faith in the living God. Samson's long intellectual struggle with the idea of breaking a prescribed code has emerged in a recognition of his failure to act freely. Milton implies that there never was a secret; it existed only as an excuse in Samson's mind, and disappears once he has discovered the true nature of his responsibility.

The conversation between Samson and the Chorus in the first act of the drama shows Samson clarifying his position by refusing to accept the more obvious kinds of guilt which can be measured by law. Even before that conversation begins, the Chorus have shown their preoccupation with ceremonial law by the nervous joke with which they celebrate Samson's feat of carrying the gates of Gaza to the top of a hill: "No journey of a Sabbath day, and loaded so" (149). We are to remember not only the many injunctions supporting the fourth commandment scattered throughout the Old Testament, such as Jeremiah's "bear no burden on the sabbath day, nor bring it in by the gates of Jerusalem" (xvii, 21), but also the way Christ frees this law from rigid and narrow interpretations.[16] The first point raised by the Chorus in their interchange with Samson is characteristically legalistic, and also appeals not to moral but to ceremonial and ethnic law peculiar to the Jewish people: "Why thou shouldst wed *Philistian* women rather / Then of thine own Tribe fairer, or as fair" (216–17). Reproachfully they point to the prescription of endogamous marriage found so often in the Old Testament (as in Deuteronomy vii, 3). But Samson turns aside their criticism, treating it as irrelevant. His first marriage, he claims, was sanctioned by an "intimate impulse" (223) from God as a step in his work as deliverer of Israel. His sin is not the breaking of a political, judicial, or ceremonial law. Nor does Samson hesitate to use his first marriage as precedent for his second: "I thought it lawful from my former act, / And the same end" (231–32). This is a reasoned conclusion, rather than an intuition prompted by God. But there is nothing inherently wrong with making a precedent out of his experience of divine direction, and using it to decide what is "lawful" in the sense of *permitted*.[17] This is the same area of casuistry in which Milton had once argued that a Christian may stay married to an unbeliever if, full of grace, he "feares not a seducing, but hopes rather a gaining" (YP II, p. 687). Thus breaking the letter sometimes fulfills the moral reason of the law. In any case, the point Samson now stresses in his reply to the Chorus is clearly correct: it was not his marriage to Dalila that was a sin, but his surrender to her (233–34).

The other criticism raised by the Chorus faults Samson for his failure to become Israel's deliverer: "Yet *Israel* still serves with all his Sons" (240). Again Samson is quick to defend himself, this time by distinguishing his sin from the guilt of others. He will not be made a scapegoat either for the nation's weak governors or for the servile people. Suffering has made him articulate. The hero who once offered deeds which "though mute, spoke loud the dooer" (248), now breaks his silence in order to educate his people and himself. The Chorus grasp the main point, as their comparison of Samson with other betrayed figures indicates, although they shy away from underlining their own responsibility.[18]

The Chorus has begun to understand that Samson's fall cannot be defined in terms of the Mosaic law. They accept his argument that he is not being punished for his marriage, and acknowledge that God can exempt the individual from "National obstriction" (312). Their comprehension is stretched but they manage to distinguish between legal impurity, waived by God's special dispensation, and the moral uncleanness which characterized the woman of Timna only after her marriage to Samson when she became the lover of his groomsman. An explanation of the hero's fall must comprehend his freedom.

Joan Bennett argues that the Chorus here posits an inscrutable God who is above law.[19] While this is the tendency of their remarks, they do manage to preserve a distinction between reason and "vain reasonings" (322), and they do believe that God's ways are justifiable to men, even if the perplexities of doubters cannot find a "self-satisfying" (306) solution (the phrase suggests that the doubters seek complete rational autonomy). We know enough about Milton's view of God's decrees (as expressed in *De doctrina christiana*, Book I, chapter 3, for example) to realize that the members of the Chorus are wrong when they stress the arbitrary nature of God's prescriptions, and right when they incline to the view that his decrees are accommodated to man's mind and actions.

Over Samson's conversation with Manoa hangs the fifth commandment: "Honour thy father and thy mother: that thy days may be long upon the land which the LORD thy God giveth thee" (Exodus xx, 12). Manoa characteristically thinks in ethnocentric fashion, finding his identity in tribe and family. For this reason Samson's marriage choices are and remain a source of bitterness to him. He did not approve of them, and he is unconvinced by the argument that they were guided by "Divine impulsion" (422). Father and son have differed in the past, and the son has refused to follow his father's wishes. They differ again now, for Samson respectfully but firmly turns down his father's proposal to ransom him.

In life, then, Samson appears to ignore the fifth commandment. Filled with inward grief when confronted with his old father, he is nonetheless resolute in refusing the kind of "filial submission" (511) which his father urges that he show God and clearly would enjoy receiving himself. Yet in death Samson fulfills the end of the commandment. While the letter of the law would only have led him astray, his determination to do the will of his heavenly father has brought about as a corollary his restoration in the eyes of his earthly father. At the close Manoa honors his son — "*Samson* hath quit himself / Like *Samson*" (1709–10) — and in doing so recognizes that Samson has not only brought honor to Israel, but also "To himself and Fathers house eternal fame" (1717).

During this conversation we are also very aware of issues relating to the first table of the law. Samson is not explicitly and personally guilty of idolatry, blasphemy, and the worship of strange gods, but by his failure he has encouraged others to indulge in these sins. The triumph of Dagon, as his father points out, is his responsibility. Samson can deny that he is at fault for Israel's military and political defeat, but he finds that he must accept responsibility for having corrupted rather than educated his people. As a failed leader, he has vicariously broken the first three commandments.

There is only a taint of actual idolatory about Samson's past behavior. Swollen with pride, he once walked about "like a petty God" (529). But he lacked Satan's egoism, and his more characteristic bent was to make a kind of idol out of Dalila. It is in terms of this servitude that Samson repeatedly expresses his failure: "Bond-slave . . . servil mind . . . servitude . . . True slavery . . . how degeneratly I serv'd" (411–19). Here again we see the inadequacy of the Mosaic law, for the law itself encourages the very servitude it condemns, teaching men to behave as slaves or bondsmen, blindly obedient to prescription. Samson's weakness, then, matches the weakness of the dispensation under which he has lived. He has not realized the freedom and rationality ("manhood," he calls it [408]) through which alone it is possible to follow the law within. Such liberty is achieved only by those who, keeping faith in God and his promises, use their full powers of comprehension. Samson has failed as a son, not of Manoa, but of God, and for this reason his instinctive refusal to entertain the scheme of release proposed by his human father is right.

Initially Dalila presents herself as motivated by penitence and conjugal affection. Urging that weakness should join with weakness, she argues that her fault arose from "the jealousie of Love" (791). Her aim was to keep Samson in safe custody, possessing him without rival in love or war, "Mine and Loves prisoner" (808). She admits that she wished to restrain his liberty, but justifies herself by claiming that she acted for "reasons in Loves law." Sensing the weakness of this argument, she adds that "Love hath oft, well meaning, wrought much wo / Yet always pity or pardon hath obtain'd" (813–14). There is a strong element of travesty here, for the phrase "Loves law" brings to mind the central doctrine that love alone fulfills the law, while the linking of love and pity recalls divine as well as human love. But while true love frees the individual from the rule of law, and enables him to realize the substance of the law through the spirit of charity, Dalila's love seeks on the the contrary to coerce and possess by laws which are entirely self-regarding. Samson is quick to point to the fallacy underlying her argument: "Love seeks to have Love" (837); that is, it only exists in a relationship characterized by faith and freedom.

Having failed to move Samson by her appeal to the laws of erotic love, Dalila tries a new tack by arguing that she betrayed her husband out of respect for civil and religious law. Magistrates and priests exhorted her to entrap an enemy of the nation and a dishonorer of Dagon. So besieged, she maintains, she had nothing to reply to such powerful arguments, although her love for Samson "combated in silence all these reasons" (864). The suggestion that this insistent, articulate woman was a mute and distraught lover is inherently implausible, and her account of how she held this long debate in silence appears to concede that love is a passion for which no rational justification can be found. Sincere love, Samson responds, would have found "other reasonings" (875).

Samson is unwavering in his assertion that Dalila should have remained faithful to her choice of husband, a choice which entailed giving up parents and country. His identification of the law of nature with the law of nations makes it clear that his appeal is not to the Ten Commandments or to the Mosaic law in general, but to that unwritten law given to the first man, of which "a kind of gleam or glimmering . . . still remains in the hearts of all mankind" (YP VI, p. 516). He thus posits a freedom to obey inner law which is analogous to the freedom achieved under the gospel. Samson's own awareness of that law is in process of being renewed in his heart by the operation of the spirit, but what is of special importance here is his recognition of its universality. The law of nature applies to all men alike, Jew or Gentile.

The seeming likeness between Samson's use of marriage for political purposes and Dalila's should not mislead us.[20] There are real differences between the two cases, the most important being that Samson does not intend to betray his spouse while Dalila's patriotism depends upon sacrificing hers. Samson's marriages would not have been divisive without the malice of the Philistines. His words to Harapha point to a road not taken: "Among the Daughters of the *Philistines* / I chose a Wife, which argu'd me no foe" (1192–93). For a moment the union of Gentile and Jew foreshadows the universality to come.

Samson is careful to answer both prongs of Dalila's argument, civil and religious. The Philistine leaders, disobeying the law of nature and nations, have lost the right to be obeyed themselves, while the Philistine gods, served by injustice, have lost the right to expect zeal of their followers. Both answers appeal to moral considerations in order to support the free conscience of the individual.

In her final pitch, Dalila conjures up a picture of careless ease and sensual pleasure as she promises to tend Samson with nursing diligence into old age. Samson, in reply, points out that what she invites him to accept is perfect bondage, in which she would have the opportunity to humiliate him further (941–44). From false wife, Dalila has become false mistress, nurse, and mother. What she offers to Samson at this point is a condition analogous to that of living under the law: a state of thraldom, servitude, and fear, in which the individual is treated as a child, not a man. Dalila is like Hagar, who in Paul's allegory of the two families of Abraham, brought forth children to slavery (Galatians iv, 24; see YP VI, p. 527).

The misogynistic outburst of the Chorus after the departure of Dalila, clearly biased and evasive, shows a warped sense of law: "Therefore Gods universal Law / Gave to the man despotic power / Over his female in due awe" (1053–55). The law to which the Chorus here appeals is the curse placed upon man as a punishment for his Fall. While Milton considers that the husband was given greater authority than the wife from the beginning, that authority was strengthened after the Fall (YP VI, p. 355; cf. *Paradise Lost* X, 195–96). But insofar as the result is despotic, it is clearly an evil, like sweat and pain, rather than a symptom of morally correct behavior. Since the purpose of the gospel is to restore through the spirit the law implanted in man at the Creation, its effect on domestic relations is to replace despotism by mutual love, support, and delight. The words of the Chorus reach back to the beginning of Scripture, but misinterpret the judgment scene by ignoring the hope which it contains. Turning the conditions introduced by the Fall into "universal Law," they fail to perceive the promise of freedom implicit in the judgment.

The giant Harapha, "bulk without spirit vast" (1238), expresses the false and debasing power of the letter. Throughout he persists in calling Samson a law-breaker, one who has been justly condemned for disrupting the league between Philistines and Israelites, for the "notorious murder" (1186) of his thirty companions at the wedding, and for the base act of robbery by which he took their robes. As a result of these crimes he has been made a slave and can expect death under the law.

Samson in replying is careful to justify his ways to the enemy, dwelling not only on the treachery of the wedding guests and the breaking of the laws of hospitality, but also on his conviction that the Philistian laws and treaties have no binding power for him since his nation was subjected by the force of conquest: "force with force / Is well ejected when the Conquer'd can" (1206–07). Releasing himself from false applications of civil law is only part of his answer, however. He now lays claim to being a fighter for freedom who locates his ultimate sanction in God's will. He acted not as a private person, but as one whose calling to free his country came from heaven. Invigorated by argument, Samson invites Harapha to combat, repeating the challenge three times. He does so with the confidence of a man who trusts his conscience rather than the formulations of man-made laws. In the very process of defying Harapha, he begins to recognize that God is merciful, that his ear is ever open and his eye "Gracious to re-admit the suppliant" (1172–73). Against Harapha's empty legalisms ("To fight with thee no man of arms will deign" [1226]), he sets freedom under the guidance of grace.

Samson dwells in sardonic mockery on the rodomontade of "glorious arms" (1130), asserting that he trusts in the "living God" (1140), not magic, for his strength. His words clearly taunt and demoralize the giant. The picture which emerges is one of fleshly might being overpowered by the spirit. This is a theme dear to Milton. It is ultimately linked to the higher heroism of suffering, as in Adam's reflections on subverting "worldly strong" by "things deemd weak" (*Paradise Lost* XII, 567–68), but in the prose such Pauline paradoxes (stemming from 1 Corinthians ix, 19; i, 25–28; 2 Corinthians i, 12) are often used to express the opposition between spirit and letter, Scripture and tradition.

The attack on the bishops provides a useful illustration. Their worldly authority and honor, argues Milton, corrupt the gospel, turning its inward power and purity into the "outward carnality" of the law, and "evaporating and exhaling the internall worship into empty conformities and gay shewes" (YP I, p. 766). That Milton associated the bishops with the Philistines is clear from his use of Samson's story in an allegory about the king in *The Reason of Church-Government* (YP I, pp. 858–59). Grounds for such a comparison include sensual idolatry, the "molten Calfe" of the mass (YP I, p. 771) providing a parallel to the feast of Dagon. Samson's encounter with Harapha is like the Reformers' encounter with the bishops in that it shows how God sends "Foolishnes to confute Wisdom, Weaknes to bind Strength, Despisednes to vanquish Pride" (YP I, p. 824). Harapha, magnifying external signs rather than the quickening power of the spirit, cowers like the bishops before the sudden assault of the spirit as it wars against "humane Principles . . . carnall sense, the pride of flesh" (YP I, p. 704). His appeal to the conventions of arms is comparable to the bishops' appeal to antiquity and custom, that "liveless *Colossus*" or "carved Gyant" which is menacing to children but "subject to the muting of every Sparrow" (YP I, p. 699). Harapha suspects magic, but the power which now begins to emanate from Samson is like those pure and powerful beams of God's word that kill the dragon of tyranny and superstition (YP I, p. 858).

The power and limits of law receive a close examination in the crisis brought by the fourth act. The public officer, with his scepter or quaint staff, appears as the visible embodiment of Philistine authority, but the law he represents is simply the arbitrary will of the lords, who through him now command Samson to appear at the feast in honor of Dagon. Samson's first reply goes directly to the point: "Our Law forbids at thir Religious Rites / My presence" (1320–21). While Samson has in mind the first three commandments, the specific reference here is to the third: "Thou shalt not bow down thy self to them [other gods or their images], nor serve them; for I the LORD thy God *am* a jealous God" (Exodus xx, 5). Even more precise in its application is the gloss provided subsequently: "Thou shalt not bow down to their gods, nor serve them, nor do after their works: but thou shalt utterly overthrow them, and quite break down their images" (xxiii, 24; see also xxxiv, 13). This not only contains the prohibition which now restrains Samson, but the injunction upon which he will subsequently act. But of course he does not yet see this.

To the "I cannot come" of absolute law, Samson now adds two assertions that "I will not come" based on the conviction that compliance would be dishonorable. How can the warrior who once aspired to deliver his country join the sword-players, wrestlers, jugglers, and mummers who entertain the Philistines? Preparing to meet a tragic end, Samson feels that decorum must be kept; he cannot bear the prospect of becoming jester for the Philistine court. By allowing Samson to expatiate on these human reasons for denying the lords, Milton draws attention to the great cost of his subsequent reversal. Samson finds that he must surrender completely his sense of personal honor and accept the humiliation of wearing the state livery of the Philistines and of playing the fool before them.[21] He resigns even the outward signs of that self-esteem which the dramatist once considered the fountainhead of all laudable enterprises (YP I, p. 841).

Samson's resolve now appears unshakable: his decision is a matter of conscience and internal peace. Alone with the Chorus, he explains that he cannot abuse the "Consecrated gift / Of strength" (1354–55) that is returning with his hair. To do so would be to reject God's renewed favor, and break the third commandment by prostituting holy things to idols. This would render him "unclean, prophane" (1362). He is alarmed by the possibility of breaking ceremonial and ritual, as well as moral, prescriptions. For a moment the distinction between circumcised and uncircumcised returns very prominently in his thinking.[22] When the Chorus observes that he has already served the Philistines by working at the mill, he sets aside the precedent with the firmness of a judge, distinguishing between spiritual and civil power and showing the ability, which Milton praised in Henry Vane, to draw "The bounds of either sword" (Sonnet XVII).

Yet it is the Chorus who point to the way out of the dilemma, although they are far from comprehending the full meaning of their words: "Where the heart joins not, outward acts defile not" (1368). Samson's first reaction is to reject the escape route suggested by this terse observation. Their casuistry, while not wrong in itself, does not apply, for "If I obey them, / I do it freely" (1372–73). But even as he speaks, he begins to see the ways of his God more clearly: "Yet that he may dispense with me or thee / Present in Temples at Idolatrous Rites / For some important cause, thou needst not doubt" (1377–79).

The idea of dispensation recalls the principle stated much earlier by the chorus ("with his own Laws he can best dispence" [314]) and based at that time on Samson's justification of his marriage to the woman of Timna. Samson's speech conveys a vivid impression of the way grace activates memory and enlightens judgment by fostering creative connections. Dispensation, once the key to interpreting his marriage to a pagan, will now admit him to the pagan temple. Samson is showing himself to be a judge in the sense of arbitrator and interpreter of the law, as well as in the sense of deliverer. In fact the two aspects of his title are converging, since he is discovering how to deliver the individual conscience from the law.

The process by which Samson moves from bondage to freedom has been presented up to this point in terms of human motivation. Now grace intervenes as "rouzing motions" (1382) dispose his thoughts to something extraordinary. He will go to the temple. As if to balance his earlier threefold repudiation of that course of action, he now asserts three times that in going to the temple he will not bring the law into contempt. These assertions are subtly varied. First he tells the Chorus that he will do nothing "that may dishonour / Our law, or stain my vow of *Nazarite*" (1385–86). Implicit seems to be a distinction between breaking the letter of the law and contravening its spirit or end. To the Officer he states the case somewhat differently: after an ironic pretense of submission, he says that he intends to comply in nothing "Scandalous or forbidden in our Law" (1409). This appears an empty reservation, since even his presence at the idolatrous rite is on a literal reading forbidden. The officer presumably takes it as such, relieved to find a face-saving formula and oblivious to the powerful but veiled irony by which Samson expresses his new spiritual freedom. The final assertion complements the first; as he will not dishonor the law, so he will not be dishonored by it: "of me expect to hear / Nothing dishonourable, impure, unworthy / Our God, our Law, my Nation, or my self" (1423–25). This last speech provides Samson's most comprehensive assertion of his determination to fulfill his responsibilities to God and man. "Expect to hear" is a suggestive way of putting the case, looking as it does to a completed action and the fame and reputation which it produces. Samson knows that something big lies ahead, for his presaging soul has told him that this day will be remarkable. He thus looks to the end, rather than the letter. The finished action or passion will contain nothing incompatible with the spirit of the law. The use of negatives ("Nothing dishonourable") suggests his humility while at the same time insisting that there will be no scandal. The line in which "Law" and "nation" are bracketed by "Our God" and "my self" effectively suggests how prescription has yielded to the law written on the heart. Deeply moved by the authority and finality of Samson's words, the Chorus pray that the spirit of God will sustain him.

The final act is full of motifs and images connected with the theme of freedom. When Manoa returns, he speaks of his efforts to ransom his son and looks forward to a triumphant homecoming. These hopes are soon blasted, and he bitterly concludes that "death who sets all free /

Hath paid his ransom now and full discharge" (1572–73). The messenger offers a new perspective on freedom, however, telling the story of how Samson escaped from bondage through a victorious death. In the choral odes that follow, it is the Philistines who are seen to have been blind and in bondage, while Samson emerges as a hero gifted with inner sight and filled with fiery virtue.

Manoa's last speech is a moving elegy which laments even while denying lamentation. Manoa argues that his son has met a hero's death and fulfilled his mission. For his country he has gained honor and the opportunity to seize freedom; for himself and his father's house he has won eternal fame (1717). The power of the speech lies in the way the old man's affirmations triumph over the emotional compulsion to cry, wail, and beat the breast. But we are also meant to realize that his speech is informed by a distinctively Old Testament point of view. Liberty is conceived in terms of national and political interests, rather than as a spiritual power located in the heart of the individual. This is not to deny that the model of heroism which he offers is a noble and religious one. Crucial to his eulogy is the fact that God restored his favor to Samson. Yet while Manoa sees an element of purgation or catharsis in his son's death, and while he also grasps that his son's example is important in the struggle for freedom, he completely misses the fact that Samson had to become a spiritual judge and interpreter in order to achieve freedom.

This is brought out strongly in the later part of his speech as he resolves to bring his dead son "Home to his Fathers house" (1733). Everything now contrives to underline the importance of the family and the tribe. The monument to the sunlike hero, appropriately surrounded by the shade trees laurel and palm, will preserve both Samson's trophies and the story of his acts. He will thus live on in the heroic youths who are influenced by the memory of his "matchless valour, and adventures high" (1740).

From the last phrase, particularly, we can see how Manoa now views the story of his son's life. The period of suffering is set aside, and the heroic Samson of the conclusion becomes one with the irresistible hero of the early exploits. What Manoa desires is a hymn of victory celebrating the rise of a deliverer to smash the enemies of Israel, something like the song of Deborah. His son is to be a patron of national liberation.

There seems no room in Manoa's vision for the kind of tragic drama which is now drawing to a close. The transition from "adventures high" to "Virgins" recalls romance, and Samson's suffering is finally reduced to a moral for those who will visit his tomb with flowers, "only bewailing / His lot unfortunate in nuptial choice / From whence captivity and loss of eyes" (1742–44). There is something comic and even reassuring in this example of the persistence of personal bias in the midst of grief. Manoa remains stubbornly unable to accept his son's marriage choices. While he has his portion of the truth, we feel the closure of his vision of things at this point.[23] He has not learned from his son, but persists in explaining Samson's fall in terms of disobedience to national custom and the laws prescribing endogamy and obedience to parents' wishes.

These limitations are implicitly recognized and set aside by the final Chorus, which looks beyond them to something larger. Acknowledging the God who hides himself and then unexpectedly returns, the Chorus understands that through this "great event" there has been a "new acquist / Of true experience" (1755–56). Their recognition that catharsis contains consolation points briefly to the internal freedom Samson has realized by his renewed faith in God.

IV

Contemporary criticism has found striking likenesses between Samson and his visitors, and an illuminating discussion by Georgia B. Christopher views the action as a process of purgation that operates homeopathically as the speeches of the visitors echo Samson's despairing thoughts. Christopher emphasizes the automatic nature of Samson's responses, especially his early ones, noting that they are emotionally charged, quite unconsidered, and often seem ordered by Providence.[24] The view that I have sought to develop acknowledges the spontaneous emotional element in Samson's responses, but stresses also his growth in comprehension. His responses to his homeopathic trials are a test of his ability to make discriminations and to reason under stressful circumstances. To embrace God's word — the promise made at his birth — is to interpret it. Thus, as we have seen, he must examine the weakness of the law as prescription, and seek a new inner freedom, and by this process begin the deliverance of his countrymen.

The last visible stage in Samson's development, when he unites his will to the will of God, occurs when the rousing motions of grace lead him to change his mind and accompany the officer to the games. The intervention of the Spirit has acted upon him forcefully and urgently ever since it first "rusht" on him in the camp of Dan (1435), and its effect here is decisive. Yet this moment also comprises the most fully conscious and deliberate choice made by Samson. The decision has been prepared for, been made apposite and meaningful, by the long process of self-examination which preceded it.[25] Imagination, instinct, nature, and reason have managed, though disturbed, to guide Samson aright, so that, as Milton puts it in the poem's "Argument," he is "*at length perswaded inwardly that this was from God.*" What he has now achieved is a spiritual condition, a state of being, rather than a program of action. As in the past, he is being led on to mightiest deeds (638), but he must still choose what form this action is to take. This he can now do freely, as a man who acts out of filial obedience, since he has been delivered from servitude to the law and to childhood prescription.

Through his encounters Samson has received illumination about sonship, love, and the spirit. Yet, as I shall now argue, there are important limits to his comprehension of the filial condition, and these center on his inability to understand that love alone fulfils the law. The absence of this doctrine contributes greatly to the sense of suffering observed to be crucial to the play's final effect by W. R. Parker, J. H. Hanford, Hugh Richmond, and many other critics.[26]

It is with reference to love that the difference between Samson and the other heroes of Milton's late poems is most immediately evident. Samson's education does not reach to the point marked by the closing words of the angelic tutor who, in telling Adam to add deeds to Faith, concludes: "add Love, / By name to come call'd Charitie, the soul / Of all the rest" (*Paradise Lost* XII, 583–85). It is love which ultimately fulfills the law, reconciling obedience and freedom. But the two great commandments of love in the gospel were only in process of being discovered in the Old Dispensation, and this helps to explain the limitation of Samson's vision. He has made remarkable progress in freeing himself from the law, but charity does not emerge overtly as the guiding principle of his education. He stands between a world that is dead, and one that is still powerless to be born.

The close appeals, not to charity, but to honor. Samson has honored truth, and brought honor to his people and to God. But love has escaped him. He has been a Nazarite indeed, one set apart from father, wife, and people. The very success of his patriotic ambitions has been dependent on this willingness to separate himself from those whom he seeks to help.

Love, of course, should not be interpreted sentimentally. Samson cares for his people, and in that care there is a degree of charity. It is nowhere more evident than in his final speeches telling them to "Be of good courage" (1381). As he assures the Chorus that he will do nothing dishonorable, he is fulfilling his responsibilities for their education, a task which he began involuntarily but has now begun to recognize. Yet care for his countrymen must be only a secondary motive at this point. His response does not sustain a strict comparison with the pattern of selfless love exemplified by the Son in the third book of *Paradise Lost*. Samson's attention is turned inward, not outward, his whole being locked in an effort to interpret providence correctly and thus reestablish his relation with God.

Nor is love a word he can use of his own response to God. His aim is to destroy idolatory and restore honor to God. This is the characteristic mission of prophets and leaders throughout the Old Testament, for whom adultery often stands for idolatry in what Milton calls the "borrow'd metaphor between God and man" (YP II, p. 673). The destruction of false worship opens up the possibility of truly loving God, but Samson does not appear to take that final step. His marriage, which has revived idolatry, ends in bitter divorce, so that human love is not allowed to function in a positive way as a metaphor for the relations between God and his church.

As we have seen, Samson's age has lost touch with the *protevangelium* and is thus unaware of the full potential of affliction. Unlike Adam, Samson does not glimpse the redeemer who provides a pattern of true heroism, even though his own suffering anticipates that future action in certain respects.[27] Thus while he has faith in God he cannot, like the Christian wayfarer, meet adversity with faith in Christ. Union in the Son, for Milton the fulfillment of love's purposes, is beyond his vision.

The sense of tragic imperfection, of a rich potential which remains unrealized, is evident in the course of the play by the handling of several important motifs. These take the form of antinomies which are deployed through the phases of Samson's career and which together build up and give substance to the underlying contrast of law and gospel. Three examples will serve to show the way such motifs reveal the tragic thwarting of the ideal; these concern action, speech, and sight.

When Samson falls into the hands of his enemies he is deprived of the freedom of action which characterizes his early exploits. Even in his final performance in the temple of Dagon, he appears as a thrall. Here his acts (heave, pull, draw, break) are of a sort that can be undertaken blindly, being expressions merely of "stupendious force" (1627). We know, of course, that he is playing the entertainer only in order to catch his enemies off-guard; to that extent he is taking the initiative. Even so, there is no realization of freedom of action here, but rather a sense of humiliation endured. Nor is there any suggestion of release as he leans as one overtired with his arms on the two massy pillars. His head is bowed, and curiously his eyes (like those of Melancholy) are "fast fixt." His gaze is turned inward to receive the light of the spirit. His last act is like a fit: "straining all his nerves he bow'd / . . . those two massie Pillars / With horrible convulsion to and fro, / He tugg'd, he shook" (1646–50). Separated from its object, the last verb describing Samson's actions seems both transitive and intransitive. It is appropriate to recall the experiences of the Quakers, sometimes called Shakers, and so identified because the Spirit manifested its presence in them by excited physical movement.

Samson fails to achieve fulfillment in speech as well as in action. In his early days he appears to have been pragmatic and laconic in his use of language. The riddle was his literary mode and silence was his "fort" (236). Through suffering he learns to express himself and becomes the teacher of his people. Finally he realizes that his "riddling days" (1064) are not over as he addresses the doomed audience of Philistines in the temple with masterful irony (1640–45). Yet we cannot find in his final words, any more than in his action, the fully developed shape of liberty. Irony provides a way of dealing with enemies, of speaking the truth and yet hiding it from tyranny and malice. Milton finds a place for such indirection even in the teaching methods of Jesus, but such veiled speech is far from the full and restorative assertion of God's word.

More important than Samson's last speech are the words we do not hear as he stands, moments before his death, silent " as one who pray'd" (1637). The great matter which he revolves in his mind is no doubt the word of God as it was revealed by the angel at his birth. There is in the very silence of the moment a tragic potential, for the true meaning of deliverance is one which Samson cannot express in words of persuasion, and the action to which he is now called will not make that meaning clear. The incompleteness of the action is matched by an incompleteness of expression, and both intensify the tragedy.

From the beginning, Samson has associated light and the word. Light is the virtual equivalent of life, and he accepts the speculation that there is light in the soul (90–91). Yet in spite of the hopes raised by the Chorus and his father, Samson has to accept blindness until the end. There is no miraculous cure for his sight. He still needs his guide to direct him so that he can place his arms around the pillars in the temple. He does not, like Oedipus at Colonus, become himself the guide. He is, however, illuminated by "inward eyes" (1689), as the Chorus puts it, so that he is able to understand how he must act in order to fulfill God's promise. The restriction by which he remains physically sightless even though illuminated within is a parallel to his inward possession of the word and his outward silence. The full meaning of his career remains a kind of riddle, one which we can only try to penetrate by extrapolating from what we have seen to what we are not able to see.

Instead of opening out into a new period of trial, like Adam's recovery at the end of *Paradise Lost,* Samson's recovery narrows to a specific call. No doubt we feel it is right that one who has seen so much should be spared further trials. From a human viewpoint, however, Samson's education appears to be still radically incomplete. In the last analysis his calling has been fulfilled — he has begun to free Israel from the Philistine yoke — but the arc of his religious renewal has been abruptly cut off. It is as if Adam's education were violently terminated after the story of the flood. There is no time for the emergence of a spiritual vision commensurate to Samson's sufferings.

The failure to achieve fulfillment in deed, word, or vision is in keeping with the violent and destructive nature of the act to which Samson is called. Milton insists on the bloody and merciless character of the event, and the suffering it brings to the Philistines. The cries of the dying are a "hideous noise" (1509), a "universal groan" (1511). Samson's body, his father imagines, is soaked in his enemies' blood and clotted gore. It is not difficult to find in the Psalms passages where the speaker takes delight in the downfall of his enemies (e.g., Psalm lxix, liv). Yet the Psalms are also full of restorative themes which, as we have seen, are either absent or muted in the tragedy. Those critics who find in the destruction of the temple the form of good works are thinking of Samson's recovered faith and his new sense of freedom and service. But the destructive and negative nature of his act, the absence from it of an informing spirit of charity, makes it inadequate as an expression either of those values which he has painfully discovered or of the meaning of self-sacrifice. Grace, which releases him from bondage, does not eradicate the past; the terms of the problem having been set by his earlier behavior, Samson's response to the opportunity granted by providence is a psychological triumph over past failure but not a creative anticipation of a new order.

There is a finely observed truth in Christopher Hill's discussion of Samson as Milton Agonistes. The aging poet continued to believe in the importance of action. Hill's point is that Milton was not "a modern liberal Christian," but a man who described hating God's enemies as a religious duty.[28] To this one might agree (but can we always identify God's enemies?) and yet still emphasize that the only way Samson can truly begin to deliver his people is by showing them the meaning of freedom. Without this truth, they will not be liberated by the fall of any number of Philistine temples. But this truth is one which Samson himself has only begun to grasp, and the Chorus struggle on far behind him.

At the close there is a disturbing impression that the new world will not be sufficiently different from the one that has passed away. Samson will be enrolled among the Old Testament saints (Hebrews, chapter xi), but at the center of his tragedy lies the incompleteness of the revelation made through his suffering. He is one of those who suffered, and "having obtained a good report through faith, received not the promise." History will bring incremental repetition, but must wait for a greater hero to provide the transformation which leads beyond tragedy and finally dissolves the law into charity, "God having provided some better thing for us, that they without us should not be made perfect" (Hebrews xi, 39–40).

University of Toronto

NOTES

Citations of Milton's poetry refer to the Columbia edition of *The Works of John Milton*, ed. Frank Allen Patterson et al. (New York, 1931–38). Citations of Milton's prose refer to the Yale edition of *The Complete Prose Works of John Milton*, 8 vols., ed. Don M. Wolfe et al. (New Haven, 1953–82), hereafter cited as YP.

1. Samuel Johnson's criticism appears in *Rambler*, No. 139, in *The Yale Edition of the Works of Samuel Johnson*, vol. IV, ed. W. J. Bate and Albrecht B. Strauss (New Haven, 1969), p. 376. Answers include M. E. Grenander, "Samson's Middle: Aristotle and Dr. Johnson, *UTQ* XXIV (1955), 377–89; A.S.P. Woodhouse, "Tragic Effect in *Samson Agonistes*," *UTQ* XXVIII (1959), 205–22; D. C. Allen, *The Harmonious Vision* (Baltimore, 1954), pp. 71–94, and many others. Stanley Fish, in "Question and Answer in *Samson Agonistes*," *Critical Quarterly* XI (1969), 237–64, revived Johnson's criticism in a new and challenging form by arguing that the gap between the play's "outer" or public plot (with its denouement in the temple scene) and its "inner" plot (complete when Samson is ready to go to the temple) is logically unbridgeable. Those who insist on the connection often interpret it in a religious context, either restricting this to the Old Testament, as does John N. Wall, Jr., in "The Contrarious Hand of God: *Samson Agonistes* and the Biblical Lament," in *Milton Studies*, vol. XII, ed. James D. Simmonds (Pittsburgh, 1978), pp. 117–39, or (more frequently) drawing Christian meanings into the design, as do (among others) the following critics: F. M. Krouse, *Milton's Samson and the Christian Tradition* (Princeton, 1949); Anthony Low, *The Blaze of Noon* (New York, 1974); Albert Cirillo, "Time, Light and the Phoenix: the Design of *Samson Agonistes*," in *Calm of Mind: Tercentenary Essays on "Paradise Regained" and "Samson Agonistes" in Honor of John S. Diekhoff*, ed. Joseph A. Wittreich, Jr. (Cleveland, 1971), pp. 209–33; Wendy Furman, "*Samson Agonistes* as a Christian Tragedy: A Corrective View" *PQ* 60 (1981), 169–81; Joseph C. Ulreich, Jr., "'Beyond the Fifth Act': *Samson Agonistes* as Prophecy," in *Milton Studies*, vol. XVII, ed. Richard S. Ide and Joseph Wittreich, Jr. (Pittsburgh, 1983), pp. 281–318. But others seeking connection between Samson's inner life and his final act find a darker emphasis on revenge or frustration, as do Kenneth Fell, in "From Myth to Martyrdom: Towards a View of Milton's *Samson Agonistes*," *English Studies* XXXIV (1953), 145–55, John Shaw-

cross, in "Irony as Tragic Effect: *Samson Agonistes* and the Tragedy of Hope," in *Calm of Mind*, pp. 289–306, and Irene Samuel, in "*Samson Agonistes* as a Tragedy," in *Calm of Mind*, pp. 235–57. Joseph Wittreich's revisionist study, *Interpreting "Samson Agonistes"* (Princeton, 1986), belongs in general to this camp. While allowing for an element of ambiguity or hesitation, Wittreich's argument leads toward the conclusion that *Samson Agonistes* subverts the heroism of Samson, portraying his last act as a second fall (p. 80) which fails to snatch spiritual victory out of natural defeat (p. 200); the tragedy thus arises out of a blunted consciousness (p. 107) which prevents the realization by Samson and his people of the values affirmed in *De doctrina christiana* (p. 308) and exemplified in *Paradise Regained* (p. 320), and this means that deliverance becomes the achievement not of the hero but of the poet who interprets the story (p. 285). Critics who find catharsis a way of reconciling tragedy with healing or consolation include Martin Mueller, "*Pathos* and *Katharsis* in *Samson Agonistes*," *ELH* XXXI (1964), 156–74; Sherman Hawkins, "Samson's Catharsis," in *Milton Studies*, vol. II, ed. James D. Simmonds (Pittsburgh, 1970), pp. 211–30; Raymond Waddington, "Melancholy Against Melancholy: *Samson Agonistes* as Renaissance Tragedy," in *Calm of Mind*, pp. 259–87; and Mary Ann Radzinowicz, "The Distinctive Tragedy of *Samson Agonistes*, in *Milton Studies*, vol. XVII, ed. Richard S. Ide and Joseph A. Wittreich, Jr. (Pittsburgh, 1983), pp. 249–80.

2. I am indebted for my approach to the essays of Arthur E. Barker, particularly "Structural and Doctrinal Pattern in Milton's Later Poems," in *Essays in English Literature from the Renaissance to the Victorian Age Presented to A.S.P. Woodhouse*, ed. Millar MacLure and F. W. Watt (Toronto, 1964), pp. 169–94. Other useful treatments of the role of the law in *Samson Agonistes* are found in Samuel S. Stollman, "Milton's Samson and the Jewish Tradition," in *Milton Studies*, vol. III, ed. James D. Simmonds (Pittsburgh, 1971), pp. 185–200, and "Milton's Dichotomy of 'Judaism' and 'Hebraism,'" *PMLA* LXXXIX (1974), 105–12; Mary Ann Radzinowicz, *Toward "Samson Agonistes": The Growth of Milton's Mind* (Princeton, 1978), especially pp. 216, 245–46, 261–65; Joan S. Bennett, "Liberty Under the Law: The Chorus and the Meaning of *Samson Agonistes*," in *Milton Studies*, vol. XII, ed. James D. Simmonds (Pittsburgh, 1978), pp. 141–63; Lynn Veach Sadler, *Consolation in "Samson Agonistes": Regeneration and Typology* (Salzburg, Austria, 1979), especially pp. 125, 273, and chapter 5; John Shawcross, "The Genres of *Paradise Regain'd* and *Samson Agonistes*: The Wisdom of Their Joint Publication," in *Milton Studies*, vol. XVII, ed. Richard S. Ide and Joseph Wittreich, Jr. (Pittsburgh, 1983), pp. 225–48.

3. Barbara Lewalski, in "*Samson Agonistes* and the 'Tragedy' of Apocalypse," *PMLA* LXXXV (1970), 1050–62, points out that in Milton's age "to judge" often meant, as Richard Rogers put it, to "revenge and redeem out of bondage." Such a definition seems to fit the exercise of dominion by which, according to Milton, "Gideon, Jephthah, and the other *judges . . .* are said to have *judged* Israel" (YP VI, p. 625). Milton follows the common practice of biblical interpretation by consistently presenting Samson as "deliverer" throughout the play. But, unlike the hero of the Book of Judges, Milton's Samson is also a judge in the sense of one who tries, appraises, and exercises his mind upon an issue so as to arrive at a correct and sound notion of it. This is a common meaning of the exercise of judgment in Milton's writing, as in *Paradise Lost* (VIII, 448), or in the account of *proairesis* in *Of Education* (YP II, p. 396). Samson, if he is to be a true deliverer, must prove himself a judge not only of himself but of his community and its laws. Wittreich argues that the play "suppresses" any mention of "judgeship," depicting a Samson who fails to act as a public person and neglects to reflect on his commission (see Wittreich's *Interpreting "Samson Agonistes"* pp. 66, 309, 152–53); but he does not take into account the preoccupation with vocation which is such an important issue throughout.

4. John Calvin, *Institutes of the Christian Religion*, ed. John T. McNeill, trans. Ford Lewis Battles (Philadelphia, 1960), pp. 429–32. Subsequent parenthetical page references to the *Institutes* are to this edition, designated *Institutes*.

5. See A.S.P. Woodhouse, *The Heavenly Muse*, ed. Hugh MacCallum (Toronto, 1972), pp. 99–123; Arthur E. Barker, *Milton and the Puritan Dilemma* (1942; rpt. Toronto, 1964), pp. 322–24 and *passim;* John R. Knott, *The Sword and the Spirit* (Chicago, 1971), pp. 106–30; Theodore Huguelet, "The Rule of Charity in Milton's Divorce Tracts," in *Milton Studies*, vol. VI, ed. James D. Simmonds (Pittsburgh, 1974), pp. 199–214. On the Old Covenant as a covenant of grace, see John T. Shawcross, "Milton and Covenant: The Christian View of Old Testament Theology" in *Milton and Scriptural Tradition*, ed. James H. Sims and Leland Ryken (Columbia, Mo., 1984), pp. 160–91.

6. See Andrew J. Bandstra, "Law and Gospel in Calvin and Paul," in *Exploring the Heritage of John Calvin*, ed. David E. Holwerda (Grand Rapids, Mich., 1976), p. 38. Bandstra discusses the approach of the *Institutes*, and notes the different emphasis of the commentaries.

7. Some representative antinomian writings are Tobias Crisp, *Christ Alone Exalted* (London, 1643), John Cotton, *A Treatise of the Covenant of Grace* (London, 1659, but containing sermons probably delivered in the thirties), and John Eaton, *The Honey-Combe of Free Justification by Christ Alone* (London, 1642). On the antinomian movement in England, see R. T. Kendall, *Calvin and English Calvinism to 1649* (Oxford, 1979), chaps. 12–13. The comparison of Milton's views with those of the opponents of antinomianism is particularly revealing, for he shares much with them in spite of his disagreement concerning the best way to describe how the gospel affects the law. See especially Henry Burton, *The Law and the Gospell Reconciled* (London, 1631), Thomas Taylor, *Regulae Vitae: The Role of the Law Under the Gospel* (London, 1631), and William Ames, *The Marrow of Sacred Divinity* (London, 1642), ch. 38.

8. Burton, *The Law and the Gospell Reconciled*, p. 2.

9. *Puritanism and Liberty, Being the Army Debates (1647–49) from the Clarke Manuscripts with Supplementary Documents* (1938; rpt. Chicago, 1965), p. [65], n.2.

10. Both terms are used by Mary Ann Radzinowicz, along with others such as "psalmic patterns" and "psalmic formulae," in her study of the importance of the Psalms to Milton's play in *Toward "Samson Agonistes,"* pp. 188–226, 368–82.

11. See Barbara K. Lewalski, *Protestant Poetics and the Seventeenth-Century Religious Lyric* (Princeton, 1979), pp. 132–33.

12. See Mary Ann Radzinowicz, "*Paradise Regained* as Hermeneutic Combat," *University of Hartford Studies in Literature* XV–XVI (1983–84), 99–107.

13. See the introduction to *The Psalms*, trans. and ed. W.O.E. Osterley (London, 1959), pp. 88–91.

14. W.O.E. Osterley, *A Fresh Approach to the Psalms* (New York, 1937), p. 228; *The Psalms*, p. 80.

15. In *Paradise Lost* the prime decree of God concerns the begetting of the Son (V, 603), as Georgia B. Christopher points out in *Milton and the Science of the Saints* (Princeton, 1982), p. 231. While the association of this decree with the royal Psalms, especially Psalm ii, 7, may be made by the reader, it does not seem to occur to Samson.

16. It is appropriate to remember the censure of Jesus by the Pharisees when he heals a man on the Sabbath by telling him to take up his bed and walk (John v, 11; vii, 23). In *De doctrina christiana* Milton associates this controversy with Jeremiah's gloss on the fourth commandment (YP VI, p. 707).

17. In *Tetrachordon* Milton observes that "Lawyers know that all the precepts of

law are devided into obligatorie and permissive" (YP II, p. 660). I remain unconvinced by Albert C. Labriola's interesting suggestion, in "Divine Urgency as a Motive for Conduct in *Samson Agonistes*," *PQ* L (1971), 99–107, that Samson's "intimate impulse" was God's reproof taking the form of an evil temptation. Rather the "impulse" foreshadows the redemption of man to "a state above prescriptions" (YP II, pp. 300, 588).

18. The tribe of Dan was singled out in the song of Deborah (Judges v, 17) for their absence at an earlier opportunity for deliverance: "why did Dan remain in the ships?" Dan's idolatry is recalled in *Paradise Lost* (II, 485) and *Paradise Regained* (III, 431).

19. Bennett, "Liberty under the Law," p. 152. On the limitations and growth of the Chorus, see also John Huntley, "A Revaluation of the Chorus' Role in Milton's *Samson Agonistes*," *MP* LXIV, (1966), 132–45.

20. Virginia R. Mollenkott, in "Relativism in *Samson Agonistes*," *SP* LXVII (1970), 89–102, argues that if Samson can justify the breaking of the law by an appeal to private inspiration, so can Dalila. But while the complex casuistry of the play is appealing to the modern mind, Milton does challenge us to distinguish between the genuine use of reason and mere rationalization. On Dalila's failure to prove a fit wife, see Dayton Haskin, "Divorce as a Path to Union with God in *Samson Agonistes*, " *ELH* XXXVIII (1971), 358–76.

21. On Samson as fool of God, see Arnold Stein, *Heroic Knowledge* (Minneapolis, 1957), p. 196; Roger B. Wilkenfeld, "Act and Emblem: The Conclusion of *Samson Agonistes*," *ELH* XXXII (1965), 160–68; Donald F. Bouchard, *Milton: A structural reading* (Montreal, 1974), pp. 152, 156.

22. Mason Tung, in "*Samson Impatiens:* A Reinterpretation of Milton's *Samson Agonistes*," *TSLL* IX, (1967), 475–92, argues that willful impatience is Samson's chronic weakness, and concludes that by rejecting the officer Samson is jeopardizing the promise of God. But while the law does foster self-righteousness, Samson's attitude at this later moment is judicious and conscientious as he stands on the verge of a new and revolutionary insight.

23. Nancy Y. Hoffman, in "Samson's Other Father: The Character of Manoa in *Samson Agonistes*," in *Milton Studies*, vol. II, ed. James D. Simmonds (Pittsburgh, 1970), pp. 195–209, stresses the fluctuating vision of Manoa: "despite the ennobling catharsis of grief, human beings remain self-centred, concerned with the ephemeral dream of earthly repute" (p. 208).

24. Christopher, *Milton and the Science of the Saints*, pp. 234, 243, 230. On parody and homeopathic cure, see also Barker, "Milton's Later Poems," pp. 177–78, and Waddington, "Melancholy Against Melancholy," pp. 269–78.

25. G. A. Wilkes, in "The Interpretation of *Samson Agonistes*," *HLQ* XXVI (1963), 363–79, maintains that the play shows how providence realizes its "uncontroulable intent" in spite of, rather than by means of, human responses, but this seems to make the depiction of psychological process irrelevant. More convincing are critics who, like Edward W. Tayler in *Milton's Poetry: Its Development in Time* (Pittsburgh, 1979), p. 121, argue that at the climax Samson's will and the will of God are united. Joseph Summers, in "The Movements of the Drama," in *The Lyric and Dramatic Milton*, ed. Joseph Summers (New York, 1965), p. 172, notes that lines 1401–07 show Samson's awareness that his "rouzing motions" have come as a command from that "master" to whom he owes "absolute subjection" (172), but it is worth adding that the command is given to a free being and fosters that freedom. Wittreich relies heavily on *Samson Agonistes*, line 1643, to support his argument that Samson acts, not with the sanction of grace, but impulsively and without appropriate deliberation (see *Interpreting "Samson Agonistes,"* especially pp. 74–75, 112, 143, 355). But Samson's assertion that he is about to undertake a new trial

"of my own accord" must be seen in terms of his audience and the rhetorical context (so different from those of the last speech we *hear* him utter), and the appropriate biblical touchstone for his response is probably not the high priest, Caiaphas (John xi, 50–51), as Wittreich argues, but Titus, who of "his own accord" does more than he is asked to do, acting out of the earnest care put into his heart by God (2 Corinthians viii, 16–17).

26. See, respectively, W. R. Parker, *Milton's Debt to Greek Tragedy in "Samson Agonistes"* (Baltimore, 1937), pp. 230–42; J. H. Hanford, "The Tragedy of God's Englishmen," in *Reason and Imagination*, ed. J. A. Mazzeo (New York, 1962), p. 26; Hugh Richmond, *The Christian Revolutionary: John Milton* (Berkeley, 1974), p. 182.

27. Many critics have contributed to the account of how the play appeals through its language to the soteriology known by Milton's Christian audience. Christian significance has been found especially in the references to ransom and the phoenix, but many other terms, such as son, father, spirit, word, home, guiding hand, and holocaust, carry Christian connotations and frequently suggest New Testament glosses. I side with William G. Madsen who concludes, in *From Shadowy Types to Truth: Studies in Milton's Symbolism* (New Haven, 1968), p. 198, that the Christian significance of such language provides an ironic counterpoint to the literal significance intended by the speakers. But while Milton assumes such differing levels of awareness, he is also concerned to show that Samson achieves a degree of freedom from bondage.

28. Christopher Hill, *Milton and the English Revolution* (New York, 1978), pp. 444–45.